CONTENTS

Until his recent death Myles Dillon was Senior Professor at the Dublin University for Advanced Studies. He formerly held the positions of Professor of Celtic, University of Wisconsin, Professor of Celtic and Linguistics, University of Chicago, and Professor of Celtic, University of Edinburgh. His previous publications include: *The Cycles of Kings, Early Irish Literature* and *The Book of Rights*.

The late Nora Chadwick was an Honorary Life Fellow of Newnham College, Cambridge. Her previous appointments included University Lecturer in the Early History and Culture of the British Isles, University of Cambridge, and Director of Studies in Anglo-Saxon and Celtic subjects in Newnham and Girton Colleges. Her publications include: *Celtic Britain, The Age of the Saints in the Early Celtic Church* and *Poetry and Letters in Early Christian Gaul*.

LIST OF ILLUSTRATIONS

ACKNOWLEDGEMENTS

The authors and publishers would like to thank the following for supplying photographs for use in this volume: British Museum, Plates 4, 6, 11, 12; Cambridge University Collection, Plate 8; Commissioner of Public Works in Ireland, Plates 16, 17, 19, 21, 32; Françoise Foliot, Plates 1, 2, 3, 22, 23; Green Studios, Dublin, Plate 30; J. A. Hedley, Plate 15; Irish Tourist Office, Plate 20; Ministry of Public Building and Works, Edinburgh, Plate 31; National Museum of Ireland, Plates 28, 29; R. Rémy, Dijon, Plates 24-7; Jean Roubier, Plates 13, 14; Dr H. Taylor, Plate 18.

LIST OF MAPS

PREFACE

The Celts were one of the peoples in prehistoric Europe who helped to create the European civilization of the past thousand years. Our purpose in this book is to trace their history from its remote beginning through the formation of the separate Celtic kingdoms in the British Isles, and down to the end of their independence. History is taken here in its widest sense, as the history of civilization. We have included not only religion and institutions, but language, literature and art.

Celtic studies have advanced so greatly in recent years that we have felt bound to present in some detail the results of this research. There are pages that have been written for the student of Celtic as well as for the common reader. Those who have no special interest in language or literary history would do well to hasten through the early part of Chapter 9, but those who have may find it worthy of closer reading.

The story of the Celts begins in the prehistoric age, when archaeology and language are our only guides. It is in the early Iron Age, beginning about 800 BC with a culture known as Hallstatt, named from a site in Upper Austria, that we can first discern them fairly clearly. The late Iron Age, called La Tène after a site in Switzerland, is the great age of the Celts on the Continent, and La Tène art is theirs and is their great achievement, as Jacobsthal has so well shown. For the early period we are involved in a terminology and in kinds of evidence that will be unfamiliar to many readers. We hope that even though unfamiliar, they may prove not unwelcome.

The distribution of work has been as follows: Chapters 1, 5, 9, 10, 11 and the Epilogue are by M.D.; 2, 3, 4, 6, 7, 8, 12 are by N.C.

We have not always been in complete agreement, and we have simply given our opinions in matters of doubt. The common opinion now is that Medb and Fergus, Cú Chulainn and Cú Roí Mac Dáire, are not historical persons. N.C. prefers to regard Queen Medb as

11

having reigned as queen at Cruachain. On the other hand, M.D. regards the druids as heirs to an ancient Indo-European priesthood, represented in India by the brahmins, whereas N.C. believes that they were not priests (Chapter 7). These are the two chief points of difference between us, and they are matters for argument. However, the book is a collaboration. We have worked together on every chapter, and we are glad to accept joint responsibility. Once we reach Britain and Ireland we are on easier ground, although there is plenty of room for doubt and disagreement.

The attempt to present the Celts in history as one people, with a common tradition and a common character, is new, and in some degree, experimental. It seems to us to have been justified beyond our expectations, inasmuch as there does emerge in the history and institutions and religion, in the art and literature, perhaps even in the language, a quality that is distinctive and is common to the Celts of Gaul, of Britain and of Ireland. We hesitate to give it a name: it makes a contrast with Greek temperance, it is marked by extremes of luxury and asceticism, of exultation and despair, by lack of discipline and of the gift for organizing secular affairs, by delight in natural beauty and in tales of mystery and imagination, by an artistic sense that prefers decoration and pattern to mere representation. Matthew Arnold called it the Celtic magic.

In a field where the harvest is rich and the labourers have been so few, we have had to turn for help to other scholars, and it has been most generously given. Professor Binchy helped us with Chapter 5, even to the extent of placing his lecture-notes at our disposal. Chapters 9 and 11 could not have been completed without the constant advice and supervision of Proinsias Mac Cana. Our friends, Ludwig Bieler, Francis J. Byrne, Glyn Daniel, Michael Dolley, David Erlingsson, Kenneth Jackson, Stuart Piggott, Terence Powell and Joseph Raftery have also been called upon. To these, and to those others who have been consulted on occasion, we wish to express our gratitude.

Our thanks are also due to the University of Chicago Press for permission to print passages from M. Dillon, *Early Irish Literature* (copyright University of Chicago 1947), to the Delegates of the Clarendon Press for permission to print two poems from G. Murphy, *Early Irish Lyrics* (Oxford, 1956) and several poems and extracts from T. Parry, *The Oxford Book of Welsh Verse*, and to the Council of the

Royal Irish Academy and the author for permission to print translations from Professor Tierney's *Celtic Ethnography of Posidonius*.

We are most grateful to Miss Máire Bhreatnach for typing and retyping with endless patience, and to Máire, Bean Uí Chinnsealaigh who kindly undertook the tedious work of revising the index.

N. K. C.
M. D.

I

Discovering the Celts

At the end of the sixth century BC the Celts were already known to Greek historians and ethnographers. Hecataeus of Miletus, writing at about that time, says that Narbonne is a Celtic town, and mentions Marseilles as being near Celtic territory. Herodotus, in the fifth century, twice mentions the Celts (the first occurrence of the name Keltoí), only to say that the Danube has its source – which he seems to suppose is in the Pyrenees – amongst the Celts, and that they dwell beyond the Pillars of Hercules and are the most westerly people in Europe except the Cynesians. But there is one written source even earlier than these, although it is preserved only in a later form. The *Ora Maritima* of Avienus (third century AD) has been shown to contain a description of the Mediterranean coast from Cadiz to Marseilles written in the early sixth century, and here too the Celts are said to dwell in Gaul and in south-western Spain.

We can go further back in time, and it appears that the original home of the Celts was east of the Rhine, in the country that is now Bavaria and Bohemia, and westwards as far as the Rhine itself. The evidence for this opinion is in a comparison of place-names with archaeology. In the Bronze Age, about the end of the fourteenth century BC, there appears in central Europe a culture marked by burial customs and by forms of decoration of weapons, ornaments, tools and pottery, that are hitherto unknown there and are found in association. The burials are in mounds (*tumuli*) of earth heaped over the grave, and some archaeologists identify this culture with the emergence of the Celts. Following on the *tumulus*-culture, there appears a new fashion of burial according to which the body was cremated, the ashes were placed in an urn, and the urns were deposited in cemeteries, known as 'urnfields'.

At the end of the Urnfield period iron tools and weapons appear, so

15

that we speak of the Iron Age, and of this early phase as the Early Iron Age or Hallstatt culture (*c.* 800–450 BC). Hallstatt is a site in Austria where many such objects have been found. The late Iron Age is commonly called La Tène, from a site in Switzerland, and the period begins *c.* 450 BC and ends on the Continent with Caesar's campaigns.

Many archaeologists would identify the emergence of the Celts with the appearance of urnfields in south central Europe, as there seems to be a cultural continuum from the time when they appear, at the close of the Bronze Age, through the Hallstatt period and down to La Tène. But this is too late, in our opinion, for the separation of Celtic as a distinct dialect, and it is better to regard as already Celtic whatever can be dated to the beginning of the second millennium BC.[1]

Over all this area, Austria, Bohemia, southern and western Germany, and France, place-names occur which are compounded with elements such as: *briga* 'hill'; *dunum* 'fortress'; *magus* 'plain'; *nemeton* 'sacred place'; *ritum* 'ford'; *seno-* 'old', *uindo-* 'white'. And these words are familiar as Irish *brí* 'hill' (Welsh *bre*); *dún* 'fort' (*dinas*); *mag* 'plain' (*ma*); *nemed* 'sacred place'; W. *rhyd* 'ford'; *sen* 'old' (W. *hen*); *find* 'white' (W. *gwyn*). The Welsh place-name *Gwynfa* in Montgomeryshire, and Irish *Findmhagh* in County Antrim are exact translations of Gaulish Ὀυινδόμαγος (*Uindo-magos*) in Gallia Narbonensis, mentioned by Ptolemy 2, 10, 6. The name of the Rhine is Celtic, and all its eastern tributaries have Celtic names: Neckar, Main, Lahn, Ruhr and Lippe. The Isar, the Inn and the Tauber are also explained as Celtic.[2] It is a probable conclusion that these names, coinciding in their distribution with the early *tumulus*-culture, were given by the bearers of that culture; and the names are Celtic. The conclusion is supported by the fact that in France and Spain, the same coincidence of Celtic place-names and river-names occurs with the Urnfield culture; for archaeology shows the spread of material cultures westwards and northwards from that Central European area.

The name 'Celtic' has been explained as cognate with Gothic *hildja* 'to fight', and this is a possible meaning. It has no prior history, as has the name *Graeci*, once proper to a small community in the Peloponnesus, or the name *Rus* 'Russian' which was originally a Finnish name for the Swedes, and perhaps meant 'rower, seafarer'.

16

But Strabo does say that it was formerly the name of the tribe of Narbonensis, and suggests that it may have come into Greek through Marseilles as a name for the whole people.[3] Caesar says that the Galli called themselves *Celtae*. The name came to be used as Strabo uses it, of a people distinguished from the Ligurians and Iberians in the west and from Illyrians and Scythians in the east. The Germans in their northern home were still unknown to the earliest Greek historians.

The Celts were distinguished in various ways, by social organization, religion, dress, methods of warfare, for these are matters of which the early historians took account; but the main distinction then, as now, will have been that of language. Tacitus says of one tribe: 'Their Gaulish speech proves that the Cotini were not Germans' (*Germania* 43). Indeed this definition by language is the only useful one, for by reference to it one can speak meaningfully of Celtic archaeology or Celtic religion. But if we do not admit language as the criterion, these terms involve a circular argument. This does not mean that there was no confusion. Tribes speaking a Germanic dialect may have been taken for Celts on account of their dress and customs, or because they were subject to Celtic overlords. The observers of the time were not professional linguists, and could not have known without careful enquiry whether the dialect of a tribe in a border area was Celtic or not.[4]

Besides place-names, the names of Gaulish chiefs and peoples tell us something of the language of the ancient Celts. Many of them can be interpreted through Irish and Welsh: Dumnorix goes into Irish as *rí an domhain* 'king of the world'; Vercingetorix is made up of *uer* 'over', *cinget-* 'warrior' and *rīx* 'king'; Anektomāros means 'Great Protector' (O.I. *aingid* 'protects'); Eporedorix 'king of horses' would be O.I. *rí echraide*; Bituriges, O.I. *ríg in betho* 'kings of the world'; Allobroges 'people from a foreign country'; Brigantes 'the exalted' (O.I. *Brigit*). Some words are mentioned by ancient writers as being the Gaulish names for things: κόρμα 'beer'; βάρδος 'poet'; δρυίδαι 'druids'; *reda* 'chariot'; μάρκα 'horse'. And the words occur in Irish as *coirm, bard, druí* 'druid', *riad* 'driving, riding', *marc*, with similar forms in Welsh. A more immediate source is provided by the Gaulish inscriptions that have been discovered in France and Italy. Some of the inscriptions of Cisalpine Gaul are in the Greek or the Etruscan alphabet, but the great majority of the inscriptions are in Roman letters. They are some sixty in number, apart from the graffiti on

17

potsherds found at La Graufesenque, and the contents of the famous Calendar of Coligny (see p. 30). More will be said about language later (pp. 257 f.).

The Celts, then, are a people who appear in history in the sixth century BC. The early writers mention them only casually, as when Xenophon writes of Celts who fought as mercenaries against the Thebans in the Peloponnesus in 369 BC, and Plato includes them in a list of barbarian peoples who are given to drunkenness. Aristotle says: 'It is not bravery to withstand danger through recklessness, as when the Celts take up arms to attack the waves.'[5]

From their home in central Europe, the Celts spread westwards to the Atlantic coast and into Spain, northwards into the British Isles, and later south into Italy and east along the Danube, and as far as Galatia in Asia Minor. The early migrations were accomplished in prehistoric times and can be dated only by archaeological evidence. The evidence is incomplete insofar as swords, brooches and potsherds cannot tell us that the men who made them spoke a Celtic dialect. We cannot hope for more than a probable opinion. It is a fact that Hallstatt or early Iron Age culture spread into Spain; we have written testimony that the Celts were already established in south-western Spain by the sixth century, and there are Celtic place-names widely scattered in Spain, and as far as the mouth of the Tagus (*Arabriga*). It is a reasonable inference that the makers of these Hallstatt weapons and tools were Celts. But the earliest Celtic migrations date from the Bronze Age, for the urnfields, which appear in south Germany and eastern Gaul after the *tumulus*-culture and are recognized as Celtic, are found also in Catalonia and as far south as Valencia. There were later separate migrations of Celts in the Hallstatt period (*c.* 600 BC) and in the second phase of La Tène culture (third century BC); and some inscriptions testify to the presence of a strong Celtic element in the population. The Celtiberi, who resisted the Roman assault for so long, and so bravely, were a mixture of Celts and Iberians as their name implies.

The Celtic settlement of the British Isles is more difficult to trace. It seems now that we must choose between two extremes. About 2000 BC came Bell-Beaker people, whose burials are in single graves, with individual grave-goods. The remarkable Wessex Culture of the Bronze Age which appears about 1500 BC is thought to be based upon this tradition. The grave-goods there suggest the existence of a warrior

18

aristocracy 'with a graded series of obligations of service ... through a military nobility down to the craftsmen and peasants',[6] as in the Homeric society. This is the sort of society which is described in the Irish sagas, and there is no reason why so early a date for the coming of the Celts should be impossible. We shall see that there are considerations of language and culture that tend rather to support it. From the middle of the sixth century BC the Early Iron Age people, builders of the hill-forts so characteristic of the insular Celtic world, begin to appear. From then until the Belgic invasion, to which Caesar refers as having occurred not long before his time, there were successive waves of Celtic immigration into Britain. But the common opinion among archaeologists seems now to be that there was no large-scale immigration into the British Isles between 2000 and 600 BC.

Archaeology has made great strides in recent years, and it is difficult for an outsider to form a personal judgement. It becomes a matter of choosing one's authority. Meanwhile important advances have been made in Celtic philology, and the great archaism of Irish tradition has been firmly established, as will appear from what follows. At present, in our opinion, either view is tenable, and we confess to preferring the early date. With the advance of research into prehistory, or perhaps even by some new discovery in linguistics,[7] a reasoned decision may be possible in the future. For the present we must be content to doubt.

With regard to the Celtic settlement of Ireland in particular, O'Rahilly in his 'Goidels and Their Predecessors', and again in his great book, *Early Irish History and Mythology*, put forward an entirely new theory. He distinguished four successive immigrations: the Cruthin some time before 500 BC; the Érainn (= Fir Bolg) perhaps in the fifth century; the Laigin (with Domnainn and Gálioin) in the third century; the Goídil who came *c.* 100 BC. The notion of a series of invasions is traditional, and is first recorded by Nennius who knew of three, those of Partholón, Nemed, and the Children of Míl.

In the Book of Invasions as we know it from the eleventh century recension there are five (or six): (Cesair), Partholón, Nemed, Fir Bolg, Tuatha Dé Danann, and the Children of Míl. But these legends are mere learned fiction, and have no value as history. Their interest is of another kind. The only bearing they have upon history is in so far as they betray a state of affairs which the literary men were trying to expound. What does appear from various references cited by

19

O'Rahilly is the presence in Ireland of at least three ethnic groups: Cruthin (or Cruithni) who were mainly in the north-east and plainly akin to the Picts of Scotland (also called Cruthin);[8] Érainn, who were mainly in the south-west and in the south-east corner (Déisi); and Goídil (*Cland Míled*) who reigned over Tara, Cashel and Croghan and were the dominant people in the early historic period. Whether the Laigin were a distinct people or merely a Goidelic tribe is not clear to us.

O'Rahilly's most novel suggestion is that his first three groups spoke Brythonic dialects, that is that they were 'P-Celts', and that the Goídil were the only Goidelic speakers, the only 'Q-Celts'.[9] And he seeks to prove this from the evidence of Irish words that are not Goidelic in form and may be Brythonic. His demonstration is not convincing, and the notion that this more archaic language was brought latest, by a migration of the Quariates from south-east Gaul, is inherently improbable. We think it more likely that Goidelic was first established in Ireland, and that Brythonic tribes made settlements there, just as Irish settlements were made in Wales both north and south. In those early centuries, when there was constant intercourse across the Irish Sea, there was every chance of linguistic borrowing. Moreover, an unknown proportion of the Irish vocabulary may be non-Indo-European, an inheritance from pre-Celtic times. The Cruthin and the Érainn, being earlier immigrants than the Goídil, probably spoke Q-dialects. However, it is right to say that no certainty seems attainable in the matter. O'Rahilly's doctrine has been accepted by some scholars[10] and dismissed by others.[11]

Meanwhile the Celts had been spreading into Italy and along the Danube towards the Black Sea. Cisalpine Gaul was settled in the fourth century, and Celtic raiders penetrated as far as Rome in 390. The shrine of Delphi was plundered in 278, and the marauders then wandered through Thrace and Macedonia. The Scordisci founded the city of Singidunum (Belgrade), and other bands even made contact with the Scythians and formed a Celto-Scythian group. Finally an army of some twenty thousand crossed into Asia Minor, Tectosages, Tolistobogii and Trocmi, and founded in eastern Phrygia the three tetrarchies of Galatia. The Tectosages occupied the site of the modern Ankara. And like the Celts of Gaul at their shrine in the territory of the Carnutes,[12] like the Celts of Ireland at Uisnech and at Tailtiu,[13] these Galatians assembled from time to time at a sanctuary called *Drunemeton* 'the sacred oakgrove', faithful in this practice to their ancient tradition.[14]

At that time a territory stretching from Ireland to Galatia was in Celtic hands. 'For two centuries,' says Grenier, 'they (the Celts) were the greatest people in Europe . . . About 300 BC the power of the Celts is at its height and seems inexhaustible in energy and in man-power.'[15]

This rapid expansion over an enormous area implies great fecundity and a great spirit of adventure. Moreover, like the Greeks in the Mediterranean, the Celts brought with them their civilization, and they imposed it upon the lands they occupied. And though they were 'barbarians' in the strict sense, theirs was no mean way of life. We have accounts of it from Polybius in the third century BC, from fragments of Posidonius who lived in the first century BC, and from Julius Caesar. Some of what Posidonius tells us is worth quoting at length, because it finds such extraordinary confirmation in later Irish sources.[16]

Polybius tells of the conquest of Cisalpine Gaul with a good deal of detail, and of the later struggle of the Romans with the Celtiberi in Spain, and the defeat of the Galatians in Asia Minor. He describes the weapons of the Celts, their preference for fighting naked, the habit of taking the head of a slain enemy, and he mentions the splendid gold torques and bracelets worn by Celtic warriors. He also says that they attached great importance to clientship as the measure of a man's rank in society.[17]

The best known passage describing the Celts is that in the sixth book of Caesar's *Gallic War*, but Posidonius, who wrote a continuation of the Histories of Polybius, is the main source of information. His works are lost, but Diodorus Siculus and Strabo have preserved a good deal of what he said about the Celts. Here is Strabo's account of the Celts of Gaul:

The whole race, which is now called Gallic or Galatic, is madly fond of war, high-spirited and quick to battle, but otherwise straightforward and not of evil character. And so when they are stirred up they assemble in their bands for battle, quite openly and without forethought, so that they are easily handled by those who desire to outwit them; for at any time or place and on whatever pretext you stir them up, you will have them ready to face danger, even if they have nothing on their side but their own strength and courage. On the other hand if won over by gentle persuasion they willingly devote their energies to useful pursuits and even take to a literary education. Their strength depends both on their mighty bodies, and on their numbers. And because of this frank and straightforward element in their character they assemble in large numbers on slight provocation, being ever ready to sympathize with the anger of a neighbour who thinks he has been wronged . . .

Among all the tribes, generally speaking, there are three classes of men held in special honour: the Bards, the Vates, and the Druids. The Bards are singers and poets; the Vates interpreters of sacrifice and natural philosophers; while the Druids, in addition to the science of nature, study also moral philosophy. They are believed to be the most just of men, and are therefore entrusted with the decision of cases affecting either individuals or the public; indeed in former times they arbitrated in war and brought to a standstill the opponents when about to draw up in line of battle; and murder cases have been mostly entrusted to their decision. When there are many such cases they believe that there will be a fruitful yield from their fields. These men, as well as other authorities, have pronounced that men's souls and the universe are indestructible, although at times fire or water may (temporarily) prevail.

To the frankness and high-spiritedness of their temperament must be added the traits of childish boastfulness and love of decoration. They wear ornaments of gold, torques on their necks, and bracelets on their arms and wrists, while people of high rank wear dyed garments besprinkled with gold. It is this vanity which makes them unbearable in victory and so completely downcast in defeat. In addition to their witlessness they possess a trait of barbarous savagery which is especially peculiar to the northern peoples, for when they are leaving the battle-field they fasten to the necks of their horses the heads of their enemies, and on arriving home they nail up this spectacle at the entrances to their houses. Posidonius says that he saw this sight in many places, and was at first disgusted by it, but afterwards, becoming used to it, could bear it with equanimity. . . .[18]

Diodorus describes the habits of the Celts of Gaul at a feast:

22

. . . the nobles shave the cheeks but let the moustache grow freely so that it covers the mouth. And so when they are eating the moustache becomes entangled in the food, and when they are drinking the drink passes, as it were, through a sort of strainer. When dining they all sit not on chairs, but on the earth, strewing beneath them the skins of wolves or dogs. At their meals they are served by their youngest grown-up children, both boys and girls. Beside them are hearths blazing with fire, with cauldrons and spits containing large pieces of meat. Brave warriors they honour with the finest portions of the meat, just as Homer introduces Ajax, honoured by the chieftains, when he conquered Hector in single combat: 'He honoured Ajax with the full-length chine'.[19]

Athenaeus, who names Posidonius as his authority, confirms the statement about the Hero's Portion:

'In former times', he says, 'when the hindquarters were served, the bravest hero took the thigh-piece, and if another man claimed it, they stood up and fought in single combat to the death.'[20]

This practice is vividly recorded in the Old Irish saga of Mac Da Thó's Pig (inf. p. 307), and it is the principal theme also of 'Bricriu's Feast'.

Another passage is of special interest from this point of view. It is the account by Diodorus of the Gauls in battle:

For their journeys and in battle they use two-horse chariots, the chariot carrying both charioteer and chieftain. When they meet with cavalry in the battle they cast their javelins at the enemy and then descending from the chariot join battle with their swords. Some of them so far despise death that they descend to do battle, unclothed except for a girdle. They bring into battle as their attendants freemen chosen from among the poorer classes, whom they use as charioteers and shield-bearers in battle. When the armies are drawn up in battle-array they are wont to advance before the battle-line and to challenge the bravest of their opponents to single combat, at the same time brandishing before them their arms so as to terrify their foe. And when some one accepts their challenge to battle, they loudly recite the deeds of valour of their ancestors and proclaim their own valorous quality,

23

at the same time abusing and making little of their opponent and generally attempting to rob him beforehand of his fighting spirit. They cut off the heads of enemies slain in battle and attach them to the necks of their horses. The blood-stained spoils they hand over to their attendants and carry off as booty, while striking up a paean and singing a song of victory, and they nail up these first fruits upon their houses just as do those who lay low wild animals in certain kinds of hunting. [21]

Here again the Irish sources match closely the description of the Celts of Gaul. The warriors of the Ulster sagas go into battle in chariots, and the challenge to single combat is the central theme in the great prose epic *Táin Bó Cualnge*. Cú Chulainn, with Loeg his charioteer, in his two-horse chariot, armed with shield and spear and sword, is a Celtic warrior just such as Posidonius describes.

And here is a description of the Gauls by Diodorus, also based, it seems, on Posidonius:

Physically the Gauls are terrifying in appearance, with deep-sounding and very harsh voices. In conversation they use few words and speak in riddles, for the most part hinting at things and leaving a great deal to be understood. They frequently exaggerate with the aim of extolling themselves and diminishing the status of others. They are boasters and threateners and given to bombastic self-dramatization, and yet they are quick of mind and with good natural ability for learning. They have also lyric poets whom they call Bards. They sing to the accompaniment of instruments resembling lyres, sometimes a eulogy and sometimes a satire. They have also certain philosophers and theologians who are treated with special honour, whom they call Druids. They further make use of seers, thinking them worthy of high praise. These latter by their augural observances and by the sacrifice of sacrificial animals can foretell the future and they hold all the people subject to them. In particular when enquiring into matters of great import they have a strange and incredible custom; they devote to death a human being and stab him with a dagger in the region above the diaphragm, and when he has fallen they foretell the future from his fall, and from the convulsions of his limbs and, moreover, from the spurting of the blood, placing their trust in some ancient and long-

24

continued observation of these practices. Their custom is that no one should offer sacrifice without a philosopher; for they say that thanks should be offered to the gods by those skilled in the divine nature, as though they were people who can speak their language, and through them also they hold that benefits should be asked. And it is not only in the needs of peace but in war also that they carefully obey these men and their song-loving poets, and this is true not only of their friends but also of their enemies. For oftentimes as armies approach each other in line of battle with their swords drawn and their spears raised for the charge these men come forth between them and stop the conflict, as though they had spell-bound some kind of wild animals. Thus even among the most savage barbarians anger yields to wisdom and Ares does homage to the Muses.[22]

The testimony of Julius Caesar, which is widely familiar, is the most valuable in some respects. He presents Gaulish society as divided into three classes, *druides*, *equites* and *plebs*, the three functions (priest, warrior and husbandman) of which Dumézil has made so much. And of the *equites* he says that the nobler and wealthier have numerous clients about them.

Caesar tells more about the druids than do the others, their twenty years of study, their oral tradition, and so on. And he says of the Gauls: *Natio est omnis Gallorum admodum dedita religionibus* 'The whole Gaulish people is much given to religion'. We are told that the druids taught the doctrine of transmigration of souls, that they were concerned with the worship of the gods, and that young men flocked to them for training.

It is said that they commit to memory immense amounts of poetry, and so some of them continue their studies for twenty years. They consider it improper to commit their studies to writing, although they use the Greek alphabet for almost everything else. . . . They have also much knowledge of the stars and their motion, of the size of the world and of the earth, of natural philosophy, and of the powers and spheres of action of the immortal gods, which they discuss and hand down to their young students.[23]

This class of professional learned men, priests and scholars, seems to share a common Indo-European inheritance with the brahmins of

25

India, for the later and fuller evidence of Irish sources shows a similar class, the *filid*, who, while shorn of their priestly office in a Christian society, have retained the scholarly functions of the druids as poets, genealogists, lawyers, and the practice of oral rather than written tradition. Both the form and content of their learning show astonishing similarity to brahminical tradition.

The archaism of this tradition can best be shown from the Irish evidence which is presented later (chap. 10), but two matters deserve mention here as requiring the assumption of a learned tradition inherited by the druids of Gaul and transmitted by them to the *filid* of Ireland.

The metres of the *Rigveda*, the earliest known forms of Indo-European verse, are based upon a line with a fixed number of syllables, of which the first half was free and the cadence was fixed in the form $\cup \cup - \cup$. It was shown long ago by Meillet that the Greek metres have the same origin, and more recently Roman Jakobson has traced it in modern Slavonic verse. Calvert Watkins has now demonstrated, we think convincingly, that the Old Irish heptasyllabic line derives from this Indo-European form, and that other Irish metres are variants of it, thus confirming the antiquity of Celtic tradition, and the common heritage of the druid and the brahmin.[24]

The second matter of importance is that of legal tradition. The earliest passages in the Old Irish law-tracts date from the seventh, perhaps even from the sixth century. They are in verse, commonly a seven-syllable line ending in a dactyl (fixed cadence), showing their oral tradition; and their content belongs to a system of customary law for which close parallels can be found in the *Mānavadharmaśāstra*, the Hindu Laws of Manu.[25]

Dr Binchy has drawn attention to the resemblances in certain points between the Irish and Indian law-books. In both countries the law consists of canonical texts, invested with a sacred origin, and interpreted exclusively by a privileged caste. There were law-schools in each case, with varying traditions of interpretation. The relations between pupil and teacher (Irish *felmac* and *fithithir*; Sanscrit *śisya* and *guru*) were similar, with eventual right of succession. The Hindu *sapiṇḍa*, a family group of four generations, descendants of a common great-grandfather, seems to have the same significance and functions as the Irish *derbfine* and the Welsh *gwely*. The basic family unit was the same in both systems.

26

The law concerning the 'appointed daughter' is a feature of both Greek and Indian legal systems. In Greece the ἐπίκληρος was appointed by her father, if he had no sons, to bear him grandsons by a chosen husband, usually her nearest agnatic relative. These grandsons became his legal heirs, and succeeded to his estate. In India the appointed daughter is called *putrikā* 'the son-like one' (*putra* 'son'), and the parallel with the Irish system is even closer, for the custom of appointing a daughter lapsed, and if there were no sons a daughter was allowed to inherit. Later she inherited only for life, and the estate reverted on her death to her paternal kin.

This is the position of the Irish *ban-chomarba* 'female heir', but there appears to have been an earlier custom by which she married a kinsman and raised up heirs to her father. In India and in Ireland the development of the law was the same, presumably a coincidence, but the original status of *putrikā* and *banchomarba* is clearly a common Indo-European tradition.[26]

Even more impressive are the laws concerning marriage in Ireland and in India. In India there were eight forms of marriage, brāhma, daiva, ārṣa, prājāpatya, āsura, gāndharva, rākṣasa and paiśāca. In the first four the daughter is given by her father without purchase by the bridegroom. The fifth is marriage by purchase, the sixth is a voluntary union of maiden and lover, the seventh is forcible abduction (proper for a warrior), the eighth is mere seduction by stealth, and is called a base and sinful rite (Manu III 20–34). In Ireland likewise there were various forms of marriage. Ten classes are recognized in the law-tract on marriage, of which only nine are explained. The first three are regular marriages, differing in the proportions of wealth brought by each party, equal proportions, wealth brought in by the man, wealth brought in by the woman. The others are temporary unions, and two of these agree exactly with two of the Indian forms, marriage by force (*lánamnas écne*) and seduction by stealth (*lánamnas tothla*). Indeed a third, 'union accepted on the man's invitation', may be equated with the *gāndharva*-marriage of the Hindus, the voluntary union of maiden and lover.

We can even claim agreement in the number of forms of marriage, for Binchy has suggested that two of the Irish 'unions' are a later development.[27]

In both systems succession to family property was in 'ideal' shares, without actual division of the property among the heirs; and in both

27

there was a distinction, with important legal consequences, between inherited and self-acquired property.

In both systems there were various forms of suretyship, which were important for the enforcing of private obligations.

Of special interest is the custom of fasting by a plaintiff against a defendant, which is discussed later. It is recognized in both systems as a legal means of enforcing a claim.[28]

The Indo-European origin of Irish metres, and the striking similarities between the Hindu and Irish systems of law, which also point to Indo-European origin, go a long way towards proving that the Irish *filid*, and therefore the Celtic druids, were heirs to the same tradition as the brahmins.

Vendryes showed long ago that a group of words associated with religion and kingship has survived in Indo-Iranian on the one hand and in Italic and Celtic on the other, and he attributed their survival to the priestly caste represented in India by the brahmins and in Gaul by the druids.[29] We may now go further and say that druid and brahmin were heirs to a common tradition of learning and culture.

Irish society was based on the family-group of four generations (p. 129), and this may be assumed for the Celts. The wider unit was the tribe. In Caesar's time there were about fifty tribes in Gaul, of which only a few still recognized the institution of kingship. Most of them had adopted an oligarchical form of government. It is, therefore from Irish sources that we learn most about Celtic kingship.[30]

About the religion of the Celts much has been written, but the picture remains obscure. Caesar tells us that the Gauls worshipped Mercury, Apollo, Mars, Jupiter and Minerva. But he is simply equating Gaulish deities with his own Roman gods. He does not give us a single Gaulish name. Other historians do give us names, and many names occur in dedications all over the vast area once dominated by the Celts, from Galatia in Asia Minor to Spain and Britain. We have more than 400 names in all, and more than 300 of them occur only once. Perhaps these are names of local deities, each tribe or group of tribes having a special cult.

One important name is that of *Lug*, Welsh *Llew*. It occurs in dedications at Avranches in Switzerland and at Asma (Tarragona) in Spain as a plural, *Lugoues*, *Lugouibus*,[31] and is common in the place-name Lugudunum, which is the name of Lyons, Loudon, Laon and Léon in France, of Leiden in Holland and Liegnitz in Silesia.

28

Lugus must have been a great Celtic god, but we do not know what his special character was. In Ireland he was the god of *Lugnasad*, 1 August, which was evidently a harvest festival, and Lug may have been the god of fertility. At Lyons the feast of Augustus was celebrated on that day, apparently in substitution for the ancient feast of Lug. Máire MacNeill has shown that his feast was celebrated all over Ireland into our own times.[32] Lug's other name was Find, 'the Fairhaired One', and he survives on the Continent as *Vindonnus*, and in a few place-names: *Uindobona* (Vienna), *Vindonissa*, etc.[33]

The poet Lucan says that Esus, Taranis and Teutates were the gods of the Celts, and two of these names are echoed in Welsh *taran* (Irish *torann*) 'thunder', and *tud* (Irish *tuath*) 'tribe'. The faintness of the echo suggests a long interval in time between the first Celtic settlement of the British Isles and the date of our Gaulish evidence. Ogmios, the god of eloquence, described by Lucian (p. 180), and Irish Ogma, who figures in the Battle of Moytura, are close in form, if not in function, although Thurneysen opposed the identification.[34]

The cult of the Mothers was certainly Celtic, i.e. Mother Earth as a source of fertility, worshipped in triple form under the title *matres* or *matronae*. The dedications that survive on monuments in Gaul are in Latin, and the figures are sometimes represented with baskets of fruit or horns of plenty, or with children in their laps. There is a Welsh place-name *Y Foel Famau* 'the hill of the mothers', which preserves the tradition.

One of the gods most often represented is a three-headed god, of whom there are as many as thirty-two effigies. In Ireland the Three Gods of Craftsmanship (*Tri Dé Dána*) are Goibniu, Luchta and Credne.[35] There are three Brigits[36] and three Finds.[37] Sometimes the god has a female companion. Sucellos (the god with the hammer) and Nantosuelta appear together on monuments, Luxovius and Brixia, Bormo and Damona. Madame Jonval, in her *Dieux et Héros des Celtes* suggests that the gods are national and protectors of the people, the goddesses local, rural spirits of fertility or of war. The marriage of the chieftain-god with the mother-goddess assured the people of protection and fertility.

Here again we are reminded of Hinduism, in which the god has a female companion, his *śakti* or source of power. Thus Indra has a spouse Sacī, Śiva has Umā, Viṣṇu has Śrī-Lakṣmī. Brahmā, Viṣṇu and Śiva form a trinity as Creator, Restorer and Destroyer, the

Trimūrti ('in triple form'). The three-headed god is, however, found in many cultures.[38]

Another feature of Celtic religion that emerges clearly is that wells, rivers and sacred trees were objects of devotion and had patron gods or goddesses. Some rivers were themselves divine. There was a sanctuary of the Dea Sequana at the source of the river Seine, and one of the Dea Matrona near to the source of the Marne. In Ireland Bóinn (the Boyne) and Sinainn (the Shannon) were goddesses. Then there were animal gods: the bull, Taruos Trigaranus, who appears on the famous Paris monument in the Cluny museum; the boar, Moccos; the goddess Epona, whose name suggests the cult of the horse; and the goddess Artio, perhaps a bear.[39] The horned god Cernunnos appears on the Gundestrup Cauldron with a stag, and the goddess Damona suggests a cult of the cow.

The priests who maintained the cult of these gods were the druids, and Caesar tells us a good deal about them. They conducted the private and public sacrifices. They taught that the soul was immortal and passed after death into another body, rather as the Hindus believed. They also thought that all men were descended from Dis, the god of the Underworld, and they were learned in astronomy and natural philosophy (sup. p. 25).[40]

After a victory, the captured animals were sacrificed to the god of war. Sometimes human victims were sacrificed, and Caesar says that criminals were preferred as being more pleasing to the gods, but that, failing them, others were chosen. This savage custom is mentioned by Lucan in a well-known passage where the gods Esus, Taranis and Teutates are said to be appeased by human sacrifice.[41] At a private ceremony or at the regular feasts of the year, there was probably a sacrificial offering, but we know little about Gaulish feasts or ritual, as the Gauls themselves have left no written records of them.

There is indeed one precious document that may be attributed to druidic learning, namely the Calendar of Coligny; for the order of the Calendar with its auspicious and inauspicious days was probably one of their duties. The Coligny Calendar is the longest single document in Gaulish so far discovered, and contains about sixty different words, some of which occur many times. It was found in 1897 in a vineyard at Coligny (Ain), and the discovery made an epoch in the study of Gaulish and of the culture of the Celts. It dates probably from the first century AD.

Many fragments of a bronze tablet were unearthed, and they proved to be a table of sixty-two consecutive months, approximately equal to five solar years. The months are of thirty or twenty-nine days, and are divided into two halves ($15+15$ or $15+14$). The months of thirty days (except EQUOS) are marked as auspicious (MAT.) and those of twenty-nine days as inauspicious (ANM.). But certain days in an auspicious month are not lucky and certain days in an inauspicious month are lucky. The second half of the month has the heading ATENOUX ('returning night'?), so that the division was apparently into a bright half and a dark half; and MacNeill has shown that the seventh, eighth and ninth days of the month were days of the full moon.[42] The lunar year of twelve months was adapted to the solar year by intercalation of an extra month of thirty days in every third year. This year had thus thirteen months, twelve named months and one extra month of thirty days, each day of which was named from one of the twelve in serial order. The extra month had, as it were, no days of its own, and was intercalated so as to bring the lunar and solar cycles into approximate accord.

There was a carefully ordered system of transference, by which the notations proper to days in a given month were transferred to the corresponding dates of the preceding month, or interchanged between two consecutive months presumably for ritual purposes.[43] The details need not concern us, but the Calendar of Coligny is evidence of a considerable degree of competence in astronomy, and may reflect the learning of the druids. Moreover in the division of the month into a bright and a dark half, in the month of thirty days with a three-year cycle, at the end of which an intercalary month was added, this Gaulish calendar resembles that of the Hindus.[44]

Learning seems then to have flourished in Gaul, though we know little directly of it.[45] Of Gaulish art we know more from the work in stone and metal that has survived. The art-form that is properly Celtic, as it seems to have been evolved by the Celts, is that of the late Iron Age, known as La Tène. Overshadowed by the prestige of Greek and Roman art and architecture, it has only gradually been recognized as a precious contribution to the culture of the West. In contrast to the realism and natural beauty of classical art, this Celtic art is imaginative, even wild, delighting in symbol and pattern, rather than in direct representation. And its affinity is with Scythian and Near Eastern forms, rather than with the Mediterranean. It derives in part, too, from abstract decorative motifs of the Bronze Age, even of palaeolithic time.[46]

To the Greeks a spiral is a spiral and a face a face, and it is always clear where the one ends and the other begins, whereas the Celts 'see' the faces 'into' the spirals or tendrils: ambiguity is a characteristic of Celtic art ... It is the mechanism of dreams, where things have floating contours and pass into other things.[47]

A fine example of this delight in pattern is the sculptured pillar from Sankt Goar, on which the human head is merely one feature in the whole field of spirals and lozenges and ropes. Another is the little bronze terret from a chariot, where the head becomes actually part of the spiral motif (Jacobsthal, *Imagery*, pl. 66). It is, indeed, in metal-work that Celtic craftsmanship is seen at its best, and the famous Gundestrup Cauldron shows pattern and imagery combined. It is not, indeed, typically La Tène, and shows archaic Greek and Oriental influence, but it is generally accepted as the work of a Celtic craftsman. A box-lid from Auvers-sur-Oise (Powell, *Prehistoric Art*, pl. 181) and the gilt helmet from Amfreville are good examples of pure decoration. The British collar and torque illustrate the love of ornament that Polybius and Posidonius attribute to the Gauls.[48]

In their coinage, too, the Celts of Gaul, while they owed much to Greek and Roman models, showed their imaginative gift and originality.

The Celts impressed the ancient historians as being impetuous and fearless in battle, easily roused and with a high sense of honour, arrogant in victory and desperate to the point of suicide in defeat, delighting in ornament, in feasting, in the recitation of poetry, *admodum dedita religionibus* 'much given to religion'. Aristotle, in the Nichomachean Ethics says: 'We have no word for the man who is excessively fearless; perhaps one may call such a man mad or bereft of feeling, who fears nothing, neither earthquakes nor waves, as they say of the Celts' (iii 7.7.). And Strabo quotes Ptolemy for the story that Celtic settlers on the Adriatic, when asked by Alexander the Great what they feared most, answered that it was lest the sky should fall. Cato the Elder says of the Celts of Cisalpine Gaul: *Pleraque Gallia duas res industriosissime persequitur, rem militarem et argute loqui* 'they have two great passions, to be brave in warfare and to speak well'.

32

The picture that we get is of a people brave and gay, physically powerful, and amazingly successful in the early period. From Galatia in Asia Minor northwest to Scotland, and south again to Andalusia, one could travel in the third century BC without leaving Celtic territory. And although there was no empire, it was one culture.

Jacobsthal says that Celtic art, in all its variety and even though spread over so wide a territory, is one culture.[49] And he adds:

> We are told that the Gauls were valiant, quarrelsome, cruel, superstitious and eloquent: their art also is full of contrasts. It is attractive and repellent; it is far from primitiveness and simplicity; it is refined in thought and technique, elaborate and clever, full of paradoxes, restless, puzzlingly ambiguous; rational and irrational; dark and uncanny – far from the lovable humanity and transparence of Greek art. Yet, it is a real style, the first great contribution by the barbarians to European art, the first great chapter in the everlasting contacts of southern, northern and eastern forces in the life of Europe.

Such were the ancestors of the peoples who emerge into history in the first centuries of the Christian era as Britanni and Hiberni, the Britons and the Irish.

NOTES

1 See p. 265.
2 A. Grenier, *Les Gaulois*, 82; see also H. Kuhn in *Völker zwischen Germanen u. Kelten* 110 f.
3 Strabo IV i 14. Cf. Diodorus Siculus V 32: 'It will be useful now to make a distinction which is unknown to most people. Those who live in the interior above Marseilles ... are called Celts, whereas those who are settled above Celtica in the area stretching towards the north ... are called Galatae.'
4 Many tribes east of the Rhine, referred to as Germanic, were Celts according to S. Feist, *Germanen und Kelten* 28 f.; and Celts were called Germans, *ib.* 9 f. See also R. Hachmann *et al.*, *Völker zwischen Germanen und Kelten* 43 f.
5 *Nicomachean Ethics* iii 7 §7.
6 Piggott, *Scotland before history*, p. 66.
7 Lexicostatistics do not provide a short-cut to the answer, see *Language* 39, 638 ff.

33

8 *E.I.H.M.* 341 f.; see, however, Jackson in *The Problem of the Picts* 159.

9 See p. 258.

10 M. A. O'Brien in *Early Irish Society* 37.

11 Vendryes, *Études Celtiques* i 352 ff.

12 Caesar, *De Bello Gallico* vi 14.

13 See D. A. Binchy, *Ériu* xviii 114 ff.

14 Strabo xii, 5, 1.

15 A. Grenier, *Les Gaulois*, pp. 99–100.

16 See J. J. Tierney, 'The Celtic Ethnography of Posidonius', PRIA LX C5 (1960), whose translations are quoted.

17 For clientship in Irish society see p. 128.

18 Strabo IV iv 2, 4; J. J. Tierney, *op. cit.*, pp. 267, 269.

19 Diodorus V 28 (Tierney, *op. cit.*, 249–50).

20 Athenaeus IV 40 (Tierney, *ib.* 249).

21 Diodorus V 29 (Tierney, *ib.* 250).

22 Diodorus V 31 (Tierney, *ib.* 251).

23 *De Bello Gallico* vi 14 (Tierney, *ib.* 202).

24 'Indo-European Metrics and Archaic Irish Verse', *Celtica* VI 194. We assume here that the Irish *fili* was heir to the poet's share of druidic learning.

25 See Thurneysen and others, *Studies in Early Irish Law* vi, 183, 223; D. A. Binchy, 'The Linguistic and Historical Value of the Irish Law Tracts', 23, 27, 30 (*Proc. Brit. Acad.* XXIX (1943)).

26 R. Thurneysen and others, *Studies in Early Irish Law* 183 f.

27 *Studies in Early Irish Law*, p. vi.

28 See p. 99. I am heavily indebted to Dr Binchy for advice about these similarities between Hindu and Irish law.

29 MSL xx 275 (1920).

30 p. 125f.

31 RC vi 488 (Bromwich, *Trioedd* p. 177); Holder, *Altkeltischer Sprachschatz* 345; *CIL* II 2812; XIII 5078.

32 *The Festival of Lughnasa*. O.U.P. 1962; see also M. Tierney, 'Lugh and Dionysius', *Éigse* x 265.

33 *DF* III lxxxii.

34 Beitr. 196.

35 *EIHM* 316. Several effigies of the Three-Headed God have been found in Ireland. There are two in the National Museum in Dublin.

36 *Sanas Cormaic* 150.

37 *DF* III lxxviii n. 5. Cf. J. Vendryes, 'L'unité en trois personnes chez les Celtes', C.R. de l'Acad. des Inscr. 1935, pp. 324–41.

38 See W. Kirfel, *Die dreiköpfige Gottheit*. 1948. But he is specially prominent in Gaul. Pettazzoni regards the Gaulish Tricephalus as a god of the sun, *The All-knowing God* 196 f.

39 RC xxi 288.

40 *De Bello Gallico* vi 13, 16, 18.

34

41 Lucan, *Pharsalia* i 444.
42 *Ériu* x 14.
43 *ibid.* 7 ff.
44 Zimmer, *Altindisches Leben* 364–71. Beside a five-year cycle, and other schemes, a three-year cycle (*idavatsara, samvatsara, parivatsara*) is mentioned, p. 370.
   The most recent study of the Coligny Calendar is by Paul-Marie Duval, ÉC x and xi.
45 Camille Jullian claims more than this: 'Toutes les formes de la littérature étaient représentées chez les Gaulois: la rhétorique, où excellaient tous leurs chefs de guerre; les épopées cosmogoniques, historiques ou éthiques, composées par les druides; les poésies lyriques ou les chants satiriques des bardes. Je vous assure qu'il y avait chez eux l'équivalent de l'*Iliade* ou de la *Genèse*, des *Atellanes* ou des odes de Pindare. Je vous assure que cette littérature était aussi riche, plus riche même, que celle de Rome avant Ennius. La langue gauloise rendait beaucoup à ceux qui s'en servaient.' (G. Dottin, *La Langue Gauloise* pp. ix–x.)
46 See chap. 12.
47 Jacobsthal, 'Imagery in Early Celtic Art', p. 10. Later he says: 'They did not decide for Greek humanity, for gay and friendly imagery: instead they chose the weird magic symbols of the east' (*ibid.* p. 19).
48 Strabo IV iv 5, see Tierney *op. cit.* 269; Diodorus Siculus V 27, see Tierney *ib.* 249
49 *Celtic Art* i 160.

35

2

The History and Geography of the British Isles to the end of the Roman Period

No written record of the occupation of the British Isles by Celtic tribes has come down to us, but we can form some idea of the period and distribution from their languages, from archaeology, and from the writings of Greek and Roman authors. The linguistic evidence has been briefly noted in Chapter 1. We have seen that in pre-historic times the Celtic-speaking peoples had entered the British Isles from somewhere in Central Europe, apparently in successive waves, at an uncertain period, but perhaps as early as the beginning of the second millennium BC. The oldest branch of these languages, referred to by modern scholars as Goidelic (or Q-Celtic), survives today in the Highlands and the Western Islands (Hebrides) of Scotland, and in Ireland and the Isle of Man; the later branch, commonly called Brythonic, to which Gaulish originally belonged, survives in Wales and Brittany. Brythonic was formerly spoken throughout south-eastern Britain also, and survives, widespread over our maps, in the names of mountains, rivers, and natural features such as forests. The survival of Brythonic in Brittany is explained as due to the colonization of Brittany from western Britain in the fifth and sixth centuries, to which we shall return later.

The oldest name under which Classical writers commonly refer to the British Isles is 'The Pretanic Islands'. They are thus referred to by Pytheas in the late fourth century BC, and by later writers – Polybius, Strabo, Avienus. The form implies for the name of the inhabitants *Pritani* or *Priteni*. The name is probably Celtic and of the Brythonic form – P-Celtic – probably Gaulish; the Gauls may have handed this

36

name on to the Greeks. The older form continued in use in Welsh texts referring to the island as a whole, *Prydain*, 'Britain' from *Pritani*; and a variant from *Priteni* is used in the form *Prydyn* in early Welsh texts referring to the people north of the Antonine Wall, the 'Picts'.[1] In the Roman period the people of the Roman province called themselves *Brittones*, perhaps a corruption of *Pritani*.

The peoples who brought the Celtic languages into the British Isles first come before us as living inhabitants in the pages and atlas of Ptolemy,[2] a Greek geographer of Alexandria who flourished about the middle of the second century AD, and whose geography, including his account of Ireland, is based on the lost work of Marinus of Tyre,[3] who lived earlier in the same century, though the information which Ptolemy gives about Ireland is believed to be derived ultimately from the work of some traveller of at least two centuries before his time.[4] The information of Marinus is probably that of the first century AD and perhaps earlier; but various strata of information can be detected, including some later details. It may be added here that in addition to Ptolemy we have a valuable source for the geography of Celtic Britain in an anonymous work of the sixth century AD known as the *Ravenna Cosmography*,[5] which makes use of sources of Ptolemy's time, and of various other periods.

From the nature of Ptolemy's record we gather that, as in pre-Roman Gaul, the Celtic peoples in the British Isles were divided into a number of separate groups, of whom the fifth century geographer Marcian states that Ptolemy enumerates thirty-three in Britain,[6] seventeen of whom belong to southern Britain. Scotland[7] therefore probably had about sixteen.[8] Ptolemy gives the names of nine 'cities' (tribes or states) with their relative positions on the Irish coast,[9] but the latter are of uncertain authenticity, and are presumably derived from sailors' records. He names none away from the coast, and all the names which have been identified belong to the east and south coasts, while for the west coast too little information is given to supply us with even an impression of its occupants. The northern and west coast of Ireland is one of the stormiest in the world, and it was probably avoided as far as possible by sailors. The cities which Ptolemy names were probably places of assembly or royal *raths* – *oppida*, like Tara and Emain Macha, and two are referred to as *regia*.[10] None can be identified with any certainty, and other names suggest close relationship with corresponding tribal names in Britain. The

37

Brigantes[11] in South Wexford can hardly be dissociated from the Brigantes who occupied most of north Britain in the Roman period. In general, the names in Ptolemy's account leave no doubt that Ireland was already Celtic-speaking when they were recorded. Very few of Ptolemy's tribal or 'city' names can be identified with names in Irish literary tradition, and therefore his Ireland is earlier than that of the Heroic Age (cf. p. 54 below). His Irish names have been derived directly or indirectly from some geographer considerably before Ptolemy's time, and Pytheas is the only competent candidate.[12]

We have no records of any languages earlier than Pictish in these islands. All our evidence – linguistic, archaeological and historical – suggests that in pre- and proto-historic times the Picts were a great nation occupying the northern part of Scotland from the Firth of Tay to the Shetlands, whom Bede knew in the eighth century AD as the Northern and Southern Picts. Their origin is unknown, but they had probably had a continuous history in Scotland from the Bronze Age until the movements of the Celts into Britain, with whom they seem to have combined. Their proper names have been preserved on about two dozen stone inscriptions evenly distributed between the Northern Isles and the Tay, almost all written in a late form of the early Celtic alphabet known as *ogam* (cf. p. 258 below). Apart from the proper names the inscriptions have never been interpreted. The evidence of the proper names, and the few Pictish words which have survived, suggest that the Celtic element in the Pictish language was nearer to Brythonic than to Goidelic, and nearer to Gaulish than to Welsh. This Pictish language continued to be spoken as late as the ninth century, till the end of the Pictish hegemony (cf. p. 147 below).

It may be conjectured that in the British Isles, as in Gaul, some of the earlier Celtic kingdoms entered on a large scale, and separated into detached groups either before or after establishing themselves here. This is possibly the explanation of the curiously wide distribution of some early identical names. Thus we find the Cornavii recorded by Ptolemy in the extreme north of Scotland, in the area of modern Sutherland or Caithness,[13] and the Cornovii on the north Welsh border with its *oppida* recorded by Ptolemy[14] as *Deva* (Chester) and *Viroconium* (Wroxeter). The first element *Corn-* appears in other places in western Britain, including of course Cornwall, as well as Cornouaille in Brittany. Another ancient name of wide distribution is that of the Dumnonii located by Ptolemy in the west of Scotland south of the Forth-Clyde line, but reaching into Stirlingshire.[15] He also assigns the whole of the south-western peninsula of England, however, including the modern Cornwall, Devon, and much of Somerset, to the Dumnonii. In Ireland a people in the ancient kingdom of Connacht and part of Leinster were known as the *Fir* (Men) *Domnann*, but not by Ptolemy.[16] Are these the relics of early Atlantic settlements? Ptolemy marks three other tribes in southern Scotland, the Novantae[17] in Galloway, south of the Damnonii; the Otadinoi[18] in Haddington and Berwickshire and south into Northumberland; and the Selgovae[19] between the two in the hill country forming the watershed between the Clyde and the Tweed.

In Wales our information of the tribal divisions before the Norman Conquest is very incomplete. The principal tribes located by Ptolemy lie along the sea-coast, and no doubt include the mountain zones in the background which receive no separate names. From Ptolemy and other writers we learn that the south-east down to the Bristol Channel was occupied by the Silures.[20] Their tribal centre was evidently at Caerwent (*Venta Silurium*). Ptolemy refers to the Demetae[21] (later *Dyfed*) as in the extreme west. For north-western Wales our knowledge is not very precise. The whole of north Wales may lie within the territory of the Ordovices,[22] and Ptolemy's information for Anglesey[23] and Snowdonia is probably defective. To the north-east were the Decangli of Flintshire, referred to by Tacitus as dwelling not far from 'the sea which looks towards Ireland'.[24]

Apart from Ptolemy's map our principal guide to the settlement of the Celtic tribes in Britain in the Iron Age is the archaeological evidence of the Celtic fortifications and the course of the Roman Conquest, which we can follow from the contemporary records left by the Romans themselves. The fortifications have been classified in two main categories: first the great hill-top fortifications of Celtic Iron Age A; and second the Belgic-type fortresses of later pattern but sometimes in contemporary use with the first type. Of these the first, and in general the earliest in Britain, are the great *oppida*, or tribal 'hill-top cities', heavily and permanently defended, but believed to have been originally intended, not for permanent occupation, but to serve as a nucleus for the protection and concentration of the scattered surrounding population in time of national danger. In Brittany a type-example is the great Campus d'Artus at Huelgoat in Finisterre, which would seem to have been formed as the rallying-point of the

Osismi in the campaign of Caesar's invasion of 56 BC.[25] Such great *oppida* were undoubtedly the tribal centres of the 'city states'. Among the most impressive that have been fully investigated in Britain are the Stanwick fortifications,[26] undoubtedly the *oppidum* of the Brigantes[27] in the North; and the great hill-top city of Maiden Castle near Dorchester.

Briefly stated the Celtic tribes of southern Britain during the Roman period consisted of old-established kingdoms found in strength chiefly inland. Of these the Cornovii[28] have already been mentioned. They occupied[29] roughly speaking Cheshire and Shropshire. Their tribal capital in Roman times was *Viroconium Cornoviorum*, now known as Wroxeter, but unquestionably a later transference from the great hillfort of the Wrekin, three and a half miles to the east, which stands like a great watch-tower, as a sentinel of the Welsh marches. Ptolemy also included within its boundaries *Deva*, the legionary fortress of Chester; and the kingdom of the Cornovii marched with the Coritani[30] of Lincolnshire and Leicestershire to the east, the great tribe of the Brigantes to the north-east, the Decangli[31] to the north-west, the Ordovices to the west, and the Dobunni to the south.

The Brigantes[32] occupied the valleys of the Pennines and the north-west of England as far as the Parisi in the east of what is now Yorkshire, and as far south as the Cornovii, and perhaps even reached up into south-western Scotland. They were a warlike people, and according to Tacitus numerically the largest in Britain. Their tribal capital, Stanwick, in the North Riding of Yorkshire, extended over an area of 850 acres of lowland enclosed in more than six miles of rampart and ditch, and its widespread and diffuse character is comparable to the early Celtic tribal centres of Gaul, comparable also to Cruachain, the capital of Queen Medb in early Connacht (cf. p. 55 below).

To the east of the Brigantes were the Parisi, with their *oppidum* Petuaria.[33] They had come from the north-eastern plains of Gaul, probably in the third and second centuries BC, and their rich graves, reminiscent of the Marnian culture (cf. p. 368 below), have been identified by their chariot burials and rich horse-trappings, representing a warrior aristocracy. To such later groups of settlers from Gaul belong also the important kingdom of the Iceni[34] of Norfolk and Suffolk, and the Trinovantes[35] in Essex, and others. These tribes were ruled by kings[36] and aristocratic military families and all

40

were centred in strong and wide-spreading hill-top citadels, and possessed some pretensions to wealth and culture. The Dumnonii were rich in minerals; the Belgic Dobunni[37] and the Iceni[38] and others minted their own coinage. Of the kingdoms of southern Britain the most advanced culturally were the Cantii, owing to their favourable position for trade with the Continent. Ptolemy refers to their *oppida* of *Londinium* (London) and *Rutupiae* (Rochester).[39]

In south-eastern and southern England the Celtic tribes of the closing centuries before the Christian era present a somewhat different pattern from the older and wider kingdoms of the earlier period. As in Gaul at the time of Caesar's invasion, political coherence was absent from the Celtic kingdoms already established in Britain. This disunity undoubtedly contributed to the penetration and supremacy of the Belgae, as it was to be the chief cause of the Roman Conquest later. When Caesar made his two expeditions to Britain in 55 and 54 BC he found that certain tribes of the Belgae had already migrated across the Channel from northern Gaul, and had gradually established an overlordship over a large part of the earlier Celtic coastal tribes of southern Britain (see map 2, below). These movements from Gaul to Britain were more in the nature of an expansion than an invasion, and Caesar himself noted that within the memory of the Gauls of his own day some of the immigrants had come into Britain as tribal units, both as plunderers and colonists, and that their British communities continued to bear names identical with those which they had left behind in Gaul.

Among the most powerful of the new kingdoms which they established on this side of the Channel was that of the Catuvellauni in Hertfordshire, with their tribal centre[40] in the vicinity of what was to become St Albans (Roman *Verulamium*). The Catuvellauni extended an overlordship over the surrounding peoples, and completely absorbed the Trinovantes[41] in Essex, between the East Anglian heights and the sea, with their *oppidum* at Colchester. In addition to the powerful Catuvellauni and their subject kingdom of the Trinovantes, Belgic kingdoms rapidly established themselves in the south and west.

Caesar's initial expedition to Britain in 55 BC had as its object an appraisement of the situation. He himself tells us (Book IV, 20) he understood that in almost all the Gallic campaigns help had been forthcoming to the enemy from that quarter, and he believed that it would be of great advantage to him to have entered the island and observed the character of the natives, and the nature of the country which was little known to the Gauls. He tells us that as soon as the Britons observed his intention of landing they sent forward their cavalry and charioteers, whom 'it is their regular custom to employ in fights', and followed them up with the rest of their forces. The chariot fighting of the Britons evidently made a deep impression on Caesar, for after relating a difficult landing and a subsequent defeat of the British forces, he pauses in his narrative to give a somewhat detailed account of the method of their chariot tactics:

Their manner of fighting from chariots is as follows: First of all they drive in all directions and hurl missiles, and so by the mere terror that the teams inspire and by the noise of the wheels they generally throw ranks into confusion. When they have worked their way in between the troops of cavalry, they leap down from the chariots and fight on foot. Meanwhile the charioteers retire gradually from the combat, and dispose the chariots in such fashion that, if the warriors are hard pressed by the host of the enemy, they may have a ready means of retirement to their own side. Thus they show in action the mobility of cavalry and the stability of infantry; and by daily use and practice they become so accomplished that they are ready to gallop their teams down the steepest of slopes without loss of control, to check and turn them in a moment, to run along the pole, stand on the yoke, and then, quick as lightning, to dart back into the chariot.[42]

Caesar had made a 'reconnaissance in force'[43] in his two expeditions to Britain in 55 and 54 BC. The actual conquest began under Claudius in AD 43, and spread northwards and westwards till the Celtic tribes of the English lowlands seem to have been over-run and subdued as far as the Severn and the Humber within three years. In 47 the Iceni were conquered, and for the most part the older established tribes, including the Iceni themselves, accepted the position of client kingdoms. In the north also Cartimandua, the queen of the Brigantes, entered into treaty relations with Rome, and accepted the position of a client state.

The ancient Celtic kingdoms beyond the periphery of Lower Britain, however, were in no sense reconciled to a conquest by the

Romans. Resistance movements and rebellions broke out whenever and wherever opportunity seemed to offer any chance of success.[44] To follow the history of the Celtic kingdoms as the Roman conquest spread is particularly difficult as our only records are those of the conquerors, and we are in the position of seeking to trace an almost universal underground movement for which we have no continuous clues. It is as if one should seek to trace the course of a series of small earthquakes without the guidance of seismological instruments. We are thankful for such surface records as Roman historians have left us.

In Wales the most powerful resistance[45] came from the tribes of the Ordovices[46] in northern and central Wales, and the warlike Silures[47] of the south-east. Sir Ian Richmond's recent study of the Cornovii[48] has shown that Roman military arrangements for the control of this western border state were dictated by the need of active measures to counter unrest, and even raiding, by the native Celtic mountain tribes to the west (cf. p. 76 below). In South Wales Caratacus raised the warlike kingdom of the Silures[49] and marched northwards to join the Ordovices, doubtless counting on an alliance with the Brigantes; but he was heavily defeated in a pitched battle in 51, and after taking refuge with the Brigantes, was handed over to the Romans in chains by Cartimandua their queen.

Cartimandua[50] is one of the outstanding women rulers of Celtic antiquity, comparable with her contemporary Queen Boudicca of the Iceni, and with the Heroic Age queen of Ireland, Queen Medb of Connacht. It is indeed impossible to have any true understanding of either Celtic history or Celtic literature without realizing the high status of Celtic women, and something of the nature of their place in society, in both Gaul and Britain. We hear from Polybius that they accompanied their husbands to battle, following them in wagons;[51] but Ammianus Marcellinus describes them as taking an energetic part in actual combat. Indeed he tells us that a whole troop would not be able to withstand one Gaul in battle if he summoned his wife to his assistance (cf. p. 195 below).

Cartimandua had been established by Claudius as queen of the Brigantes. She repudiated her husband Venutius, who apparently commanded wide territories to the north, and her only hope of survival lay in Roman protection. Her marriage with her husband's standard-bearer Vellocatus was doubtless a matter of policy, for Venutius, formerly loyal to Rome like herself, was now found to be

43

disaffected and leading a resistance movement. It has been suggested with high probability that if the Brigantes could have been united as a strong buffer state, the cost to the Romans of occupying northern Britain might have been saved. This however was not to be. The conquest of the Brigantes was completed by Agricola, who established Chester, now a legionary fortress, as his base, and from there completed the conquest of Wales soon after his arrival in Britain in 77 or 78.

Already in AD 61, however, the Roman general Suetonius Paulinus had inflicted a severe local defeat on the Welsh tribes – perhaps the Ordovices – on the shore of the Menai Straits, and Tacitus has left us a vivid account of the encounter between the Roman soldiers and the druids of Anglesey in one of his most studied melodramatic passages:

On the opposite shore stood the Britons, close embodied and prepared for action. Women were seen rushing through the ranks in wild disorder, their apparel funereal, their hair loose to the wind, in their hands flaming torches, and their whole appearance resembling the frantic rage of the Furies. The Druids were ranged in order, with hands uplifted, invoking the gods, and pouring forth horrible imprecations. The novelty of the sight struck the Romans with awe and terror. They stood in stupid amazement, as if their limbs were benumbed, riveted to one spot, a mark for the enemy. The exhortations of the general diffused new vigour through the ranks, and the men, by mutual reproaches, inflamed each other to deeds of valour. They felt the disgrace of yielding to a troop of women and a band of fanatic priests they advanced their standards, and rushed on to the attack with impetuous fury. The Britons perished in the flames which they themselves had kindled. The island fell, and a garrison was established to retain it in subjection. The religious groves, dedicated to superstition and barbarous rites, were levelled to the ground.[52]

Meanwhile Boudicca, the queen of the Iceni, led a powerful rebellion in East Anglia, in which the Trinovantes joined, and Suetonius was forced to return at speed, leaving the conquest of Wales to be finally completed by Agricola.[53] Under Boudicca's husband Pratugasus, and indeed probably before, the Iceni had of necessity

44

become a client state, sacrificing their independence perforce for the protection of Rome, to whom their loyalty became due in consequence. As a client king Pratugasus could not appoint his successor in the kingdom, but he bequeathed half of his property to Rome and the remaining half to each of his two daughters. The royal family and the nobility were treated as a conquered kingdom, and the Romans did not appoint Boudicca to inherit the rule of the client kingdom. They further alienated the British nobility by treating the grants which had been made to them by Claudius as loans, and before absorbing the kingdom into the Roman province they proceeded to divide the legacy at the hands of the military and fiscal officials. No doubt some resistance was offered, but the brutality with which Boudicca and her daughters were treated involved the honour of the whole tribe, which rose in rebellion. The Trinovantes, who also had their own financial sources of grievance, joined the Iceni.

Dio Cassius has left us a portrait of Boudicca, which has been justly called 'the most dramatic picture of a Celtic heroine in classical literature':[54]

> She was huge of frame, terrifying of aspect, and with a harsh voice. A great mass of bright red hair fell to her knees: she wore a great twisted golden necklace, and a tunic of many colours, over which was a thick mantle, fastened by a brooch. Now she grasped a long spear, to strike fear into all who watched her . . .[55]

To judge from Cartimandua and Boudicca the British women hardly fall short of their Gaulish sisters in force of personality and political and military prestige. Suetonius, by prompt action and skill in military tactics, succeeded in quelling the rebellion, but not without great difficulty, and the rebels were treated with such severity as might be expected. Suetonius was recalled shortly after, and Roman policy was able to concentrate on strengthening the defences of the frontiers.

Meanwhile the unrest of the Brigantes – the largest confederation of native tribes in Britain among the Roman client kingdoms – compelled Agricola, on his appointment as governor of Britain, to postpone the final subjugation of Wales – now virtually conquered by Suetonius – and turn his most concentrated efforts to the north. On his northward route he negotiated the difficult Lancashire country between the Pennines and the sea, founding his fort at Ribchester, guarding the entrance to the River Ribble, and so over the Pennines to his fort at Elslack en route for Ilkley and York, and also from his fort at Manchester leading to a network of Pennine routes into Yorkshire.[56] It was masterly strategy to impede both cross-country communications by the Brigantes, and Irish raiding from across Morecambe Bay against the Roman forts in Yorkshire.[57]

In AD 80 he began his famous campaign in southern Scotland, quickly reaching as far northward as the Tay, and establishing a line of temporary forts along the Forth-Clyde isthmus, encompassing the Celtic (British) kingdoms of the Selgovae and the Votadini in the south-west and south-east respectively, and penetrating and fortifying Galloway and Ayrshire. Reluctantly as he looked at the opposite coast of Ireland, clearly visible, he abandoned, or perhaps rather postponed, the dream of conquest yet further westward. As Tacitus, who was in a position to know, tells us, 'He saw that Ireland . . . conveniently situated for the ports of Gaul, might prove a valuable acquisition', and Tacitus goes on to tell us that one of the Irish kings, who had been forced to flee owing to local political troubles, was received by the Roman general, and, under pretence of friendship, detained to be of use on some future occasion.[58]

'I have often heard Agricola declare', adds Tacitus, 'that a single legion, with a moderate band of auxiliaries, would be enough to complete the conquest of Ireland.'[59] But Agricola's dream was never fulfilled. Instead he took precautionary measures against Irish invasion of south-western Scotland.

The extent of the Roman occupation of Scotland is still a matter of enquiry, but north of the Highland Line the country of the Highland clans was apparently never penetrated. In order to protect the Lowlands from raids or conquest from the north, Agricola penetrated into Perthshire and built the great legionary fortress of Inchtuthill ten miles from Perth, a strong position as a permanent base for winter quarters, but not for strategical purposes. Beyond this point his northern progress seems to have been chiefly through the great plain of Strathmore north of the lower Tay. Forts were built up the east coast as far as Kintore on the Don, and even further.[60] But progress northwards was checked by the powerful tribe of the Caledonians at the famous battle of Mons Graupius,[61] an unidentified place[62] apparently further north than the Perthshire Highlands, but almost certainly approached along the east coast. The Roman fort of Raedykes near Stonehaven has been shown to be the most likely site of the battle,[63] and the native tribes, the Caledonians assembled for the battle, would presumably therefore be Picts. In a preliminary engagement the Caledonians had made a night attack on the Roman camp where the ninth legion was unprepared. The attackers succeeded in penetrating into the very heart of the camp, and had not Agricola arrived for the timely relief of the legion the Caledonians would have carried the day. Tacitus tells us, however, that they were put to the rout, 'and if the woods and marshes had not served to protect them that single encounter would have been the end of the war'.[64]

The Caledonians were by no means dispirited, however, and to judge from their tactics they seem to have been more advanced in both their political and military methods than the Britons of the south. Tacitus, whose general account of the campaign is regrettably vague, leaves us nevertheless some significant details.[65] He tells us, for example, that the Caledonians sent their wives and children to a place of safety, which we have seen to be contrary to ancient Celtic tradition; and he stresses their newly acquired sense of the importance of unity:

They listed the young men of their nation, and they held public conventions of the several states, and . . . formed a league in the cause of liberty. . . . Experience had taught them that the common cause required a vigorous exertion of their united strength. For this purpose, by treaties and alliance, and by deputations to the several cantons, they had drawn together the strength of the nation.

Tacitus adds that nearly thirty thousand men appeared in arms, and that their strength was increasing every day. Their chieftain, most renowned by birth and valour, was Calgacus, who harangued the assembled troops before the battle in a speech which Tacitus claims to have reported verbatim, and which we can hardly doubt reflects the well-known compelling characteristic Celtic eloquence:

The extremity of the earth is ours, . . . but this is the end of the habitable world . . . The Romans are in the heart of our country . . .

No submission can satisfy their pride ... While the land has anything left it is the theatre of war ... They make a desert and call it peace.

Meanwhile Agricola selected his site in a close place between the hills and the sea, and stationed his troops, the infantry in the centre, numbering, according to Tacitus, about eight thousand men, the three thousand horse in the wings, the legions in the rear. The Caledonians were stationed on rising ground, with their charioteers lower down on the plain. 'The Britons', says Tacitus, 'wanted neither skill nor resolution. With their long swords and *cetrae* (small light shields), they managed to elude the heavy weapons of the Romans, and at the same time to discharge a thick volley of their own.' But the chariots seem to have obstructed the movements of the native soldiery in the narrow ground; the army on the heights at first descended slowly, hoping to take the Romans in the rear, then rushed down swiftly, but were forced to retire at speed:

The vanquished Britons had their moments of returning courage, and gave proofs of virtue and of brave despair. They fled to the woods, and rallying their scattered numbers, surrounded such of the Romans as pursued with too much eagerness. ... It is a fact well authenticated that some laid violent hands upon their wives and children, determined with savage compassion to end their misery.

The battle of Mons Graupius, which took place in AD 84, ended the seventh and last campaign of Agricola in Scotland. It was the culmination of his effort to conquer the country, and he was recalled soon after. The result of the whole northern campaign was to leave the Romans in possession of all lowland Scotland; but the Highland tribes retained their freedom and were never penetrated by the Roman legions. Scotland has remained for ever an unconquered country.

Meanwhile the Highland tribes were by no means subdued, and as soon as the Roman power showed signs of weakening they were ready to take full advantage of the change by a series of acts of aggression and raids which culminated in the gradual withdrawal of the Roman defences southwards. The cause of the change was, of course, neither local nor British, but lay in the military crisis in the heart of the empire, necessitating the withdrawal of troops from the western frontiers. The change began in the Scottish lowlands soon after AD 100. The advanced garrisons were given up, and all the forts north of the Cheviot, and perhaps north of the Tyne-Solway gap, were evacuated. In 117 a powerful rising of the Celtic peoples in Scotland and northern England took place, serious enough to bring the Emperor Hadrian to England, and between 122 and 128 or 129 the great stone wall or, better, *vallum*, from Tyne to Solway was built in the hope of forming an impenetrable barrier.[66] An interesting inscription, apparently from the eastern end, seems to record the completion of the building of this great *vallum*, by Hadrian, as a *limes*, a 'barrier' erected as a 'necessity'.[67] In 139–42 a forward movement was again resumed, and a turf wall was built from Forth to Clyde under Hadrian's successor, Antoninus Pius. Nevertheless the second half of the second century saw the gathering of the Celtic forces in the Scottish Lowlands and the north of England. Revolts in 155–8 and 181 destroyed the walls and almost all the forts, and in 196 a large part of Britain was overrun. In 208 Septimius Severus arrived with his younger son Geta and subdued the 'Caledonii' and the Picts of Strathmore and Strathearn; but after the death of Severus in 211, Caracalla withdrew all Roman permanent garrisons to Hadrian's wall,[68] and further measures of defence were taken, chief of which were new advanced posts manned by irregular units or frontier patrols, the *exploratores*, e.g. at High Rochester, Risingham, Bewcastle and Netherby. The main burden of the northern defences was henceforth delegated to the Britons of the north, supported by Roman resources. The success of this measure can be gauged from the fact that during the third, and still more the fourth, centuries Roman Britain enjoyed her most prosperous period, when the villas flourished and town life developed.

The Roman occupation of Britain can best be likened to a great flood tide, and the close came, as the tide recedes, not by a sudden event, not even by a series of events, but by a gradual process, as the ebb-tide leaves the shore. It was in a sense part of a world crisis, the overthrow of a great civilization by the inroads of barbarians from the north. In 406 the barbarians crossed the Rhine and in 410 Rome, 'the mistress of the world', fell to the Goths. The same year the Anonymous Gaulish chronicler records a specially heavy raid on Britain.

During the third and fourth centuries the *pax Romana* had lulled

49

southern Britain and Gaul alike into a sense of security. There can be no doubt that in Lower Britain the Celtic and the Roman peoples had to some extent settled during the centuries of the occupation into a community whose best hopes of continuing peace had lain in unity. Their interests were by now combined, and their hope for the future lay in preventing raids from across the frontiers and permanent settlement by alien populations. To the Celtic peoples of the north and west however the situation presented a very different aspect. The weakening of the Roman hold on Britain, and the gradual withdrawal of the Roman forces, opened the way to hopes of conquest and occupation, not only to the Teutonic peoples of north-western Europe – the Angles and Saxons, the Jutes and the Frisians – but also to the unconquered Celtic kingdoms of northern Britain and Ireland.

The Barbarian invasions of the Continent, which brought Roman rule to an end, were not isolated from raids in Roman Britain. The history of the fleet is obscure at this period,[69] but a Roman admiral Carausius, who was in command of the English Channel, certainly reconditioned the fleet before he was murdered in 293 after setting himself up in Britain as emperor. His successor Constantius, who came to Britain in 296, constructed a new fleet, and before his death[70] in 306 either he or Carausius built and heavily defended some at least of the twelve forts along what is – perhaps ambiguously – called the 'Saxon Shore'[71] in south-eastern Britain, extending from Brancaster on the Wash to Portchester in Hampshire, while a corresponding series was built on the French coast and on the Isle of Alderney.

Meanwhile the Picts of the far north, and the Irish, both of whom had been immune from the Roman conquest, were gaining in strength and boldness as the Roman strength weakened. Both possessed fleets more numerous and powerful than is commonly realized, and both were attacking British coasts throughout this period. Gildas recognized the heaviness of the Pictish attacks by sea 'de curucis' (from their 'curraghs', the Gaelic word for the native sea-craft), and the fourth-century writer Vegetius has left us an interesting section on the new British coastal patrols attached to the fleet, with their expertise in camouflage and maritime guerrilla tactics.[72]

During the fourth century, raids by the Picts of Scotland became more formidable, and in 367 occurred the greatest disaster which had yet befallen Roman Britain, in which a simultaneous attack was made on all three fronts at once – by the Irish from the west, the Picts from the north and the Saxons from the east. Ammianus Marcellinus, a contemporary informant, describes it as a *conspiratio barbarica*.[73] The immediate effect of the attack was devastating though its effect has been exaggerated. The wall forts were repaired by Count Theodosius, but the outposts beyond were permanently abandoned, and the raids by sea continued. Signal stations were set up along the Yorkshire coast, probably by Theodosius also; but were destroyed by Saxon raiders in 390, and Stilicho's expedition of 395 brought defences still further south. The Gallo-Romans were still anxiously watching bulletins from Britain, now their chief defensive outpost against the barbarians, and in 399 or 400 the poet Claudian in his poem against Eutropius[74] declares that

> The Saxon is conquered and the seas are tranquil,
> The Pict is broken and Britain is safe.

How deluded!

The chief name which has come down to us in both history and tradition from this period of crisis in Britain is Magnus Maximus. The part which he actually played is matter for conjecture.[75] We cannot take any firm stand on the late and delightful Welsh medieval tradition of his marriage to a Welsh bride,[76] or his unsatisfactory pedigree.[77] On the other hand the brief entry in the almost contemporary *Anonymous Gaulish Chronicle*, s.a. 392 is weighty: 'Maximus strenuously overcame the Picts and Scots'.[78] His achievement was evidently outstanding as a check to the Celtic and Pictish attacks, for in 383 the army in Britain proclaimed him emperor and crossed with him to Gaul, where he set up his court in Trèves in 384 or 385. His troops were evidently the *Seguntienses*, 'the men from *Segontium*' (Caernarvon) who are named among the *auxilia palatina* (evidently his personal bodyguard) serving in Illyricum,[79] where he was killed (at Aquileia) in 388, and where an inscription undoubtedly records the event.[80]

In Britain the end came quickly. The governor Constantine was forced by the army in 407 to usurp the title of Emperor and apparently by friendly arrangement with the Emperor Honorius he crossed to Gaul, taking some British troops with him. This is our last farewell to a Roman governor. Procopius tells us that he was subsequently defeated in battle and slain together with his sons; and he adds:

'Notwithstanding this the Romans were never able to recover Britain which henceforth continued to be ruled by tyrants'.[81]

On the whole it would seem that this was virtually the end of at least the Roman military occupation.[82] Zosimus, a Greek writer who is believed to have obtained his information from Olympiodorus, a very reliable source, tells us that the Barbarians from beyond the Rhine:

> . . . ravaging at will, forced the people of Britain and some of those of Gaul, to secede from the Roman Empire and act independently, no longer subject to the laws of the Romans. The Britons took up arms and defended themselves, and, struggling bravely, freed themselves and repelled barbarian attacks. The Armoricans, encouraged by the example of the insular Britons, had thrown off the Roman yoke. This British-Gallic secession occurred in the time of the Emperor Constantine.[83]

In 410 came the famous rescript of Honorius informing the 'cities' ($\pi\acute{o}\lambda\epsilon\iota\varsigma$) ('city states') of Britain that they might look after themselves.[84] The correct interpretation of this probably is the formal withdrawal of the Roman prohibition of the natives from bearing arms. The precise year of the official evacuation is of small account. By the middle of the fifth century Britain had become an independent country, ruled over once more by independent Celtic princes.

In consequence of her seclusion and inviolability Ireland has preserved in miniature for future ages the economy and institutions of the ancient Celtic world of the Iron Age. She is the microcosm of the early Celtic race. The art of the La Tène style continued without a break to form an organic element in the Irish art of the Middle Ages. The intellectual classes of Gaul reappear in ancient Ireland to carry on the intellectual life and historical traditions by oral transmission till written records begin with the introduction of Christianity and Latin learning. In the absence of Roman penetration of Ireland her political geography changed only slowly, and we lack the external evidence of either contemporary Latin documents or early vernacular written records to help us to trace the early settlement and population groups.

On the other hand Ireland possessed a greater wealth of carefully preserved oral tradition from the earliest period of our era than any other people in Europe north of the Alps. For this reason the foundation of her early history from traditional materials is of general interest far beyond her geographical and political area, and second only to that of the ancient Greek and Roman world. Further, archaeologically speaking Ireland is a museum of the ancient world. The Industrial Revolution which changed the face of Britain left the Irish countryside inviolate, a paradise for the archaeologist and place-name specialist. The absence of Roman disruption and of recent industrial development combine with the discipline of modern scholarship to enable us to reconstruct conjecturally something of the early settlement of Ireland before the days of written history. The process of reconstruction is under way, and it may well add centuries to the history of the periphery of western Europe.

When the Irish historical period begins early in the fifth century the dominant peoples of Ireland were the so-called Goidels, with strong-holds at Tara in Meath, Croghan in Connacht, and Cashel in Munster. The chief Irish families claimed to be of 'Goidelic' origin, and to be related to one another closely through the parent stock. They were a group of leading families, 'over-kings', who held their lands free of rent or tribute, while themselves exacting tribute from the provincial subject kingdoms.

Our oldest genuine traditions, however, relate to a period which has been credibly shown to be that of Ireland during the previous period, and in fact to be, not learned speculation, but genuine oral tradition, embodying a reliable picture – within certain well-defined limits – of Ireland as she was before the introduction of writing, of European culture, and before the dominance of the dynasty of Meath over the north. The historical geography and political institutions of this traditional picture of Ireland offer a remarkable contrast, on the one hand to the picture artificially built up by the late 'pseudo-historians', working in the interest of the historical dynasty of Tara, and an equally strong contrast on the other to those conditions known from genuine historical records to have prevailed from the fifth century onwards, as we shall see. This traditional picture is that of a heroic society in the late Iron Age, much like that of Gaul before the Roman conquest. It has been preserved for us intact by the exceptionally high quality of Irish oral tradition. This phase of Ireland which immediately preceded the historical period merits our keen interest and attention. It offers us a picture of Celtic society which is unique in Europe.

53

This earlier oral tradition claims to extend reliable Irish history back to the Heroic Age, and it can be shown to be appropriate to a period as early as the fourth century AD. Many traditions may even be authentic for the close of the third century, for example the person and some of the stories about Cormac mac Airt, who according to tradition reigned as king of Ireland from 227 to 266. Our fullest and most authentic picture of Ireland in the earliest historical period, however, is the great prose saga of *Táin Bó Cualnge*, 'The Cattle-Raid of Cooley', which has preserved for us an intimate record of a European society in the late Iron Age.[85] Ireland is already a Celtic country in this story, as the proper names prove. We must realize, however, that the story has come to us through various centuries of oral transmission, during which the earliest tales, originally formulated in the Heroic Age, had been recast in a final artistic form, first oral and finally, probably in the early eighth century, in written form. The storyteller recognizes the period as belonging to the far past, but the allusions and traditions have been preserved with great fidelity, as can be seen from the consistency of the internal evidence, and from comparison with other Irish heroic stories.

In the *Táin* Ireland is divided into four provinces, already called *cóiceda*, 'fifths', each province consisting of one 'fifth'; but the tradition is so conservative that the fifth province, known in historical times as Meath (*Mide*), and which seems not yet to have come into existence, is never mentioned. The Ireland of the *Táin* is the Ireland of the *Érainn*, the earlier Celtic inhabitants, and it is thought that the fifth province, Meath (Ir. *Mide*, 'the Middle Province') was added later after the establishment of the supremacy of the Uí Néill ('descendants of Niall Noígiallach') in central and northern Ireland in the fifth century.[86] The four provinces known to the *Táin* tradition were large kingdoms, like the oldest Celtic provinces of Gaul and Britain, and they bore the names *Ulaid*, *Connachta*, *Laigin* and *Mumu*. The names of the four-fold division have survived till the present day as Ulster, Connacht, Leinster and Munster. The province of the *Ulaid* ('people of Ulster') consisted in the *Táin* of the whole of northern Ireland, including Donegal in the far west and Dunseverick on the Antrim coast. It was a great monarchy with its chief *ráth* or 'court' at Emain Macha, two miles west of Armagh, and its king was Conchobar mac Nessa, a prince of the *Érainn*.

The second of the *Cóiceda* at this period was Connachta (modern

54

Connaught), with its centre of power spreading widely over the hill of Cruachain. In the *Táin Connachta* is ruled by a woman, Queen Medb, whose consort is Ailill, and the province of *Connachta* is the rival and enemy of the *Ulaid*. South of the *Ulaid* were the *Laigin* (modern Leinster) (cf. p. 19 above). The *Cóiced* of *Mumu* (modern Munster) is ruled by small kings of whom the chief is Cú Roí mac Dáiri, whose seat is in West Kerry, and who has close relations with the heroes of the Ulster Cycle. As yet the Eóganacht dynasty of the great rock citadel of Cashel has not arisen.

The tradition represented by the *Táin* and its framework of the four great provinces gives us our first introduction to early Irish history, comparable to our picture of Britain at the time of the Roman conquest. Christianity is unknown. Tara plays no part. The Goidels are never referred to. Everything in the *Táin* suggests that the political and religious conditions preserve an unbroken tradition from before the fourth century, a 'Heroic Age' civilization of the sub La Tène period. For these reasons the oral traditions preserved in the *Táin* may be said to represent the earliest period of Irish history, which dates from the fourth century while the Heroic Age was still a living memory.

Moreover, the sympathies implied in the *Táin* are all with the *Ulaid* and therefore with the *Érainn*, not with the later dynasty of Tara. The Ulster places and the Ulster heroes are more familiar to the narrator than those of Munster and Connaught. This suggests that the *Táin* is an Ulster composition, and as the monastery of Bangor, Co. Down, was a centre of historical studies in the seventh and eighth centuries, it is probable that the *Táin* may have been finally written down in this monastery. And the motive for the compilation of this great prose epic? Perhaps we may suggest that it is a proud assertion of the past greatness of the *Érainn*, the ancient Celtic rulers of Ireland, against the parvenu line of the Uí Néill of the Tara dynasty, and the northern Uí Néill, who had destroyed Emain Macha and reduced the *Ulaid* to a small territory in northern and eastern Antrim. It may be suggested that the final formulation of the story and its record on vellum was inspired by a political motive.

Subsequently to the period represented by the *Táin*, a new dynasty arose with its royal *ráth* at the prehistoric sanctuary of Tara in Meath. It was apparently the founding of this kingdom which established the division into five 'fifths' (*cóiceda*). This was indeed of short duration.

55

The founder of the new dynasty was Níall Noígiallach, and his descendants subsequently ruled all the centre and northern half of Ireland. The southern half, consisting of half Leinster and all Munster, was never subject to the Uí Néill ('descendants of Níall'), but at a later date was ruled by a branch of the Munster dynasty from the great rock citadel of Cashel. It is believed that the new dynasty of the Uí Néill and the province of Meath rose to prominence as the result of invasion, and that they were Goidels. Who were the Goidels?

The ancestry of these Meath 'Goidels' is traced in late pseudo-historical texts to a certain fictitious *Míl Espáine* who was supposed to have come from Spain. Hence the name *Milesians*, by which name the Goidelic conquerors are commonly referred to in modern histories. *Míl Espáine* is evidently a translation from Latin *miles Hispaniae* 'the soldier from Spain', and in the Book of Invasions he is given a fictitious pedigree going back to an eponymous ancestor, *Goídel Glas*. In fact the name *Goídel* is borrowed from Welsh *Gwyddel* 'Irishman'. It may be derived from Welsh *gwydd* 'wood, forest'.

The late Professor O'Rahilly categorically stated that the people of this last invasion of Ireland and the Goidelic form of the Celtic language were introduced simultaneously into Ireland at a comparatively late date, and he uses the term Goidelic of both the people and their language (p. 20 above). He expressed the view that: 'If anything is certain about the Goidels, it is that they reached Ireland direct from the Continent', and he held that they 'must have come to Ireland from Gaul', and suggested that their migration was from south-eastern Gaul, perhaps from Gallia Narbonensis, whence they passed to the western coast not later than 120 BC, and migrated to Ireland towards 50 BC.[87] The late date and the course of events suggested by O'Rahilly are difficult to accept in view of the silence of Roman historians on so long and important a migration at this late date. The question must be regarded as at present unsettled. A more acceptable theory would be that the Milesians (Goidels) did come from Spain, as the Book of Invasions says. The discovery of Q-Celtic inscriptions in Spain by Tovar shows that in that lateral area the older forms had survived.[88]

If, however, we accept the provisional date suggested in Chapter 1 (p. 19 f.), that is to say some time early in the second millennium BC, for the spread of the Celtic peoples to the British Isles, it becomes reasonable also to accept the conclusion that the differentiation of the

Celtic languages into two principal groups, known as Goidelic (commonly called Q-Celtic) and Brythonic (commonly called P-Celtic, cf. p. 258) originally took place, not, as formerly believed, exclusively somewhere on the Continent, but also in the British Isles at some period between *c.* 2000 and 600 BC. Very possibly analogous changes may have been taking place throughout the whole Celtic world, and the Quariates may have represented a backward mountain dialect. But, language apart, who are the peoples commonly known as the 'Goidels of Meath' and commonly regarded as the latest immigrants into Ireland large enough to form a distinct population group?

At present this question cannot be answered with confidence; but the following facts are significant:

1. Although only four provinces are known in the earliest Irish traditions of the Heroic Age, they are known in the earliest written sources as the *cóic cóiceda*, 'the five provinces'. Therefore one has been added in the earliest historical period.

2. The political institutions of the earliest historical period imply a dominant dynasty in Meath, with military off-shoots in the north and west. Therefore Meath was probably the 'fifth' province of the *cóiceda*, with its centre at Tara.

3. Whether by external invasion, or by internal stimulus, the dynasty of Tara became predominant in the northern half of Ireland, as the dynasty of the rock of Cashel did in the south. Tara was an ancient heathen sanctuary. The subsequent Christian history of Cashel suggests that sanctity doubtless gave prestige to Cashel as to Tara.

4. Consistent tradition suggests that the ruling dynasty of northern and central Ireland obtained their power by military conquest, in the late fourth and early fifth century AD. This does not necessarily imply a movement of people. It was the time of the barbarian invasions, and Meath, a rich agricultural province with a wealthy sanctuary, would be a tempting prey to a military invading group. But the invasion may have taken place much earlier, and the Goidelic rise to supreme power may have been a gradual process. We do not know.

57

During the fifth century and earlier the weakening power of the Roman Empire gave a great impetus to the movements and expansion of the Insular Celtic peoples, always seeking to extend their territory. The Irish in particular took advantage of the military weakness of the Roman defences of western Britain to penetrate the western promontories of Britain. We have seen from the statement of Ammianus Marcellinus that already during the fourth century Irish raids were no less formidable than those of the Picts and Saxons from the north and east. The Irish Sea had always been, and continued to be, a purely Celtic area, both politically and culturally. Here the Romans had no part, and there was no unified Celtic power to preclude the free transit and transport of the individual Celtic communities to and fro across this Celtic Pond.

Among the most significant of these Irish expansions was the occupation of south-western Wales, the area of a wider Pembrokeshire, later known as the kingdom of Dyfed. This area was occupied by a dynasty from Leinster, who led a migration and settled in sufficient numbers to render the population bi-lingual in the fifth century, and to form what was virtually a little Irish kingdom. The pedigree and the story of its foundation are exceptionally well preserved, and these and other traditions enable us to trace also Irish settlements from the same quarter all the way along the south coast of Wales and the Bristol Channel, and even into the little mountain kingdom of Brecknock in the interior. At the same period Irish penetration of the Caernarvonshire peninsula has left abundant traces in place-names, and in the archaeological evidence of Roman defences. We have already traced some of these late Roman defensive measures in the preceding pages.

The peninsula where this Irish influence is strongest is Dyfed. It would seem indeed that Dyfed, and perhaps the peninsula of Lleyn in Caernarvonshire also, were bilingual at this period, and certainly in Dyfed, the ruling class were Irish-speaking. Inscriptions in the *ogam* alphabet, which is characteristically Irish, are more numerous here than anywhere else in Wales. Their number suggests a strong Irish aristocracy on the spot, which extended to the neighbouring area of Carmarthenshire, the county which has the largest number of Ogams after Dyfed.

Moreover the Irish settlers seem to have been well established and continuous in Dyfed. A unique family group of three generations is

58

commemorated by four inscribed stones in the area. A stone in Llandeilo churchyard commemorates in both Latin and *Ogam* letters a certain Andagellus, son of Cavetus.[89] Another pillar-stone in the same churchyard commemorates in Latin, Coimagnus, son of Cavetus;[90] another at Maenchlochog commemorates Curcagnus, son of Andagellus.[91]

Interesting confirmation, both of the intensive settlement of the Irish in south-west Wales at this time, and of the Roman appointment of barbarian princes to protect the outlying provinces, is afforded by a stone inscription on a round-headed tombstone believed to date from *c*. 550.[92] It is now in the Carmarthenshire Museum, but formerly stood in the entrance to Castell Dwyran graveyard. The inscription in Latin lettering is in three horizontal lines and runs:

Memoria
Voteporigis
Protictoris.

The round head of the stone is original and not due to weathering, for on the left arc at the top an *ogam* inscription is cut which translates the Brythonic (British-Welsh) name into Goidelic (Irish) and reads:

Votecorigas.

It will be remembered that the Irish language has *c* corresponding to Welsh *p*.

Voteporigis of the inscription is believed to be the *Vorteporius* whom Gildas attacks in the first half of the sixth century as the *tyrannus* ('tyrant') of the Demetae ('the men of *Dyfed*' or Pembrokeshire). The word *tyrannus* at this time is commonly used of usurpers (cf. p. 69 below).

These memorial stones are especially common in the districts known to have been occupied by the Irish in historical times, and it is therefore interesting that *Voteporix* (gen. *voteporigis*) is of Irish descent and in a Déisi (i.e. Irish) district, and that the Irish form *Votecorigas* is also given and in Ogam writing. The implication is that both Welshmen with a knowledge of Latin, and also Irish speakers, are expected to be equally interested in this early ruler, the 'Protector'. For our immediate purpose, that of watching the change from Roman

59

to native Celtic rule in Britain, and the measures taken by the Romans in the latter part of their rule in Britain to train and make use of their native Celtic elements, the important thing about the inscription is the word *protictor*, 'protector'. This is not a grateful adjective, or a laudatory epithet, but a Roman title. It is the title given by the Romans to the barbarian princes honoured with the status of *foederati*, i.e. 'protectors' of the frontiers on behalf of the Romans. *Voteporix* in the sixth century doubtless bore it hereditarily. No one would be so well qualified to keep the Irish out of Dyfed as an Irish dynasty with Irish subjects.

The peninsula of Caernarvonshire, and also Anglesey and West Merioneth, were settled by Irish about the same time as Dyfed, and the Irish language was spoken all over the area, perhaps in remote parts down to the Norman Conquest,[93] and is deeply embedded in place-names. At the head of Afon Lledr in Caernarvonshire is *Llyn Iwerddon*, 'Lake of Ireland'. Lower down, near the falls of the Conway River is a hill or place called *Iwerddon*, 'Ireland', and half-way between is *Dolwyddelan*, 'Gwyddelan's meadow', Gwyddelan being derived from *Gwyddel*, 'a Gael', an Irishman.[94] Even as late as the fourteenth century one Welsh poet could say of another that his Welsh was *diseisnig* and *diwyddelig*, 'uncontaminated by English and Irish'. The old view that the Irish element in west Wales is a relic of the ancient Goidelic population is now completely discredited. The Irish of Caernarvonshire, however, came apparently from further north than those of Dyfed, for the northern peninsula was known, and is still known today, by the name of *Lleyn*, from Irish *Laigin*, 'the Leinstermen', while the little village on Nevin Bay still bears the name *Porth Dinllaen*, 'the harbour of the fort of the Leinstermen'.[95] The choice of Aberffraw on the west coast of Anglesey as the capital of North Wales at a later date was probably dictated by fear of an *adventus Scotorum* (an 'Irish occupation'). The gravity of this fear lies behind the tradition of Cunedda and his sons.

According to late Welsh tradition, preserved in what is believed to be the oldest part of the *Historia Brittonum*, and dating perhaps from the seventh century though finally compiled by Nennius in the early ninth century, a certain Cunedda came to North Wales with his eight sons and grandsons from Manau Gododdin, the ancient territory of the Votadini, to the south of the Firth of Forth, and 'they drove out the Irish with immense slaughter from those regions, who never returned again to inhabit them'. The passage is our sole authority for the expedition. The tradition – if it can be trusted – implies a military movement, presumably along the thirty-seven miles of the Antonine Wall and then by ship from Dumbarton to Anglesey. It is not true that the Irish were in fact driven out of Wales, but these British chiefs from the north have presumably come with the intention of settling, and later traditions have been at pains to specify the kingdoms which they were believed to have founded in northern and western Wales. The establishment of these kingdoms came to form an important element in the early history of Wales.

By far the most important of the Irish expansions of the fifth century was that from north-eastern Ireland to the islands and coast of the south and south-west of Scotland. The coast of either country is clearly visible from the other, and we have seen (p. 46 above) in Tacitus how the Roman general Agricola had looked across from the Ayrshire coast and speculated on the ease with which Ireland could be conquered. On the other hand as we trace the Irish settlements up the west coast of Britain, and the defensive measures adopted by the Romans against Irish penetration, the expansion of the Irish from the Antrim coast into western Scotland in the fifth century becomes a natural sequel. Irish consolidation on a wide scale in western Britain was only possible beyond the Roman frontier of the Antonine Wall. Here a permanent Irish kingdom was founded in the fifth century, but whether by military or peaceful penetration is uncertain, though no tradition of military conquest has come down to us. The expansion and consolidation of this Irish settlement and Irish dynasty as the kingdom of Dál Riata will be traced in the following chapters.

In south-western Britain the most important movement and expansion was that of the Britons of the Devon-Cornwall peninsula and the Severn Sea into Armorica, the most westerly peninsula of Gaul. Prior to its conquest by Caesar in 56 BC the powerful sea-faring tribe of the Veneti in the south-east had had close transmarine relations with western Britain. We have seen that according to Zosimus the weakening power of the Roman Empire had stimulated the people of Armorica to follow the example of the Insular Britons and throw off the Roman yoke. During this period, probably already in the fourth century or earlier, the colonization of western Armorica from the south-west of Britain began to take place, and continued without apparent opposition from the Romans till the British language superseded that of the original Gallo-Roman peoples of Armorica. The British emigration has commonly been attributed, on the testimony of the sixth century British historian Gildas, to the settlement and establishment of the West Saxons in eastern England. A closer study of the pressure and penetration of the Irish on the western peninsulas of Britain, however, leaves no room to doubt that the British emigration was yet another result of the Irish pressure on western Britain at this period. In a later chapter we shall trace the development of this British immigration in the rise of the kingdom of Brittany.

NOTES

1 K. Jackson, 'The Pictish Language' in *P.P.*, 134 f.; 159. Cf. also H. M. Chadwick, *E.S.*, 66 f.
2 The latest edition for the section relating to the British Isles is that contained in C. Müller's edition of *Claudii Ptolemaei Geographia* (Paris, 1883) Vol. I, Lib. II, caps. ii Hibernia: iii Albion. My references throughout are to this edition.
3 For an account of the ancient geographers who have left records of the British Isles, see especially E. H. Bunbury, *History of Ancient Geography* (2nd ed. London, 1959) II, 595 ff.
4 O'Rahilly, 'The Goidels and their Predecessors', P.B.A. XXI (1935), 323 ff.
5 The British section has been published by I. A. Richmond and O. G. S. Crawford in *Archaeologia* XCIII (1949) 1–50, and separately by the Society of Antiquaries of London (Oxford, 1949).
6 These are enumerated by Ptolemy *ed. cit.* in Cap II, p. 74 ff.
7 A valuable study of Ptolemy's sources and methods with particular references to Scotland is given by I. A. Richmond in *R.N.N.B.*, 133 ff.
8 See W. J. Watson, *C.P.S.*, 15
9 Ptolemy (*ed. cit.*), p. 74 ff.
10 II, ii. 9.
11 II, ii. 6; Cf. O'Rahilly, *E.I.H.M.* pp. 33, 34.
12 O'Rahilly, *E.I.H.M.*, p. 40 f.
13 II. iii. 11.
14 II. iii. 8; cf. W. J. Watson, *C.P.S.*, 16.
15 II. iii. 7; cf. Watson, *C.P.S.*, p. 15.
16 Watson, *C.P.S.*, p. 24.
17 Ptolemy, II. iii. 5.
18 Ptolemy II. iii. 7. This form of the name is generally preferred to the alternative reading *Otalini*. The corresponding form in the *Ravenna Cosmography* is possibly *Volitani* (? for *Votilani*); but the

form *Votadini* would seem to be favoured by the early medieval form *Guododin* (see p. 60).

19 Ptolemy II. iii. 6.
20 Ptolemy II. iii. 12.
21 II. iii. 12. Cf. further Pliny, *Nat. Hist.* IV, 102.
22 Ptolemy, II. iii. 11.
23 Cf. Tacitus, cap. 18.
24 *Annals*, XII, 32.
25 Wheeler and Richardson, *Hill-forts* 23 f.
26 Excavated by Sir Mortimer Wheeler in 1951–2. See his account in *Stanwick*.
27 Ptolemy II. iii. 10.
28 The most recent study of the *Cornovii* is that of Sir Ian A. Richmond, in Foster and Alcock, *C.E.*, 251 ff.
29 Ptolemy II. iii. 11.
30 *Ibid.*
31 See Richmond, *C.E.*, 252, n. 8.
32 Ptolemy (II. iii. 10) notes as one of their oppida *Cataractorium*, believed to be identical with Catterick in Yorkshire (cf. p. 114 below).
33 Ptolemy, II. iii. 10
34 Ptolemy, II. iii. 11.
35 *Ibid.*
36 Tacitus, *Agricola* XII. Cf. *Annals* XII, 36; *Histories* III, 45.
37 See Chapter V by Derek Allen in E. M. Clifford, *Bagendon*.
38 Richmond, *R.B.* (2nd Ed., London, 1963), p. 15.
39 Ptolemy, II. iii. 12.
40 Ptolemy II. iii. 11. '*Catuvellauni* in quibus oppida *Salinae, Urlanium* (*Verulamium*),' Identified with Wheathampstead. See R. E. M. and T. V. Wheeler, *Verulamium*.
41 Ptolemy II. iii. 11.
42 *De Bello Gallico* iv 33 (transl. Edwards).
43 Collingwood, *R.B.E.S.*, 22.
44 Tacitus, *Agricola* XV.
45 *Agricola* XV f.
46 *Ibid.* XVIII.
47 *Ibid.* XVII.
48 'The Cornovii', in Foster and Alcock, *C.E.*, 251 ff.
49 Perhaps after an interval spent among the Belgic *Dobunni* in the Cotswolds. See Clifford, *Bagendon*, 160.
50 The story of Cartimandua is related by Tacitus, *Histories* III, 45: *Annals*, XII, 36, 40. See recent commentaries on the situation by Ian Richmond, 'Queen Cartimandua', J.R.S. XLIV (1954), 50 f.; also *ibid.* Appendix to Sir Mortimer Wheeler, *Stanwick*, 61 ff. See further Chadwick, S.G.S. VIII (1955), p. 60 ff.
51 *Histories*, V, 78.
52 *Annals* XIV. xxx (translation by A. Murphy); cf. *Agricola* XIV.

53 Tacitus, *Agricola* XVI.
54 G. R. Dudley and G. Webster, *The Rebellion of Boudicca* (London, 1962), 20.
55 Dio Cassius, *Roman Histories, Epitome* of Book LXII, 3, 4.
56 G. Simpson, *Britons and the Roman Army* (London, 1964), 18 f. See also her map of the Agricolan forts in the southern Pennines, fig. 4.
57 Richmond, *R.N.N.B.*, p. 113 f.
58 Tacitus, *Agricola*, XXIV.
59 *Ibid., loc. cit.*
60 For a discussion of the eastern advance and the forts, see O. G. S. Crawford, *T.R.S.* and the map in the binding.
61 Tacitus, *Agricola* XXIX.
62 For a recent discussion, see Crawford, *T.R.S.*, p. 130.
63 Crawford, *T.R.S.* 108 ff., and passim.
64 *Agricola*, XXVI.
65 The campaign and battle are reported at length by Tacitus, *Agricola*, XXIX–XXXVIII.
66 For a recent brief recapitulation of the events leading to the building of the northern walls, see G. Simpson, *B.R.A.*, 34 ff.
67 The inscription appears to be contemporary, and is of exceptional interest. See the study and interpretation by I. A. Richmond and R. P. Wright in A.E., Ser. iv, vol. xxi (1943), 93–120, and Plate III.
68 See Dio Cassius lxxviii. 1.
69 For some accounts of the fleet, see D. Atkinson, 'Classis Britannica' in *Historical Essays in Honour of James Tait* edited by Edwards, Galbraith & Jacob (Manchester, 1933) p. 1 ff.; more recently C. G. Starr, *R.I.N.*
70 According to the '*Origo Constantini imperatoris*', alternatively known as the *Anonymus-Valesianus*, Constantius died at York in 306, *Monumenta Germaniae Historica*, Vol. IX, *Chronica Minora* (Berlin, 1892), p. 7.
71 The most recent study of the Saxon Shore is that of Donald A. White, *L.S.* Cf. also the important review by S. S. Frere in *Medieval Archaeology* V–VI (1962–3), p. 350 f.
72 Flavius Vegetius Renatus, *Epitoma Rei Militaris* (Berlin, 1885), Book IV, cap. 37. It has been suggested that South Shields may have become a naval base under Constantius of a system of coastal defence in the north similar to that of the Saxon shore forts.
73 XXVII. 8. 1. *Britannis indicabat barbarica conspiratione ad ultimam vexatas inopiam.*
74 *In Eutropium* XXVIII. 3. 7.
75 See the study by C. E. Stevens 'Magnus Maximus in British History', É.C. III. p. 86 ff.
76 Related in 'The Dream of Maxen Wledig', translated by Lady Charlotte Guest in *The Mabinogion*, and by Ellis and Lloyd

(Oxford, 1929), Vol. I, 135 ff.; also Gwyn Jones and Thomas Jones (London, 1949), 79 ff.

77 Pedigree no. II in MS. Harl. 3859.

78 'Incursantes Pictos et Scottos Maximus strenue superavit.' Mon. Germ. Hist. Auctorum Antiquiss., IX, Chronica Gallica, p. 646.

79 See N.D., ed. O. Seeck . . . in partibus Occidentis, V, 65 (p. 118); 213 (p. 124); VII 49 (p. 134).

80 See C. E. Stevens, 'The British Sections of the Notitia Dignitatum', A.J. XCVII (1940), p. 134, and note 5.

81 Vandal War I. ii. Procopius was a Byzantine historian of the first half of the sixth century.

82 See M. P. Charlesworth, L.P., 35 f.

82 Zosimus V. cap. 5, 6.

84 Ibid., cap. 10.

85 The historical basis of the Táin was first demonstrated by Sir William Ridgeway, 'The Date of the First shaping of the Cuchulainn Saga', P.B.A. II (1905–6). For a more recent and fuller study with corrections see K. H. Jackson, O.I.T. We are further indebted to Professor Jackson for an earlier personal loan of his notes on this subject.

86 E.I.H.M., 172 ff.

87 E.I.H.M., 207–8.

88 See Mac White, ZCP xxv 16.

89 Nash-Williams, E.C.I.W., no. 313.

90 Ibid., no. 314.

91 Ibid., no. 345.

92 Jackson, L.H.E.B., 139.

93 W. J. Gryffydd, Math, 342 f.

94 W. J. Watson, C.P.S., 228.

95 W. J. Gryffydd, Math, 343, n. 90.

3

The Celtic Revival

When the Celtic princes became the independent governors of Britain their principal problem was to maintain their national Celtic integrity against the encroachment of peoples from outside – the Teutonic peoples from the east, the Picts and Dalriadic Scots (Irish) from the north, and the Irish from the west. With the withdrawal of Roman organization and protection, the island of Britain stood like a great pharos off the Atlantic coast of Europe, and like the Celtic peoples of Gaul faced a struggle for existence against the shock and breakers of barbarian advancing tides. This problem of the Celtic independent princes was the principal fact in the history of Britain in the fifth century. Our first concern is to examine the situation among the Celtic kingdoms within Britain, and to enquire what measures they took to consolidate their political integrity and to meet their frontier difficulties. Our next concern is to survey the history of the Celtic peoples on the outer periphery of Celtic Britain.

We have seen that these peoples on the western fringe of Europe, like the Teutonic tribes to the north, were restless and seeking expansion. Unable to expand further to the west and north they, again like the contemporary Teutonic tribes, were seeking to encroach on British borders. The history of the Celtic peoples of the periphery of Britain and of Europe during the fifth and sixth centuries is the history of a people seeking new lands to settle in, new kingdoms in which to establish authority and to enforce their settlement rights. This, after all, is practically what the Teutonic peoples in the east were seeking also, as the history of Gaul shows. Military conquest was merely a means to an end. The Celtic peoples were not essentially militant, and, as their history shows throughout, military aims were always secondary, and resorted to chiefly, perhaps exclusively, when peaceful penetration was not practicable. Naturally Roman records distort the picture, for the Romans encountered the Celtic peoples almost exclusively as relentless military opponents.

As yet the entire north and west of Britain had retained its Celtic population virtually unchanged. Scotland, north-western England, Wales and Cornwall and all the islands to the west were wholly Celtic. Of these areas the Lowlands of Scotland, northern England, Wales, and the Cornish peninsula spoke British, developing about this time into what we know as Welsh. North of this British periphery the Picts were at least half Celtic, the Irish to the west wholly Celtic. If the Picts should succeed in permanently occupying southern Scotland, and even penetrating further south; if the Irish should succeed in establishing a kingdom for themselves on the west coast of Scotland, and smaller territories on the western peninsulas of Wales, our islands would remain none the less a Celtic area. Ultimately the principal struggle for existence was to be within this unconquered western stronghold of all the Celtic peoples – 'the edge of the habitable globe' – to maintain its integrity against the new Teutonic element penetrating this last stronghold of the Celtic civilization from the east.

It was on the whole a close fought rearguard movement on three fronts for the British peoples. They stretched in an unbroken line from the Firth of Forth to Land's End, with no central organization or coordination. They had to defend themselves against Saxon penetration from the east, Pictish from the north, Irish from the west. In the present chapter we shall attempt to show what steps they took to maintain their new-found independence, and how far they were successful. It may perhaps be said here in anticipation that they ultimately succeeded in preventing large-scale occupation by the Irish in the west, south of the Highland Line, even while founding a new colony overseas in Armorica. On their eastern front they were able to offer a stubborn resistance initially, and even, at least in the north, to take the initiative in attacking the Saxon invaders; but the absence of centralization and unity among the Celtic peoples, and their failure to make common cause with the powerful Pictish kingdoms to the north, combined with geographical difficulties of communication in hill country, eventually brought it about that the whole of Lowland Britain fell into Saxon hands.

The first task of the Celtic independent kingdoms in their struggle to maintain Celtic integrity was for the British princes, now the independent rulers of southern Britain, to establish some form of stable government and central organization with the aim of defending the Borders. In this they were apparently successful, for no hint of anarchy following upon the Roman withdrawal has come down to us in our traditions of the period. Our first enquiry must be as to the nature of the new measures, and how far continuity was maintained from Roman times.

One of the most marked developments in the recent attitude to the Roman occupation of Britain is a fuller realization of the continuity which persisted throughout the period between the earlier Celtic tribal life and that which emerged when the last Roman military convoy left the Island. On the whole the country had probably not drastically changed fundamentally. We have seen the persistence of the old tribal areas in the north and in Wales throughout the occupation, and we can trace how the vitality and experience of the British tribes of Lowland Scotland in particular gradually qualified them to take their place as early as the late Roman period as the most effective northern defence against the powerful Pictish kingdom of northern Scotland.

It would seem that the Roman amenities and civilization had hardly affected Britain in depth beyond the part of central and south-eastern England, generally included in the term 'Lower Britain'. This was the principal area of the villas and the towns – London, Canterbury, the country towns such as Silchester, Verulamium, Bath, Cirencester, Gloucester, Caerwent. In general the traditional Celtic life seems to have been little disrupted or even transformed. The Romans appear to have interfered little with the religious, domestic, and civil life of the native Celtic peoples. The ancient Celtic kingdoms seem to have continued as *civitates*, political 'cantons' for administration, carried on by an *ordo*, a permanent executive 'council', which functioned in the cantonal capital, consisting of *decurions* or ex-magistrates who had been elected by the city. The native religion lived on apparently without interference side by side with Roman cults, and native temples and shrines continued to be built.

Despite the desire of Agricola to encourage education he never introduced the art of writing to the Celtic peoples, or put them in a position to record their own traditions or institutions. These continued throughout the Roman occupation to be carried on by a

68

vigorous oral cultivation and transmission; and when, centuries later, the Celtic peoples, under the tutelage of the Christian Church, had learnt the Roman alphabet, and could write fluently enough to place on record in the vernacular their native Celtic civilization, it was not the Roman laws, but the native Celtic laws which they codified; the ancient literature of their own people, both poetry and prose, which they wrote in their manuscripts; and after the departure of the Roman rulers, it was the genealogies of their own chiefs and leading families that they recorded. Most significant of all, the Roman language never gained wide currency in Britain, and unlike Gaul, has left relatively few traces behind from the period of the Roman occupation. Much has been made of *graffiti*[1] scratched on small objects, such as the word *'satis'* scratched on a single tile at Silchester, and attributed to a weary brickmaker by Haverfield,[2] and charmingly translated by M. P. Charlesworth as 'Time to knock off'; but is not this slender trace of workman's Latin more probably the 'exeat' of a satisfied Roman foreman with his 'Work to rule'?

In regard to the civil government of Britain in a wider sense after the departure of the Romans, we are largely dependent on conjecture. The letter of Honorius sent to Britain in 410 (cf. p. 52 above) is said to have been addressed to the 'cities' (πόλεις) in Britain. The word probably signifies *civitates* or 'city states', and refers to the separate Celtic kingdoms, which had retained their identity and some measure of modified self-government throughout the Roman period, much as in Gaul. The passage from Zosimus quoted above (p. 52) implies that the military organization was in the hands of the *civitates*. But what was the central authority which alone could render them effective to maintain the political integrity of Britain?

Procopius, writing *c.* 550, states with reference to the revolt of the Britains under Constantine in 407: 'The Romans were never able to recover Britain; but from this time it continued to be ruled by tyrants (τυράννοις)'. In Latin works of that period this term usually signifies 'usurpers' or rulers who had no legal rights to their position, and this seems to be the type of native ruler who governed the Celtic provinces of Britain before and after the Roman period.

In a treatise which claims to be contemporary, and which bears the title *De Excidio Britanniae*, and is generally regarded as the work of an early sixth century ecclesiastic, Gildas, we are told (cap. 23) of a powerful British ruler, a *superbus tyrannus*, whom the writer has handed down to us with much obloquy as responsible for the introduction of the Saxons into Britain. Gildas himself tells us, however, that while the Britons were being harried by the Picts *de curucis* ('in their sea-going craft') all the councillors, together with the supreme dictator (*omnes conciliarii cum superbo tyranno*) invited the warlike (*ferocissimi*) Saxons into the country. The responsibility for the invitation is clearly stated to lie with the *conciliarii* – by whom we are probably to understand the *civitates* – with the *tyrannus* at their head. The invitation was an official one and the Saxons were first invited in to act as mercenaries against Pictish raids, receiving their keep in fixed monthly supplies (*annonas, epimenia*). The procedure as depicted by Gildas was perfectly regular, and in accordance with continental Roman practice in relation to the Franks and other barbarian peoples, and the act of the *tyrannus* was a completely constitutional one. Gildas's account suggests that the ravages of the Saxons only began when their payment failed or proved inadequate to their demands. Moreover it implies a stable government, anything but anarchy. The *superbus tyrannus*, the native British ruler in charge of the defences, acting with the authority of all his councillors, presumably members of the *ordo*, was taking constitutional measures for dealing with a crisis inherited from the preceding period. Gildas's term does not mean 'a proud tyrant' in the sense in which it is usually interpreted, but the leading or most important ruler, the *superbus tyrannus*, the 'highest dictator'.[3] No name is given to him, but Bede in his *Historia Ecclesiastica* calls him *Vurtigernus*,[4] which is generally regarded as a proper name, but which in fact simply means 'overlord'.

Few certain facts are known about Vortigern; but he seems to have been the leading Celtic figure in Britain *c.* 425, and it is very possible that he formed a buffer state on the Welsh Border – possibly at a time when the outlying peninsulas had already passed largely into Irish hands (cf. pp. 57–61 above). It seems reasonably certain that he had authority to strengthen the native military defences of his own country with Saxon *foederati*. He became the subject of a large number of unfavourable legends, among others a fantastic story of his encounters with St Germanus;[5] but what stands out with some clarity is his position as a powerful Romano-British prince of Roman Britain who played an official part in cooperation with the governors of the provinces in hiring Saxon mercenaries to protect Britain against barbarian inroads from the north after the removal of the

Roman army of occupation. But there is no suggestion anywhere that his Celtic sympathies imply anti-Roman politics, and he seems to have acted in the capacity of a Roman official as leader of the *civitates*.

Our next important consideration must be to examine the principal problem which faced the other independent British princes, namely the defence of their borders as the only means of maintaining the freedom of the country and the independence of its Celtic rulers. What was the nature and extent of this threat to the borders of Celtic Britain, and what steps did they take for this purpose of defence?

It is perhaps in regard to the Anglo-Saxon occupation of eastern England that opinion has undergone in recent years the most marked change. In our own generation archaeology has supplemented our documentary evidence, and the picture which has emerged is a very different one from that of Gildas.

The picture so far presented by archaeology is that the Saxons came in the first place, not as invading armies, but in a series of civil settlements, beginning before the end of the second century and under Roman auspices. How far there may also have been independent private or trading settlements is at present *sub judice*; but Roman employment of the Saxons as *foederati*, 'mercenaries', is beyond question, and is, of course, fully in accordance with the Roman practice on the continent. Roman military use of the Saxons as *foederati* had taken place between 390 and 400, and it has been pointed out that east of a line between York and Bedford there is scarcely a Roman walled town apart from the Saxon shore forts and similar sites in the Lincolnshire Wolds, without an accompanying Anglo-Saxon cemetery, while pottery of fourth century date in Roman technique and Saxon decoration points to close association of Roman and Saxon in both the neighbourhood of the 'Saxon Shore' forts and the East Riding near to York. We have reason to believe that by the end of the third century the 'Saxon Shore' had already been partially settled, or that the forts themselves were partly manned, by Saxons, or were the focal points of more or less organized trade relations with the Teutonic tribes across the North Sea.[6] There is no evidence of a general massacre of the native population, and the possibility may be dismissed as most improbable on practical grounds. After the departure of the Romans, however, the

71

encroachments became military. Here, as in Gaul, what apparently began as numerous relatively small-scale Teutonic enterprises and settlements, developed, as Roman power weakened, into military conquest, and the creation of an alien barbarian kingdom displacing Roman and Celtic dominion alike.

After a lurid description of the depredations of the Saxons, Gildas tells us (cap. 25 f.) that a remnant of the Britons took up arms and challenged their victors to battle under a certain Ambrosius Aurelianus, whom he praises as 'the last of the Romans', and to these men came a victory.

Ambrosius seems to have represented the rearguard of the withdrawing Roman army, and he is described by Gildas as a *vir modestus* and a *dux*. Nothing more is known of him from early sources, but he is very probably the *Emreis Guletic* whom Nennius in the *Historia Brittonum* relates to have been victorious in a series of hostilities against Vortigern, in the course of which Vortigern was driven to take refuge in Snowdonia. These legends are in the nature of folk-tale, and doubtless arose at a time when mounting hatred against the Saxons was heaping obloquy on Vortigern.

In recent years a growing body of opinion tends to regard King Arthur as historical,[7] and some would identify him with Ambrosius Aurelianus, though the questions are in reality quite distinct. We have no satisfactory evidence for a historical Arthur. Nevertheless cumulatively the amount of legendary evidence is arresting, and there may have been a British commander in the late fifth or the sixth century who bore the Roman name Arthur (*Artorius*).

Turning now from the Saxon penetration of the east to the northern frontiers, it has been suggested above that the chief defences against Pictish incursions from the north were the British tribes of southern Scotland, who had apparently been entrusted already in the Roman period with the defences of the northern border, and had probably been to some extent trained and equipped for this purpose by Roman military methods. For the British of southern Scotland[8] we are largely dependent in the last instance on Celtic tradition, as we shall see. We have, however, in addition one all-important contemporary Latin document which is our safe conduct – so far as we can interpret it – through the change-over from Roman to Celtic rule in southern Britain, and which is especially significant in its negative evidence in regard to the border defences in the north and west. This is the

Notitia Dignitatum,[9] a document believed to have been drawn up in the chancellery of the Eastern Roman Empire in the late fourth or early fifth century, giving under each province of the Empire the lists of returns furnished from time to time by local officials throughout the Empire. The document is therefore not a survey representing the civil and military conditions of the Roman Empire at any given moment, but something resembling a card index kept over a period of time. It is a dynamic register, and for the closing phase of Roman rule in Britain it is our most illuminating document. Its bare entries can be supplemented from Celtic traditions by the genealogies of the princes of the frontier kingdoms on the northern border. These genealogies show significant changes in the names during the fourth and fifth centuries, from those of Pictish appearance, to names suggesting Romanized Britons, and these again give way to names of Celtic princes standing proudly on the theshold of the historical period in the fifth century, in their own right as native princes and leaders of Celtic Britain. The *Notitia Dignitatum* shows no entry for the *dux*, an old office of the Roman military leader of the northern defences. If his duty had been delegated to the north British *foederati* it is natural that no returns would have been sent in for him, and his place would have been taken by some British leader. Perhaps after Stilicho had finally withdrawn the chief Roman supply base in the north to York some powerful British chief may have succeeded him as *dux*. With the help of the Latin document of the *Notitia* and the Celtic genealogies the course of history on the northern border is reasonably clear.

During the closing years of the Roman occupation of Britain, and especially in consequence of the great raid of 367, the Romans had sought to ensure that the unconquered northern tribes were contained beyond the range of the impoverished Roman power, and they followed here the policy already inaugurated on the Continent[10] of training and incorporating native troops to police their northern frontier, probably furnishing them to some extent with Roman equipment and perhaps bestowing on them Roman insignia. We have here no direct contemporary authority, but this at least would seem to be the position as suggested by the *Historia Brittonum*[11] of Nennius and by the Welsh genealogies. Although these texts are not earlier than the beginning of the ninth century, Nennius has made use of records going back to the seventh century or even earlier, while the genealogies are derived from conservative and carefully preserved oral tradition.

A study of these records suggests that the Romans either established, or at least supported, a native dynasty to guard each end of the northern (Antonine) wall, – a distance of only thirty-seven miles. The genealogies of these dynasties have fortunately been preserved.[12] On the whole the best authenticated and the most stabilized of these dynasties is that of Strathclyde, with its stronghold at Dumbarton. The most eminent name in the Dumbarton dynasty at the close of the Roman period is that of a certain *Ceredig Gwledig*, generally identified with the *Coroticus* whose soldiers were accused by St Patrick in his famous letter of having carried off newly baptized members of his flock from Ireland, doubtless as slaves. Dumbarton was still described by Bede in the early eighth century as a *munissima urbs*, 'a very strongly fortified place'. The branches of this dynasty can be identified as far away as Galloway. The genealogy has probably been preserved with official care, for its genuineness can be checked from external historical sources. The most famous king among them, Rhydderch Hen, figures in later traditions of both St Kentigern and the prophet Myrddin (later *Merlin*), as well as in Adamnán's *Life of St Columba*. Ceredig's immediate ancestors bear names which look like corruptions of Roman names, and before these come three which apparently have a Pictish character.[13] This would suggest that the dynasty began shortly after the raid of 367, and that first Pictish chiefs, then later local British chiefs, had been employed as *foederati* by the Romans to guard the western end of the Antonine Wall, as the result of the raid. The static epithet of the dynasty *hael*, 'generous', 'wealthy', perhaps contains a hint of Roman payment in gold; and the slave raiding of Coroticus in Ireland in the fifth century might be construed as providing the practical resources of these princes when Roman financial resources failed. This at least is Gildas's explanation of the Saxon raiding on Britain when the *epimenia* due to them as Roman *foederati*, were no longer forthcoming. Indeed, the British princes of Dumbarton to the north would be no more eager to be overrun by the powerful Picts than were the Romano-Britons further south.

At the eastern end of the Antonine Wall was the old kingdom of the Votadini, the name which survived later in that of *Manau Guotodin*, the original home of Cunedda[14] (cf. p. 60 above). The name *Cunedag*

74

is puzzling, being neither Roman nor British, and unknown elsewhere in Welsh. Can it be Irish? According to the Welsh genealogies Cunedda's name, like that of Ceredig, is preceded by three Roman names, Ætern (L. Eternus), Patern (L. Paternus, to which is added the epithet peis rut, 'of the red cloak'), and the third Tacit[us]. Before these come a series of two pairs of names which resemble the curious lists of pairs of names on the pedigrees of the Pictish kings.[15] The territory of the Votadini stretched from south of the Firth of Forth to Berwickshire while to the north of the Firth was the kingdom of the powerful Southern Picts.

It is tempting to hazard a guess that the important fifth century treasure from Traprain Law in Haddingtonshire[16] is pirate's loot, and that the Roman foederati of this great stronghold, like their fellow princes of Dumbarton, had taken to piracy when Roman subsidies failed at this time. The epithet peis rut has been thought with great probability to refer to the red cloak denoting the official insignia of a Roman cavalry officer. It seems probable that both Ceredig and Cunedag were Romanized Britons guarding the narrow isthmus at each end of the Antonine Wall between the Forth and the Clyde against the Picts. Possibly both these dynasties are of Pictish origin. Following the three generations of Roman names which succeed the Pictish on these pedigrees the names are of British form. These succeeding lists would on a normal computation carry us back to the fourth century, and the evidence leads us to surmise that as a result of Pictish raids, and especially the great Pictish raid of 367, the Romans had 'authorized' native princes – first Pictish, later Romanized British – to guard the northern defences on behalf of the Empire as foederati. Then in the fifth century, during the so-called 'national revival', native British names succeeded the Roman.

What was the general position in the west, where the Celtic peoples had never been fully Romanized? Here again the Notitia Dignitatum fails us, for no returns of any kind were sent in from the Welsh marches, or indeed from western Britain at all. This is the more remarkable since we know that Caernarvon (Segontium) was occupied till as late as 383 when Magnus Maximus departed with his Seguntienses; and Manchester and Ribchester show coins till the same date. Chester had been occupied by the Twentieth Legion and Caerleon by the Second, and only a part of the latter had been removed to Richborough at an earlier date. How then can we account for the total

75

silence of the *Notitia* in the fifth century with regard to Roman officials on the western border?

Part of the explanation perhaps lies in the fact that when Magnus Maximus removed some at least of the regular troops from the west to Gaul he left the entire western defences in the hands of the native troops. This period corresponds roughly with the devolution, the change to the *foederati* on the northern border, and there is some corroborative evidence that by a similar devolution the Romans transferred a part of the responsibility in the west to native princes, more especially on the western sea-board.

Just as the peril to the northern frontiers came from two distinct peoples, the Picts and the Irish, so on the western frontier the peril came independently from two distinct peoples, the Welsh and the Irish. It has recently been convincingly demonstrated by Sir Ian Richmond[17] that the Cornovii, the chief ancient tribe of the western border provinces, were in a position of great insecurity, owing to the disaffection and mountain raids of the Ordovices immediately to the west. Consequently they already held exceptional responsibility and exceptional privileges under the Romans. They were the only British tribe that gave its own name to the unit of Imperial auxiliary troops; and this unit, also contrary to custom, continued to serve in its own province.

From the official Roman records of the Cornovii we may perhaps turn to the later British traditions of the period comparable with those of the north British *foederati*. We have seen that Gildas represents a powerful native prince, a *superbus tyrannus*, to whom later writers gave the name Vortigern, as taking control of lower Britain, and cooperating with such native officials (*omnes consiliarii*) as still functioned after the withdrawal of Roman authority. This was in the period of our Celtic Revival. His British name and all our traditions imply that he was a native of the Welsh border, and his genealogy is preceded by three generations of Romanized forbears, while his great grandfather bears the name *Gloiu*, apparently an eponym for Gloucester, to which is added the epithet *gwalltiu*, 'of the long hair', possibly reminiscent of the long horse-hair of the Roman cavalry officer's helmet. The traditions and pedigree suggest that he was an important British prince who had become Romanized, and by analogy with the north it may be conjectured – it can be no more than conjecture – that in the late period of the Roman occupation he had been granted *foederati* status in succession to the Cornovii, who were under Roman control. The absence from the *Notitia Dignitatum* of an entry for the western defences would in this case be in no way remarkable, but consistent with the absence of an entry for the *dux* on the northern border.

The chief peril to southern Britain came, however, from the Irish, and thus a major consideration of the defences, first by the Romans, and later by the independent British princes, was always the defence of the western shores. We have already seen that several Irish settlements on the western peninsulas of Wales were already taking place on an intensive scale during the Roman period. We have seen that the evidence of an early inscription in Dyfed (Pembrokeshire) records the title of *Protector* as having been held by a native prince, and this is an official Roman title bestowed on *foederati* responsible for defending the frontiers. The later genealogies attach the same title to Magnus Maximus and his son and grandson.

The Romans had long been alive to the Irish menace, and from the third century onwards the Romans and the Britons of Wales found themselves menaced by a common foe. In south-eastern Wales the chief defences were no longer at Caerleon and Caerwent, to act as defences against the Welsh, but at Cardiff, where a late large fort was built in the third century against the Irish on the site of a second century one. In Caernarvonshire the early fort of Segontium built on the hill above Caernarvon was abandoned and a new one built at the mouth of the river by the shore to protect the valuable Roman trade of the Anglesey copper mines from Irish raiders,[18] while the late small fort at Holyhead was probably built at this period against the Irish.[19] Further the line of defence of the Saxon Shore forts of the east and these Welsh ones on the west was continued in the north – in Lancashire, on Morecambe Bay, and even east of the Pennines.

An early tradition of Irish kingdoms on the coasts of the Severn Sea in Wales and south-western Britain is preserved in an Irish text known as *Sanas Cormaic*[20] ('Cormac's Glossary'), a kind of encyclopedia and glossary believed to date from the ninth century. Here it is claimed that from the time of St Patrick the Irish had had divided kingdoms, the more important halves being in Britain, and that they had held that power long after the coming of Patrick:

The power of the Irish over Britain was great, and they divided Britain between them into estates . . . and the Irish lived as much

77

east of the sea as they did in Ireland, and their dwellings and their royal fortresses were made there. Hence *Dind Tradui* . . . that is, the triple rampart of Crimthann Mór,[21] son of Fidach, king of Ireland and Britain as far as the English Channel . . . From this division originated the fort of the sons of Liathán in the lands of the Britons of Cornwall (*Dind map Lethain, dún maic Liatháin*) . . . And they were in that control for a long time, even after the coming of St Patrick to Ireland.[22]

The source of Cormac's information is not known, but although the tradition is referred by him to several centuries before his time, the statement that the situation which he describes survived to a time 'long after the coming of Patrick', suggests that his information is fairly recent and it is certainly consistent with such other evidence as we have. Cormac's reference suggests that *Dind map Lethain* is on or near the northern shore of the Dumnonian Peninsula. The tribe is probably to be identified with the Irish Uí Liatháin of Munster, and Cormac is evidently using a Welsh source which he feels under the necessity of translating for his Irish readers: 'Dún maic Liatháin – for *mac* is the same as *map* in British'.

Nennius, writing about the same time, is probably relying on the same Welsh source when he tells us (*Hist. Brit.* cap. 14) that 'the sons of Liathán occupied the region of Dyfed, Gower and Kidwely'.

Traditionally, then, all the South Welsh seaboard was occupied in the fifth century by a closely related Munster tribe[23] which Cormac locates on the opposite shores of the Severn Sea, and this tribe, or certain Irish kingdoms, command all the approaches to the south-west of Britain – south and south-western Wales, the Bristol Channel and the Dumnonian Peninsula.

It is against five British princes of these troubled western maritime kingdoms that Gildas (cap. 28) hurls reproaches early in the sixth century. They appear to be his older contemporaries, rulers of wide territories on the western sea-board, and he addresses them by name, apparently in geographical order, beginning with Constantine, 'tyrant' of Dumnonia (the Devon-Cornwall peninsula) and continuing round the Welsh coast till he reaches the 'island dragon', Maglocunus. The three western princes can all be identified on the Welsh genealogies, Maglocunus being the great Maelgwn Gwynedd, great-grandson of Cunedda, and ruler of North Wales and Anglesey.

Gildas has named the wide British kingdoms from Devon to Lancashire which must have been the bulwarks against Irish penetration in depth. Archaeology and tradition alike reflect the danger of an *adventus Scotorum*.

It was precisely at the period of the departure of the Romans from Britain, the assumption by the Celtic princes of the rule of Britain, and the mounting threat of Saxon, Pict and Irish to British independence, that the colonization of Britanny from western Britain was taking place in force.[24] It had doubtless already begun not later than the fourth century, and proceeded with impetus throughout the fifth century, reaching its climax in the sixth. Linguistic evidence indicates that the language of the immigrants was most closely allied to that of Cornwall, but a large proportion of the colonists are believed to have gone from Devon, because the rapidity with which Devonshire acquired English place-names suggests that this Celtic area was only thinly populated by Britons when the English arrived there; and indeed the Irish settlements on the Severn Sea would make British emigration from Devon more than likely. The late Breton hagiographical traditions, however, associate the princely leaders of the movement and the ecclesiastics with east central, central, and even western Wales.

It is commonly assumed that the cause of the migration was the pressure of the Saxon invasions, and this is the impression conveyed by Gildas. The *De Excidio*, attributed to him, is our earliest native authority for the evacuation from Britain. In cap. 25 he refers to 'part of the population' emigrating sorrowfully across the sea, chanting 'beneath the swelling sails' a passage of lamentations from the Psalms instead of sailors' shanties. He does not actually state that they were sailing to Armorica, but the historical evidence for this is overwhelming. In the light of what has been said above of the Irish penetration, however (cf. pp. 58 f. above), the imminent fear of an *adventus Scotorum* must have been even greater to the inhabitants of Cornwall, Devon and Wales, and especially to all living on the Severn Sea, than fear of Gildas's *adventus Saxonum*. These people were in a pincer movement, but the Saxon threat as yet touched them only remotely.

Only slightly later than Gildas we have a statement by Procopius of Caesarea[25] that large numbers of independent Britons and others, ruled by their own kings, were sent annually to the land of the Franks, who planted them as colonists in the thinly populated areas. Procopius clearly obtained his information from Frankish envoys at the court of Constantinople, where he held office in the first half of the sixth century, exactly the time when the colonization of Brittany was at its height. The serious Saxon raids in Gaul would naturally make the Frankish kings view friendly immigrants favourably. Moreover, it has been pointed out[26] that if we can trust the statement of Procopius, and the statement of Gildas (cap. 26) about the long peace that followed the Siege of Mons Badonius (cap. 26), the Saxons cannot have extended their frontier far to the west during this period, and we cannot assume that the threat to the Britons was as yet crucial. The Frankish chroniclers, it is true, attributed the British immigration to Saxon raids, notably Eginhard, friend and biographer of Charlemagne, and Ermold le Noir, who had accompanied Louis on an expedition to Brittany in 824; but the literary nature and the late date of these statements rob them of their value as evidence. Their source may very probably have been derived ultimately from Gildas himself, for he was well known and widely read in Brittany in the ninth century.

Meanwhile the nearest refuge of the Britons harried by the Irish in the south-west of the British Isles was western Brittany. Yet during the fifth century the Romans in Brittany were suffering from Saxon attacks no less than Britain, and to meet the emergency the Roman administration introduced changes in their defensive system, seeking to concentrate the defences as near as possible to the eastern border, and also to protect the coastal areas and the estuaries of the rivers.[27] The *Notitia Dignitatum* (cf. p. 73 above) shows extensive changes, the military command having now been removed from the interior to the coast, the defence of the whole coast being reorganized to oppose Saxon landings. No measures seem to have been taken to protect the west, and this must have facilitated small-scale landings and settlements by the incoming Celtic population. The Saxons never succeeded in making a permanent kingdom here as they did in Britain, but they succeeded in destroying much of the Roman civilization, especially round the coasts.

Yet the fact that the Saxons had not succeeded in displacing the Breton immigrants suggests that some kind of internal organization still existed. We have no clue as to the nature of this organization. In the absence of any shred of evidence, and with the course of events in

Britain before us, one is tempted to guess. Can the Gallo-Romans have acted as the *superbus tyrannus* and his *conciliarii* are said to have done in Britain, and encouraged the British immigrants to enter as *foederati* to help against the common foe? We have seen evidence that the British chiefs of the Welsh Marches lacked neither experience nor valour in such warfare. And this is precisely the area which, according to Breton tradition, furnished the leaders of the immigrant Bretons.

The Romans were fast losing their hold on Armorica. Already in 409 Armorica had revolted, and Zosimus tells us that 'encouraged by the example of the insular Britons, they had thrown off the Roman yoke' (cf. p. 52 above). From this it would seem that there was close political intercourse between Britain and Armorica already before the beginning of the fifth century, apparently of an organized kind. This is doubtless the underlying motive of St Germanus's visit to Britain in 429, for we are told by his biographer Constantius[28] that before he was made bishop of Auxerre he held the office of *dux tractus Armoricani*, and we know from the evidence of the *Notitia Dignitatum* that as such he would be responsible for the *litus tractus Armoricani*,[29] and the Saxon devastations in Armorica would be his main concern. We know that the Gallo-Romans of Armorica were in a state of rebellion, not only in 409 and 429, but throughout the fifth century,[30] and Constantius refers to them as 'a fickle and undisciplined people', led by a certain Tibatto whom the anonymous *Gaulish Chronicle* twice mentions, first s.a. 435, where he is referred to as the leader of an independence movement on the part of 'Gallia Ulterior' (i.e. Armorica), and again in 437 where he is referred to as having been among those captured and slain when the rebellion was put down. The movement seems to have been at its height following Germanus's visit to Britain in 429.

At the same time that the Gallo-Roman centres of Armorica moved eastwards, the new Celtic population entered Armorica by sea, concentrating on the coast-lands and occupying large tracts of the interior of the country, especially in the west. The chief Roman centres of Nantes, Vannes and Rennes, i.e. the eastern border states, had adopted Roman defence measures and remained Roman in character and institutions, and enclosed themselves in defensive walls owing to the Saxon scare;[31] but all the rest of the peninsula gradually changed its character and its language from Gallo-Roman to a form of Celtic closely related to Cornish and Welsh, Cornish more particularly. The country changed from Armorica, a peripheral Gallo-Roman province, a shabby outpost of the Empire, facing east, to a country with its back to Gaul, and its contacts, its culture, its political sympathies, its social relations, its Church and its population closely united with those of Celtic Britain, especially western Britain. It became once more a Celtic country.

Passing from the Ireland of the late Iron Age, and at the dawn of history, to the opening of the historical period, is a dramatic experience. It is the change from a country developing in isolation on its own traditional lines to a country open to the influences of an outside and higher civilization. It has already been emphasized that the high development and professional devotion of the intellectual classes of ancient Ireland have preserved for us their oral records of a native civilization on the periphery of the ancient world till their traditions passed into the crucible of Latin letters. This revolution in culture came about by the opening up of contacts with more advanced civilization to the east. In Ireland some isolated hoards from Roman Britain, such as the silver hoard from Balline, give concrete evidence of direct contact across the Irish Sea in the fourth or fifth century.[32] This is a different and much more immediate contact than Ireland's earlier foreign contact with the outside world by way of the longer Mediterranean sea-routes in the Bronze Age, or that of the earlier centuries of our era, perhaps as early as the third century, when Gaulish warriors, probably exiles, crossed to southern Ireland and entered the service of Irish kings,[33] or that of cultural contact directly stimulated by the barbarian invasions of Gaul.

We have seen (p. 54 above) that with the traditions of *Táin Bó Cualnge* and other sagas of the Heroic Age we leave the Ireland of the Ancient World behind, and with the fifth century we enter a new phase of history. The prestige of written records claims to displace oral tradition, and though we now know that our written annals and many records of institutions of the early millennium are themselves based on oral tradition, the fact of their subsequent written form when incorporated into the annalistic histories gives them a place for the first time in the historiography of Europe. How far these records are to be depended on is a very difficult question and one which is at the moment much debated.

This change from what we may call the Iron Age form of recording

82

history, the traditional oral saga, to the chronicle style which reached Ireland through Latin channels under ecclesiastical influence, is startling to the student of Irish historical records. Events are henceforth recorded in chronological order in the form of annals on foreign models. The entries are brief and laconic, and are generally in Latin, though sometimes interspersed with entries in Irish, as in the *Annals of Tigernach*. History is now the work of clerics educated in the Latin tradition, trained in a Continental type of education, and in chronology – the root of historiography.[34]

But the clerics, like their predecessors the *filid*, could only do their work under patronage, whether monastic or more directly princely. In either case their work was invariably written for a direct purpose, under direct political influence. Propaganda is never absent, even though unavowed. This principle underlies all our early Irish annals and has coloured the record of our early historical period. The same influence has virtually ignored the province of Munster and flood-lit the family of Níall Noígiallach and their rise to power in Ulster. This does not mean that genuine history is absent from the annals. It means that it is difficult to assess correctly.[35]

The early traditions of the family of Níall Noígiallach form a bridge between the older purely oral records of prehistoric Ireland and the later written records, and it is with the rise of Níall and his family to the chief power in central and northern Ireland that Irish history really begins. The traditional dates[36] of Níall are given as 379 to 405, or more probably 428. The pedigree[37] of Níall and his family is unreliable; but Irish tradition, derived from early Munster poems, especially elegies, fragments of which have survived,[38] claim that he was the son of Eochu Mugmedón and of 'Cairenn, the curly black-haired daughter of Sachell Balb of the Saxons' (cf. below). This is apparently the only occurrence of the name *Cairenn*, an Irish transformation of L. *Carina*. The term *balb*, 'stammerer' is used elsewhere of people of foreign tongue. Presumably Níall's father obtained his wife from Roman Britain. It was widely believed that Níall met his death abroad,[39] and that he met it while raiding in Britain is by no means improbable. Traditions of activities and death abroad are also attributed to Dathí,[40] a prince of Connacht, Níall's nephew and immediate successor as 'king of Ireland', according to the later genealogists. Foreign contacts were a marked feature of the family in later generations also. In the *Additamenta* by the scribe Ferdomnach

83

in the *Book of Armagh*, Níall's own grandson Fedelmid has married the daughter of a British king, and she and her son are able to converse in the British tongue with St Patrick's British nephew Lomman. We shall see the first fruits of this contact overseas in the migration of St Columba, a member of the family of the northern Uí Néill, to Scottish Dál Riata, in the following century.

Our earliest traditions of Níall associate him closely with contemporary poets, and it is from poets that we obtain our most personal references to him. An eighth or ninth century poem, purporting to be an elegy, claims that Níall was the foster-son of the famous Munster poet Torna Éices, 'Torna the learned'. The poet refers to Níall's father Eochu Mugmedón and his grandfather Muiredach, and claims that, now Níall is dead, the enemies of Ireland (i.e. the Saxons) will ravage. The opening verse recalls his mother's British name and stresses Níall's fair hair. Tuirn son of Torna laments:

> When we used to go to the gathering with Eochu's son,
> Yellow as a bright primrose was the hair on the head of Cairenn's son.[41]

A saga[42] on the death of Níall adds the comment:

> Cairenn, the curly black-haired daughter of Sachell Balb[43] of the Saxons was the mother of Níall.

In the same saga his own official poet is said to have been the well-known early Munster poet Ladchenn mac Bairchedo, whose surviving genealogical poem is ascribed by Kuno Meyer to the seventh century.[44] These poems and poets and their relations with Níall illustrate very well the importance of early Irish poetry for the reconstruction of early Irish history. It is significant that this famous head of the Goidelic dynasty was remembered in after times as a heroic warrior, with his heroic poets to celebrate him and his ancestors; and it is doubtless to these poets and their close association with Níall and his family that we may attribute the exalted and indeed even exaggerated prestige of the Uí Néill in the later annals. This in itself would account for the support of the cause of the poets by Columba (cf. p. 227 below), himself a member of the northern Uí Néill. There can be no doubt, however, that Níall and his family owe their importance to a fundamental change which came about in the political divisions of Ireland in their time, and for which they are mainly responsible – the disappearance of the political divisions of Ireland represented by the *cóiceda* (cf. p. 54 f.).

The chief change in the development from the age-old political geography which took place during the early historical period was the destruction and partitioning, about the middle of the fifth century, of the ancient *cóiced* of the *Ulaid*, which had included the whole of northern Ireland from Donegal to Antrim. Tradition claims that this process had begun at least as early as the time of Cormac mac Airt;[45] but as a broad fact, according to our so-called historical records, the change was brought about by the northward and eastward expansion of the family of Níall, with their allies from Connacht. The result was the dismemberment and finally the conquest of the Érainn in the north, in all probability by the three sons of Níall himself, Eogan, Conall and Enda, and at Níall's instigation.[46]

An early stage in this dismemberment was the conquest of a group of peoples between the eastern and the western Ulaid known as the Airgialla ('Oriel', 'subject peoples'),[47] ultimately by the Uí Néill and their Connacht allies. Their territory consisted of the modern counties of Armagh, Monaghan, Tyrone, and most of Fermanagh and Derry. Its possession by the Uí Néill carried with it Emain Macha (two miles from Armagh), the ancient capital of the Ulaid. The conquest of Oriel had placed most of Ulster under the Uí Néill. Of the old independent Ulaid there now remained unconquered by the new 'Tara dynasty' only Donegal and the north-eastern coastal strip from Antrim to Dundalk – in the north and north-east were the little kingdoms of Dál Riata and Dál Fiatach; to the east of Lough Neagh, the kingdom of Dál nAraidi.[48]

A further step in this dismemberment of ancient Ulster was the conquest c. 428 of Donegal, the country which still remained independent to the west of Oriel, and the formation on the spot of the new kingdom of Ailech or Fochla (lit. 'north'), by two of Níall's sons, Eogan (d. 465) and Conall. The new province later formed the nucleus of the kingdom of the northern Uí Néill. These two sons of Níall now occupied territories known later respectively as *Tír Conaill* in the Donegal mountains to the west; and Tyrone (*Tír Eógain*) to the east. Their capital was Ailech.[49] In 563 they gave a crushing defeat to the Dál nAraidi, whose country seems to have

85

become the possession of Eogan's line, as we understand *A.U.* 562 (recte 563).

From the fifth century onwards the ruling dynasty of northern and central Ireland were the Uí Néill,[50] the descendants of Níall Noígiallach. The next in succession to Níall at Tara was his son Loegaire who was reigning at Tara in St Patrick's time,[51] and who is the first Irish king whose dates are regarded as approximately established (cf. p. 83, n. 36). According to the traditional history[52] the succession as head of the dynasty from 506 to 734 alternated between the descendants of his two sons Eogan and Conall, jointly known as the northern Uí Néill, who had founded the kingdom of Ailech in the north, and the descendants of a third son, Crimthann, known as the southern Uí Néill, who claimed their capital at Tara.[53] The two dynasties of the kingdom of Ailech are represented as having held together in unity, alternating in their turn with the southern Uí Néill, till the Cenél Eógain overcame the Cenél Conaill in battle in 734. From 734 to 1036 the succession is represented as alternating between the Cenél Eógain and the southern Uí Néill of Meath. In the rivalry between the Cenél Conaill and the Cenél Eógain the former had the advantage of the natural fastnesses of the Donegal mountains, while the Cenél Eógain could expand eastwards and southwards till the power of Oriel, their eastern neighbours, was broken in 827 by Níall Caille, king of Ailech, and Oriel became subject to the kings of Cenél Eógain, known later as the kings of Tyrone. It was possibly an earlier phase of this eastward expansion of the Uí Néill of Ailech which prompted the movement of members of the dynasty of Dál Riata on the Antrim coast overseas to Scottish Argyll (cf. p. 97 below).

The chief kingdoms which had formed constituent but independent kingdoms in the wider over-kingdom of Ulaid consisted of (1) the small kingdom of Dál Riata in the extreme northern coastal strip of Co. Antrim, who had their dynastic stronghold on the rocky promontory of Dunseverick, at the terminus of the *Slige Midluachra*, the ancient royal route north from north Leinster and Meath.[54] Their ruling dynasty, it will be remembered, claimed to be of Érainn stock; (2) the Dál Fiatach on the eastern sea-board of Co. Down, also Érainn and perhaps the true Ulaid of the Heroic Age tradition, though this is disputed; (3) the Dál nAraidi, remains of the ancient Cruithni, between the Dál Riata and the Dál Fiatach, occupying a wide area

86

around Lough Neagh. They were the largest and most powerful people in these parts, and constituted a portion of the eastern Oriel (Airgialla) conquered by the sons of Níall in the fifth century,[55] and made into a dependent state. In the sixth century their most important king was Mongán (d. 624), who is widely celebrated in the very considerable corpus of sagas and poems relating to him. His residence was at Moylinny, practically the modern town of Antrim on the eastern shores of Lough Neagh. The capital of the ancient Ulaid, Emain Macha, which manifestly gave birth to Armagh, only two miles away, came into the possession of the Uí Néill,[56] on the conquest of the Ulaid.

The destruction of the old *Cóiced* of Ulster and the annexation of its centre of power by the dynasty of the Uí Néill, is the most important fact in early Irish history. Henceforth the chief power is in central Ireland, where the southern branch of Níall's descendants claimed to occupy the prehistoric sanctuary of Tara, and are commonly referred to as the 'Tara dynasty'. By their annexation of the ancient Ulaid capital of Emain Macha about the middle of the fifth century they had gained a stronghold close to St Patrick's sanctuary of Armagh, and with it the patronage of the chief saint of the defeated Ulaid. Moreover, as this is claimed as the centre of the earliest learning and of the introduction of the art of writing and Latin culture into Ireland, its possession may have given to the Uí Néill the control of spiritual and intellectual, no less than of political, prestige, and of the teaching and writing of history.

Our literary texts recognize two great divisions of Ireland, known as 'Conn's Half', comprising northern Ireland, and 'Mug's Half', comprising Munster and Leinster. The names originate in a fictitious story claiming that Conn Cétchathach ('of the hundred battles'), ancestor of the Uí Néill (*Connachta*) and Mug Nuadat ('slave of Nuadu') whose proper name was Eógan (ancestor of the Eóganacht) had divided Ireland between them. This conception was undoubtedly the creation of the historiographers. It appears in annals and genealogies, but not in the Book of Invasions.[57]

The literary tradition undoubtedly reflects a historical division between the territory dominated by the Uí Néill and that which developed from the old *cóiceda* of Munster and Leinster from the fourth to the tenth centuries. Our traditions for this 'southern half' ('Mug's Half') are on the whole less full than those of the north; but

87

we can trace in the annals and genealogies of Munster a class of historiographers attached to the interests of the dominant line of the Eóganacht of Cashel comparable to those working in the interests of the Uí Néill in the north. Literary evidence suggests on the whole, however, that from the fifth century onwards Munster was developing intellectually perhaps even more than by military and territorial expansion, and that her outlook was continental rather than insular. It may well be that in fact during the early historical period Munster was the most civilized part of Ireland.

Whereas in the Heroic Age the seat of the chief king, Cú Roí mac Dáiri, was in west Munster, we find that in the early historical period the chief dynasty of 'Mug's Half' was the Eóganacht with their chief seat at Cashel near the borders of Leinster. The Munster dynasty of the Eóganacht formed a consolidated realm, generally peaceable and flourishing, and probably, as suggested above, always in touch with the continent. The culture of both Munster and Leinster was high. It is claimed that writing in the vernacular had already begun in Munster by 600, and that panegyric poetry from Munster has been preserved in written form from the second half of the sixth century,[58] and contact between south-eastern Ireland and Gaul had evidently had an unbroken sequence from at least as early as the third century, and was actively stimulated between Aquitaine and southern Ireland during the barbarian invasions of Gaul.[59]

The growth of the power of the Eóganacht had been rapid. In the earliest period they are never heard of. By St Patrick's time their chief branch are already ruling on the great rock of Cashel though other branches of importance are located in the west in Cork and Limerick. Cashel is indeed the 'Tiryns' of southern Ireland, which commanded the routes from western to eastern Munster, and again the northward route to Leinster. The growth of their strength in east Munster is in some measure at the expense of the old kingdom of Leinster, which had been greatly reduced by the expansion of the power of Meath.[60] The conquest of north Leinster by the dynasty of Tara had been accompanied by the imposition of a heavy annual tribute, which according to a continuous tradition[61] was resisted in a series of battles lasting for centuries. According to tradition King Loegaire of Tara, son of Níall Noígiallach, met his death in 462 or 463 in seeking to exact it, and the last heroic saga, that of the Battle of Allen,[62] fought c. 722, records the death of Fergal, son of Mael

88

Dúin, king of 'Conn's Half', who had invaded Leinster and perished seeking the tribute.

The reduction of the power of the Lagin by the growing power of Meath in the fifth century evidently facilitated the growth of strength of the Eóganacht of Cashel. The tribal histories and genealogies enable us to trace the means by which the eastern Eóganacht gained control, by the fifth century, over the provincial kingship of Munster at the expense of the Érainn of West Munster, who had hitherto been the overlords. This growth of power the Eóganacht appear to have achieved by enlisting various tribes, including both Lagin and some sections of the Érainn themselves, as allies in conquering the dominant sections of the Érainn and in consolidating their own position against them.[63] The principle was analogous to the Roman establishment of *foederati* on their frontiers. Of these federate allies of the Eóganacht the most interesting are the Déisi.[64] Rival traditions assign the rise of Cashel to power variously to the eastern and western divisions of the Eóganacht. Strife between the two branches continued from the fifth to the ninth century, and is said to be the main feature of Munster internal politics in the early historical period. Both branches were powerful, and although those located at Cashel in east Munster were generally in a position to claim the kingship of Munster,[65] the claim did not always pass unchallenged.

According to the tradition, which was obviously fostered by the eastern branch, the Eóganacht of Cashel rose to power with the help of the Déisi, who had been expelled from Tara as the result of a quarrel with Cormac mac Airt. While part of the Déisi migrated to Pembroke-shire, under their leader Eochaid Allmuir ('from overseas'), the rest settled in south Leinster near the Munster border, where they were known as the *Déisi*[66] (mod. Ir. *Decies*) after the name *Déisi Breg*, the district from which they had come. The grand-daughter of their chief married the king of Cashel, Oengus mac Nadfroích,[67] and the Déisi helped him to conquer eastern Munster, where they were settled by him as *foederati*.[68] The incorporation of the Déisi territory of South Leinster into Munster is thus closely bound up with the growth of the power of Munster and of the stronghold of Cashel. Oengus mac Nadfroích is in fact the first king of Cashel mentioned in the annals.[69] The size of Leinster is still further reduced, but the intermarriage of these ruling families and the position of the frontier troops ensured peace, and was a source of strength to both provinces, and this eastward extension and consolidation of Munster power was of importance for the subsequent history of Ireland. It is claimed in the *Tripartite Life of St Patrick* that Oengus mac Nadfroích was baptized with his sons by the saint at Cashel, and that Patrick prophesied that none of his descendants should ever die of a wound, which was tantamount to declaring them clerics, and the same source adds that no one is king of Cashel until Patrick's successor instals him and confers ecclesiastical rank upon him.[70]

A variant tradition ascribes the initial rise of the Eóganacht, not to Oengus mac Nadfroích but to the legendary ancestor of the Eóganacht, Conall Corc, son of Lugaid, who was fostered by Crimthann Mór mac Fidaig, and succeeded him as king of Munster. According to this tradition, which has survived in Scotland till modern times, Conall Corc, having been treacherously banished by his uncle Crimthann, eventually reached the palace of the Pictish king Feradach Findfechtnach, king of Cruithentuath on Turin Hill above Forfar,[71] and married his daughter Mongfind. Eventually Corc returned to Munster, taking her and their sons, and succeeded to the throne. The story occurs in several variant forms, and it is interesting to note that Corc's uncle is the Crimthann Mór mac Fidaig to whom Cormac's Glossary refers as 'king of Ireland and Britain as far as the English Channel' in the passage quoted on pp. 77–8 above in which reference is made to the double kingdoms of the Irish kings of this period, and of their royal residences in Britain. One of these, Dind Tradui, explained as 'the three-fossed fort of Crimthann Mór mac Fidaig', is specified. The story of Corc cannot be regarded as historical, but it has interesting traditional elements.[72] The marriage of a Pictish princess with a foreign prince is fully in accordance with what we know of Pictish exogamy, while Scottish clan tradition claims that the Eóganacht clan of Mag Gerginn and also the earls of Lennox are descended from Corc and Mongfinn.[73]

The most powerful of the pre-Norse kings of Cashel was Cathal mac Finguini (*c.* 721–42) to whom the *Annals of Inisfallen* (s.a. 721) claim that Fergal, son of Mael Dúin, King of Tara, made submission. Indeed these annals, which are, of course, of Munster provenance, claim in his *obit* s.a. 742 that he was 'king of Ireland', whereas the *Annals of Ulster*, which are of northern provenance, refer to him only as *rex Caisil* ('king of Cashel'). The Battle of Allen took place in the time of Cathal mac Finguini. It was a violation of a truce previously made between Cathal and Fergal.[74] Accordingly, as in honour bound, Cathal returned the head of Fergal, which had been cut off in the battle, to the Uí Néill, in compensation for the breach of the truce that had been made between them.

It has been claimed, nevertheless, that during the early Christian centuries, Munster was on the whole perhaps the most consolidated realm in western Europe.[75] Political changes, migrations and dynastic strife are of relatively limited intensity, and the fact that only two or three of the score or so of kings who ruled Munster at that period died violent deaths demonstrates her relatively peaceful condition.[76] This quiet political history of Munster is to be interpreted in direct connection with the history of culture and the church. It is in Munster that we find the thickest concentration of ogam inscriptions – a sure sign of a cultured and wealthy aristocracy; our earliest records of writing; our earliest cultured monastic contacts, as demonstrated by the 'Irish Augustine' at the monastery of Lismore on the Blackwater (cf. p. 221 below); and finally the ecclesiastical associations of the kings of Cashel, who, during the historical period, were sometimes bishops. Tradition claims that this unique combination of the status of king and bishop dates back to the time of the consecration of Oengus mac Nadfroích by St Patrick. The tradition is late, but the fact of this close association of the kingship and bishopric of Cashel is undoubtedly the key to the history of the southern half of Ireland throughout the early historical period.

NOTES

1 Evidence for *graffiti* is collected by A. Burn, *The Romans in Britain* (Oxford, 1932). See also Haverfield, *R.R.B.* 28 ff.; cf. Charlesworth, *L.P.*, 67.

2 Haverfield, *R.R.B.*, 30.

3 On the significance of the title, see N. K. Chadwick 'Bretwalda, Gwledig, Vortigern', B.B.C.S. XIX (1961), 225 ff.; also 'Note on the name Vortigern', *S.E.B.H.*, by H. M. Chadwick and others, 34 ff.

4 The most important of the early references to him are cited by C. A. Raleigh Radford in *Antiquity* XXXII (1958), p. 19. Cf. also H. M. Chadwick, *O.E.N.*, 37; and *S.E.B.H.*, 21; cf. further 'Note on the name Vortigern', *S.E.B.H.*, 34 ff.

5 *Historia Brittonum*, caps. 39, 41, 48.

6 We are chiefly indebted to Dr J. N. L. Myres for the conclusions briefly stated above. Supplementary matter has also been added by K. Dauncey and the late R. R. Clarke; cf. also P. Hunter Blair, *Roman Britain and Early England* (Edinburgh, 1963), 162 f. The principal references to all these preliminary studies are entered by N. K. Chadwick in 'The British or Celtic Part in the Population of England', in *A.B.*, 138 ff.

7 Sir John Rhŷs, *Celtic Britain*, 238. See Sir F. Stenton, *A.S.E.*, 3; Sir J. E. Lloyd, *H.W.* I, 125 f. Collingwood, *R.B.E.S.*, 321 f. The most recent and authoritative studies are those of K. H. Jackson, 'The Arthur of History', and 'Arthur in Early Welsh Verse', in R. S. Loomis (editor), *A.L.M.A.*

8 For the Britons of Southern Scotland at this period the best accounts are those of K. H. Jackson, 'The Britons in Southern Scotland', *Antiquity* XXIV (1955), 77 ff.; and more recently 'Angles and Britons in Northumbria and Cumbria', in *A.B.*, 60 ff. See further Salway, *F.P.R.B.*, 198 f.

9 Edited by Otto Seeck (Berlin 1876). For valuable studies see C. E. Stevens, A. J. XCVII (1940); E. Birley, T.C.W.A.S. XXXIX (1939), No. XIV, 190 ff.; more recent research by A. H. M. Jones, *L.R.E.*, III, Appendix II, p. 347 ff.

10 For the system here suggested see P. Hunter Blair, *O.N.*; M. P. Charlesworth, *L.P.*; H. M. Chadwick, *E.S.*

11 The chief edition is that of Mommsen, *MHG, Auctores antiquissimi*, t. XII, (Berlin, 1898), 112 ff. A more recent edition is that of F. Lot, *Nennius et L'Historia Brittonum* (Paris, 1934). A useful English translation by A. W. Wade-Evans, *Nennius and the History of the Britons* (London, 1938) contains also the *Annales Cambriae* and the Genealogies of the British (Welsh) princes. These texts, published in English by Wade-Evans, constitute the compendium of texts contained in the British Museum MS. Harleian 3859, and are an important historical document in their own right.

12 Cf. p. 122, n. 23.

13 An interesting tradition of a Pictish ruler of Dumbarton is recorded – for what the record is worth – in the Welsh (Latin) *Life of St Cadoc*. Text and translation by A. W. Wade-Evans, *V.S.B.G.* (Cardiff, 1944), 24 ff.

14 The Old Welsh form is *Cunedag*.

15 See H. M. Chadwick, *E.S.*, 3.

16 A. O. Curle, *T.T.*

17 'The Cornovii', in Foster and Alcock, *C.E.*, 251 ff.

18 Richmond, *R.B.*, 155.

19 *Ibid.*, *R.N.N.B.*, 113, and fuller references in n. 5.

20 Edited by K. Meyer, *S.C.*, No. 883, s.v. *mug-eme*, p. 75 f. Cf. also W. Stokes, *T.I.G.*, p. 62. The passage is translated on p. xlviii.

21 His traditional dates are 366–379.

22 I have followed the translation of K. Jackson in *The Celts* (edited by J. Raftery, Dublin, 1964), 75.

23 See the valuable map of the various 'tribes' of Ireland by Liam Price in *L.C.*

24 The most authoritative account of the colonization of Armorica is that of J. Loth, *E.B.*

25 *De Bello Gothico* IV, 19.

26 F. M. Stenton, *A.S.H.* (2nd ed., Oxford, 1950), 6.

27 For the Roman city states and the changes in the Roman defence system in Armorica, see R. Couffon, 'Limites des cités gallo-romaines et Fondations des évêchés dans la péninsule armoricaine', *S.É.C.*, Tome LXXII (1942); F. Merlet, 'La Formation des Diocèses et des Paroisses en Bretagne', *M.S.H.A.B.*, Tome XXX (1950), Tome XXXI (1951).

28 The life of St Germanus by Constantius has come down to us in two versions. The shorter and better, which is believed to be the older, is edited by W. Levison, *Mon. Germ. Hist.*: *Script. Rer. Merov.* VII (1920), 225 ff.

29 The offices attributed by Constantius to St Germanus present a difficult problem, and are not wholly free from suspicion. See Gaudemet, 'La Carrière Civile de St Germanus' in the volume of studies issued at Auxerre by G. Le Bras and E. Gilson, *St Germain d'Auxerre et son temps* (Auxerre, 1950), p. 111 ff. For a brief discussion of the question as it relates to the defence of Armorica, reference may be made to N. K. Chadwick, *P.L.*, p. 263 f.

30 For an account of the rebellions of the Armoricans, see W. Levison, *Neues Archiv* XXIX, 139 ff.

31 On the erection of defensive walls around the Gaulish open towns of this period, see Jullian, *Bordeaux*, 34, 43 ff.; *La Gaule* IV, 594, n. 4, and references. Cf. also the brief but valuable account of O. Brogan, *Roman Gaul* (London, 1953), 221 ff.

32 See S. P. ÓRíordáin, 'Roman Material in Ireland', P.R.I.A., LI, Section C, No. 3 (1947), p. 39 f.

33 For evidence and references see Kuno Meyer, *Ériu* IV (1910), 208; and cf. *Learning in Ireland in the Fifth Century* (Dublin, 1913), 7 f., and notes 15–17.

34 On this subject see the illuminating study of Cennfaelad by E. MacNeill, 'A Pioneer of Nations', *Studies* XI (1922).

35 As J. V. Kelleher has pointed out, 'Early Irish History and Pseudo-History', S.H., no. 3 (1963), 113 ff.

36 His dates are a matter of considerable uncertainty. He is believed to be the father of Laegaire, whose accession in AD 427 or possibly 428, and whose death in 462 or 463 are believed to be our first secure dates of an Irish king. See O'Rahilly, *E.I.H.M.*, 209. But the chronology of the fifth century is very uncertain. See O'Rahilly, *loc. cit.*, and for an important discussion see J. Carney, *S.I.L.H.*,

330 ff.; cf. also H. M. Chadwick, *E.S.*, 133 ff.

37 This is given by O'Rahilly, *E.I.H.M.*, p. 221.

38 For the texts see K. Meyer, *Otia Merseiana* II (1899), p. 88 ff.; 'Totenklage König Níall Noígiallach' in *F.W.S.*, p. 1 ff.; *ÄID* I, p. 14 ff.; II, p. 21 f.

39 On the variant traditions of his death cf. O'Rahilly, *E.I.H.M.*, p. 217 f.

40 O'Rahilly dates the death of Dathi or Nathí in AD 445, *E.I.H.M.*, p. 215.

41 K. Meyer, *A.I.P.*, p. 69.

42 Edited and translated by Kuno Meyer in *Otia Merseiana* II, p. 84 ff.

43 See *E.I.H.M.* 216 n. 3.

44 *ÄID* I, p. 15 f.

45 MacNeill, *Phases*, 124 f.

46 O'Rahilly, *E.I.H.M.*, 223, 227 f.; Binchy, *S.H.*, no. 2 (1962), p. 150.

47 On the subject of the establishment of Oriel see O'Rahilly, *E.I.H.M.*, 225.

48 O'Rahilly, *E.I.H.M.*, 234.

49 The splendid fortress known today as the Grianán Ailech, just inside the eastern border of Donegal.

50 The *Uí Néill* are the descendants of Níall Noígiallach. The term is to be sharply distinguished from *O'Néill*, which is proper only to the descendants of Niall Glúndubh, who fell in battle against the Norsemen on the Liffey in 919. See McNeill, *C.I.*, 90.

51 As we learn from Muichu's *Life of St Patrick*.

52 For the biassed nature of the sources of this tradition see Kelleher, S.H., no. 3, 120 ff.

53 On this claim see Kelleher, S.H., no. 3, 123.

54 See Colm Ó Lochlainn, 'Roadways in Ancient Ireland' in *E.S.E.M.*, 465 ff., and map *ad fin*.

55 See O'Rahilly, *E.I.H.M.*, 222 f.; cf. D. A. Binchy, 'Patrick and his Biographers', S.H. no. 2 (1962), 150.

56 See Binchy, 'Patrick and his Biographers', *S.H.*, no. 2 (1962), p. 150. On the early relationships of these three independent kingdoms to the over-kingdom of *Ulaid* see E. MacNeill, *Phases*, 185; *ibid.*, *C.I.*, 185; O'Rahilly, *E.I.H.M.*, 222 f.

57 *E.I.H.M.* 191–2.

58 R. Flower, *I.T.*, 184.

59 See the brief but impressive studies of this subject with fuller evidence and references by Kuno Meyer, *L.I.F.C.*, p. 7 f.; 'Gauls in Ireland', *Ériu* IV (1910), p. 208.

60 The stages by which Tara traditionally extended its sway over Leinster are outlined by E. MacNeill, *Phases*, p. 120 ff., and more especially p. 187 ff.

61 See 'The Boromean Tribute', text and translation by Standish H. O'Grady, *S.G.*, no. XXVIII.

94

62 Text and translation by Whitley Stokes, *R.C.* XXIV (1903), p. 41 ff.
63 Ó Buachalla, C.H.A.J., LVII (1952), p. 113.
64 *Ibid.*, p. 116.
65 See the *Frithfolaith Chaisil fri Tuatha Muman* 'Reciprocal Services of Cashel and the Tribes of Munster', an important document for Munster history (YBL. col. 339 and elsewhere), probably compiled as early as 800, Irish Texts i. This tract, though brief, is more authoritative than the *Lebor na Cert*, which is hardly earlier than the eleventh century. The *Frithfolaith* is an account of the reciprocal services between the king of Cashel (i.e. of Munster) and the kings of the various Munster states. It depicts the Munster of the period preceding the rise of *Dál Cais* (cf. p. 165 below) to power after 950. See Liam Ó Buachalla, C.H.A.J., LVI (1951), 90 f., *ibid.*, LVII (1952), 81 ff.
66 According to MacNeill *Déssi* (*Déisi*) means 'vassal communities', in this case those dwelling around Tara, perhaps identical with the Luaigni, the chief fighting force of north Leinster in the *Táin Bo Cuáilnge*.
67 Slain in 490 according to the *Annals of Inisfallen*, s.a. 492.
68 The situation is clearly summed up by Ó Buachalla, *op. cit.*, vol. LVII (1952), p. 116. The text of the saga of 'The Expulsion of the Dessi', believed to have been first written down *c.* 750, was printed by Kuno Meyer in *Y Cymmrodor* XIII & XIV (1900, 1901), p. 10 ff., and the text with references to variant versions and commentaries was reprinted by Meyer in *Ériu* III (1907), p. 135 ff. Cf. further the text of a different and later version, also edited by Meyer, in *Anecdota from Irish MSS* I (Dublin, 1907), p. 15 ff. Cf. more recently S. Pender, 'Two unpublished versions of the Expulsion of the Déssi' in *Féilscríbhinn Torna*, edited by S. Pender (Cork, 1947), 209 ff.
69 Ó Buachalla, C.H.A.J., LVII (1952), p. 73.
70 *Tripartite Life* I, 194 f.
71 The earthen rampart of the fort on Turin Hill still stands.
72 The text of the story in saga-form is incomplete. For references to the sources and a discussion of the bias and historical elements in these Eóganacht traditions see Ó Buachalla, C.H.A.J., LVII (1952), 116 ff. Cf. also Dillon, *C.K.*, p. 34 ff.
73 For references see H. M. Chadwick, *E.S.*, 41, n. 2.
74 *Annals of Inisfallen*, s.a. 721.
75 MacNeill, *Phases*, 12.
76 Ó Buachalla, C.H.A.J., LVI (1951), 87.

4

The Formation of the Historical Celtic Kingdoms

In the preceding chapter we have traced the emergence of organized Celtic realms on the western periphery of Europe following on the decline and withdrawal of Roman power. The whole of southern Britain was now once more governed by native Celtic dynasties, who carried on the internal administration of the country, and defended the borders, which were beset on all sides by neighbouring peoples, Teutonic, Pictish, and Irish, all seeking expansion and permanent settlement in Britain after the withdrawal of Roman defences. During the sixth and following centuries the earlier political fragmentation of the Celtic peoples developed into more extended and unified communities. We have seen that the Celtic peoples on the borders of southern Scotland and throughout southern Britain had already established native dynasties ruling wide kingdoms; and we have also seen that these kingdoms spoke a single Brittonic language, throughout all Scotland, south of the Forth-Clyde line, and northwestern England, Wales, Cornwall and now on to Brittany.

Beyond the area which had been under Roman rule lay two great Celtic realms which the Romans had never conquered. These were the powerful Picts of the Highlands and islands of Scotland, protected by their mountains; and the Celtic peoples of Ireland, immune in their isolation across the Irish Sea. We have seen that the conquests and emergence of the Goidels during the fifth century had welded the kingdoms of Ireland under two great dynasties – northern Ireland under the control of the descendants of Níall Noígiallach, southern Ireland under the Eóganacht of Cashel. In the present chapter we shall trace the development of the Picts during the sixth and seventh centuries into the two powerful divisions, referred to by Bede as the

96

'Northern and Southern Picts, separated by steep and rugged mountains.' We shall also trace the development of the last and greatest of the Irish settlements in western Britain, which succeeded in establishing an important kingdom in the west of Scotland to the north of the Roman defensive line of the Antonine Wall. The relations of these Pictish and Irish settlements with one another and with the Britons to the south of them, and later with the Angles settled to the south and east of them, are the nucleus of the modern kingdom of Scotland, while the British dynasties of southern Scotland combined with those of north-western and western Britain to develop later into the much smaller but more consolidated kingdom of Wales.

In tracing the conquests of the Uí Néill in northern Ireland we recognized that two little independent kingdoms which had formed a part of the ancient *cóiced* of the Ulaid had remained independent and developed a future importance for the countries across the Irish Sea far in excess of their role in insular Irish history. Both claimed to be of Érainn or pre-Goidelic stock. The first of these is the little kingdom of Dál Riata, whose dynasty claimed to be of the 'seed of Conaire Mór', their pre-historic king. This remnant of the Ulaid now had their chief seat at Dunseverick on the small strip still left to them on the north coast of Co. Antrim. We know little of the dynasty till St Patrick's day, but in the ninth-century text of the *Tripartite Life of St Patrick* the kingdom is governed by Erc and his sons, Loarn and Fergus, the latter of whom is blessed by the saint, and Patrick prophesies to him that one of his descendants shall occupy the throne of Dál Riata and Fortrenn for ever. Fortrenn is the name of one of the kingdoms of the Southern Picts in historical times, but seems to be used here for Scotland as a whole. We also hear of the expansion of the kingdom of Dál Riata under the sons of Erc in the *Annals of Tigernach*: 'Fergus mór mac Erca (*sic*) with the people of Dál Riata held part of Britain and died there.'[1] Here the event corresponds to one which in the *Annals of Ulster* is recorded s.a. 502. It probably took place about the middle of the fifth century or possibly a little later. Meanwhile the kingdom of Dál Riata in Ireland from which they had come still continued; but little is heard of it after the Battle of Mag Rath (Moira) in or about 634, when they fought in alliance with the Dál Riata of Scotland in an unsuccessful encounter against Domnall, son of Aed, king of Tara. Henceforth the history of Dál Riata and the 'seed of Conaire Mór', as they called themselves,

97

belongs to Scotland, where the term continued to be used in relation to the dynasty of Scottish Dál Riata as late as the twelfth century.[2]

The other survival of the old Ulaid which remained independent was the kingdom of Dál Fiatach, traditionally related to Dál Riata, and claiming descent from the same stock. Having lost their ancient citadel of Emain Macha, they occupied the sea-board of Co. Down and part of Co. Antrim. The dynastic name, *Dál Fiatach*, is derived from their legendary ancestor, Fiatach Find.[3] Their ruling dynasty lasted down to the Norman Conquest, but it plays comparatively little part in the Irish annals, and, like Dál Riata, its more notable historical associations lay eastwards and overseas. Their most outstanding king was Baetán mac Cairill (d. 581), who is said to have compelled Aedán mac Gabráin, the contemporary king of Scottish Dál Riata, to submit to him at the battle of Rosnaree on Belfast Lough,[4] and to have subdued Manu (the Isle of Man).[5] (Cf. p. 106 below.)

In tracing briefly the relations recorded from the early historical period of the small kingdoms in north-eastern Ireland which survived from the prehistoric fragmented Ulaid we are in reality entering on a new area, this time a maritime one. Its centre of culture was an island, the Isle of Man, which we have not yet brought into the picture because no early records have been preserved, and it is only from the evidence of the later historical period that we are able to trace something of the early history of the island. The key to this lost history is contained partly in the language, partly in the local stone inscriptions and archaeological remains, but most of all in the history of the surrounding countries – Ireland, Scotland, north England and Wales – with all of which the Isle of Man was in close communication. Before passing to a fuller consideration of northern and southern Britain in the sixth and seventh centuries therefore, we will pause to take a brief survey of the Isle of Man, Ellan Vannin, to give it its Manx name.

In prehistoric and early historical times, when the sea offered a quicker and easier means of transport than land routes, the Isle of Man occupied a key position. In these times of the rapid backward and forward voyages between Ireland, Scotland, and Wales, the Irish Sea and the waterways to the north of it were busy intersections of sea-routes, the northern extension of the Atlantic coastal route of pre-historic times, and the Celtic peoples were no mean seafarers.

Throughout the historical period the narrow and stormy straits between Ireland and the Hebrides and south-western Scotland were traversed readily, and the Irish Sea afforded a lively communication, sometimes friendly, sometimes hostile, between all the lands in its coastal areas. It was a great land-locked lake, and has been the true focus of Celtic civilization from before the Roman occupation of Britain, and the most important distributing centre for the closely related literary and mythological traditions shared by the countries fringing its shores.

In view of this key position, and perhaps even more owing to its genial climate and fertility, the Isle of Man has had colonists from both Ireland and Wales from pre-historic times.[6] We have no early vernacular records,[7] but much can be deduced as to its early history from the annals of the Celtic countries in its orbit, for it undoubtedly played a part of very considerable importance in the struggle between the fragments of the Ulaid, that is to say the new Irish kingdom of Dál Riata in western Scotland, and those of the relatively large and important kingdom of Dál nAraide around Lough Neagh, and again the small but by no means inconsiderable kingdom of the Dál Fiatach on the north-eastern coast of Ireland. Something of its history and its relationship with all the surrounding countries is also reflected in the language, or rather languages, which we can trace on the stone inscriptions, of which the island possesses a considerable wealth in the Ogam and runic alphabets as well as in Latin.

It is suggested that there may have been some colonization from Ireland in the fourth and fifth centuries, about the time when the Irish immigration into Scottish Dál Riata was at its height, and this is very probable. The island seems to have been British-speaking at an earlier time, but there were Irish speakers there at least by the fifth century.[8] The language spoken in the Island today is not of the Brythonic Group, but Goidelic. We know that Gaelic was spoken in Man at least as early as the fifth century AD, because several Ogam inscriptions of this period in the island show Gaelic linguistic characteristics, and the language was brought to Man in the fourth century, just as it was probably brought at this time to the Highlands and islands of Scotland and the western peninsulas of Wales (cf. p. 59). There are signs, however, that British (Welsh) was also spoken in Man in the period of the Ogam inscriptions and both languages were probably spoken there in the Dark Ages.[9]

99

The Gaelic of Man is not an independent survival from the original parent Goidelic stock, however, but is closely linked to medieval Irish and Scottish Gaelic, nearer to Scottish Gaelic than to Irish. The two latter were not seriously differentiated before the sixteenth century, and from the Viking period till the late thirteenth century the Isle of Man had close political relations with western Scotland. Scottish Gaelic was spoken in Galloway, less than twenty miles from the Isle of Man, as late as the seventeenth century, and both historical and linguistic indications point to close communications between Man and Galloway from at least the early ninth century onwards. The close relationship which still subsists between the Manx language and the Scottish Gaelic of today reflects the time when the Gaelic of Galloway provided a connecting link between the two.[10]

We shall see that Welsh historical records suggest incursions into North Wales from Galloway across Morecambe Bay (cf. p. 150 below), and in the early ninth century a dynasty in Gwynedd.

Before the occupation of Argyll by an Irish dynasty in the fifth century the whole of Scotland north of the Antonine Wall, including the northern and western islands, had been ruled by the powerful dynasties of the Picts, and apart from Argyll the Picts continued to be the rulers till as late as the ninth century. Their language, which has survived only in proper names and inscriptions, has never been interpreted, but is now thought to be an amalgamation of an earlier form of Celtic, akin to British, with an indigenous non-Indo-European language, probably descended from a language of the Bronze Age.[11] We have already seen that in the earliest period of which we have record, groups or tribes known as the Cornovii and the Dumnonii – names also familiar to us from south-western Britain – occupied the north-western and the south midland areas of Scotland respectively.

The word Pict is a somewhat general term which covers a number of peoples in Scotland, known to Latin writers both on the Continent and in this country as *Picti*,[12] and in our earliest vernacular sources as *Cruithni*. But some of the peoples of Scotland are referred to by classical writers under more specific names. In Roman times two of the important tribes who were certainly 'Picts' were the *Verturiones* concentrated on the upper Forth and the river Earn, known later as the 'men of Fortrenn' (cf. p. 97 above), and the Caledonii in the valley of the Upper Tay with their capital at Dunkeld, 'the *dún* ('stronghold') of the Caledonii'. Their centre of activity was round Mount Shiehallion ('the Shee-hill' or 'sacred mountain of the Caledonii').

We know little about the organization of the Picts in the early centuries of their history. Bede, writing in the early eighth century, evidently visualized the Picts as divided into two main bodies whom he distinguished as the Northern and the Southern Picts, for he mentions that 'the provinces of the former are separated from those of the latter by steep and rugged mountains'; and he tells us further that St Columba arrived in Britain in the ninth year of the reign of Brideus son of Meilochon,[13] the *rex potentissimus* of the northern Picts, and that he converted them to Christianity. The Southern Picts, who live 'on this side of the mountains' (*qui intra eosdem montes habent sedes*), adds Bede, had been converted long before by the preaching of St Ninian. The mountains which separated the Northern from the Southern Picts were Druim Alban and the Mounth. Bede's division was probably a political reality. Land communication between the Northern and the Southern Picts must always have been very difficult and hazardous, especially after the establishment of the kingdom of Dál Riata.

Direct statements of relations between the northern and the southern Picts are rare in the early annals. Through the whole of the historical period the southern Picts appear in our records as divided into four separate provinces or kingdoms, all of them enclosing the valley of the Tay.

1. *Atholl*, roughly the Perthshire Highlands and the carse of Gowrie, the old kingdom of the Caledonii, with its capital at Dunkeld, dominated by Shiehallion, which was possibly their sanctuary. This kingdom controlled the valley of the upper Tay and during the Pictish historical period its capital was at Scone.

2. *Circinn* or *Girginn*, i.e. Forfar, now Angus, and Kincardine or the Mearns, i.e. Strathmore, the northern territory of the Lower Tay Valley and the eastern seaboard to the watershed of the river Dee. Strathmore is a very rich agricultural area and its capital must always have been near Forfar, close to the foot of Turin Hill (cf. p. 90 above), known popularly today as *Dunnechain* (the '*dún* of Nechtan').

3. *Fortrenn* (the genitive case of *Fortrinn* (pl.), later used as a nominative),[14] situated to the south-west of the Tay, and including the upper waters of the Earn and the Forth, with its confluents.

4. *Fib* (Fife), the rich corn-growing country between the Tay and the Forth. Traditions of fifth century saints and of early kings with their seat at St Andrews point to its seaboard concentration. The earliest name of St Andrews was *Kilrymont*.

This general collection of Pictish kingdoms, or states, or provinces was known in later Latin medieval records as *Pictavia*; in native speech and records as *Cruithentuath*, 'the people of the Cruithin'.

Both the Picts of Atholl and those of Fortrenn were on through routes to the Irish kingdom of Dál Riata in the west, and for this reason play a larger part in Irish records than the Picts of Fife or Circinn. Yet the rich agricultural kingdom of Circinn (Angus) was probably always the most important centre of power. The finest and most advanced of the famous Pictish sculptured stones are scattered throughout this area; and as one stands on the great Iron Age hill fort of Castle Law above Abernethy on the south bank of the Tay and surveys the line of hill forts along the north, the whole Tay valley comes into view as a nucleated area, surely always the heart of Pictavia.

We are in the dark as to the precise political relations between the Northern and the Southern Picts at the time of which Bede speaks. It is just possible that in the sixth century the centre of Pictish power was in the neighbourhood of Inverness under Bride mac Maelchon, Brude mac Maelchon as he is generally called in later records, Bede's *rex potentissimus*. He had a fleet, and certainly controlled the northern isles and the Hebrides. Adamnán, in his biography of St Columba, speaks of the saint meeting a *subregulus* of the Orkneys at his court, and it is inconceivable, in view of Columba's relations with him, that the saint could have established his sanctuary on Iona had not the control of the Hebrides been with Brude.

But the situation does not suggest that even in the late sixth century the Northern Picts held any ascendancy over the Southern Picts. A century later, when Ecgfrith of Northumbria sought to destroy the Pictish power in 685, he was slain at Forfar in Circinn (Angus), though his opponent, Brude mac Bile, is called king of Fortrenn in the annals. Perhaps the two kingdoms of Fortrenn and Circinn were united already at this time; but clearly Circinn, as Ecgfrith's objective, was the heart of Pictavia.

The kingdoms known collectively as *Cruithentuath* were the earliest native power in Scotland, a strong and, in some ways at least, a highly developed civilization into whose western seaboard the kingdom of Dál Riata had penetrated, growing into a powerful kingdom itself, even waging aggressive warfare in *Cruithentuath*. From the sixth century onwards the struggle for supremacy between the Picts of both north and south on the one hand, and the Irish kingdom of Dál Riata, later called Argyll, on the other, forms the most important theme of the history of Scotland till the union of the two peoples in the middle of the ninth century, and with the union, the beginning of what we mean today by the country of Scotland. A subordinate but important theme during the whole period, is the relations, now friendly, now hostile, between the Irish kingdom of Dál Riata and the Britons of southern Scotland. Meanwhile the Anglian dynasty of the Bernicians of Northumbria were gradually extending themselves northwards, and making heavy inroads into the British territory of south-eastern Scotland.

Although all indications confirm our traditions of the Picts as a powerful nation we are very much in the dark as to their internal history. About two dozen Pictish inscriptions exist, and their distribution covers the north and east of Scotland and corresponds closely with that of Pictish art represented on the 'symbol stones' to be described later. With two or three exceptions, in which the inscriptions are written in Latin letters, the Pictish inscriptions are written in a late form of the Ogam alphabet, and have not been translated.

It is uncertain at what precise period the Picts as a whole became literate in the common use of the term. We have occasional references to 'the ancient documents of the Picts',[15] but this is thought probably to have reference to brief notices in calendars kept in the Pictish churches. A number of versions of what is commonly called a 'Pictish Chronicle' have come down to us,[16] but these contain for the most part little more than lists of early kings, sometimes with brief notes attached. From *c.* 550 these lists appear to be fairly trustworthy, for we can check them by the frequent references to the same kings in trustworthy Irish, Welsh, and English records. Before 550, however, the Pictish king lists cannot be regarded as historical.

103

Succession among the Picts was through the female. Moreover there are indications in the traditions of the Picts that the fathers were often, if not usually, members of unrelated clans, sometimes foreign princes on a visit. Reference has already been made (p. 90 f. above) to Corc, son of Lugaid, nephew of Crimthann mac Fidach of the *Eóganacht* of Munster, who is said to have made his way to the court of the Pictish king Feradach on Turin Hill above Forfar and to have married his daughter *c* 400, and subsequently to have returned with her and their three sons to Munster. The story is interesting as reflecting traditional Pictish customs, all the more so since the clans of Mar and Lennox traced their ancestry to Corc and Feradach's daughter,[17] and a branch of the *Eóganacht* of Munster is traditionally recorded to have been settled in Mag Gerginn (i.e. Angus and the Mearns or Kincardineshire) in early times, and to have been the ancestral clan of Oengus, king of Alba, most probably Oengus mac Fergusa, who died in 761.

We are in a stronger position to trace the outline of the history of the Scottish kingdom of Dál Riata.[18] In the first place our sources from neighbouring peoples are much fuller. The Irish annals throughout our period and down to *c.* 750 serve as a useful check on Scottish events, especially the events of Dál Riata. Moreover, the Scottish kingdom of Dál Riata, Irish in origin, had kept a short Chronicle,[19] probably on the Island of Iona, from the seventh century at latest.

All our authorities, with the exception of Bede (cf. p. 148 below) are in agreement that the kingdom was founded by Fergus mac Eirc ('Son of Erc'), at a period believed to be towards the close of the fifth century. An interesting document, containing a survey or inventory of the 'houses' and general muster for sea and land, attributed to Dál Riata, has survived (cf. p. 107 below). The inventory is preceded by a brief narrative giving some details of the invasions and the landing, and the document may well be based on some institution of later times – perhaps a basis for taxation or personal (?maritime) service – and so probably preserves echoes of earlier tradition. The fleet is said to have carried a hundred and fifty men, led by three brothers – Fergus Mór, Loarn and Oengus Mór. Little is known of Loarn himself, but his family, known as Cinél Loairn, occupied the northern part of Argyll, with their chief seat on the rocky promontory now occupied by the ruin of Dunolly Castle at Oban. The site was well placed for ready communications with Ireland, and the external relations of the Cinél Loairn are chiefly with Ireland. The rivalry of the Cinél Loairn and the Cinél Gabráin formed the chief internal incidents of Dalriadic history.

Of Fergus Mór himself nothing is known, save that his family occupied Islay. Fergus's grandson Gabrán, who had Kintyre and Knapdale, with his chief stronghold on the rock of Dunadd in the midst of Crinan Moss, was killed in 557 in a serious clash with the Picts under Brude mac Maelchon, and was succeeded by his cousin Conall. It was during Conall's reign that St Columba settled on Iona and as a result of a visit to Brude's court, which we may interpret as a diplomatic mission, is said to have converted the Picts to Christianity.

The eventual rise of the Cinél Gabráin to pre-eminence in Dál Riata is doubtless to be ascribed to the political sagacity of St Columba. He was undoubtedly the great man in the expansion of Dál Riata during the sixth century. His biographer Adamnán would have us picture him as a recluse saint; but his relations with the Picts must have secured the tenure of the new colony of Dál Riata. His monastic settlement on Iona may have been dictated by the contemporary religious habit of the monks of the Celtic Church of making their sanctuaries on solitary islands; but one cannot fail to be struck by its excellent strategic position for communications with the northern and perhaps also the eastern Picts and all parts of Dál Riata, both Irish and Scottish. Despite late Irish traditions to the contrary, Columba more than once returned to Ireland on political missions on behalf of the new Scottish kingdom of Dál Riata. Of these the most famous was to the Convention of Druim Cett (575) which was held under the Irish king, Aed son of Ainmirc, and on this occasion Columba was accompanied by the king of Dál Riata, Aedán mac Gabráin.

The kingdom in Argyll grew in area and importance, even penetrating further eastwards into the ancient area of the Caledonii in the Perthshire Highlands. The true founder of this expanding Irish kingdom was Aedán mac Gabráin himself. He remained Columba's firm friend to the end of his life and there can be little doubt that it was their joint statesmanship which guided the destiny of the little Irish-speaking kingdom of Argyll till, partly by conquest, and probably still more by alliances, gradually under Aedán's descendants it amalgamated ultimately with the kingdom of the Picts to form the united kingdom of Scotland.

His own personal record is largely maritime. In 575 he and St Columba jointly attended the Convention of Druim Cett in northern Ireland and Aedán evidently possessed, or had some control of, an Allied fleet, for according to the *Annals of Ulster* s.a. 579 (recte 580) he made an expedition to the Orkneys, which at this time were apparently in the control of the king of the Northern Picts. In 578[20] the Irish annals record a battle in Manau in which Aedán was victorious, and the battle was evidently widely known since it is mentioned in the Irish annals. Aedán's maritime activities are puzzling. He certainly had access to the sea from his seat on Dunadd by way of the Crinan River; but his position was hardly an ideal one for a seagoing fleet. On the other hand our records tell us almost nothing of Oengus mac Eirc after his settlement on the island of Islay. Here, however, a fleet would have been a necessity to him, and it is just possible that he and Aedán made joint maritime expeditions, and that the Dalriadic panegyrists, whose poems must have formed the basis of all the later Scottish annals of this period, would credit the expeditions solely to Aedán. The question of Aedán's seafaring activities are particularly interesting for their bearing on his warlike relations with Baetán mac Cairill (d. 581 or 582, cf. p. 98 above) including their rivalry for the Isle of Man. At this period Baetán was the most considerable of the kings of Dál Fiatach, the remnants of the old Ulaid on the east coast of Antrim, and we have seen that it is at this period also, the sixth century, that the Isle of Man begins to figure in the authentic history of the Irish Sea and the surrounding countries, and to appear under her own name *Manau* in the Irish and Scottish annals, and in the *Annales Cambriae*, and even in the Northumbrian history recorded by Bede. The whole record is obscure owing to variant readings both in the tribal histories and in the annals, but it seems probable that Baetán first compelled Aedán to submit to him, perhaps at the famous battle of Rosnaree on Belfast Lough, and that Baetán then conquered the Isle of Man, which Aedán re-took two years after Baetán's death, i.e. in 582 or 583. The dates are not wholly reliable and are undergoing drastic revision at the moment.[21]

Apparently a struggle was in progress between Scottish Dál Riata and the king of South Ulster, first on the shores of Belfast Lough, then in the Isle of Man – doubtless a struggle between these two branches of the same Érainn stock for supremacy in north-eastern Ireland, perhaps resistance to the Uí Néill. In these obscure but important relations of the kings of Dál Riata and Dál Fiatach at this period it is probable that Dál nAraidi around Lough Neagh played a part. An interesting Irish saga relates that Aedán received military help from their king Mongán (d. *c*. 624). The Isle of Man would have formed an important base for both Aedán and Baetán, and indeed Aedán's maritime power must have been considerable. This is doubtless true of all Dál Riata, and is, in fact, indicated by the Irish document referred to above which enumerates the units forming the fleet.[22]

Aedán's most permanent achievements, however, were his activities against the Picts, especially in the east of his dominions, and though he suffered some heavy reverses he seems to have gained control of some Pictish territory.

Aedán has left his impression on history as Dál Riata's greatest king. Already in 628 the *Annals of Ulster* refer to his successor, Eochaid Buide, as *rex Pictorum*. Meanwhile the growing power of the Bernician kings, and the advance of Aethelfrith of Northumbria northwards, prompted Aedán to march south against him with a large army, doubtless in alliance with his southern neighbours, the Britons; but he was severely defeated by Aethelfrith at a place which Bede (*H.E.* 1. 34) calls *Degsastán* in 603; and, adds Bede, 'from that day until the present no king of the Scots in Britain has dared to make war on the English'.

The outline of the early history of Scotland is a particularly difficult one to trace owing to the fact that at the dawn of the period of our contemporary written records, from at least as far back as the early seventh century, Scotland was divided among four nations, differing widely from one another in origin, and all speaking different languages. Of these the Picts of the north and east are the most archaic, both in language and institutions, while the kingdom of Dál Riata (Argyll) in the west is comparatively new. The Britons occupied the whole of the south between the two walls at least from Roman times and probably earlier. By the middle of the sixth century a new Teutonic dynasty had superimposed itself in the north-eastern territory of Roman Britain, founding the Anglian kingdom of Bernicia, and this new political element rapidly extended its authority up south-eastern Scotland, annexing the British area of Manau Guotodin and the whole of the old area of the tribe of the *Votadini*.

The British kingdoms that the Bernicians superseded had emerged as a result of the withdrawal of the Romans from the northern defences. But when they enter history in the sixth and following centuries under independent native princes the territory of these British-speaking peoples seems to have corresponded in some measure with that of the Roman territorial units whom they superseded and probably preceded. In all probability they developed with no great change of territory, or of range of influence or change of dynasties into the group of independent kingdoms known to later Welsh records as *Gwŷr y Gogledd*, 'The Men of the North'.

These Britons of southern Scotland, developed into a number of independent kingdoms of varying size and importance, each governed by its own native dynasty, but capable of forming temporary alliances. Those in the east were known as the *Gododdin*, keeping their old name, derived from the *Votadini*, and it is from this area that Cunedda and his sons are said to have migrated (cf. p. 60 above), though Cunedda is nowhere referred to as a king, or even a *dux*. The kingdoms in the west stretched from the Clyde probably to the borders of Mercia. The most important of these western British kingdoms were those of Strathclyde ('the watershed of the Clyde'), and Cumbria immediately to the south of it, Cumbria reaching from the Clyde right down north-western England till it joined the Welsh of Wales on the Welsh border. It is probable that these independent western dynasties were originally members of large and important British families, whose genealogies are derived in Welsh records from a certain Coel Hen to the south, and Dyfnwal Hen, further north.

Perhaps we should speak of both Strathclyde and the British countries to the south of it under the single term of *Cumbria*, and their language as *Cumbric*, for Latin writers speak of them as *Cumbri* and *Cumbrenses*, which is a Latinization of the native word *Cymry*, the meaning of which is 'fellow-countrymen', and which both they and the Welsh of today use of themselves. But however the two areas were divided, they were quite distinct from one another, as references in Early Welsh poetry make clear. Of the Welsh kingdoms which composed the confederation of Cumbria probably the most important during the sixth and seventh centuries was that known in early Welsh sources as *Rheged*. Its precise extent and boundaries are unknown, but its capital was almost certainly Carlisle, and its sphere the coastlands of the Solway Firth and Morecambe Bay, and it seems to have extended a wider political influence to the borders of Strathclyde in the north, Galloway in the west, Gododdin in the east, and Lancashire and perhaps north-west Yorkshire in the south. Its wide influence and what we know of its area and history would suggest that it constituted a kind of 'over-kingdom', like the Irish *cóiced*, perhaps a continuation of the ancient Celtic wide kingdoms of Western Britain like Dumnonia, and again like those of pre-Roman Gaul.

These North British communities have left no written records, but at some period annals relating to the sixth and seventh centuries seem to have been kept in a North British scriptorium and have been incorporated into our Welsh annals, and into the *Historia Brittonum* by Nennius early in the ninth century,[23] and also into an eighth century document incorporated in Symeon of Durham's *Historia Regum*;[24] but no wholly independent records have survived, even from the Church, though later traditions and the clear evidence of inscriptions on their tombstones prove these 'Men of the North' to have been Christians. In addition to these early written records incorporated into later Latin works, we have a great wealth of vernacular traditions composed in the form of oral poetry, largely panegyric and elegiac. These North British poems have not survived in the North[25] but were preserved and transmitted orally by a highly trained class of official court bards, such as are referred to in this period in the *Historia Brittonum* (ch. 62) where we are told:

Then Talhaern Tataguen ('father of inspiration') gained renown in poetry, and Neirin and Taliesin and the bard Bluch, and Cian, 'the wheat of song', gained renown together at the same time in British poetry.

These bards, or their successors at a later date, probably after the Anglian annexation of Cumbria, sang their songs afresh in the courts of their southern neighbours, and in Wales the poems were written down at a still later date in manuscripts of which four have survived to our own time.[26]

The picture thus transmitted to us by a highly cultivated and jealously guarded conservative tradition[27] enables us to know at first hand many of the ruling families[28] of the North and their history, and gives us the entrée into these little courts, though it is not always easy to locate them precisely. Our general impression is that of a confederation of small local princes, and a society living in conditions which characterize heroic society everywhere. There was no central government or organized state. Accordingly there was no developed trade or coinage, no architecture except in wood or earth and rough stone forts. Society was based on a military aristocracy, with its emphasis on *noblesse oblige*. The prestige of birth and heredity was great, but was equalled by the spirit of individualism which pervaded society, and the heroic honour which stimulated effort, and was inseparable from the princely standard. A prince and his followers constituted a *teulu* ('warband'). In time of peace they lived in close proximity to one another, sharing the evening feast and its accompaniment of music and song. In time of war they moved as one man, led by the chief unquestioningly to victory or to death. Of policy, of any conception of a state, we hear nothing. The most famous of their battles, recorded in the Welsh annals, and widely celebrated in poetry, was fought, not against external enemies, nor against their powerful neighbours, the Irish of Dál Riata or the Picts to the North, or the encroaching Anglians of the east and south, but among the Britons themselves. This was the battle of Arthuret, recorded in the *Annales Cambriae* s.a. 573 as *Bellum Armterid*. From Welsh traditions we gather that it was fought between one of these British princes, Gwenddoleu and his cousins Gwrgi and Peredur, and that Gwenddoleu was killed. It is said to have been 'fought for a lark's nest', which may perhaps refer to Caerlaverock, an important strategic harbour in early times commanding the approach to the Solway on the northern bank. The site must have been near the modern village of Arthuret on the outskirts of Longtown not far from the Roman *Castra Exploratorum* and if the local place-name Carwinley represents an earlier *Caer Gwenddoleu*, as seems probable, we may associate Gwenddoleu with the Roman fort. For most of us the battle has the more romantic interest that it is claimed in Welsh poems that the prophet Myrddin (Merlin) fought and won a gold torque in the battle of Arthuret, in which his lord Gwenddoleu was slain, and that as a result of the battle he lost his wits and afterwards lived the life of a wild man in the forest of Celyddon in Scotland (p. 334). There are some grounds for regarding Merlin as the domestic bard of Gwenddoleu.

The North British princes were nevertheless able to form temporary alliances among themselves, and under these circumstances they were still strong enough to take the offensive against the Angles of Bernicia. In Ch. 63 of the *Historia Brittonum*, which is evidently based on seventh century written material recorded in some northern scriptorium, possibly at Carlisle itself, Nennius tells us that Urien of Rheged and his son fought against Theodric, son of Ida, king of Bernicia (572–9). He also tells us that Urien with three other British princes – Riderch (i.e. Rhydderch) *Hen* ('the old') and a certain Guallauc, and Morcant – fought Hussa, Ida's son, king of Bernicia (585–92), and besieged him in the Island of Metcaud (i.e. Lindisfarne) for three days and nights; but Urien was betrayed by Morcant out of jealousy (*invidia*) and killed, because he was the greatest war leader of them all. And so in their first brilliant encounter with the Angles, the Britons were in a position to take the initiative and wage aggressive warfare against them; but they were never able to combine permanently. We possess a splendid collection of poetry from a generation later, known as the *Gododdin* (cf. p. 269 below), commemorating a disastrous expedition of the men of Manau Gododdin into Northumbria and the battle of Catraeth, probably near Catterick or Richmond in Yorkshire, in which they were annihilated almost to a man. This is the last forward movement of the North Britons against the Angles. If they could have formed a united British kingdom in the North, and combined with the Picts, no Anglian dynasty could have stood against them.

From now onwards the history of the North Britons is that of a rearguard movement. The new Anglian kingdom of Bernicia had been founded in the middle of the sixth century. Probably the name itself, and certainly the population, were British, but the dynasty, of unknown origin, appears to have been Anglian. The first ruler of whom we hear was Ida (*c.* 547–59), and the capital was at Bamburgh. After the murder of Urien of Rheged, and the breakdown of the British offensive under the four princes, the British princes of Manau Gododdin were over-run by the Angles of Bernicia, and in the seventh century the Angles of Bernicia were already in possession of the whole country between the Tees and the Forth, including Manau Gododdin. Bede tells us (I, 34) that their king Athelfrith 'conquered more territories from the British than any other king, either making them tributary, or expelling the inhabitants and planting Angles in their places'. The Anglian expansion westwards with the gradual elimination of the British kingdoms south of the Highland Line was more tardy. Indeed the expansion into Rheged may have been a peaceful one, the result of a royal marriage between King Oswy of Northumbria (642–71) and Riemmelth, perhaps, a grand-daughter of Urien,[29] prince of Rheged. The British kingdoms were by this time reduced to Strathclyde, which nevertheless retained its independence till early in the eleventh century. The northward extension of the Angles was checked a generation later at Forfar in 685 when Oswy's son Ecgfrith met his death in his northward thrust against the Southern Picts in the Battle of Dunnichen Mere, and the English Border had to fall back on the line of the Forth. Nevertheless it was the gradual extension northwards and westwards of the Anglian territory and the Anglian speech which ultimately created the Scottish Lowlands and the gradual encroachment of the Anglo-Saxon language.

Owing to sparsity of records for North-western England we have little direct evidence in the early period for communication between the Britons of the North and those of Wales, but a sense of unity would seem to be implied by the two Welsh terms *Deheubarth* (from L. *dextralis pars*, literally 'the right hand' or 'southern part') commonly used to denote south Wales, and *Gwŷr y Gogledd* (literally the 'men of the left', or 'north'), denoting the North British, or, as we may interpret the term, 'our northern half'. A glance at the map of the kingdoms of Wales in the earliest traditions, and the dynastic genealogies of which we have record, shows a large number of small kingdoms, each independent and ruled by a royal house claiming inheritance from father to son. The pattern looks very similar to that which prevailed in Cumbria and Strathclyde and also earlier in Gaul – in fact a common Celtic type resulting from the fragmentation of the wider pre-Roman kingdoms. As we trace the separate history of these small kingdoms to the gradual unification of Wales under the house of Merfyn Vrych and his son Rhodri Mawr in the ninth century, and finally in the person of Hywel Dda in the tenth, we shall be surprised at the length of the history of most of these little kingdoms, and the long period during which they were able to maintain their identity. Some of their ruling lines had a life of more than 500 years. This is strong evidence that the Welsh were not originally and inherently a warlike people till forced to defend their land against foreign invasion.

The districts which modern historians believe to owe their origin to the sons and grandsons of Cunedda (cf. p. 60 above) are those which still bear their names in the late lists which are recorded; but the names have probably been created as eponyms of the little Welsh kingdoms of northern and western Wales – Rhufon from Rhufoniog, i.e. southern Conway; Dunod (L. *donatus*) from Dunoding, round Harlech (where the line persisted till 900); Ceredig from Ceredigion; Edeyrn (L. *Aeternus*) from Edeyrnion; Meirion (L. *Marianus*) from Meirionydd, etc. During the ninth century, native historians in all the Celtic countries created eponymous ancestors in the fifth century where the genuine traditional pedigrees ceased. We may compare the pedigrees of the ruling family of Argyll (Loarn, Gabrán, etc.) and also the eponymous *Cruithne* and his sons, and certain surveys of the Picts which are wholly antiquarian in character and origin. The Welsh list is of later authority than the original notice of Cunedda[30] and may be based on a mnemonic like the list purporting to record Arthur's battles.

Moreover the statement of the total and final expulsion of the Irish (cf. p. 60 above) credited in the original notice to Cunedda and his sons cannot be accepted at its face value, for we know that the Irish formed a prominent element in the population of north Wales long after the fifth century. Indeed it may be added that the districts in which the sons of Cunedda are supposed to have settled are not in all cases areas where the Irish are likely to have settled in concentration. The orthodox view is, however, that the sons of Cunedda formed the earliest ruling dynasties of the principal kingdoms of the northern and western seaboard of Wales, and that they established themselves there shortly after the middle of the fifth century.

We can trace the history of many of the Welsh dynasties and their descendants, and thus follow in some measure the political history of Wales, from the sixth century – the period of Gildas's princes and the early phase of the establishment of the Saxon dynasties in Britain – till the South Welsh prince Hywel Dda ('the Good') submitted to Edward the Elder in the tenth century. Of these Welsh dynasties by far the most outstanding is the line of *Maglocunus* who, we are told in the *Historia Brittonum*, ruled over the Britons in the region of Gwynedd (*apud Brittones regnabat, id est in regione Guinedotae*) and of whom Cunedda is here stated to have been his *atavus*. The founder of the dynasty, Einion Yrth (*Girt*) had his seat at Rhos, where he seems to have been succeeded by one of his sons, the father of Cynlas, identified with *Cuneglasus*, one of the 'wicked' princes singled out for censure by Gildas. Einion's other son, Cadwallon Llaw Hir ('Cadwallon of the long hand'), the father of Maelgwn (Gildas's *Maglocunus*), ruled on

Môn (the modern Anglesey). This line, with its seat at Aberffraw, had a history of 800 years from the fifth century to 1282, and under Maelgwn the dynasty was destined to become the most influential in Wales.

The Maglocunus of Gildas is a typical heroic prince surrounded by his court bards. The whole dynasty were zealous Christians, for the little church of Llangadwaladr, two miles from Aberffraw, the royal church of this little capital of the dynasty, still preserves a Latin inscription in memory of King Cadfan to which we shall refer later. The monument to Cadfan, with its ambitious rhetorical phraseology, is witness to an interesting continuous history of the family on the spot, suggesting that Aberffraw had already become the chief seat of the dynasty. It was Cadfan's son, Cadwallon II, who in 633, in alliance with King Penda of Mercia, overthrew and slew Edwin of Northumbria, the first English king to invade Wales. For a time it seemed as if the Welsh might destroy the Northumbrian kingdom; but in the course of a determined march to the North with this end in view Cadwallon was slain in 634.

Many of the most interesting of the Welsh kingdoms did not claim origin from the sons of Cunedag but developed quite independently. The most important is Powys, the 'Garden of Wales', as the Llywarch Hen poet describes it, which is believed to have developed directly from the ancient kingdom of the *Cornovii*, and which in early historical times comprised the valleys of the Severn and the Dee. In the early Middle Ages the southern portion of Powys included Builth and Gwrthrynion on the upper Wye. The royal line of Builth had an undisputed claim to be descended from Vortigern. It had its own royal line, and a king of this line, Fernmail, was still ruling when Nennius was writing *c*. 830. *Gwrthrynion* is a name formed from *Gwrtheyrn*, of which *Vortigern* is the older form. The romantic little kingdom of Brecknock in south Central Wales was never conquered and retained its independence from the fifth to the tenth century. Its royal pedigree[31] claims to be derived from a native princess Marcell (L. *Marcella*) who married an Irishman. Their son Brychan[32] is evidently an eponym. Other Irish names occur in the pedigree.[33]

In addition to Powys, Builth and Brecknock, the whole of South Wales continued to be ruled by independent kings down to the time of Hywel Dda. The kingdom of Dyfed, as we have seen (p. 59 above), was ruled by a line of princes whose origin was almost certainly Irish,

114

and the dynasty lasted from the fifth to the tenth century. Three genealogies are extant.[34]

South-eastern Wales was always independent and formed the distinct kingdom of Morgannwg. This was the most Romanized part of Wales, with a good climate and fertile land, and included Cardiff, Caerleon and Caerwent, and also the early Christian monastic centres of Llanilltud, Llancarfan and Llandaff. The history of this kingdom is chiefly interesting from its early and important ecclesiastical influence. It remained under its own princes till the eve of the Norman Conquest.

Wales is essentially a sea-board country. The great mountain masses inland made communication between north and south difficult, and from the earliest times a political division between north and south makes itself increasingly a force in the historical life of the country. The communications and sympathies of the north Welsh linked them with the British of Cumbria and Galloway, a link reflected in the term *Gwŷr y Gogledd*, which implies 'our northern neighbour'. The link with the north was strengthened rather than weakened when the power of the kingdom of Northumbria qualified them to be valuable allies against a threatened Viking conquest of north Wales. On the other hand the relations of Deheubarth had always been closer with southern England, and during the Viking Period the South Welsh kingdoms gradually came to a realization that safety lay in alliance with their stronger eastern neighbours. We shall trace the gradual union of the small Welsh kingdoms into a constructive political unity in chapter 6.

In concluding this brief outline of the formation of the Celtic kingdoms in the historical period a word may be added on the nature of the Breton settlements and the formation of the independent Breton kingdoms. We have seen that the settlers brought with them their native British language, having its nearest affinities with that of Cornwall, a poor country whence the majority of the colonists must have been drawn. On the other hand, for what Breton traditions are worth – and in this case they are in general consistent and in no way inherently improbable – the leaders of the migrations, both aristocratic and ecclesiastical, were chiefly drawn from eastern and southern Wales.

Whatever the object of St Germanus in his journey to Britain (cf.

p. 81 above), if he had any political hope of cutting off her intercourse with Armorica he had no success, for the colonists continued to pour into Brittany throughout the fifth and sixth centuries, and by the sixth they had established British kingdoms round the entire coast of Armorica, which ceased to be called by its old name *Armorica* ('along the coast'), and became known as *Brittany*, a name which first occurs in a letter of Sidonius Apollinaris. In Britain it is known as *Britannia Minor*, 'Little Britain', in Latin writers, and also as *Lledau*, *Letavia* – probably the native name – and the people as *Lidwiccias*.[35]

The names of two of the three great British kingdoms in Armorica contain echoes of their British connexion. In the north the wide kingdom (later 'duchy', 'county') of *Domnonia* covered almost all northern Brittany, including, after 530, the province of Léon in the north-west, which was at first independent. In the earliest of the Breton saints' *Lives*, that of St Samson of Dol, Domnonia is referred to as *Prettonaland* (i.e. 'Brittany') – a tribute to its early importance. The country was traditionally founded by a king Riwal of the royal stock of Gwent, in south-eastern Wales. No early account of the settlement of Cornouaille in the south is historical before the ninth century, and our legends are chiefly contained in the *Lives* of the local saints, Guénolé, Corentin, and Ronan, and in the forged charters of the great abbey of Landévennec. Legend claims early communication between Cornouaille and western Wales. It may be added that it is popularly assumed that *Domnonia* brought its name with colonists from the *Domnonian* peninsula of Devon and Cornwall; but neither the names of the British *Cornwall* nor the Breton *Cornouaille* occur before the ninth century. In fact we do not know precisely whence the immigrants of either Domnonia or Cornouaille came, or how the names arose.

The third of the great kingdoms is *Bro Waroch* ('the land of Waroch'), which comprised the whole of the rest of southern Brittany, including the western part of Vannes. East of this limit the area was still Roman and long known as *Romania*. This is the wealthiest part of Brittany, the old kingdom of the *Veneti*, conquered by Caesar, and having an early connexion with Britain, on whom they were said to have been accustomed to draw for their naval supplies. Perhaps they gave their name to Gwynedd. Most of our traditions point to Wales as the region whence the leading settlers came. A particularly striking example is that of St Gwrthiern, whose name and story, despite his

Breton sanctity, correspond closely to the British 'tyrant' Vortigern.

No contemporary records of the conditions of the settlement have come down to us; but Breton scholars have come to realize that the 'saints', i.e. the non-militant educated elements, were the true organizers of the expeditions and settlements. 'The Immigrants organized themselves, and in this essential task everything conspires to give us the impression that the spiritual leaders enjoyed the principal rôle.'[36] Indeed traditions of the migration point to close association throughout our period of the princely leaders and clerics, who were often members of the same family, and went to Brittany together, prince and cleric forming the hard core of the migration movement.

We may be assured that the Gallo-Romans would not have allowed the Britons to occupy their land and eat them out of house and home if they had not a fair return from the immigrants. Late traditions, preserved in Latin medieval saints' *Lives*, such as those of St Leonorus and St Méen, relate how the Britons cleared the land, which even to this present day shows evidence of having been in earlier days largely covered by forest and heath. These traditions reflect their forestry methods, especially the *Life of St Méen*, a saint from Archenfield, in south-eastern Wales, who had perhaps learnt his forestry in the mysterious Forest of Dean, and who established a great monastery in the Forest of Brocéliande in eastern Brittany. He was of the royal family of Archenfield and throughout his life kept his close relationship with the king Judicaël of *Domnonia*, a descendant of the legendary King Riwal. Judicaël eventually retired to end his life in Méen's monastery in the Forest of Brocéliande, not very far from the spring where tradition tells us that Vivien enchanted Merlin. The real importance of the monastery – the greatest of many early, small forest monasteries in Brittany – lay in the fact that it was remote from the attacks of the barbarians. And this immunity continued down to Viking times, for it is on record that a bishop of Dol retired there for safety.

These *vitae* borrow freely from one another, and in the *Life of St Malo*, we learn that in the process of clearing, St Leonorus had found a golden ram, doubtless of Roman workmanship, thrown up by the moles, and this he took to Paris while on a diplomatic mission to King Childebert (d. 558), asking for the exact value of the ram in land, and also security of tenure. He argued that the land had been a wilderness till they had cleared and tilled it, and that it was only fair that they should occupy it without hindrance – a request which the king granted. The interest of this tradition lies in the picture of the cleric as diplomat and lawyer on behalf of the settlers; in the nature of the relations implied with the Frankish king; in the steps taken to ensure permanent legal tenure; in the fact that Leonorus in effect bought the land, asking only the exact value of the ram. Another interesting point in these stories is that not only in the original home in Wales, but also after the migration, the narratives suggest that prince and cleric – often relatives – continued to work together in Brittany. All this suggests close organization. The emigrations were not haphazard; and the stories imply that these royal and clerical combinations were not confined to the earliest generations.

The importance of Brittany to the Celtic Church in our own islands must have been especially high at this time as affording communication with the Continental Church, and as avoiding the necessity of the more dangerous crossing of the Straits of Dover. This Breton route was, of course, the route taken by St Columbanus (cf. p. 233 below). We have also to bear in mind that in general the sea was a great unifying factor. It joined rather than divided. We have seen the claim in Cormac's Glossary that at this period certain Irish kingdoms extended on both sides of the Irish Sea. In traditions of the settlement of Brittany we again come upon traditions of such double kingdoms. Tradition claims that King Riwal, the legendary founder of the kingdom of *Domnonia*, came with a great fleet in the time of the Frankish king Lothair 1 from his kingdom in eastern Wales and 'continued to rule as *dux Brittonum* on both sides of the sea till his death'.[37] We are led by a certain amount of evidence to think that a tyrant of Domnonia, Cunomorus, Count of Poher and of Carhaix, the great Roman centre in Western Armorica, may also have ruled simultaneously in British Domnonia.

All that we learn from Breton traditions shows it as an expansion of western Britain. Communication was kept up between the royal families who migrated and the old stock. The so-called 'missionaries' were the educated men who negotiated the settlements and organized the colonists, attending to their spiritual and legal needs. The Frankish court encouraged them, and in general the intellectual life of the colonists must have been relatively high, possibly owing to contacts with the Gallo-Roman population. We possess a number of saints' Lives, written in Latin and dating from the ninth century, whereas the earliest Welsh Life – that of St David – dates from the late eleventh century.

Our picture is not that of a fleeing host of emigrants under a highly spiritual leader, but a political expansion of peoples, organized from leading Welsh princely families, whose political rights and privileges and spiritual integrity are in the charge of literate clerics. As our principal sources are monastic and late, it is not surprising that some of the early princes have been transformed into saints. The most striking case is that of Vortigern who, as already mentioned, appeared in the records of Quimperlé as St Gwrthiern. [38]

Meanwhile in Brittany, as in our own islands, the sixth and seventh centuries were the period which saw the rise of the historical kingdoms. It is a matter of regret that the contemporary narrative of Gregory of Tours does not concern itself to any serious extent with the two Breton states of Domnonia and Cornouaille, for the history of which we are largely dependent on records of ecclesiastical institutions and the less reliable narratives of saints' Lives. In the earliest of the latter, the *Life of St Samson* of Dol, Domnonia (*Prettonaland*) is not referred to as a kingdom, but a realm, a duchy or county, and in Frankish sources it was ruled by a 'royal count', though these seem to have inherited from father to son. In this Life we have a vivid account of the relations of the Domnonian princes with both the Frankish king Childebert, and also with the regent Cunomorus, who is said to usurp the kingdom during the minority of the young prince Judual who died *c*. 580. St Samson conducts us to the sixth century Frankish court to solicit the help of Childebert for young Judual, and we witness the triumph of the rightful heir – so we are assured – and the downfall of the usurper. [39]

Cunomorus is the most interesting figure in early Breton history, which may be said to begin with his relations with the Frankish kings. By origin he was one of the small ruling Breton chiefs, having his stronghold in Pou-Castel, today Carhaix, and his 'county', or little city state, was the surrounding country, now Poher. His traditional dates, first as regent, then as usurper of Domnonia, are calculated as approximately 540–54. He seems to have been a Christian in early days, but having incurred the enmity of the Church he has come down to us in tradition as a usurper, a murderous tyrant, and even a Bluebeard. By his usurpation of Domnonia, and as master of Poher and Léon, he already possessed half Brittany, and was evidently aiming at the supremacy of an independent principality. However, on the triumph of Judual, Domnonia rose against the 'tyrant', who was defeated and slain in his native Poher, whither he had retired in the hope of finding refuge and reinforcements.

While the Bretons were occupying the peninsula, the Franks had been gradually extending over Gaul, and under Clovis (c. 481–511) the Gallo-Roman cities of Armorica formally recognized the Frankish authority. The Franks regarded themselves as the true successors of the Roman rulers, and refused to recognize the Breton independence in the rest of the peninsula, while the Bretons on their part refused to accept the Frankish claim, and on the contrary sought to extend their own independence eastwards.[40] According to the contemporary Gregory of Tours[41] the successors of Clovis deprived the Breton rulers of the title of king, substituting that of 'Count', the title borne by the Frankish officials responsible for administering the various city-states on behalf of the Frankish kings. Nevertheless, under the title of counts, the Breton chiefs continued to defy the authority of the Merovingian kings. This was the period in which the Gallo-Roman state of Vannes was in process of becoming *Bro Waroch*, 'Territory of Waroch', from the name of a Breton chief Waroch 11 (577–94), under whom the town became Breton in 579. Waroch was, in fact, a particularly formidable adversary of the Franks, and the pages of Gregory are lively reading as he traces the sensational military career of this redoubtable prince and his political relations with the Frankish rulers. In 587 he invaded Nantes and in the following year Rennes and again Nantes; and although in 590 a powerful Frankish army invaded Vannes, the event proved a disaster to the Franks, whose army was defeated and partly destroyed by Waroch's son Canao.[42] It is in no way surprising under these circumstances that the picture presented to us by Gregory of Tours is that of violent rulers, Breton and Frankish alike, constantly at war with one another, the Franks seeking to enforce control, the Bretons of *Broërech* laying waste the Gallo-Roman border city-states of Rennes, Nantes and eastern Vannes.[43]

The struggle between Bro Waroch and the Frankish kings lasted for centuries. Sometimes the armies of the Frankish kings suffered disaster at Breton hands; but the Breton chiefs were unable to consolidate their gains. Charlemagne ordered no less than three expeditions into Brittany, and Louis the Pious came in person twice.

Finally Louis the Pious appointed Nominoë, a native Breton, first as count, later duke; but in 846 Nominoë himself forced Charles the Bald to recognize the independence of Brittany. Charles was indeed glad of the help of the Bretons as allies no less than as subjects, for he now had to face the far more serious problem of the Viking invasions. In 849 Nominoë openly rebelled, but he died in 851 in a campaign near Chartres.[44] His son and successor Erispoë was assassinated in 857 by order of the famous Salomon, who succeeded him. From 863 Salomon recognized the Frankish hegemony and promised to pay homage to Charles the Bald, though he soon withheld both his tribute and his loyalty, and paid for his crimes and treachery with his life in 874. With Salomon Brittany had entered upon the feudalism of the Middle Ages.

NOTES

1 RCxvii 124.
2 Cf. H. M. Chadwick, *E.S.*, 35, n. 2.
3 O'Brien, *Corpus Gen. Hib.* 136a, 46.
4 *Ros na Ríg in Semne*, Island Magee (O'Rahilly, *E.I.H.M.*, cf. n. 5 below).
5 For references see O'Rahilly, *E.I.H.M.*, 504.
6 For a brief account of the prehistoric evidence see R. H. Kinvig, *H.I.M.*
7 The earliest written Manx is the translation of the Prayer Book *c.* 1625.
8 For the evidence given below see K. H. Jackson, P.B.A., XXXVII (1951), 77f.
9 K. H. Jackson, in *E.C.*, 209 f.; T. F. O'Rahilly, *E.I.H.M.*, 504, n. 1.
10 T. F. O'Rahilly, *I.D.P.P.*, 117.
11 See K. H. Jackson, in F. Wainwright (ed.) *P.P.*, ch. VI and Appendix.
12 Reference may be made to a paper by N. K. Chadwick: 'The name Pict', S.G.S. VIII (1958).
13 The name is basically identical with that of Maelgwn, the ruler of North Wales (cf. p. 79 above).
14 *E.I.H.M.* 26.
15 Reference may be made to a suspicious document claiming to be an ancient record of the foundation of St Andrews, which assures us that the scribe has copied the contents as they are found *in veteribus Pictorum libris*. See Chadwick, *E.S.*, 28. Cf. M. O. Anderson, *S.H.R.* XXIX (1950), 17.
16 Most of the texts of the early *Chronicles* were published by W. F. Skene, *P. and S.*, and discussed by him in *C.S.*, Vol. I. For detailed

extracts, translated into English, see A. O. Anderson, *E.S.S.H.*, I, *pass.*, and cf. especially the Bibliographical Notes, p. xiv ff. For a general study of the subject see H. M. Chadwick, *E. S.*, *pass.* A more recent and quite indispensable study is that of M. O. Anderson in three contributions to S.H.R. XXVIII. 1 and 2 (1949), XXIX (1950). The best version of the Pictish king lists is that of Skene, *P. and S.*, p. 4 ff.

17 Cf. Chadwick, *E.S.*, 96, 98, and important references there cited. Nearly all the king lists are printed in full in Skene, *P. and S.*

18 The clearest general outline is that of H. M. Chadwick, *E.S.*, p. 121 ff., though this study now needs to be checked by the later researches of M. O. Anderson, especially as indicated in the references to the S.H.R., n. 16 above.

19 On this subject see M. O. Anderson, S.H.R. XXIX (1950), 18.

20 Cf. O'Rahilly, *E.I.H.M.* 237, n. 3; 504, and cf. F. J. Byrne, S.H., no. 4 (1964), 58.

21 There can, I think, be no doubt that O'Rahilly's interpretation of the Irish annals is correct as against those of some earlier scholars. See O'Rahilly, *E.I.H.M.* p. 504. Cf. further F. J. Byrne, S.H., no. 4 (1964), 58.

22 Ed. J. Bannerman, *Celtica* vii 142; see also *P. and S.*, p. 308 ff.

23 See K. H. Jackson in Chadwick, N. K. (Editor), *Celt and Saxon*, p. 20 ff. Cf. 27 ff., 53 f.

24 See P. Hunter Blair, in *S.E.H.B.*, p. 86 ff.

25 See I. Williams, *Early Welsh Poetry*, 22. Three stanzas of Old Welsh poetry were, however, written down in the first half of the ninth century on the upper margin of a folio in the Juvencus MS. of the metrical version of the Psalms, preserved in the Cambridge University Library. See Williams, *E.W.P.*, 28, 72.

26 A valuable brief account of the process outlined above is given by R. Bromwich, 'The Character of the Early Welsh Tradition' in *S.E.B.H.*, Ch. V.

27 See H. M. and N. K. Chadwick, *G.L.*, I, 163 f.; H. M. Chadwick, *E.S.*, 143.

28 A number of the genealogies are recorded in Harl. 3859; also Jesus College (Oxford), MS. XX; and Hengwrt 356, and are published by W. F. Skene, *F.A.B.W.* II (Edinburgh, 1868, p. 454). Cf. further H. M. and N. K. Chadwick, *G.L.* I, 149.

29 See the *Historia Brittonum*, ch. 57. Although it is not specifically stated, the *Rum* (*Run*), father of Riemmelth here mentioned, is probably Run, son of Urien.

30 Cf. J. E. Lloyd, *H.W.* I, p. 118.

31 In Jesus College (Oxford) MS. XX, viii, the genealogy is confused with that of Dyfed, which is not surprising in view of the Irish elements in the tradition. See further *Y Cymmrodór* viii, 85.

32 For legends about Brychan and his son Rhain, see Lloyd, *H.W.* I, p. 270f.

33 See Wade-Evans in the *De Situ Brecheniauc, V.S.B.G.*, p. 313.
34 See K. Meyer, 'The Expulsion of the Déisi', *Ériu* III 135 f.; *Y Cymmrodor*, XIV 101 f.
35 See Plummer, A.-S. *Chronicle* II 404.
36 Waquet, *H.B.*, 20.
37 See Baring-Gould and Fisher, *L.B.S.*, III, 343, n. 2.
38 For St Gwrthiern see the note in Chadwick and others, *S.E.B.H.*, 39 ff.
39 For a discussion of the historicity of the narrative see Durtelle de Saint-Sauveur, *H.B.* I, p. 52 f.
40 *Ibid.*, I, p. 46 f. and references.
41 *Hist. Franc.* IV, 4.
42 *Ibid.*, X, ix.
43 *Ibid.*, IX. 17; X. 9; cf. de la Borderie, *H. de Bretagne*, I, p. 442 ff.
44 For a brief account of Nominoë, see A. Rebillon, *H. de Bretagne*.

5

Secular Institutions: Early Irish Society

The sources of information about the secular institutions of Ireland are plentiful, but they have not yet been fully explored. Much can be learned from the sagas, and a great deal more from annals, genealogies and, above all, the ancient law-tracts. The Irish law-tracts are probably the most important documents of their kind in the whole tradition of western Europe, by reason of their mere extent, and of the archaism of the tradition they preserve. Their roots are not in Roman Law, but in ancient Indo-European custom (p. 260).

The basic unit of territory and administration in Ireland was the *tuath*, and it seems sometimes to correspond in area to the modern barony.[1] The word means 'tribe, people', and is used also for the territory they inhabit. Many names of baronies are ancient *tuath*-names; but the Book of Rights, in the eleventh century, lists only ninety-seven *tuatha* as against the two hundred and seventy-three baronies of today.

It would be a mistake to suppose any close connexion between *tuath* and barony. The barony was a Norman tenure, and when Strongbow or De Lacy granted estates in barony they may have taken advantage of existing territorial divisions as rent-bearing units, so that a barony might consist of one or of several *tuatha*. But in the areas which were shired later, the barony was probably a newly delimited area with no tradition behind it.

A larger unit was the *trícha cét* 'thirty hundreds' which was originally a military term for a force of three thousand men. MacNeill suggested that it may preserve a very old tradition and have a common origin with the Roman legion, also three thousand in its earliest form.[2] The term is later used in a territorial sense and we have the names of twenty-nine *trícha cét* from various sources.[3] But it never occurs in the text of the Laws, and is equated by the glossators with *tuath*, which shows that by their time the term was obsolete.[4]

Each *tuath* was ruled by a king (*rí*), 'originally a sacred personage, tracing his descent from one or other of the ancestral deities and mystically invested with sovereignty by means of immemorial inauguration rites'.[5] The inauguration of the king was a symbolic marriage with Sovereignty, a fertility rite for which the technical term was *banais rígi* 'royal wedding'.

Sovereignty was imagined as a goddess whom the king must wed, presumably to ensure the welfare of his kingdom. We are reminded of the Hindu *śaktī* (p. 26), and of the female companions of some of the Gaulish gods. The notion is perhaps a development from the primitive idea of a marriage of the tribal god and a goddess of the earth, or of water, as the source of fertility.

There are many Irish tales in which this idea is expressed, and it persisted into modern times. Probably the earliest is *Baile in Scáil* 'The Phantom's Frenzy', in which Conn, king of Ireland, finds himself in a fairy dwelling where a phantom prophesies the future kings of Ireland, and a woman seated on a crystal throne pours out a cup of ale for each king that is named (p. 197). In several others an old hag is transformed into a beautiful girl by the embrace of the future king. This story is told of Niall of the Nine Hostages, and also of Lugaid Laígde, father of Lugaid Mac Con.[6] In the *Dindshenchas* version the maiden says to Lugaid:

Atbér-sa fritt, a meic mín,	I will tell you, gentle boy,
limsa foït na hairdríg:	With me the high-kings sleep;
is mé ind ingen seta seng,	I am the graceful, slender girl,
flaithius Alban is Hérenn.	the Sovereignty of Scotland and Ireland.[7]

The legendary queen Medb, whose name means 'intoxication', was originally a personification of sovereignty, for we are told that she was the wife of nine kings of Ireland, and elsewhere that only one who mated with her could be king. Of king Cormac it was said: *nocor faí Medb lasin mac/níba rí Érenn Cormac*, 'until Medb slept with the lad, Cormac was not king of Ireland'.[8] The lesser kings too were wedded to their kingdoms. As late as 1310 the Annals record the espousal of Fedlimid Ó Conchobhair (Felim O'Connor) to the province of

Connacht. In the seventeenth century Ó Bruadair refers to a king as 'the spouse of Cashel'. Even in the eighteenth century the poets called Ireland the spouse of her lawful kings.

Giraldus Cambrensis describes a ritual, reported to him as still practised in one of the northern kingdoms, which involved the sacrifice of a mare. The king-elect went through a symbolic union with the slaughtered animal and then bathed in the broth of its flesh and drank thereof.[9] This account has been discredited by some scholars, but there is little doubt that it is well founded. It resembles closely the Hindu rite of *aśvamedha* in which the queen goes through a symbolic union with the slaughtered stallion, plainly a fertility rite. In this northern Irish kingdom it was the king who sought fertility for himself and his tribe by means of the ancient ritual. The cult of the goddess Epona of the Gaulish pantheon seems here to have survived in Ireland in the twelfth century. But the ordinary form of inauguration of a king was by giving him a white rod in token of sovereignty. The rod was given to a high king by his principal vassal king, to a vassal king by the high king.[10]

In early times the king was hedged about by taboos (p. 139). No man who was physically blemished was eligible for kingship. The king was bound too by the magic power of Truth (*fír flatha*); and if he was guilty of injustice, disaster might overtake his people, just as the sins of Prometheus were visited upon Thebes. It is told of the famous king Cormac, when he was in fosterage at Tara, that king Lugaid Mac Con gave judgement against a man whose sheep had grazed the woad-garden of the queen. Lugaid adjudged the sheep as forfeit. The side of the house in which he sat fell down the slope. 'No,' said Cormac, 'the shearing of the sheep is enough in compensation for the grazing of the woad, for both will grow again.' The house then stayed and fell no further. 'That is the true judgement,' said all, 'and it is the son of the true prince who has given it.' For a year afterwards Lugaid remained king of Tara, and no grass came out of the ground, nor leaves on the trees nor grain in the corn. Then the men of Ireland expelled him from the kingship, for he was a false prince; and Cormac became king.

Two points are here worth noting, first that the land became waste from the king's falsehood, and second that the house began to fall and was then stayed by the true judgement. This notion of the magic power of Truth appears in other Irish tales, and forms another

126

curious link with Hindu tradition. Lüders showed in a famous article the Hindu belief that the mere utterance of a true statement could work wonders, and there are clear traces of the same belief in Ireland.[11]

The king was ruler of his peoole in times of peace and military leader in war. He presided over the annual assembly (*oenach*) which was held at a sacred burial-ground, but he was not above the law. He had a special judge (*brithem ríg*) whose duty it was to decide cases in which the king's rights were involved. This judge might also act in disputes between different kindreds within the *tuath*, but recourse to him was not compulsory: the parties were free to choose any qualified judge.

The king (*rí*) of the *tuath* was bound by personal allegiance to a superior king (*ruiri*) who in turn was similarly bound to a 'king of superior kings' (*rí ruirech*), the king of a province, the highest king known to the Laws. The notion of a King of Ireland to whom the provincial kings owed allegiance was a later development, perhaps not earlier than the tenth century. The inferior king gave hostages to his overlord, and received from him a stipend in token of his dependence. He was bound to certain services, notably tribute and 'hosting' (help in war), and the suzerain was, presumably, obliged to help him in his own quarrels. But the bond between them was solely one of personal fealty: in theory, at least, the over-king had no authority over the territory and people of his subordinate. We have, in the eleventh century Book of Rights, detailed lists of the tributes paid by the kings and the stipends they received, but they are probably mere invention, an antiquary's attempt to present traditional customs, the practice of which had been partly forgotten. Later sources mention tributes of food, which were sometimes commuted into ounces of gold or silver. The form of the stipend is uncertain.[12]

As there were three degrees of kingship, so there were three kinds of *oenach*:

A fair convened by an overking, to whom the rulers of several *tuatha* owed allegiance, might be attended by tribesmen from these petty kingdoms also. Such for example was *Oenach Raigne* for the tribes of Ossory. Most important of all was the provincial fair held in the neighbourhood of the chief stronghold and attended by all the tribes of the province; it lasted for several days, and there was an elaborate program of public business and entertainments.[13]

Such were Oenach Tailten in the great kingdom of Uí Néill, Oenach Emna in the kingdom of the Ulaid, Oenach Carman in the kingdom of the Lagin, Oenach Téite (Nenagh) in Mumu (Cashel), and Oenach Cruachan in Connacht.

After the king came the nobles (*flaithi*), who were the warrior-class and patrons of the 'men of art' (*oes dána*), poets, historians, lawyers, leeches and craftsmen. The third estate was the *grád féne*, the ordinary free-men who tilled the soil and paid a tax of food-rent to the king. The free-man was normally a *céle*, bound by clientship (*célsine*) to a nobleman 'who, in return for a fixed render of provisions and a certain amount of unpaid labour gave him stock to graze his land and guaranteed him a limited protection against the violence of powerful neighbours.'[14]

Clientship seems to have been the basis of a nobleman's prosperity and of his social standing. The law-tracts distinguish two sorts of clientship, according to the terms of the contract, 'free' clientship and 'base' clientship. The relationship between lord and client consisted of the granting of a fief (*rath*) of cattle by the lord in return for a fixed rent, in kind and in service, from the client. The rent was calculated as an annual payment for seven years equal to one third of the value of the fief. In 'base' clientship, which is more commonly mentioned, the client received, in addition to the *rath*, a payment equal to the lord's honour-price, and the lord thus acquired additional rights in his regard – for instance, he was entitled to a third share of the penalty if the client were killed. But the 'base' client, like the 'free', remained a free man. The relationship was a contract, and could be repudiated by either party on certain conditions.

Much of the tract on 'base' clientship is devoted to details of fief and rent. The annual rent for six cows is a calf of the value of three sacks of wheat, a salted pig, three sacks of malt, half a sack of wheat and a handful of rush candles. For twenty-four cows the rent is a fat cow, a salted pig, eight sacks of malt, a sack of wheat, and three handfuls of rush candles. The prominence given to clientship in the Irish law-tracts reminds us of what Polybius and Caesar tell us of the Gauls (pp. 21, 25). We need not doubt that it was an old Celtic institution; but the Welsh law-books do not mention it.

There were slaves (*mug* m., *cumal* f.), perhaps mostly captives of war, but they do not appear to have been a large element in the population.

The word *aire* means 'free-man' and is an inclusive term for both *flaith* and *aithech*.[15]

In Ireland there was a special class, which may be regarded as a sub-class of nobles, the *oes dána*, whose art ennobled them. The *oes dána*, or learned class, included the judge, the leech, the joiner, the metal-worker, and, most important of all, the poet (*fili*), who seems to have inherited much of the prestige of the druid of pagan times. His duty was first of all to praise his patron, but also to preserve his genealogy, to be learned in history and literature, and to be a master of the craft of poetry. There are tracts prescribing the metres he must learn, the number of tales he must know, and the other learned works he must study, during a course of twelve years. He demanded rich rewards for his service, and he was likely to satirize a thrifty prince or nobleman. The *fili* was honoured and feared, like the brahmin in India. He was no longer a priest in this Christian society, but he had means of divination akin to magic. Or at any rate, he had had them in the pagan past, and the tradition of his magical power survived.[16]

This is the tripartite society of priest *fili* (*drui*), warrior (*rí*) and husbandman (*aire*) that Dumézil has traced so successfully in many areas of the Indo-European world. In Gaul *druides*, *equites* and *plebs* are the classes recognized by Caesar, so that early Irish society maintained the old Celtic, and apparently the Indo-European pattern.

The only officer of state whose name we know was the *rechtaire*, who controlled the king's revenues.

Within the *tuath* the important unit was the family, not the individual, and for most legal purposes the family of four generations (*derbfine*), descendants of a common great-grandfather; and this group was originally the unit in Welsh law too.[17] Land was owned jointly by the group, and in matters of inheritance and of liability all members of the *derbfine* had a share. And this was also true of succession to the kingship. An uncle or a grand-nephew could succeed as well as son or grandson, so that in theory there was a good field from which to choose the best man. In practice there were often several unscrupulous rivals seeking to maim or kill each other in order to secure the kingship for themselves.

Beyond the *tuath* lay the wider provincial kingdom, governed by a *rí ruirech* or *cóicedach*. In prehistoric times there had been five such provinces, Ulaid, Lagin, Mumu, Connachta and Mide,[18] roughly corresponding to Ulster, Leinster, Munster and Connaught of modern times, but with Meath and Westmeath as a separate central kingdom, having the sanctuary of Tara as its capital. This division into five kingdoms has given us the word *cóiced* 'fifth' for 'province', but it was already a thing of the past when history begins in the fifth century. By that time there were three kingdoms in the north, Ailech, Airgialla and Ulaid; and in the south-east Osraige (Ossory) was a powerful kingdom, sometimes owing allegiance to Caisel (Mumu), sometimes to Lagin, but always with a will of its own. Later on, in the eighth century, the central kingdom of Mide fell apart, and a separate kingdom of Brega, corresponding to the present County Meath, south Louth and north Dublin, was established. The Brega dynasty seems to have come to an end by the eleventh century, and Brega was joined again to Mide.[19]

This is the political state of Ireland, as it appears from the old law-tracts, some of which date from the seventh century. But from the ninth century onwards, there were attempts by several powerful kings to establish themselves as masters of the whole country by taking hostages from the other provincial kings. This ambition was finally realized by Brian Boru in 1002, and from then until the Norman invasion, the Kingship of Ireland, at least as an idea, may be said to have prevailed.

In such a society commerce consisted of barter, an exchange of goods and probably personal service, not unlike the practice that may still be observed among Irish farmers. The great occasion for this trade was the annual *oenach*, but private bargains can be made at any time. The unit of value was the *sét*, half the value of a milch cow and upon it were based these commercial transactions, and the various tariffs prescribed by the law as fines, honour-price or compensation.[20]

As there were no towns, and society was entirely rural, and since there was no public enforcement of law, and no use of money, the duties of the state were few and simple. The main source of wealth was in cattle, for there was no individual ownership of land, the land being joint property of the *derbfine*.

When a dispute arose between members of the *tuath*, the aggrieved party had various procedures open to him, but the affair was conducted privately between plaintiff and defendant. Normally they would agree to go before a judge, whose business it was to arbitrate, and he took a fee for his service. The law-tracts prescribe procedure for distraining the property of the defendant, the notice that must be given, the witnesses that must be present and so on; and there was an elaborate system of suretyship, enabling the wronged party to enforce a contract, if the other party should fail to perform his part. Even in a case of homicide, the crime was treated as a private wrong.

In Ireland distraint played a large part in legal affairs, for it was the normal way of compelling one's neighbour to submit to arbitration. When arbitration was agreed, the case was heard in the judge's house. Both parties employed lawyers to do the pleading. The judge's fee was one twelfth of the amount involved. Then the question of procedure arose, and it was complex; for there were five modes of procedure ('The Five Paths of Judgement'),[21] according to the matter in dispute; and the plaintiff's lawyer had to find the right one. There was a fine for changing from one 'path' to another.

The law-tracts also expound the capacity of witnesses, and the law of evidence and of proof. Finally, both parties had to find sureties for their abiding by the judge's decision.

Where the enforcement of law was not a function of the state, the institution of suretyship was of great importance. There were three kinds of surety, *naidm*, *aitire* and *ráth*. The *naidm* undertook only to join the creditor in enforcing payment, pledging his honour. The *aitire* pledged his own person and freedom in case the debtor should default. The *ráth* undertook to compel a debtor to pay his debt, and failing that, to pay the debt himself. In some cases all three kinds of surety were required.[22]

A point of special interest in legal procedure is the use of fasting as a means of securing redress. In certain cases where a defendant was of privileged rank (*nemed*), a plaintiff was obliged to fast in front of the defendant's house before making distraint, and this placed a grave obligation on the defendant to give pledges that he would submit to arbitration. The plaintiff came at sunset, and fasted until sunrise. The defendant was bound to fast too, and if he broke his fast he became liable for double the amount claimed. If he wished to take food, he was obliged first to offer food to the plaintiff, and to give a pledge that he would pay or that he would submit to arbitration. If he did

131

neither of these things within three days, he could be distrained upon like a commoner.

Such a defendant, if he simply disregarded the fast and refused to pay, lost his honour; he could not enforce any claim of his own: 'He who does not give a pledge to fasting is an evader of all. He who disregards all things is paid by neither God nor man' (*AL* i 113).

This usage is closely paralleled in Hindu law, where the procedure is called *dharna* (*dharaṇa*). A creditor may sit fasting at the door of the debtor, until the debtor, lest he be liable for the death of the other, yields compliance.[23]

Compensation for a wrong was estimated according to the damage suffered and also according to the rank of the injured party. The fine (*díre*) was measured according to the honour-price (*lóg n-enech*, *eneclann*) of the victim.[24]

Besides the tracts dealing with clientship, distraint, suretyship, and the 'Five Paths of Judgement', there are tracts on marriage, on water-rights and on the ownership of bees, on 'sick-maintenance' (the liability of one who has inflicted corporal injury upon another to have his victim nursed back to health at his charges),[25] and on many other matters.

The law of marriage in early Ireland is of special interest, as it shows in great measure the persistence of ancient custom in spite of Christian teaching. Divorce is freely allowed. Indeed there is a trace of annual marriage. A marriage may always be ended by common consent. This freedom would explain the career of the famous Gormlaith, who was first the wife of Olaf Cuarán, Norse king of Dublin, then of Malachy, king of Meath, then of Brian Boru, and was later offered in marriage to Sigurd, Earl of Orkney.[26] As late as 1339 the Annals of Ulster record that Turlogh O'Conor, king of Connacht, took to himself the wife of an Ulster nobleman, and put away his own wife, a daughter of O'Donnell.

More remarkable is the fact that concubinage, as we would call it, is legally recognized: a man may take and maintain a second wife in the life-time of his 'principal wife'. The purpose of this was presumably to obtain sons, if the first wife were barren, but even this is not stated in the law-tracts. The law regulates the relationship of the secondary wife to the principal wife, and the compensation payable to the husband for a wrong done to her. But no such compensation was payable by the principal wife who was moved by lawful jealousy

132

of her, even to the shedding of blood. This was one of the seven bleedings that did not cause liability. Moreover, she was known by the ugly name, *adaltrach* 'the adulteress'. The tract recognizes ten kinds of union, ranging from permanent marriage to temporary sexual relations. (Of these, two seem to be late, so that we are brought close to the eight forms of marriage in Manu, see p. 26.) How far these provisions represent actual practice in the Christian period may remain doubtful. But there is evidence for divorce, and the frequent mention of the secondary wife in the commentaries can only mean that she was of common occurrence. [27]

The practice of placing one's children in the care of foster-parents was a normal feature of Irish society, and it was not confined to the noble class. Sometimes children were fostered for love, but usually a fosterage-fee was paid, and it varied, according to an early text, from three *séts*[28] for the son of a freeman of lower rank to thirty *séts* for the son of a king. The commentary says that boys were taught riding, swimming, the use of the sling, and the playing of board-games; the girls learned sewing and embroidery. Or for children of lesser rank, it was herding and farm-work for the boys; the quern, the kneading-board and the sieve for girls. But it may be that here the commentator is indulging his fancy, as those commentators loved to do. He knew that there was an exact program of training for a boy who should enter the household of a *fili*, and he wished perhaps to imitate it. In practice, of course, the children in fosterage would pick up these accomplishments anyway. The time of fosterage ended for boys at seventeen, for girls at fourteen, and they returned home. But the tie of fosterage remained close: there was an obligation on the part of the children to support their foster-parents in old age, and those who had been fostered together were bound in close companionship. This relationship with one's *comaltae* is a recurring motif in the sagas. The tragic climax of *Táin Bó Cualnge* is Cú Chulainn's fight with his foster-brother, Fer Diad. In 'The Destruction of Da Derga's Hostel', the tragedy is the greater because the death of Conaire is at the hands of his own foster-brothers.

In Wales the practice of fosterage existed, and it is referred to in the laws several times incidentally, but there is no separate chapter devoted to it. The normal event was for a nobleman to send his son to fosterage with a *taeog* or serf, and the law says that the foster-son shares the inheritance of the serf like one of his own sons.[29] The word *cyfaillt*, which came to mean 'friend', is identical with Irish *comaltae*.

One other chapter of Irish law is of special interest, as it preserves very old tradition, namely the obligations of maintenance of the sick. There are two tracts on the subject, which were discovered in a fifteenth century manuscript from the Phillipps Collection, acquired by the National Library in 1930, and both are very old, not later than the eighth century. One is entitled 'Judgements in Blood-Lyings' and the other 'The Judgements of Dian Cécht'. In many legal systems there was a rule that one who injured his neighbour physically was obliged to pay not merely the appointed penalty but also the cost of healing his victim, the leech-fee of the Anglo-Saxons. In early Ireland the offender was obliged himself to provide for the cure of his victim. Nine days after the wound is inflicted, a leech pronounces his verdict. If he says that the patient will recover, the defendant must take him into his house, or to the house of a kinsman, and provide for him till he recovers. The diet and the treatment of the patient are set forth in detail. Diet varies with his social standing. Besides a basic ration of two loaves a day and an unspecified quantity of fresh meat, to which every patient is entitled, a member of the 'noble grades' receives honey, garlic and especially celery, for its peculiar virtue as a remedy, salt meat every day from New Year's Eve till Lent, and twice a week from Easter to the end of summer. A member of the 'freemen grades' gets salt meat only on Sundays until Lent, and not at all after Easter. Celery is prescribed for all.

The prescriptions as to lodging are quite exacting. Fools, lunatics and enemies are not to be admitted. No games are played. Children are not to be beaten, nor may there by any fighting. There is to be no barking of dogs nor grunting of pigs. The patient is not to be awakened suddenly, and people may not talk across him as he lies in bed. There must be no shouting or screaming. But all this is only a part of the defendant's liability, for he must also entertain the retinue of his patient throughout the period of his sickness. Every freeman had the right to a company of followers according to his rank on certain occasions, and sick maintenance was one of them. Retinues of four and more, to as many as eight persons, are mentioned. And finally the defendant must find a substitute to do the patient's work during his absence.

Dian Cécht was the Irish god of healing, and the second tract is piously attributed to him. It deals largely with the amount that is to

134

be paid to the leech, and this varies with the gravity of the wound, or, according to another doctrine, with the amount of the wergild, that is to say, with the status of the victim. One point of interest is the manner of measuring wounds by grains of corn. And there is a curious catalogue of twelve doors of the soul, parts of the body where wounds are specially grave.

This tract, 'The Judgements of Dian Cécht', is one of the very early ones and contains passages of verse that are probably as early as the sixth century. It has recently been edited by Professor Binchy.[30] The archaic custom of sick maintenance was already obsolete by the eighth century, for *Críth Gablach*, which cannot be later, declares that there is no such practice now, and goes on to describe the old procedure as we find it in *Bretha Crólige* ('Judgements in Blood-Lyings').[31]

In Wales the picture is very different, and it is only with the aid of the Irish evidence that one can see traces of the old Celtic system showing through the Welsh texts as we have them. For there is a Welsh law-book, declared to have been compiled and published in the tenth century under Hywel Dda, whereas in Ireland there is merely a record of ancient custom, going back in part to the sixth or seventh century, with gloss and commentary to explain it. The Welsh tales, which also tell us something about institutions, are not earlier than the twelfth century.

The earliest manuscripts of the Welsh law-book were written c 1200, long after Norman interference had begun, and the prestige of Norman institutions must be allowed for when we compare them with the Irish tracts.[32] In the time of Hywel, there was close contact between the great Welsh king and the royal house of Wessex. He often attended the Witenagemote; and Asser, the biographer of King Alfred, who was a Welshman, used to divide his time between the court of Wessex and his home in Dyfed. There was therefore a strong Anglo-Saxon influence at work even before Hywel's day, and this too will have left its mark upon the laws.

The Welsh legal manuscripts fall into three main 'families' or recensions, all of them presumably based on the original law-book issued under Hywel's authority, but containing much additional material supplied by later jurists, which affords interesting evidence of the subsequent development of Welsh law, including its adoption of Anglo-Norman institutions. These recensions are known as the

Book of Iorwerth, the Book of Blegywryd and the Book of Cyfnerth; none of the extant manuscripts is older than the thirteenth century, and the information they supply as to earlier conditions is not always reliable. Thus the account which all three of them give of the circumstances in which the 'Laws of Hywel' were drafted and promulgated is full of anachronisms. The earliest surviving manuscript (late twelfth century) is in Latin, but this would seem to have been translated from a still earlier Welsh text.[33]

The many small kingdoms that we find in post-Roman Wales of the fifth and sixth centuries, presenting the same state of affairs as in Ireland, were gradually brought under the rule of a single dynasty descended from Cunedda, and in the ninth century Rhodri Mawr was king of approximately all of Wales that was to remain Welsh during the Norman period. On his death in 877, his kingdom was shared among his three sons, Mervyn, Anarawd and Cadell. From Anarawd the line of Gwynedd in the north is descended; and from Howel the Good, son of Cadell, came the lines of Powys and Deheubarth. This division into three kingdoms is the state of Wales reflected in the Laws.

Lloyd says at the beginning of his discussion of early Welsh institutions, that four institutions supply the framework, *cenedl, tref, cantref* and *brenin*, kindred, hamlet, tribe and chief (king). The corresponding terms in Irish are *fine, baile, tuath, rí*. But while the first two may fairly be equated, the Welsh *cantref* (or *gwlad*, which is the older name) had come to differ widely from the Irish *tuath*. The king in Wales maintained a Court with a whole body of courtiers whose duties and rights were laid down; and he administered a system of public law, and derived revenue from it in fines. The *cantref* itself, and the commotes (W. *cymwd*) into which it was divided, seem to have been late administrative divisions, which arose after the old *gwlad* had ceased to be a separate kingdom. Lloyd says that 'the larger *gwlads*, such as Môn, Ceredigion, Brycheiniog, Ystrad Tywi, were divided into *cantrefs*, the smaller, such as Meirionydd, Dyffrin Clwyd, Buellt, became *cantrefs* themselves, and thus the *cantref* everywhere took the place of the tribe as the means of enforcing justice and as the link between people and crown.'[34] This situation probably arose after the establishment of the three kingdoms.

Each *cantref* had its law-court, and in the south this was the old assembly of free-men. This assembly could even pass judgement on

136

the king's conduct, and, by *dedfryd gwlad* or 'judgement of the people', declare him to have acted oppressively. It also retained the ordinary judicial powers of the court. But in Gwynedd and Powys there was a professional judge in each commote who did the work, and the freemen who sat on either side of the king as assessors of the court were a mere survival and had no judicial function. There seems to have been no fixed place of meeting, and the court could thus meet wherever it was most convenient.

While the old customary law, based on the blood-feud, is traceable in the law of *galanas* or compensation for homicide, the notion of delicts as offences against the state is fully developed in Wales. For serious crimes the normal penalty was a fine of twelve cows, the term for which was *dirwy* (Ir. *díre*): for lesser offences the fine was three cows. These fines were paid to the king, not to an injured party. Evidence consisted mainly, as in Ireland, of oaths sworn on either side in accusation and denial, the accused person having to produce compurgators who swore in support of his testimony. Beside the court of the commote or of the *cantref*, there was a higher court in which matters concerning the king and his household were decided. And inferior courts were also held by the *maer*, or steward, and by the *canghellor*. Moreover, the bishop and the abbot had their separate courts. Law and procedure were the same for all these courts.

Three chapters of the Book of Iorwerth are devoted to homicide, arson and theft respectively, and these preserve some features of the old customary law. The penalty for homicide, called *galanas*, varied with the status of the victim, and was paid to the kin (of both father and mother). Honour-price (*gwynebwerth*) was also payable, and if the amounts were not paid in full, the slayer might be slain with impunity. Something of the old blood-feud here survives. The payment of honour-price in addition to the fine is a point of agreement with Irish custom and must be of common origin with it. The distinctions of degrees of responsibility in cases of theft or arson show affinity with Irish law, but these matters are beyond our competence and must be left to experts in legal history.

Kingship survived in Wales until the end of Welsh independence. By the tenth century there were three kingdoms, Gwynedd in the north, with the royal dwelling at Aberffraw in Anglesey, Deheubarth in the south with its capital at Dynefwr, and Powys in the east with its capital at Pengwern (Shrewsbury).[35] The king had an elaborate court, according to the law-books, and numerous officials. He appointed the judges and justice was administered in his name. But all of this seems to have been borrowed from Anglo-Saxon England. In the *Mabinogion*, and from some technical terms in the law-books, one can recognize traces of the old Celtic system. For example, the word *alltud* 'foreigner' (lit. 'from another tribe') shows that the *tud* (Ir. *tuath*) was the original unit of population, as in Ireland, before the three kingdoms were established. The family of four generations, and family-ownership of land were as in Ireland. Also the custom of fosterage (*cyfaillt* 'friend' = Ir. *comaltae* 'foster-brother'), and the system of suretyship were probably in origin the same.

One illustration, which is of special interest, may be given to show how ancient custom lies almost hidden in the Welsh texts. The Irish law of distraint has been discussed already, and distraint was normally of chattels, that is to say of livestock. Land could not be seized, as it belonged to the family-group. But if a man had a claim upon land – if he had been wrongfully deprived of his share – then he could make formal entry on the land by means of an archaic procedure (*tellach*). There were three 'entries' with fixed intervals: on each successive occasion the claimant brought with him an increased number of witnesses and a larger amount of stock. At the third entry they remained on the land overnight, and the claimant kindled fire. Then if the occupier of the land still refused to submit to arbitration, ownership was vested in the claimant.[36]

An action of title to land in Welsh law presents a complete contrast. The claimant comes before the Court which fixes a date for hearing. The occupant is notified. Both parties are represented by counsel, and there is a regular court procedure. Here we have a comparatively modern process of law, whereas the Irish form is a conventionalized method of forcible seizure.

But the Welsh texts record another legal means of vindicating title to land, namely by uncovering the fire on the ancestral hearth (*dadannudd*). It was apparently obsolete, for the jurists themselves did not clearly understand it; but it remains as evidence of the former practice of old Celtic customary law.[37]

The Irish sagas tell us more about the life of the people than do the tales of the *Mabinogion* for Wales. Among the free classes honour was a man's most jealously guarded possession, more precious than life.

In the saga of the 'Exile of the Sons of Uisliu', Derdriu puts Uisliu on his honour, and he cannot refuse to take her away. His brothers try to dissuade him, but when they learn that it is an affair of honour, they promise to join him. So too in 'The Feast of Dún na nGéd' it was the insult offered to Congal at the feast that led to the Battle of Moira. 'The most important element in the legal status of every free-man is his "honour-price",'[38] and upon it depended the amount that was due to him in compensation for a wrong.

The honour of a nobleman, even of a king, was threatened by the satire (aer) of a poet, and this was greatly feared. Refusal of a poet's request or failure to reward him adequately for a poem, might bring a satire upon one, and in the sagas a poet's satire might even disfigure a man. The demands of the poets, and the willingness of others to accede to them, whatever the cost, are a recurring theme.

The term for the formal request of a poet is ailges (ail 'reproach', ges 'request'). The word ges, geis (pl. gessa) alone has acquired the special meaning of 'taboo, prohibition', and expresses an idea that is familiar to us all in the simple form of superstitious avoidance of certain acts or circumstances. But in early Irish society geis was of great importance, and yet it is hard to define. It could attach to rank, as to a king, or to a place or thing: it was geis for anyone to turn the left side of his chariot towards Emain Macha; gessa may be peculiar to a spear or a sword.[39] But commonly they were restrictions on an individual. It was geis for Fothad Canainne to drink ale without having the heads of the slain in his presence. It was geis for Cú Chulainn ('The Hound of Culann') to eat dog's flesh, and for Conaire, whose father was a bird, to hunt birds; but Conaire was subject to many other gessa, and he perished by transgressing them.[40] An old tract on the gessa of the kings of Ireland contains some curious pro-visions. It is geis for the king of Tara to be still in bed at sunrise in the plain of Tara, or to break a journey on Wednesday in Mag Breg, or to travel over Mag Cuilinn after sunset. The king of Leinster may not stay for nine days on Mag Cualann, nor travel over Belach Duiblinne on a Monday, nor sleep between Dublin and the Dodder River with his head to one side. The king of Connacht may not make a circuit of Cruachain on the feast of Samain. The king of Ulster may not eat the flesh of the bull of Dáire mac Dáire: he may not drink the water of the river Bó Nemid between dawn and nightfall. These are only some of the gessa, for there are seven for the king of Tara and five for each of the other kings.[41]

Kings and nobles dwelt in fortified enclosures of earthwork (*dún* or *ráith*), within which were several wooden buildings. Beside the enclosure was a lawn (*faithche*), which was probably the home pasture.

Many of the sagas describe the feasting habits of the Irish, 'The Story of Mac Da Thó's Pig', 'Bricriu's Feast', 'The Feast of Dún na nGéd; and we have in the Book of Leinster a description, and even a plan, of the banquet-hall at Tara, in which the places assigned to the guests, and the portions allotted to them, are set down. While these sources are not historical in the simple sense, they do tell what was accepted as traditional by a medieval Irish audience.

Bread and porridge were the normal diet, but beef and pork were served at feasts, and beer (*coirm*) was drunk. Mead (*mid*) was also drunk, and wine was served on great occasions. The principal meal was taken in the evening. In a royal dining-hall the fire was in the centre, and the cauldron. The drinking-horns were filled from a vat of beer. The guests reclined on couches (*imdae*) arranged in rows from the wall to the fire. Places of honour near the king were assigned according to rank.

In *Fled Dúin na nGéd* (eleventh century?) we are told that when a king of the southern Uí Néill was High King the king of Connacht was on his right hand, and when a king of the northern Uí Néill was High King, the king of Ulster was on his right and the king of Connacht on his left. In 'The Battle of Mag Rath', which is somewhat earlier, there is a conflicting and more detailed account: the High King sits in the middle of the hall, with the king of Munster on his right in the south end, the king of Ulster on his left in the north end, the king of Connacht behind him to the west and the king of Leinster before him to the east. Here the kings occupy places corresponding to their geographical order, but we may doubt whether such an assembly of guests ever took place.

The garments worn by men and women were the *léine*, a linen shirt worn next the skin, the *inar*, a short tunic, and over them a square woollen cloak (*brat*), fastened with a brooch (*delg*), which was sometimes a precious ornament. Rings, bracelets and torcs were of gold, silver and electrum (*finnruine*).

Warriors were armed with shield (*sciath*), sword (*claideb*) and spear (*gae*, *sleg*); and other weapons mentioned are *bir*, *foga*, smaller spears, and *mánais*, a heavier weapon, which O'Curry says was for thrusting.

As regards warfare, the sagas of the Ulster Cycle preserve a tradition that corresponds closely to the descriptions of Gaulish custom given by ancient writers. The warriors drove into battle in chariots. The challenge to single combat and the taking of heads of the slain are frequently mentioned. Raiding for cattle was then, as later, the commonest occasion of fighting.

In historic times, while the old heroic customs will have become obsolete, the weapons and armour may have remained much the same until the Norse invasions presented a new challenge and introduced new fashions. But no comprehensive study of the matter has been made since the days of O'Curry and Joyce.

Hunting and cattle-raiding were the chief employment of the nobles. At home they listened to the poems of the *filid* and the bards, and to the tales of the storytellers. Board-games were a common pastime. The game most frequently mentioned is *fidchell* (Welsh *gwyddbwyll*) 'wood-sense', and other such games were *brandub* 'raven-black' and *buanfach* 'long striking'. Of *fidchell* we know only that the game was played for a stake, and that there were two sets of figures on a board divided into black and white squares.

The boys played a ball-game, sometimes called *áin phuill* 'driving a hole'. In one early account in *Táin Bó Cualnge*, each player has a ball, and one side attacks and the other defends the goal alternately.

The year was divided into two periods of six months by the feasts of *Beltine* or *Cétsamain* (May 1) and *Samain* (November 1), and each of these periods was equally divided by the feasts of *Lugnasad* (August 1) and *Oimelc* or *Imbolg* (February 1). The first name contains the word for 'fire' (*tene*, i.e. 'Bel's Fire'?), and there is a tradition that on that day the druids drove cattle between two fires, as a protection against disease.[42] The second feast, Samain, was the great feast of the year, probably a harvest festival. The word may mean 'end of summer', but this is not certain.[43] *Lugnasad* means 'feast of Lug', and *oímelc* seems to mean 'sheep's milk', which would be a name for the lambing season.

The dominant feature of society in both Wales and Ireland is its rural character. There were no towns, nor even villages in the English sense. Urban civilization remained foreign to the insular Celts until it was imposed upon them by conquerors. After the Roman legions were withdrawn from Britain, the British abandoned the cities and camps, and resumed their rural way of life. In Ireland, even after the Norman invasion, the towns were Norman strongholds from which the native Irish were excluded. The old cities, Dublin,

141

Waterford and Limerick, were built by the Norse invaders; later ones such as Trim, Kilkenny and Clonmel, by the Normans. The town, with its market-place for commerce, with its corporate rights and duties, was foreign to Celtic society. The earliest Irish coins were struck for Sihtric III of Dublin about the end of the tenth century. Hywel Dda was the first king to strike coins in Wales. There was no native Irish coinage before the Norman invasion. Trading was by barter, with values reckoned in cattle, and the chief place of trade was the popular assembly, in Ireland the *oenach* which has given its name to the modern Irish cattle-fair. The Welsh laws do assess penalties in money, for they are late, but the memory of an older practice survives. The law says: *ar warthec y telyt pob tal gynt,* 'every payment was formerly made in cattle'.[44] In Ireland, even late commentators continued to reckon in cattle long after the Norman Invasion, when coinage must have been in use. But, indeed, the Irish may not have taken readily to coinage, for commutations are sometimes made not into currency, but by ounces of gold and silver, even in the sixteenth century.[45]

This conservative character of insular Celtic society gives it a special interest, and something of it is still with us. The countryside of Wales or of Ireland with its scattered homesteads, and the close pattern of fields, reflects even today the old rural pattern, when the kin-groups were owners of the land. Evans in his *Irish Heritage* and Arensberg in *The Irish Countryman* have shown, for Ireland at least, now slowly change comes in this environment.

NOTES

1 See Binchy, *Críth Gablach* p. 109; MacNeill IPG 88 f.
2 IPG 104.
3 See Hogan, 'The Trícha Cét and Related Land-Measures' pp. 191 ff. (PRIA xxxviii C 1929).
4 Giraldus Cambrensis has been credited with the statement that there were a hundred and seventy-six *trícha cét* in Ireland in his day. But this is an error. He does not mention the *trícha cét*, and his reckoning of 'cantreds' in Ireland is fanciful. See Top. Hib. III v (ed. Dimock p. 145).
5 D. A. Binchy in *Early Irish Society*, p. 56.
6 *CK* 38 f.
7 *MD* iv 142. 125.
8 ZCP xvii 139. See also O'Rahilly, *Ériu* xiv 14 ff., where other reff. are given; and J. Weisweiler, *Heimat u. Herrschaft*. The most recent discussion is by Professor Mac Cana, 'Aspects of the

142

Theme of King and Goddess in Irish Literature', ÉC vii 76 ff.; 356 ff.; viii 59 ff.

9 *Top. Hib.* III xxv.

10 J. O'Donovan, *Tribes and Customs of Hy Fiachrach* 425; *Medieval Studies presented to Aubrey Gwynn S.J.* (Dublin 1961), 197; cf. the rod of Agamemnon, *Il.* ii 101, as Professor G. Huxley reminds me. J. Carney has shown that the Feast of Tara was the inauguration ceremony of the king of Tara, SILH 334 ff. See also Binchy, *Ériu* xviii 134.

11 'Die magische Kraft der Wahrheit im alten Indien', ZDMG xcviii (1944), 1; 'The Hindu Act of Truth in Irish Tradition', *Modern Philology* xliv (1947), 137; Maartje Draok, 'Some Aspects of Kingship in Pagan Ireland', *The Sacral Kingship* 651–63 (Leiden, 1959).

12 See *LC* p. xvii.

13 Binchy, *Ériu* xviii 125.

14 Binchy, *EIS* 58. For much of the material in this chapter I am indebted to unpublished notes lent me by Dr Binchy. A Welsh text says: 'There are three kinds of persons, a king, a brëyr and a bondman', Melville Richards, *Laws of Hywel Dda* 26.

15 It is hardly to be doubted that the word is akin to Sanskrit *arya-*, although Thurneysen suggested an alternative explanation, ZCP xx 353. Binchy has pointed out to me that the genitive *airech* is to be explained by analogy with *ruire* 'over-king', gen. *ruirech*.

16 For references see O'Rahilly, *EIHM* 340.

17 See Binchy, P.B.A. xxix 223.

18 O'Rahilly points out that the name *Mide* is late. The old name of the central province is uncertain, *EIHM* 166, 174 n. 4. For the Five Provinces see also O'Rahilly, *Celtica* I 387 f.

19 *EIHM* 166.

20 Binchy, *Proc. International Congress of Celtic Studies* (Dublin, 1962) 121.

21 See Thurneysen, *Cóic Conara Fugill* (APAW 1925, Phil.-Hist. Kl. 7).

22 See Thurneysen, *Die Bürgschaft im irischen Recht*, 35 ff. (APAW 1928, Phil.-Hist. Kl. 2). Binchy *EIS* 63.

23 Thurneysen, 'Das Fasten beim Pfändungsverfahren', ZCP xv 260 ff.; Jolly, *Grundriss der indo-arischen Philologie* II 8, 148; L. Renou, Le jeûne du créancier dans l'Inde ancienne', JA 1943–5, pp. 117 ff.

24 See Binchy, *CG* 84 f.

25 See Binchy, *Ériu* xii 1 ff., and *inf.* 104.

26 She is the Kormlöd of whom the Saga of Burnt Njal says: 'she was endowed with great beauty and all those attributes which were outside her own control, but it is said that in all the qualities for which she herself was responsible, she was utterly wicked.'

27 Thurneysen and others, *Studies in Early Irish Law*, p. 16 ff., 240 ff. Here again I owe much to unpublished notes of Dr Binchy.

28 The *sét* was a unit of value equal to half the value of a milch cow.

29 See Melville Richards, *Laws of Hywel Dda* 77.

30 *Ériu* xx 1 f.

31 *Críth Gablach*, ed. Binchy, 11. 47 ff.; *Ériu* xii 82 f.

32 The late date of the manuscripts is not the decisive point, for the Irish manuscripts are, with one exception, very much later. In Ireland the native tradition proved stronger at first than Norman influence, and, as is well known, the Normans soon took to Irish ways.

33 Hywel D. Emanuel 'The Latin Texts of the Welsh Laws' in the *Welsh History Review* 1963 pp. 25–32.

34 *HW* i 302.

35 See *Wales through the Ages* p. 107.

36 See *AL* iv 18.

37 Here I am specially indebted to Professor Binchy's unpublished notes.

38 Binchy, *Críth Gablach* 85.

39 See J. R. Reinhard, *The Survival of Geis in Medieval Romance*, 56 f.

40 *EIL* 27 f.

41 See 'The Taboos of the Kings of Ireland', PRIA liv C pp. 1 ff. Also J. R. Reinhard, *op. cit.*, 106 f.

42 Binchy, *Ériu* xviii 129. The mythical king Beli of Welsh tradition may preserve the name, but no Irish god Bel is known.

43 See Vendryes, *La Religion des Celtes* 313 (Mana. Introduction à l'histoire des religions 2, Paris, 1948).

44 *ALI* II xxi 10.

45 See *Studia Celtica* i 1 ff.

6

The Early History of the Modern Celtic Kingdoms

The entente between the ruling houses of Dumbarton and Dál Riata (p. 107 above) must have broken down after Aedán's death. In 642 his grandson, Domnall Brecc, undertook a disastrous expedition against the Britons in the upper valley of the Carron under their king, Owen of Dumbarton, a collateral descendant of Rhydderch Hen (cf. p. 74 above), and the triumphant British bards sang how 'the ravens tore the head of Domnall Brecc'[1] – an interesting hint of a British panegyric poem on the victorious British leader. After this we hear no more of Dalriadic aggression for the time being. For about a century the history of Dál Riata is largely a record of internal struggles for supremacy between the Cinél Loairn, and the Cinél Gabráin.

But the penetration of the Scots eastward into Pictish territory continued gradually. As early as 628 the *Annals of Ulster* speak of Aedán's son, Eochaid Buide, as *rex Pictorum*, so it is possible that the Dalriadic dynasty had been enforcing its influence, if not its actual conquests, eastwards among the Picts for several generations. The name *Atholl*, derived from *Ath-Fótla*, 'second Ireland', or 'New Ireland',[2] must have been given to this district by the Scots themselves already by the beginning of the eighth century.[3] It was originally one of the kingdoms of the Southern Picts with its capital at Scone.

Towards the middle of the eighth century Dál Riata came to a clash with Oengus mac Forgusa, the most powerful of all the kings of the Southern Picts. His precise origin is unknown, but he seems to represent a new line. During the century which preceded the union of the Picts and Scots (see below) the four kingdoms of the Southern Picts (cf. p. 101 above) had been struggling for supremacy among themselves with varying success, but the outcome resulted in the establishment of Oengus mac Forgusa,[4] whose chief seat seems to have been traditionally at Forteviot in Fortrenn, but with whom the Picts of Fife and their capital at Kilrymont or St Andrews, were evidently associated. It is indeed possible that at this period the term Fortrenn also included the modern county of Angus as well as Fife, and that the Pictish kingdom of Angus, with its capital at Forfar, has preserved his name. Already between 706 and 717 its king, Nechtan IV, had been able to negotiate independently with Bishop Ceolfrith of Jarrow in Northumbria in what must have been fundamentally a political entente.

In 741 the Irish annals record a *percussio Dál Riatai* (a 'devastating attack') by Oengus on Dál Riata. In this year, nevertheless, began the long and brilliant reign of Aed Finn in Dál Riata, and in 749 we hear of the 'ebbing' of the power of Oengus, and in 768 of an invasion of Fortrenn by Aed of Dál Riata whom Flann Mainistrech[5] calls 'Aed the Plunderer', and the *Duan Albanach*[6] ('The Scottish Poem') calls *Aed ard-flaith*, 'Aed the high sovereign'. A serious aggression against the Picts is therefore being conducted from Dál Riata, and it seems likely that this is the period when the Scots of Dál Riata penetrated deeply into Atholl and Fife.

The period between 765 and 973 is very obscure because the Irish annals, hitherto our chief guide to Dalriadic history, now fail us. The period, however, must have been a momentous one, for we are on the eve of the union of the Picts and Scots; but the Picts have left few reliable records even at this late date. The union must indeed have come about as a gradual process, largely through intermarriage, and some time after 781 the royal lines of Dál Riata and the Picts seem to have become in some measure united, for after the death of Fergus, successor of Aed Finn, four of the nine kings of Dál Riata between him and Kenneth mac Alpin (see below) have Pictish names, and this cannot be the result of conquest because these Pictish names do not begin till after 781 (the year of the death of Fergus), when there is no hint in the annals of a conquest to account for it. Moreover all the Pictish kings known to have been ruling in Dál Riata have Dalriadic names except Constantine (d. 820). There can be no doubt that the Pictish law of inheritance through the female, together with patrilinear succession by tanistry among the royal family of Dál Riata, must have greatly facilitated a union of the two peoples by intermarriage. The actual union of the Picts and Scots, which gave us our modern 'Scotland', seems to have taken place somewhere about the middle of the ninth century under Kenneth mac Alpin (d. 858), perhaps as a gradual process; but the Vikings' attacks were now in full swing. The twelfth century English chronicler, Henry of Huntingdon, who probably derived material from documents of the reign of David I, evidently attributes Kenneth's initial success over the Picts to his having attacked them immediately after they had suffered a heavy slaughter at the hands of Danish pirates.

Little is known of the rise to power of Kenneth's family. Alpin's father belonged to the royal line of Gabrán, but his name indicates a Pictish mother. He had reigned in Dál Riata during the first half of the ninth century, but his home and origin are unknown. Henry of Huntingdon states that in 834 'Alpin, king of the Scots' had fought successfully against the Picts and many of the nobles of the Picts were slain; but that three months later he was killed in another battle, 'being elated with success', and the Picts cut off his head.[7]

Kenneth is said by Henry of Huntingdon to have attacked the Picts and secured the monarchy of Alba in 834, and to have fought successfully against the Picts 'seven times in one day'. It is clear that both Alpin and his son Kenneth were celebrated in elegiac poetry which has left its echoes in our records. This is what we should expect from an Irish kingdom like Dál Riata, and due caution must be exercised accordingly. The Chronicle of the united Picts and Scots, which dates from the tenth century, states that Kenneth ruled the Picts happily for sixteen years, after he had wiped them out (*delevit*); and other texts also speak of a *destructio* of the Picts. It is remarkable that no hint of such a conquest is given by records of Irish, British or English provenance. The *Annals of Ulster* call Kenneth king of the Picts in recording his death in 857 (recte 858), and the title remained in use by the Irish and even the Welsh annalists till the time of his grandson. But the actual subjects of Kenneth himself and of his successors are referred to as 'Scots', and the Picts soon came to be thought of as a people of the past.

The Irish kingdom of Argyll also gradually imposed its language over the north and west of Scotland, and this has been known since the seventeenth century as Gaelic.[8] After the ninth century the Pictish language disappeared, and the language of southern Scotland remained the British which had been spoken there from prehistoric times. The English language had not yet superseded British in the eastern lowlands. Did the widespread superimposition of Gaelic take

147

place between the fifth and the ninth centuries? It is not impossible; but one is tempted to suggest that the new Irish influence had perhaps begun earlier than the immigration of the sons of Erc in the fifth century AD. In fact we may even suggest that the Irish had crossed the narrow seas at an earlier period, and that the record of the sons of Erc is in reality not the beginning of an immigration, but the last stage, and with it the record of a new dynasty. Without discussing the difficulties which such a view admittedly raises, we may recall that Bede, in describing the early inhabitants of this island (H.E. I, v) mentions that 'Scots' from Ireland migrated hither under their leader *Reuda*, and 'either by fair means or by force of arms secured for themselves those settlements among the Picts which they still possess. From the name of their commander', he adds, 'they are to this day called *Dalreudini*; for in their language *Dal* signifies a part.' Can Bede be right, and was the arrival of an Irish dynasty in Argyll earlier than the fifth century? Bede gives no date, but the passage is of special interest because some names given by him have an archaic form of *c.* 700 which Bede must have got from contemporary sources in his own life-time.

However and whenever the Irish came, the Scottish 'Irish' element, though numerically far inferior to the Pictish, now becomes dominant over the whole of Scotland, and Dál Riata itself becomes unimportant. From the ninth century the western sea-board kingdom of Dál Riata plays little part in history. The centre of power shifts from the west to the east, and the Scottish element in the aristocracy of Scotland seems to prevail though their numbers may have been small. The ecclesiastical capital was already at Dunkeld in the shadow of Mount Shiehallion on the bank of the Tay a few miles north of Perth, whither it had been transferred by Constantine, king of the Picts (d. 820). [9] The Dalriadic kings now live and rule in the old Pictish kingdoms. Flann of Monasterboice says that Kenneth mac Alpin 'was the first king of the Gaedhil (i.e. the Irish), who possessed the kingdom of Scone (i.e. Atholl)', which was already virtually Irish. It would seem, however, that, like the Bernician kings, the royal family was not entirely stationary, for we find them also at Abernethy, Forteviot, and Rosemarkie – all in Southern Pictavia – and apparently the various members were not always together in one place. Kenneth himself died in his palace at Forteviot in Fortrenn. Henceforth however the chief royal seat is at Scone, near the Roman camp of Grassy Walls in

Scone Park in Atholl on the lovely bank of the Tay a short walk above Perth. The mound in the grounds immediately behind Scone palace still marks the old site of the traditional dwelling of the Pictish kings – the kings of Cruithentuath.

We now pass to one of the most interesting phases of Welsh history, leading up to the control of North Wales by Rhodri Mawr (d. 878), whose grandson Hywel Dda (d. 950) was the first to submit to an English king. In this phase of Welsh history the most important features are, first the gradual process by which the unification of the various Welsh kingdoms was effected within a few generations by a series of royal marriage alliances; secondly the defeat of the Danish army and the death of their king Gormr at the hands of Rhodri Mawr; and thirdly, the end of Welsh isolation, and the beginning of her intellectual development and entry into relations with Wessex and the wider continental sphere. Of great importance also is the part played by the House of Wessex in Welsh politics, especially by Alfred the Great. The importance of the Celtic sympathies and the influence of Alfred in Welsh politics is one of the most important unwritten chapters in the early history of our country. We shall not find Alfred's Celtic political concerns fully recognized in the Anglo-Saxon Chronicle, for the annalist had quite other interests; but we shall find them set forth in Asser's *Life of King Alfred*, a prime authority on this question, more especially as it affected South Wales.

Early in the ninth century, either in 816 or 828,[10] something of a change took place in the patrilinear succession of Gwynedd.[11] Merfyn Vrych (d. 844), was the son of Ethyllt, who was a direct descendant of the 'Island Dragon' Maelgwn, and the Catamannus of the famous Anglesey inscription (cf. p. 114 above), and also of the great Cadwallon, slayer of Edwin of Northumbria. His mother's was the most distinguished line in Wales. His father's line is not well authenticated in Welsh historical records, but Welsh poetry and genealogies suggest that he belonged to the 'Men of the North' and was a descendant both of the famous line of Coel Hen and of that of Dyfnwal Hen of Dumbarton, whose dynasties had given effective protection to our northern frontiers during the late Roman period. The family traced its ancestry to Llywarch Hen, a cousin of the great Urien of Rheged, and to others whose names occur in Merfyn's immediate family, but are not common elsewhere in Wales, though

149

they occur among the 'Men of the North'. Probably the Northumbrian expansion westward had displaced branches of the old dynasties, especially from Galloway, causing them to expand across the narrow seas to Ireland and the Isle of Man.[12] The Irish *Annals of Ulster* s.a. 657 (recte 658) record the death of *'Guret (Gwriad)*,[13] king of Alcluathe' (Dumbarton), while the famous Manx Cross, inscribed Crux Guriat,[14] of approximately Merfyn's date, suggests that the family may have come to Gwynedd more immediately from the Isle of Man.

In the poem known as the *Cyfoesi*, we find a reference to 'Merfyn Vrych from the land of Manau',[15] and in Triad no. 68 we read of 'Gwriad son of Gwrian in the North', probably with reference to the Guriat on the contemporary Manx Cross. The name is also that of Merfyn's father *Guriat* and that of his son or grandson.[16] It seems clear that Merfyn's own ancestors were among various chieftains of the 'Men of the North', and that the names of their immediate family in Wales were among the ancestral names of his father's line. Whatever his immediate place of origin, Merfyn established himself in Gwynedd, and allied himself to the royal house of Powys by marrying Nest, the sister of Concenn or *Cyngen* (d. 854), the last king of the old line of Powys. After this the kingdom of Powys apparently passed to the line of Merfyn Vrych, and on his death to his son Rhodri Mawr.

Merfyn was an outstanding king. We possess from a manuscript preserved at Bamberg in Bavaria, based on a ninth century original, the opening sentence of a letter – perhaps the earliest Welsh letter in existence – from Merfyn of Gwynedd to Concenn or Cyngen, king of Powys, his brother-in-law: *Mermin rex Conchen salutem*, 'Merfyn the king salutes Conchen.' The letter contains a learned cryptogram,[17] and in the letter itself Merfyn addresses the neighbouring king of Powys in polished terms, and it is clear that his court (referred to as *arx*) is a cultivated one, where a degree of education was established – some Latin, possibly a modicum of Greek, and at least two Celtic languages were spoken. The *arx* of Merfyn is evidently on a regular through route from Ireland to the Continent, for it is assumed in the letter that other travellers will follow. This is, in fact, the period of the great opening of the activity of Irish scholars in the scriptoria of the continental libraries, and we know that there were recognized hostels for Irish and also for British *peregrini* en route. When therefore we learn that Merfyn's brother-in-law Concenn, king of Powys, to whom this letter is addressed, died at Rome in 855, we know that he is only one of a long series of pilgrims from Britain and Ireland at this time. Alfred the Great from Wessex made the journey to Rome twice.

Intellectually the reign of Merfyn[18] seems to have been of the highest importance. This is the period when the *Annales Cambriae* appear to have been drawn up in their present form,[19] and also the most important text of the *Historia Brittonum*. The genealogies of the North British princes seem to have been originally drawn up at the same period and in the same milieu.[20] Taken as a whole the evidence suggests that in Wales a school of antiquarian activity flourished in Gwynedd about the beginning of the ninth century and was fostered throughout that century at the courts of Merfyn and his son Rhodri, and from the beginning of the ninth century Wales evidently had something of a continental public, or at least audience.

This is also the period to which we owe our knowledge of the earliest Welsh poetry. We have seen that in chapter 62 of the *Historia Brittonum* 'Talhaern *Tataguen* ("Father of poetic inspiration") was a renowned poet, and Neirin (Aneirin) and Taliesin, and the bard Bluch, and Cian Gueinth Guaut ("kernel of song") were all at the same time renowned for British poetry.' The great collection of the earliest Welsh poetry claims in its title in our only extant manuscript to be the work of Aneirin himself. One other extant collection of poems claims to be the work of Taliesin, but they can hardly date from his period (cf. p. 270 below). The contents of the poems lead one to conclude that Aneirin and Taliesin were the official bards of the courts of Manau Guotodin and of the court of Urien of Rheged respectively. We do not know where these poems were first written down, but on linguistic grounds it was most probably somewhere in Wales in the ninth century. We do not even know where our extant manuscripts were written, but again it was almost certainly in Wales or, less probably, Cumbria. The contents of the poems must have been well known to the literary circle in Gwynedd, and in all probability the first written records of the poems from oral tradition were made in the same milieu as that which recorded the traditions and the annals and the pedigrees of the northern princes, i.e. in North Wales in the ninth century. As in Ireland, Latin learning was brought into requisition to record in writing the oral traditions of the past, probably in the interests of the reigning dynasties. Gwynedd was a centre of culture and of native oral tradition, and the court, first of Merfyn, and later of his son Rhodri Mawr, was evidently largely responsible for having the records made. Here more than anywhere else the importance of exalting the northern ancestry, the splendid northern traditions and history, and the oral literature of the early members of the line of Merfyn's ancestors becomes obvious. They would be invaluable assets to the prestige of the new dynasty claiming descent from Llywarch Hen from the north.

We may believe, though we cannot prove, that the great intellectual achievement of the reign of Merfyn and his son Rhodri was the recording in written form of the ancient traditions of the north, the North British Heroic Age. In so far as their dynasty was partially a new one in North Wales, and also in support of their anti-English policy, the traditions of their heroic past in the north must have been invaluable in gaining them the support of their immediate followers and of the wider population of the country of their adoption.

The important part played by the court of North Wales at this period has hardly been fully appreciated. First Merfyn, then his son Rhodri, brought Wales from her isolation into the intellectual life of Europe. In politics no less than in literature Merfyn and Rhodri made a permanent contribution to the future history of Wales, working deliberately for the unification of the country, not by violence but by policy, in a series of diplomatic marriages. We have seen that Merfyn came to the throne by the marriage of his father Gwriad to Ethyllt, the daughter of Cynan, the last king of the island line of Gwynedd, and that Merfyn married Nest,[21] sister of the last king of the old line of Powys.

The son of this union was Rhodri Mawr, 'Rhodri the Great'. On his mother's side, therefore, he was heir to Powys, as Merfyn had inherited Gwynedd through Ethyllt, and on the death of Cyngen in Rome in 855[22] Rhodri acquired Powys,[23] in addition to Gwynedd. Soon after 872 Rhodri himself married Angharad, sister of Gwgon, king of Ceredigion and thus seems to have found himself in possession of the large kingdom of Seissyllwg, a kingdom which had been formed more than a century earlier by the addition of Ceredigion to Ystrad Tywi, cutting off the little 'Irish' kingdom of Dyfed (cf. p. 58 above) or Pembroke from the rest of Wales. Dyfed had nothing to look forward to but slow strangulation at the hands of the sons of Rhodri. She was in a pincer movement. However, Rhodri's grandson, Hywel Dda, son of Cadell, son of Rhodri and Angharad, relieved the apprehensions of Hyfaidd (*Hemeid*), king of Dyfed, and turned an enemy into a friend by marrying his grand-daughter Elen, so that on the death of Hyfaidd's son, Llywarch, in 892 [24] Hywel added Dyfed to Seissyllwg, now part of his own domain, and ultimately, in succession to the sons of Rhodri Mawr, he also annexed Powys.

The dynasty is indeed a remarkable one. By a series of diplomatic marriages, and apparently without striking a blow, they had made themselves masters of most of Wales in four generations. Already by the middle of the ninth century Rhodri was the greatest man in Wales and the founder of a great family. But Merfyn had already set the stage for him. His marriage with Nest of Powys must have taken place just at the moment when both Powys and Gwynedd were suffering devastating attacks from the Mercians; and Mercia was getting help from Wessex. It was doubtless with the object of presenting a united front against English aggression that Merfyn had allied himself with his neighbour in this, the richest and most vulnerable part of Wales. The history of these marriages perhaps suggests that in earlier times in Wales, as among the Picts, inheritance may have passed through the female, and literary prose stories in the *Mabinogion* also lend some colour to such a suggestion. This history of the gradual unification of Wales, no less than the long life of many of the early Welsh dynasties, demonstrates the fallacy of regarding the Celtic peoples as inherently war-like.

Yet Rhodri's military achievements are hardly less important than his policy of consolidation. In 855 (recte 856) the *Annals of Ulster* record the death of 'Horm' (Norse *Gormr*), leader of the Danes, at the hands of *Ruadri*, son of Meirminn, 'king of the Britons'. This outstanding achievement probably reached the ears of the court of Charles the Bald at Liège, who about this time was gravely intimidated by the Vikings, for Sedulius Scottus ('the Irishman'), a member of Charles's court (cf. p. 237 below), composed an ode on a victory over the Danes. [25] In 876 the *Annales Cambriae* record the 'Sunday battle' in Anglesey, fought no doubt against the Danes, and this is doubtless the explanation of annal 876 (recte 877) in the *Annals of Ulster*, which record how *Ruaidhri*, son of Muirminn, king of the Britons, came to Ireland, fleeing before the Black Foreigners (i.e. the Danes); and the following year the death of Rhodri, and also his son [25] Gwriad, at the hands of the Saxons is recorded in the *Annales Cambriae*. His realm was inherited by his sons severally, Anarawd, probably the eldest, taking Gwynedd and Anglesey, Cadell probably having Seissyllwg, where his descendants ruled for many generations. The shares which may have fallen to the four remaining sons are unknown.[26]

Rhodri, like the Men of the North, had been forced to fight on two fronts. His death was the heaviest blow that the Welsh could have suffered at this time. On the west the Danes were still a rising power; on the east the English in both Mercia and Wessex had been, and still were, an ever increasing menace. By Rhodri's inheritance of Powys he had fallen heir to the richest part of Wales, but also to the age-old feud along its borders, to which Offa's Dyke, built during the closing years of the eighth century, bears witness. Early in this century, in the lifetime of Elisedd, the king of Powys (commemorated on the cross near Llangollen commonly known as Eliseg's pillar), the Welsh had been strong enough to gain some ground; but in 822 the *Annales Cambriae* record the destruction of Degannwy by the Saxons, who 'took the region of Powys into their own power' (*in sua potestate*). In the year 828 the *Anglo-Saxon Chronicle* reports Ecgbriht, the West-Saxon king conquering Mercia and reducing the Welsh to submission, thus bringing Wessex into direct conflict with the Welsh for the first time.

A generation later in 853 the *Anglo-Saxon Chronicle* tells of the Mercians under their king Burgred obtaining the help of Aethelwulf, father of Alfred the Great, and making an expedition into Wales and reducing the country to subjection. It is this period of the subjugation of Powys by Burgred of Mercia, with help from Wessex, that Sir Ifor Williams has suggested as the background of the sad poems purporting to be the work of Llywarch Hen (cf. p. 273 below). There can hardly be any doubt that this moment of great political intensity and poignancy was the occasion of Cyngen's pilgrimage to Rome.

Rhodri's death at the hands of the Saxons brings to an end the long struggle for power, not only between Powys and Mercia, but also in its later stages between Gwynedd and Wessex. Asser fully appreciated the contribution of the dynasty of Gwynedd towards the creation of a unified Wales, in that the dynasty had brought a congeries of little states into a closely-knit realm. The annexation of Powys by Hywel Dda, Rhodri's grandson, was only the final stage. Asser says pointedly that after Rhodri's death, his sons worked together in unison against the other southern states, and it is the Wales of Rhodri's sons,

154

Gwynedd in the north and Deheubarth (cf. p. 112 above) in the south that Asser has in mind more particularly when he refers to Wales by the grandiose epithet *Britannia*. In the reigns of Merfyn and Rhodri the brilliance of the 'Men of the North' was destined to flower again and to find its fullest expression, both politically and intellectually. It is in the earliest genealogy of this family[28] that we first meet with Rhodri's epithet *Mawr*. The *Historia Brittonum*, compiled in this century, lays great emphasis on the traditions of the Romans preserved in Wales. In the reign of Alfred, Asser of St David's emphasizes the persistent effort of Rhodri's son and heir Anarawd to make a compact with the Northumbrians. There can be no doubt that in all this Rhodri and his sons were aiming at a united British nation and an ultimate conquest of the Saxons, as their ancestor Cadwallon had done. It is partly in the light of these ideals, and bearing in mind the common bond of race and language, that we must view the prominence given to the traditions and the poetry of Cumbria and the northern Britons in the Gwynedd of the ninth century. All the memories of the heroic past were called on to serve this great end, which even after Rhodri's death sent its fiery cross throughout all the Celtic lands in the last great Welsh heroic poem, the *Armes Prydein*[29] ('The Prophecy of Britain'), composed not before *c.* 900 or later than 930 (cf. p. 277 below).

It would be interesting to know how Asser first came into contact with Alfred. His own words suggest that he came as a refugee, for he speaks of his own king Hyfaidd of Dyfed, who often plundered the monastery of St David's and expelled the inmates; and he speaks of his own relative, bishop Nobis, and of himself also, as having been expelled.[30] Yet it is striking that both Alfred and William the Conqueror should have found it imperative to establish permanent relations with Dyfed and the church of St David's. Was it the Irish menace? We must surely associate Alfred's interest in St David's – a church and monastery wholly Irish in character – with his contributions to the Irish Church, of which we hear from Asser, (ch. 39) and also with other indications which Asser gives us (chs. 76, 91) of Alfred's interest in Ireland. In addition we have the unique record of the visit of three Irishmen to his court, and the notice of the death of the Irish scribe Swifneh (of Clonmacnoise), both related in annal 891 in the Parker Text of the *Anglo-Saxon Chronicle*.[31] Living on the Welsh border, Alfred could not fail to realize that Wessex and Mercia could never hope to remain secure from invasion from the west with a permanent and implacable enemy on their rear.

Hywel Dda began his career as joint heir of Seissyllwg with his brother Clydog, but probably ruled alone there after this brother's death, which took place two years after their submission to Edward the Elder. Hywel doubtless acquired Dyfed by his marriage with Elen, grand-daughter of Hyfaidd Hen (see p. 153 above). Early in life he visited Rome, and after his return he was closely associated throughout his life with the English court. In the *Anglo-Saxon Chronicle*, MS. D., s.a. 926, we read that Hywel of the 'West Welsh',[32] and Owen of Gwent, in fact the whole of South Wales, submitted to Athelstan. When, some ten years later, the tributary princes leagued themselves against Wessex, only the South Welsh seem to have stood aside, doubtless due to Hywel's influence.

Hywel had no claim on North Wales for most of his life, for the evidence of charters makes it clear that he and his cousin, Idwal Foel ap Anarawd, ruled North and South Wales separately under Athelstan. But in 942 Idwal and his brother, or possibly his son, Cingen, were slain in battle against the Saxons. At this point Hywel seems to have annexed Gwynedd and doubtless Powys also, thus gradually by inheritance and marriage becoming the sole ruler of Wales under Athelstan.

Hywel's English sympathies are fully attested both in the part which he took in English legal procedure and in the English influence on his own Welsh institutions (cf. p. 135 above). Athelstan often summoned the *subreguli* to meetings of the *witan* when they were approving grants of land, and the names of Welsh princes appear from time to time among the witnesses; and from 928-49 Hywel's name appears on every charter containing Welsh signatories, and always the first in order. One of these grants made at Luton in 931 bears the testimony:

† *Ego Howael subregulus consensi et subscripsi.*

The cross doubtless represents Hywel's mark, doing duty for his signature. This English influence on his institutions is seen again in the silver penny now in the British Museum, the first pre-Conquest example of a silver penny struck by a Welsh king, which bears on the obverse the legend *Howael Rex.*

It is interesting to speculate as to what the history of Wales might have been if Rhodri had not been killed in warfare against the Saxons. He had failed to win Dyfed though he had succeeded in hemming it in; and it was from this corner of Wales that Alfred managed, with Asser's help, to inaugurate a pro-English policy among the South Welsh princes, a policy which was to bear fruit in the alliance between Rhodri's grandson, Hywel Dda, and Alfred's grandson, Athelstan in the following century. When Alfred obtained the services of Asser, and the homage of the South Welsh princes in opposition to the ambitions of the Sons of Rhodri, the battle between opposing policies of the North and South Welsh princes – between Celtic political separatism and hopes of freedom from the Saxons on the one hand, and on the other union with England in face of the common danger from the Danes – was virtually over. The annexation of Powys by Hywell Dda, his submission to Alfred's son, Edward the Elder in 918, and his later submission to Athelstan are only the final stages.

There is a similarity in the aims and achievements of Rhodri Mawr and Alfred the Great. As a result of Viking pressure both had succeeded in developing from a group of small units into relatively consolidated states, each struggling for survival while threatened by foreign enemies. Each was the first in the history of his country to win the epithet 'great', probably after the example of the great western Emperor Charlemagne. Indeed each had some knowledge of continental affairs. The death of Rhodri, while Alfred was rapidly rising in power, undoubtedly facilitated the task of uniting under Alfred and Athelstan, first the South Welsh princes, and ultimately the whole of Wales, under an English king. In traditions of North and South Wales at this period we have passed from the heroic ideals of the north to the realistic political vision of the south. But we have also stepped out of the Old World into a new era.

We have seen how, at the close of the Classical Period, and after the Barbarian invasions had transformed the Roman Empire, two peoples of north-western Europe had continued to develop on their own traditional lines with comparatively little upheaval. The Teutonic peoples of Scandinavian lands and the Celtic peoples of the British Isles, though never wholly isolated from the Continent and the new conditions resulting from the downfall of the Roman Empire, were not at first directly affected politically. They continued to progress on their own lines in relative isolation. Here the growth of power of the kingship developed from within rather than by external agency, leaving the integrity of the Celtic lands unaffected except for the outer fringes.

During the eighth century a new Barbarian irruption took place from Northern Europe sweeping east over Russia and west over the British Isles and the peripheral countries of Western Europe. The wide scope and devastating impact of this movement can be inferred from the fact that it is universally known to historians as the 'Viking Age'. The eastern or Swedish activities of the Scandinavian Vikings concentrated chiefly on Finland and, more especially, Russia, where the great river systems of the Dniepr, the Don and the Volga served them as highroads to the richer lands of the south and east, for expansion, colonization, and the formation of city-states. The western Vikings in the early period set sail for the most part from Norway, and their nucleus may be gauged from the names by which they were commonly known in the Irish records of the period – *Lochlannachs*, people of *Lochlann* (Rogaland), the country round the Stavanger Fjord in south-western Norway; and perhaps *Hiruath*, the people of Hörthaland, immediately to the north of Rogaland.[33]

The cause of the Viking Age, as of all such barbarian irruptions, was food shortage. Norway in particular, with its long narrow axis consisting of a great mountain spine, and a narrow coastal strip, could not support a vigorous growing population. Emigration in some form was inevitable. The more precise dating has been attributed to various causes, one of which, it has been suggested, was the invention of the keel *c*. 600,[34] which must have had a far-reaching effect on ocean-going ships in the west. Scandinavian tradition emphasizes the effect of the policy of King Harold the Fair-haired (died *c*. 945)[35] who from his original kingdom of Vestfold in the south-east of Norway aimed at uniting the whole country under his rule. Many independent rulers emigrated to win for themselves land elsewhere, especially in Iceland, the Faroes and the Northern Isles of Britain.

The Celts themselves must have been intrepid seafarers for, as we shall see (p. 235 below) the Irish monk and scholar Dicuil, who wrote the treatise *De Mensura Orbis* about the year 825, probably in Iona, speaks of islands, probably the Faroes, in the ocean to the north of Britain, which had been inhabited by Irish anchorites for about a century, but had become deserted owing to Viking raids. He also refers to the island of *Thile* (evidently *Thule*, Iceland)[36] which had been described to him about thirty years earlier by priests who had spent some months there. Later, when the Norsemen settled in Iceland in the late ninth century, they found certain Irish hermits still living there whom the Norsemen called *papar* (literally 'priests').[37]

In all probability the ultimate causes of the avalanche from the north on the British Isles were external. Of these the first was the disappearance of the Pictish fleet from northern waters. Gildas spoke of the attacks of the Picts on southern Britain in Roman times (cf. p. 50 above). We know from Adamnán that in the sixth century the Orkneys were ruled by a *subregulus* under Brude, the powerful king of the Northern Picts, who evidently held supreme power throughout the Hebrides – a hegemony which can only have rested on his fleet. In the west this may have been threatened by new Celtic fleets, for we have seen that already by the fifth century seafarers had established the kingdom of Dál Riata in western Scotland from their home in northern Ireland, and we have traced the importance of their fleet after the establishment of the kingdom in Scotland. The *Annals of Ulster* record an expedition (*fecht*) to the Orkneys by Aedán mac Gabráin *c*. 580 from Scottish Argyll. The Pictish power in the west was now challenged. In the east the seas were policed in the seventh and eighth centuries by the Frisians, who doubtless restricted the Picts to northern waters, and thereby curtailed their power. It may be taken as certain that the destruction of the power of the Frisians by Charles Martel in 734, and their final subjugation by Charlemagne, gave the freedom of the seas to the Vikings in southern waters.

But long before the Viking Age[38] the settlement of the Scottish Islands had taken place on a wide scale, partly it would seem by peaceful penetration. The family of Rögnvaldr, Earl of Möre, a large province in western Norway, south of Trondhjem, settled in the *Northreyjar*, 'the Northern Isles', i.e. Orkney and Shetland, probably as early as *c*. 860, and the Earldom of Orkney and the *Northreyjar* became their hereditary possession.[39] From there the kingdom spread over the whole of northern Scotland, and the power and wealth of its court is attested by the number of *skalds* or 'poets' who thronged to the court, and whose panegyric and elegiac poems have formed the basis of the historical sagas of the Orkney jarls – the *jarlasaga*, incorporated into the *Orkneyinga Saga*.[40] This great earldom was the key to the Viking world in the west, and it was only a matter of time before dreams of expansion and permanent rule led them to hopes of Ireland. Nothing less than such a dream accounts for the sagas and poems, and for the whole picture of the Battle of Clontarf[41] as the death of Viking hopes in Ireland. But this is to reach the Celtic winning post before we have made the start. A long and bitter agony was to intervene.

The earliest of the Norwegian Kingdoms in the British Isles probably dates from still earlier times. It consisted of a kingdom comprising the Hebrides, known as the *Suthreyjar*, the 'Southern Isles' (later *Sodor*) to distinguish them from the *Northreyjar*, and it included also the Isle of Man. The precise date and origin of the Hebridean kingdom are unknown,[42] but from the number of Norse place-names it seems likely that already in early times a gradual Norse infiltration had penetrated into a basic Celtic population.[43] The Celtic people and the Norsemen had lived side by side in the Hebrides for many centuries. The Gaelic dialects of the Northern Outer Hebrides had Norse elements from about AD 800,[44] and the people of the Hebrides were recognized during the Viking Age as a distinct people with the name *Gall-Ghaedhil* (literally 'Foreign-Irish') to distinguish them from the original Gaelic population.

We know that this did not prevent the churches – Iona, and probably Eigg[45] and the Faroes[46] – from being among the victims of the earliest Viking raids; and in the ninth century our internal history of the Hebridean kingdom is limited to families who migrated to Iceland.[47] From the intervening position of the Inner Hebrides, between the Earldom of Orkney and Ireland, we may suppose that the Kingdom of the Hebrides was probably in some measure dependent on the Earls of Orkney. This would account for the sparsity of Hebridean records and for the apparent absence of a central court with a body of panegyric poets. On the other hand no Hebridean contingent is recorded among the followers of Earl Sigurðr of Orkney at the Battle of Clontarf in 1014, while a Hebridean kingdom, centred in the Isle of Lewis, was operating in western Ireland in the thick of the Viking onslaught. The Isle of Lewis was more Norse than any other part of the Hebrides or of Gaelic Scotland elsewhere, and the density of Norse place-names is greater in Lewis than in any other part of Celtic speaking Scotland.[48]

The fiercest impact of the Viking attacks on Celtic lands was on Ireland. In the early ninth century it had brought the age of the

Saints to an end, first by destroying the island sanctuaries on a wide scale, notably Inishmurray off the Sligo Coast, and Skellig Michael off the Kerry Coast, and the islands at the mouth of Wexford Harbour, and also the monastic coastal settlements and headlands, such as the famous Monastery of St Comgall at Bangor, Co. Down. By a swift crescendo in the same century these sudden and devastating plundering raids were followed by penetrating incursions into the interior, where bases were established for raiding inland.

In this early period the Norwegians were the leading Viking power in the attacks: the front door into Ireland was Limerick, and the Shannon the chief waterway leading to the north and east. Fleets were stationed on Lough Neagh and Lough Ree, whence the great religious centre of Armagh was annexed and desecrated, and the western monasteries of Clonmacnoise, Clonfert and Terryglas, were burnt. It was from the west that the chief raids first penetrated to Leinster and the east coast, and it seems that the Kingdom of the Hebrides, more specifically the Kingdom of Lewis, may have been the immediate basis for this western thrust into the heart of Ireland in the first half of the ninth century. In the latter half of the tenth century, when the Limerick Vikings were expanding into a realm wholly independent of Dublin, and concentrating their activities on forming their own colonies in Munster, their immediate connexion with the Outer Hebrides is demonstrated, at least in Irish tradition, by reference to a certain Morann, son of 'the sea-king of Lewis', who is said to have been killed in Limerick in battle against the Irish, while the recurrence of the names *Manus* (Old Norse *Magnus*), and *Somarlid* (O.N. *Sumarliði*) in both royal families suggests close connexion, possibly intermarriage, even possibly a double kingdom.

Throughout the ninth and tenth centuries Norse colonization continued on a wide scale, and proceeded to spread along the east and south coasts. Dublin had been fortified in 841, and Norse sea-port towns were founded in Wicklow, Wexford, Waterford, and Cork. In the tenth century each had its own independent king and was prepared to make independent alliances, whether by marriage or for plundering raids, with their own people or with the Irish chieftains indifferently. No central government existed, whether of the Irish or the Norsemen; but about the middle of the ninth century a resistance movement led to a series of Irish victories and the Norwegian supremacy crumbled. Simultaneously a great Danish fleet arrived in the east, probably from England, and captured Dublin, while their leader defeated the Norwegians in a great battle following their landing at Carlingford Lough. In the third phase of the Viking occupation which followed, the basis of operations was in the east and the attacks came from the Irish Sea.

The course of events which follows suggests that the main objective of the Danes was the destruction of the Norwegian power in Ireland, and it has even been suggested that they were hired by the Irish as mercenaries with this end in view. It is not easy to see a sound economic basis for such a supposition, but undoubtedly Leinster combined forces with the Danes now and with the Norse later at Clontarf, in pursuance of their ancient enmity against Meath. The Danes evidently had a formidable fleet, but in 852 (recte 853) the *Annals of Ulster* record the arrival of Amlaim (Norse *Ólafr*), the son of the king of Lochlann[49] (possibly *Ólafr* 'the White'), who regained possession of Dublin. Again s.a. 870 (recte 871) the same annals record how Ólafr and Imar (Norse *Ívarr*) came again to Dublin from 'Alba'. These two Norwegian leaders together made Dublin the chief Viking centre in Ireland, and the base for their fleet, operating against the coasts of the surrounding countries. The arrival of Ólafr from Lochlann close on the Danish victory in 854, is only one of a number of indications that the Norwegian settlements in Ireland were a part of a deliberate policy of expansion and colonization from south-western Norway.

The arrival of Ólafr and Ívarr and the establishment of their base about the middle of the ninth century again shifted the balance of power, and for some forty years Ireland seems to have been free from further invasions, though the two Norse leaders plundered the grave mounds and sanctuaries, sometimes with the help of the Irish local rulers. The help may have been given under duress, and the Norwegian rulers must have been forced to find gold to pay their followers, if they were to maintain their newly-won lands in the British Isles. It was during the closing years of the ninth century and the opening years of the tenth that the Danes were establishing their kingdom in Northumbria and East Anglia. The danger to the Norwegian kingdom of Dublin from the east was a very real one.

Ólafr sought to meet it by attacks from Scotland. In 866 he invaded Fortrenn and pillaged this, the most southerly of the Pictish provinces. The *Annals of Ulster* tell us that in 869 (recte 870), the two kings of the Norsemen (*duo reges Normannorum*), i.e. the two rulers of Dublin, overcame the great rock citadel of Dumbarton, which gave them control of the entrance to the Clyde and to Strathclyde and Cumbria to the south. The destruction of Dumbarton is also recorded in the *Annales Cambriae* s.a. 870. This may have been merely a precautionary measure, for its does not appear that the monastery of Hoddom in Dumfriesshire was desecrated, while in 875 both Strathclyde and Galloway were harried from the Tyne.

In general the poverty of Wales and her mountainous interior gave her some immunity from any permanent occupation by the Vikings, though small Scandinavian colonies existed in South Wales.[50] It was inevitable, nevertheless, that Anglesey, the 'granary of Wales', should be devastated by the 'Black Gentiles', as the *Annales Cambriae* tell us, s.a. 853 (recte 855), doubtless under their leader Gormr, who is believed to have led the great Danish fleet to victory against the Norse forces in Ireland at Carlingford Lough, and probably the Danish force which had sacked Paris and held Charles the Bald and his Frankish realm in terror. In the year following the devastation of Anglesey, however, Gormr was slain, and the relief to the tension is echoed, not only in the Irish Annals, but, it would seem, on the Continent, to judge from eulogies on a certain *Roricus* – in all probability Rhodri Mawr – composed at the court of Charles the Bald himself (cf. p. 153 above).

The Isle of Man is exceptionally rich in Viking remains, including a wealth of runic inscriptions, and it is just about the period of Norse supremacy in Ireland – the middle of the ninth century – that the first permanent Norse settlements seem to have been established. It is believed that the starting point was Dublin, especially after the expulsion of a large number of Norsemen recorded by *A.U.* s.a. 901 (recte 902); but the Hebrides and Galloway probably contributed, for again the strong hand of the Orkney earldom shows itself when the Isle of Man was eventually conquered by Sigurðr the Stout, Earl of Orkney, the romantic owner of the famous raven banner, who perished at the Battle of Clontarf in 1014. The conquest of Man was undoubtedly a factor in his ambitious project of a southern kingdom, a western parallel to Normandy. The opening of the Manx historical period may be said to begin with the Viking conquest, for in later times the island came into the possession of Godred Crovan, a

Hebridean (King *Gorry* or '*Orry*' of Manx tradition), and his successors were known as kings of 'Man and the Isles' till the cession of the island in 1266. But although under Norse rule, and with a heavy Norse intake of immigrants, it remained, like Ireland, a Celtic country and a Celtic-speaking island to the end – even to our own life-time. It was, in fact, the last Viking kingdom to survive in our islands with a Celtic-speaking population.

In 902 Dublin was retrieved by the Irish and many of the *gennti* (foreigners, Vikings)were expelled. It may have been as a result of this resistance movement that about this period, and perhaps under these conditions, an unchronicled major settlement of Cumberland[51] and Lancashire[52] took place on a scale amounting to an invasion, though no records of conflict entered our annals. Our evidence comes chiefly from place-names, which suggest a Norwegian population with a strong Celtic element in their language. They practised agriculture on an intensive system, and have left Norse place-names almost to the exclusion of any others along the Lancashire coast, between the sea and the foot-hills of the Pennines from the Dee northwards. The villages seem to be the homes of squatters, draining and cultivating small patches of unwanted land which has become in consequence jet black and richly fertile, and these villages are so close to one another that a day's walk, even today, will cover an area of villages with purely Norse names without a single intervening Saxon name – Ainsdale, Birkdale, Meols Cop, Blowick, Scarisbrick, Bescar, Ormskirk, Burscough, Hoscar, Skelmersdale. The Saxons seem to have occupied the river banks and, still more, the higher and drier land between the Viking squatters and the hills, and here the names again reveal the settlement plan – Preston, Rufford, Whalley, Churchtown, Croston, Eccleston, Wrightington, Worthington, Shevington, Parbold, Appley Bridge. And the Saxon dairy farms have left traces of their summer pastures and transhumance in the hill country on the sunny, western slopes of the Pennine foot-hills. The absence of a written record in chronicle or annals is probably due to the fact that no wealthy monasteries with scriptoria had been established in north-west England. Burscough Priory near Wigan was not founded until *c.* 1190 and was an inconsiderable foundation.

The silence of our records on the extensive Norse settlements on the east of the Irish Sea helps us to realize that the picture of the Viking Age in Ireland is an exclusively monastic record. The monasteries, by their concentration and wealth, were the agonized victims of armed raiders. The record which they have left is unfortunately only too true. In the early stages of the invasions it may indeed be the whole of the truth. In Brittany we know that the monastery of St Méen in the Forest of Broceliande was especially favoured and developed to serve as a refuge for the bishops of Dol from Viking attacks.

In 919 Dublin was recaptured, and Niall Glúndub, with twelve other kings and those who formed the core of the resistance movement, lost their lives, though the northern Uí Néill continued to put up a brave resistance. It was in the period immediately following that the Vikings developed the sea-port towns. Dublin grew in importance and was strengthened by closer intercourse with the Danish kingdom of York. Limerick, hostile and governed independently, probably by its original dynasty, consolidated its colonies in Munster. But towards the close of the century a certain Cellachán (d. 954), a ruler of the Eóganacht dynasty of Cashel, put new life into the Irish resistance, while in western Munster Dál Cais on the borders of Co. Clare was able to enlist the help of Connacht against the Limerick Vikings. By the middle of the tenth century the supremacy had passed from the Eóganacht dynasty of Cashel to Cennétig, the ruler of Dál Cais, and his two sons Mathgamain and Brian Bórama were strong enough to lead the offensive against the Vikings which culminated in the great Battle of Clontarf in 1014 and the end of the Viking supremacy in Ireland.

The importance of the Battle of Clontarf is sometimes disputed. The issue was by no means clear cut between the Irish and the Norse. Sihtric, the Norse king of Dublin, took no part in the conflict. In pursuit of their traditional jealousy of Meath, Leinster supported the Dublin Vikings, and the Limerick Vikings, always hostile to the Dublin dynasty, seem to have been on Brian's side. Even the Irish victory was marred by the death of Brian; and although the battle concluded as an undoubted Irish victory the break was not sudden and complete. The Norse settlements lived on under their own institutions, and even carried on trade with the English ports on the Bristol Channel. Moreover two centuries of adjustment in a small country had tended to bring the two peoples closer together. Frequent intermarriage and the conversion of many of the leading Norsemen in Dublin to Christianity, including Ólafr Cuarán and his son Sihtric 'Silken-beard', indicate the sympathy which had been growing between them. Brian had married Sihtric's mother, and perhaps gave his own daughter to Sihtric in exchange. The leading bards of the Irish and Norse courts were fraternizing. The true fundamental significance of Clontarf lay in the death of Sigurðr the Stout, the great Orkney Jarl, bearing with him into the battle 'his own devil' – the ill-omened raven banner; for the death of the Orkney Earl put to an end to the supreme effort of the Norwegians to annex and exploit Ireland as another Normandy.

It was this ultimate spiritual, rather than the immediate political, effect of the battle which gave it unparalleled importance at the time. In communities where the spoken word rather than written propaganda is widely influential, the contemporary bards and saga tellers are the most trustworthy witnesses for the impact of contemporary events on the people living at the time. For scholars sifting evidence a thousand years later the emotion and the significance have become clouded. The Battle of Clontarf inspired in Irish and Norse alike both poetry and saga. To the Norse poets and saga-tellers particularly, the battle was fought not only by the Irish and the Norsemen, but between supernatural powers of the air. The old saga convention of the *Battle of Allen*, where the issue is fought out between St Bridget and Columcille, here reappears. Men throughout the Celtic world saw dreams and portents, while a man in Caithness beheld the ghastly vision of supernatural women weaving the great web of battle on a loom of slaughter, where men's heads were the weights, men's entrails the warp and woof.[53] In Ireland the prose narrative 'The War of the Irish and the Foreigners'[54] is imbued with emotion and picturesque quality equalled elsewhere only in the saga of the *Battle of Allen*, and with a rhetoric even more hectic in its excited flow. Probably no battle ever fought in north-western Europe has inspired such a glowing celebration in the poetry and prose of its own day.

There could be no going back. The Viking régime had brought changes in the economic life and institutions of the country which were fundamental. They had dreamed of settling in a pastoral country with a rich internal food-producing economy, self-supporting, and free from external commitments, and with an ancient, unquestioned system of inheritance and government more practical and dependable than any theoretical legislative system which could be readily devised. The Norse tenure had proved precarious, their dreams fallacious. The dispersed and elementary and conservative life of the ancient Celtic Iron Age, which was still the economic basis of life in Ireland, defeated the centralizing methods of the new-comers whose only chance of survival in a new land was in concentration.

Ireland had had no towns as we understand the term. Her royal raths – Tara, Cruachain, Emain – were more like permanent camps than royal cities and centres of bureaucratic government. She had no sea-ports. The Vikings gave her her coast-line, with development of harbours and town life, especially in the cities of Limerick, Dublin, Waterford, Wexford and Cork. It is a matter of common knowledge that the Irish terminology of ship-building and trade, and of their accompanying weights and measures, consists largely of Scandinavian borrowings. The first coinage struck in Ireland was that of the Viking kingdom of Dublin. It was no fault of the Vikings that Ireland did not become a commercial nation. They at least brought her into the orbit of the commercial world which they knew. And there they left her.

The influence of the Viking régime on the internal economy of Ireland is more subtle and more difficult to assess owing to the extreme conservatism of the Irish tradition embodied in the surviving written texts. This conservatism is especially remarkable in the Irish law-texts which were treated by the jurists as inviolable, and preserved with so great a fidelity that it is possible to trace, not only the original medium of oral tradition from which the written texts are derived, but even, in places, the oral poetical form in which they had been transmitted through centuries (cf. p. 259 below). Unlike the Welsh laws, which received certain modifications owing to the influence of their Anglo-Saxon neighbours, the Irish laws had never been subjected to serious modification from neighbouring peoples. Clearly changes were inevitable under the impact of a foreign occupation, and as early as the tenth century, radical changes had come about. Indeed the challenge which the Norse occupation offered to the traditional order of Irish society has been described as 'a watershed in the history of Irish institutions'.

Thus, indirectly, the Vikings brought it about that the Irish kings entered into the fellowship of those whose genius entitled them, each after each, to gather their people into a nation – Charlemagne in 800; Rhodri Mawr c. 850; Kenneth mac Alpin about the middle of the ninth century; Alfred the Great shortly before 900; and last of all, Brian. Thus tardily and under Viking pressure the little off-shore island was brought into the political development of the western continental world.

The damage done to the artistic and intellectual life of Ireland was great. Both had been dependent on the monastic centres which had fostered them and inspired and stimulated them. Many of the monasteries had been burnt and pillaged and their treasures scattered, and many of the scriptoria with all their inherited traditions and techniques, all their mastery of the art of superb manuscript illumination, had been destroyed. The loss was incalculable and much of it irrecoverable. High creative art, like high intellectual achievement, can only flourish in an atmosphere of security. The monasteries were always dependent on the support of the governing chiefs. The chiefs themselves, however, were less liable to be pillaged than the wealthy monastic foundations. They were in a large measure necessary to the very subsistence of the invaders, who were themselves non-productive and depended on the traditional native Irish pastoral economy and the organized food-producing powers exercised by the native chiefs. They and their heirs survived, and so eventually the great monasteries revived and lived again. It is a remarkable fact that the period immediately following on the Viking occupation was so productive of artistic works, especially in metal, that it has been claimed as something of a Renaissance.[55] Here also the Viking influence contributed something, not only stimulating and revivifying, but even bringing in new artistic motifs.

The ravaging of the monasteries drove many of the monks overseas, and the lasting gain to European scholarship which resulted from their inclusion in continental monasteries[56] and their influence on European scholarship is widely recognized.[57] This movement of Irish, and indeed of Welsh scholars also,[58] to the Continent is no new thing. It was probably known to Notker Balbulus in the time of Charlemagne. The *Gesta Caroli Magni* tell of the arrival of extremely learned Irish monks who had come with some 'British merchants' to Gaul, and who were welcomed by Charlemagne and entrusted with the education of the young nobility. One of these scholars remained in Gaul, the other resided in the monastery of St Augustine in Pavia in Italy.[59] The *Anglo-Saxon Chronicle* records (s.a. 891) the arrival in a curragh on the coast of Cornwall of three Irish monks who at once went to King Alfred's Court. Aethelweard adds[60] that they then went to Rome, intending to go to Jerusalem. The entry in the *Anglo-*

Saxon Chronicle does not state that they were scholars, but a later addition to the text adds that Swifneh, 'the greatest scholar in Ireland died'. He has been identified[61] with Suibhne mac Maíle Humai, anchorite and scribe of the Abbey of Clonmacnoise on the Shannon, whose obit appears in this same year in the *Annals of Ulster* s.a. 890 (recte 891). His tombstone, now lost,[62] was still extant at Clonmacnoise in Petrie's time,[63] and the spelling of his name in the *Anglo-Saxon Chronicle* makes it clear that the chronicler received the name in an oral form. The notice of Suibhne's death was almost certainly brought by the three pilgrims.

It is surely an error to suppose, as is commonly done, that the Irish monks took their books with them when fleeing from Ireland during the Viking raids. This was undoubtedly done in some cases, but circumstances of travel at that time would certainly preclude the removal of monastic libraries to the continent on a large scale. The great gift of the monks to the continental centres, as innumerable references make clear, is their intellectual capital, which they had acquired in Irish monastic centres, of which Clonmacnoise was the most notable example in the west, as Bangor in Co. Down was in the east. The wanton destruction of the monastic libraries, especially through fire and exposure to weather, must have been enormous; but effective efforts to save them must have been chiefly made by hiding them near at hand. It is in no way surprising to find little topical occasional poems inspired by the Viking Terror, like the one expressive of the comfort to be derived from stormy weather which would prevent a Viking raid from the sea:

> Bitter is the wind tonight,
> It tosses the ocean's white hair:
> Tonight I fear not the fierce warriors of Norway
> Coursing on the Irish sea.[64]

NOTES

1 The reference occurs in a stanza of a Welsh poem in the *Gododdin* (cf. p. 269) and is believed to be a later interpolation.
2 The derivation appears to be *ath* – with the sense of Latin *re*, denoting repetition – and *Fótla*, one of the names of Ireland. See Watson, *C.P.S.*, 228 f.
3 For the evidence see O'Rahilly, *E.I.H.M.*, 371.
4 Skene, *C.S.* I, 305 f.

5 An eleventh-century Irish scholar, a synchronist and historian.
6 Edited and translated by K. Jackson, S.H.R., XXXVI (1957), 125 ff.
7 For the text see Skene, *P. and S.*, 209, cf. *ibid.*, *C.S.*, I, 306.
8 K. H. Jackson, 'Common Gaelic, The Evolution of the Irish Language', P.B.A., XXXVII (1951).
9 See Skene, *C.S.* I, 302; cf. Chadwick, *E.S.*, 10 and *passim*.
10 On the date of Merfyn's accession see J. E. Lloyd, *H.W.* I, 231; cf. also *ibid.*, 224, n. 145.
11 Lloyd believed that with the accession of Merfyn Vrych in 825 'a stranger possessed himself of the throne of Gwynedd and of the royal seat of Aberffraw'. See however N. K. Chadwick in *S.E.B.C.*, 74 ff.
12 Cf. Chadwick, *E.S.*, 146.
13 Whitley Stokes equated the name of Merfyn's father *Gureat* (recorded in the *Hanes Gruffydd ap Cynan*) with L. *Vireatus*; cf. further Jackson, *L.H.E.B.*, 345. Skene identified the name with the Pictish Ferat (*F.A.B.W.I.*, p. 94).
14 See J. Rhŷs, 'A Welsh Inscription in the Isle of Man', ZCP, I (1897), p. 48 f., with plate of *Crux Guriat*.
15 Skene regarded the expression *dir Manaw* as more applicable to the 'land' (*dir*, *tir*) at the head of the Firth of Forth (*F.A.B.W.*, I, p. 94); but see Bromwich, *Triads*, p. 396.
16 The reading of the MS makes the precise relationship here uncertain.
17 For a fuller notice of the letter and cryptogram, and references, see N. K. Chadwick, *S.E.B.C.*, 94 ff.
18 For a fuller study of the intellectual level and contacts of the court of Gwynedd at this period, with full references, see N. K. Chadwick, *S.E.B.C.*, p. 29 ff.
19 Chadwick, *G.L.* I, 146 ff.
20 N. K. Chadwick, *S.E.B.C.*, 46 ff.
21 See the MS in Jesus College, Oxford, XX, Pedigree 20. This account, harmonizing with MS Harleian 3859 in the British Museum, is to be preferred to the one which reverses matters and makes Nest the mother of Merfyn, and Ethyllt his wife.
22 See Lloyd *H.W.* I, 325, n. 17.
23 See Lloyd *H.W.* I, 325.
24 See Wade-Evans, *V.S.B.G.* genealogy I.
25 On the bearing of Rhodri's victory on events at Liège, and on the odes, see N. K. Chadwick, *S.E.B.C.*, 83 f.
27 So MS A.; but MS B has *frater*, so also the *Brut y Tywysogyon*, MSS. *Peniarth* 20; and *Red Book of Hergest*. See the editions by Thomas Jones, Cardiff, 1952 and 1955 respectively.
27 See Lloyd, *H.W.* I, 326 and n. 27.
28 This pedigree was published from Jesus College (Oxford) MS 20 by E. Phillimore, *Y Cymmrodor*, Vol. VIII (1887).

29 Edited by Sir Ifor Williams (Cardiff, 1955).

30 See Asser's *Life of King Alfred*, cap. 79, edited by W. H. Stevenson, new impression with article on recent work by D. Whitelock (Oxford, 1959).

31 On this annal, and the identity of Swifneh, see Plummer's note *ad loc. T.S.C.* II, p. 105.

32 Plummer understands this to refer in general to the Cornishmen. See *T.S.C.* II, p. 452 s.v. *West Wealas*. This interpretation seems to me improbable in this context however; cf. further Plummer's note, p. 135 f.

33 C. J. S. Marstrander, *Bidrag til det norske sprogs historie i Irland* (Kristiania, 1915), p. 56 ff. cf. also A. Bugge, *Contributions to the History of the Norsemen in Ireland* (Christiania, 1900), 4.

34 A. Brøgger and H. Shetelig, *The Viking Ships* (Oslo, 1951), 52 ff.

35 On Harold's dates see G. Turville-Petre, *The Heroic Age of Scandinavia* (London, 1951), 116.

36 For two important articles on Dicuil and his work see M. Esposito in *D.R.*, Vol. 137 (1905), 327 ff.; *Studies*, Vol. III (1914), 651 ff.

37 The account is given in the Icelandic Preface to the *Íslands Landnámabók* ('The Book of the Settlement of Iceland'), part of which dates from the twelfth century, and is on the whole accepted as a source of high authenticity.

38 On the early dating of the settlements in the Northern Isles see A. Bugge, *Vesterlandenes Indflydelse i Vikingtiden* (Christiania, 1905); A. W. Brøgger, *Ancient Emigrants* (Oxford, 1929); T. D. Kendrick, *History of the Vikings* (London, 1930); H. Marwick, *Orkney* (London, 1951), 36.

39 See H. Shetelig, *V.A.G.B.I.*, Part I (Oslo, 1946), 22 ff. Cf. H. Koht, *Inhogg og Utsyn i Norsk Historie* (Kristiania, 1921), 34.

40 See *The Orkneyinga Saga* edited by S. Nordal (Copenhagen, 1916); translation and study of the saga by A. B. Taylor (Edinburgh, 1938); translation and a valuable introductory study by Vígfússon in the Rolls Series, Vol. I, 1887; Vol. II, 1894.

41 For a general account of the battle see 'The Battle of Clontarf' by the Rev. John Ryan, J.R.S.A.I., Vol. VIII, 7th Series (1938), 1 ff.

42 For a general account see E. MacNeill 'The Norse Kingdom of the Hebrides'. S.R. XXXIX (1916) 254 ff.

43 See R. L. Brenner, *Saga-Book of the Viking Club* III (1902-4), 373.

44 M. Oftedal, 'Norse Place-names in Celtic Scotland', *Proceedings of the International Congress of Celtic Studies* (Dublin, 1962), 48.

45 See A. Sommerfelt, *De Norsk-irske Bystaters Undergang* 1169-71 (*Avhandlinger utgitt av det Norske Videnskaps-Akademi i Oslo* II. Hist. Filos. Klasse 1957, No. 4), 5.

46 See p. 158 above. Dicuil reports these islands as deserted in his day (the early ninth century) owing to Viking raids (*causa latronum nortmannorum*).

47 See Shetelig, *V.A.G.B.I.*, 31.
48 M. Oftedal, *op. cit.*, 44f.
49 i.e. Rogaland, an early kingdom in western Norway.
50 For Viking activities in Wales see B. G. Charles, *Old Norse Relations with Wales* (Cardiff, 1934). See further Melville Richards, 'Norse Place-names in Wales', *I.C.C.S.*, 51 ff.
51 See B. Dickins, *The Place-names of Cumberland*, Vol. III (Cambridge, 1952), p. xiii.
52 See an important paper by F. T. Wainwright, 'The Scandinavians in Lancashire', T.L.C.A.S. LVIII (1945–6), p. 71 ff., and the references there cited. Cf. also Ekwall, 'The Scandinavians and Celts in the North-West of England' (London, 1918); *Place-names of Lancashire* (Manchester, 1922).
53 This forms the subject of the Norse skaldic poem, the *Darratharljóth*, edited and translated by N. K. Chadwick in *Anglo-Saxon and Norse Poems* (Cambridge, 1922), 111 ff.
54 *C.G.G.*, edited and translated by J. H. Todd (London, 1867).
55 Cf. F. Henry, 'The Effects of the Viking Invasions on Irish Art', in *I.C.C.S.*, p. 61 ff.
56 See Zimmer, *Keltische Beiträge*, III, 108.
57 For an excellent general account of Irish scholars on the Continent from the eighth to the tenth centuries, and their sojourn and work in Continental monasteries, see L. Bieler, *Ireland*, 65 ff. See further J. M. Clark, *A.S.G.*, 18–54, especially p. 33. Cf. further for St Gall, J. F. Kenney, *Sources*, 594.
58 See Clark, *A.S.G.*, 30; cf. also Chadwick, *S.C.B.C.*, 94 ff.
59 See Clark, *loc. cit.*
60 See D. Whitelock, *A-S.C.*, p. 53.
61 C. Plummer, *T.S.C.*, Vol. II, p. 105.
62 See Pádraig Leonard, 'Early Irish Grave-Slabs', P.R.I.A. Vol. 61, Section C, No. 5 (1961), 161.
63 See Petrie, *The Round Towers of Ireland*, p. 328 where a wood-cut of the tomb-stone with Suibhne's name occurs.
64 English translation by Kuno Meyer, *A.I.P.*, 101 (new edition 1959).

7

Celtic Religion and Mythology and the Literature of the Otherworld

The Celtic world is exceptionally rich in memories of religion, mythology and the supernatural. In Gaul religious life was evidently very intense (cf. p. 28 above). Ireland has preserved the richest store of mythological traditions of any country north of the Alps, not even excepting Iceland. Yet the evidence for the supernatural conceptions for these two Celtic realms is somewhat paradoxical, and disparate. Gaul has much to tell us of the religion of the Celts. We have already seen in chapter 1 that memories of the ancient Gaulish gods and spirits have survived in innumerable dedications at local sanctuaries of rivers and springs, sacred lakes and forests. Many records have survived in the writings of Classical authors, in place-names, and in material remains in metal-work, in coins and inscriptions. Native Celtic temples of the late Classical period have been excavated, and statuary in both wood and stone now witnesses to a native Gaulish conception of the gods in human form at least from early in our era. Our knowledge of religion in Gaul as a living belief and practice is therefore considerable.

On the other hand in Gaul, as in ancient Greece and the Teutonic world, there is no close connexion between religion and mythology, as the mythology has come to us in later and more fully developed stages. Mythology is always to some extent an artificial creation, an artistic expression of religious emotions or beliefs which are in the nature of things formless. Mythology is, in fact, an attempt to define the infinite and the indefinable, and what it offers is not a definition but a symbol. The mythology of the Gauls, the artistic symbolism of their religion, has not survived, owing to the fact that no Gaulish literature has survived. Their oral traditions, including their mythology, were never written down. As a result of the Roman conquest Gaul rapidly adopted Roman culture, including the art of writing, and the oral traditions died quickly.

In contrast to this, the oral literature of ancient Ireland, including the mythological traditions, survived, as we have seen, till a much later period. The archaism of Irish culture, virtually untouched by Roman culture till nearly half a millennium later than Gaul, preserved its oral traditions intact, including its mythological traditions, till the art and fashion of writing had become general in the Christian monastic *scriptoria*, from the sixth century AD onwards. The heathen religion was by this time a thing of the far past, and the Christian monasteries had no will to record it. For Gaul we have a wealth of evidence for Celtic religion but no developed system of mythology. For Ireland we have a wealth of mythological tradition in a highly developed literary form, but practically no evidence directly bearing on heathen religion.

Yet the hiatus is more apparent than real. Celtic Britain forms a bridge between the two Celtic realms of Gaul and Ireland. In material remains she has much in common with Gaul from which she has been directly influenced; in mythological traditions she has retained fragments which can be shown to be identical in origin with those of Ireland. Owing to the Roman conquest of Britain both material remains and mythological traditions are relatively sparse; but they are both relevant and valid, and we shall refer to them briefly here, to demonstrate both the fundamental unity of Celtic religion and mythology and also the essential unity of the Celtic realms in their heathen spiritual life.

In tracing the unity between the continental religion and mythology of Gaul and their remains in the insular Celtic countries to the west we find links in the traditions of sacred islands off the Atlantic coast of Britain and Ireland – links which also remind us of earlier Greek stories of the 'Islands of the Blest' west of the Pillars of Hercules, and the magic island of Circe in the western seas. These sacred islands have a continuous history from the time of Homer to the Age of the Saints, when they were used as sanctuaries for Christian anchorites. Strabo (IV. iv. 6), writing in the first century BC, reports on the authority of Posidonius that a community of women occupied a small island off the mouth of the Loire, from which men were excluded, though the women crossed the sea to join their husbands from time to time and then returned. Once a year it was their custom to remove the roof of the temple of their god and to cover it again the same day. Should one of them let fall the materials she was carrying she was at once torn to pieces by her companions. The Irish *immrama* (cf. p. 241 below), some of which describe islands occupied solely by women, are hardly more remarkable than this ancient Gaulish tradition.

In the first century AD the Roman geographer, Pomponius Mela, speaks of nine priestesses called *Gallizenae*[1] under a vow of perpetual virginity on the island of Sena (the modern Île de Sein) within sight of the south-western tip of Brittany. They possessed magical powers, could raise storms, change at will into animal forms, cure the sick, and foretell the future to sailors who came to consult them. We shall find a meteorological station similarly credited in Irish mythological tradition to the god Manannán mac Lir in the Isle of Man. Again Plutarch, writing *c*. 83 AD, speaks of a certain Demetrius who had reported that among the islands lying near Britain many were isolated and had few or no inhabitants, and some bore the names of gods or heroes. He had voyaged to the nearest of these which had only a few inhabitants, holy men held inviolate by the Britons. Soon after his arrival a violent storm had arisen which the inhabitants told him signified the passing of the mightier ones.[2] Plutarch also informs us that in that part of the world – 'five days off from Britain' – there is one island in which Cronus is confined, guarded in his sleep by Briareus; for his sleep has been devised as a control for him, and around him are many demigods as his attendants and servants.[3] The identity of Demetrius is uncertain, but he is believed to have been a native of Tarsus, a literary man sent by the Emperor Domitian on some mission to Britain – probably the Demetrius who dedicated two bronze tablets with Greek inscriptions, now in York Museum.[4]

As late as the sixth century AD the Byzantine writer Procopius has left us a remarkable echo of the Western World as the last home of the traditions of the Celtic lands of the Continent. He tells us that the people of Armorica had the task of conducting the souls of the dead to our island. In the middle of the night they heard a knocking on the door, and a low voice called them. Then they went to the sea-shore without knowing what force drew them there. There they found boats which seemed empty, but which were so laden with the souls

175

of the dead that their gunwhales scarcely rose above the waves. In less than an hour they reached the end of their voyage, and there in the island of Britain they saw no-one, but they heard a voice which numbered the passengers, calling each by his own name. Breton folk-lore has located the place of departure as the Baie des Depassés on the south-western tip of Brittany.[5]

The basic facts of the religion of the continental Celts have already been stated in chapter 1, and need not be repeated here. Here we shall confine ourselves to a brief summary of the corresponding features of Celtic religion in Britain, and to a somewhat fuller picture of one or two Gaulish cults which Classical authors have recorded in some detail in their native setting. It is hoped that in this way the essential unity of Gaulish and British religion will be made clear, and a background established for the development of the Celtic mythological literature recorded from the western Celts, especially from Ireland.

We have seen in chapter 1 that one of the most fundamental features of Gaulish religion is the wide prevalence of sanctuaries connected with natural features, especially springs, rivers, lakes and forests. The Gauls were not city dwellers, and their native sanctuaries are those of a nature religion. Strabo (IV.i.13) tells us – again on the authority of Posidonius – of a vast votive treasure of the tribe of the Volcae Tectosages which had been stored away in sacred enclosures (ἐν σηκοῖς ἀποκείμενα) and part in sacred lakes (ἐν λίμναις ἱεραῖς). He adds that there were many places where treasures of gold were stored in *Celtica*, and that heavy masses of gold and silver were submerged in lakes because there the treasure was most inviolable. This was evidently in the neighbourhood of Toulouse, where there was a great sanctuary (a 'temple', a ἱερὸν ἅγιον) containing very great treasures, for many had dedicated them and no-one dared lay hands on them. One recalls the hoard from Llyn Cerrig Bach in Anglesey recovered in 1943. The site had been part of a lake into which had been thrown a large number of weapons, chariot furniture, tools, slave-chains, portions of trumpets, cauldrons, and fragments of bronze decorated with La Tène designs. The whole is believed to have been the site of sacrificial offerings made between the mid-second century BC and the second century AD.[6]

An important sanctuary of the goddess Sequana existed from Gaulish times near the source of the Seine, and here in the marshlands numerous pieces of wooden sculpture, have recently come to

176

light, including a number of statues dating from the second century AD. The sanctuary will be discussed more fully in chapter 12 below, but here we may compare the sanctuary at the spring of the native British goddess Coventina at the Roman fort (Fort VII) of Brocolitia (Carrawburgh)[7] on the south side of Hadrian's Wall. The spring, which still bubbles up, was originally covered by a temple of Celtic type which contained a well or basin, and into this had been thrown a great number of money offerings, and, even in the fifth century, altars and sculptured tablets from the temple – perhaps by Christians.[8] Among these are a marble slab with an inscription 'to the goddess Coventina', and a bas-relief depicting Coventina herself reclining on a water-borne leaf, holding a water-plant in her right hand, and a flowing goblet in her left. One of the sculptured bas-reliefs represents three water-nymphs, each holding a vase from which an abundant stream is flowing.

The most impressive passages about the Gaulish forest sanctuaries occur in Lucan's *Pharsalia*. In l. 452 f. he refers to the Gaulish druids 'who dwell in deep groves (*nemora alta*) and sequestered uninhabited woods', and who 'practise barbarous rites and a sinister mode of worship', to which the scholiast adds:

'They worship the gods in woods without making use of temples.'[9] This reference in the *Pharsalia* to sacred woods recalls another passage in the same poem (l. 399 ff.) where Lucan relates how Caesar felled a sacred wood near Marseilles in which trunks of trees are crudely sculptured to represent gods (*simulacra maesta deorum*). Here, says Lucan, barbarous rites are practised in honour of the gods, and the altars are heaped with hideous offerings, and every tree is sprinkled with human blood; and he tells of the water which fell in abundance from dark springs and of the coverts where wild beasts would not lie down in this motionless thicket. A priest (*sacerdos*) officiates for the spirit of the place (*dominus loci*).

It is an eerie spot:

The people never frequented the place to worship very near it, but left it to the gods . . . The priest himself dreads the approach and fears to come upon the lord of the grove.

Even after making due allowance for Lucan's fine rhetoric in this passage we cannot doubt the existence of the sacred wood near Marseilles felled by Caesar, and the superstitious dread of the natives

177

who were called upon to cut down the trees 'untouched by men's hands from ancient times'.

In Britain our evidence for woodland sanctuaries is less ample, but Dio Cassius states that the Britons have sanctuaries (ἱερά) under Boudicca, and offer human sacrifices to the goddess of victory *Andraste* or *Andate* in a sacred wood (ἄλσος).[10] We may refer also to the groves on the island of Anglesey which Tacitus tells us[11] had been devoted to barbarous superstitions, and which were destroyed by Suetonius Paulinus shortly before AD 61 (cf. p. 44 above). The occurrence of the element *nemet* in British place-names again links up these British sanctuaries with those of Gaul (cf. p. 16). One of the most interesting of the links is a late name in the eleventh-century Breton cartulary of Quimperlé, where a forest in Finisterre is referred to thus: 'Quam vocant nemet'.[12]

We do not know when native temple structures first made their appearance in Gaul, though the new technique of the excavation of wooden remains[13] may throw light on this. A single wooden prototype of pre-Roman Iron Age temples of typical form has come to light, not in Gaul, but at Heathrow in Middlesex in Britain.[14] Caesar never mentions temples in Gaul, although Suetonius accuses him in vague terms of having robbed Gaulish *fana* and *templa*.[15] Greek and Roman writers do not use the words ναός, *aedes* to denote Celtic temples, and we have no description of Gaulish altars, for which Latin writers use the terms *arae, altaria*. During the Gallo-Roman period, however, structural sanctuaries become widespread in both Gaul and Britain, and in both countries, in Britain especially, local wayside shrines have left many traces. Certain Celtic temples in the estuary of the Rhône have been excavated. These temples will be described more fully in chapter 12 below. Here we will only mention that the porticos of the larger temples are of monumental structure, 'veritable *propylaea* of Hellenic conception', and the ambitious architecture, combined with native Celtic features, notably the cult of the human head, suggests an adaptation of Classical architectural building tradition to a Celto-Ligurian religious cult.

The structural plan of the many native Celtic stone-built temples from the Roman period in both Gaul and Britain remains constant, though there is some variety in shape. The normal form was a square box-like building consisting of a *cella* or sanctuary, sometimes raised and surrounded by a portico or verandah, which might be closed or

178

with low walls designed to carry columns. The *cella* was small, entered by a door, and lighted by small windows above the portico, and the public were evidently excluded from the *cella*. The whole was sometimes contained in a square enclosure. Both in Gaul and Britain, however, both round and polygonal temples existed while retaining the same scheme of *cella* surrounded by a peristyle.[16]

Many of the wayside shrines in Britain, which are common in the neighbourhood of Roman roads, are associated with Roman gods; but dedications to native gods are also common in Britain, especially in the north. In several cases later Roman structures have been superimposed on earlier Celtic sanctuaries. A famous example in Britain of the persistence of a native dedication is that at Gosbecks Farm near Colchester, where a Roman temple of Celtic pattern had been substituted for an original large ditch surrounding the same rectangular plot, and contained pre-Roman rubbish. Here a bronze statue of Mercury gives us the clue to the later dedication.[17] At Frilford, north-east of Abingdon, two Romanized shrines have been superimposed on an earlier wooden building which had consisted of a circular ditched enclosure containing an open wooden shed. This had been razed to the ground in the Roman period and replaced by a circular enclosure, while a new temple of the common Celtic box-like design was built beside it.[18] The sanctuary continued in use into the fifth century.

The most important native dedication of a Romano-British temple in Britain is that of Lydney on the precipitous west bank of the River Severn in Gloucestershire. It is in origin a forest sanctuary, being situated in the Forest of Dean. The god of this temple is *Nodons* or *Nodens*, who is undoubtedly Nuadu or Nuada *Argetlám*, 'Nuadu of the Silver Hand'.[19] Lydney was a therapeutic temple of Aesculapian type and a pilgrim sanctuary, and its most important period is later than 364. It is a large complex of buildings of the type of Classical sanctuaries of healing, and included a long portico like a cloister divided into compartments to accommodate the patients; a courtyard building with further apartments and a reception hall; and ample baths. It is interesting to reflect that Irish mythological tradition explains the epithet of Nodens by his having an artificial hand made of silver. The association with the Lydney therapeutic temple is clear; but Lydney was a wealthy temple and it is possible that the 'silver hand' owed its origin to the rich offerings made to the god. The name *Nuadu Argetlám* is also known to Welsh tradition as *Lludd Llaw Ereint* ('Lludd of the Silver Hand') whose daughter *Creiddylad* is the original of Shakespeare's *Cordelia*, and whose son was *Gwynn ap Nudd* (Irish *Finn*).

The local nature of most British sanctuaries and the distribution of dedications show that the religion of pre-Roman Britain, like that of pre-Roman Gaul, was essentially a nature religion.

The wide distribution of statuary, both in the round and in relief, makes it clear that the Gauls sometimes pictured their gods as human beings, though this is perhaps a relatively late development. Among statues of Gaulish gods a number occur in groups of three, that is to say triads of gods, as well as tricephalous and even bicephalous statues of native divinities, and traces of supernatural triads are also found occasionally in Britain, e.g. at Brocolitia (cf. p. 177 above). We have seen (p. 28) that Caesar has specified the names of four Roman gods whom he equated with Celtic gods, without, however, giving us any Celtic names; and we have also seen that Lucan on the other hand names three Celtic gods by their native names. These lists suggest that the particular gods in question were conceived in human form; but neither in Gaul nor in Britain have we anything suggestive of any conception of an all-powerful universal god, or on the other hand anything approaching a pantheon. In Gaul, however, certain cults have a wide distribution, and of two of the gods, Belenus and Ogmios, Roman writers have left us notices which suggest that a rich literature of the gods must have been current in Gallo-Roman circles, and has even left its impress on native art, such as frescoes and coins.

The Greek writer Lucian, who was born at Samostata on the Euphrates in the second century AD, relates that as he was travelling in Gaul, apparently in the neighbourhood of the Atlantic, he came upon a picture of an old man, clad in a lion's skin, leading a group of followers whose ears are attached to his own tongue by little gold and amber chains of great beauty and delicacy. The men are not being forced along, but follow him eagerly and heap praises on him, and it is clear that they would regret their liberty. A Greek-speaking Gaul who was standing near explained to him that the old man represents eloquence and is pictured as Heracles, clad in his lion's skin, because the Celts believe that eloquence is of greater power than physical strength, and also that eloquence attains its climax in old age. His name is Ogmios. [20] A temple to Hercules and the Muses is said to have been erected at Autun by M. Fulvius Nobilior after his capture of Ambracia in 189 BC because he had learned in Greece that Heracles was a musagetes.[21] Traces of this pictorial conception of eloquence still linger in Irish mythology and saga. Reference may be made to the entry of the 'cauldron of covetousness' in *Cormac's Glossary*, s.v. *bóige*,[22] and a passage in *Táin Bó Cualnge*[23] describing a dark man, apparently supernatural, who is carrying seven chains round his neck, to the end of which seven heads are attached. It would be interesting to know the relationship between these traditions and the designs on certain Breton gold coins which show human heads attached to a cord surrounding the large head in the main field of the coins.

We have a valuable reference to another purely native Gaulish god, Belenus, from the Gallo-Roman poet Ausonius of Bordeaux in the latter part of the fourth century. Ausonius tells us that a certain Phoebicius, grand-father of his own contemporary Delphidius, himself a famous teacher of the University of Bordeaux, had been *aedituus* or 'temple priest' of the god Belenus. Belenus is attested as the chief god of Noricum, and as highly venerated at Aquileia, where he was equated with Apollo.[24] The name is found on inscriptions in the Eastern Alps, in northern Italy and southern Gaul, and among the Ligurians. It has been suggested – quite gratuitously as it would seem – that Ausonius has here introduced an exotic name without local foundation. Against this we would urge the wide southern distribution of the name in areas subject to considerable Greek influence; the equation of Belenus with Apollo at Aquileia; and the Greek associations of the names of his own son Attius Patera and his grandson Delphidius, both famous for their eloquence. The family claimed to be descended from the druids of Armorica, and it will be remembered that Caesar records that although the druids transmitted their learning exclusively in oral form, yet they made use of the Greek alphabet for almost all the rest of their correspondence. The entire picture of a Gaulish god Belenus, equated with Apollo, and his temple-priest and two succeeding generations of the priest's family all bearing names of Delphic associations, all famous for their eloquence and claiming descent from a backward druidical stock of remote western Gaul, is as convincing as it is picturesque, a welcome glimpse of a Gaulish god and his attendant priest in the twilight of Gaulish heathendom. Both the cult of Belenus and Lucian's vignette of Ogmios are among our more interesting and less common traces of Greek influence among the gods known in southern Gaul.

Irish mythology is derived through the Atlantic sea-routes from a much earlier age than our earliest mythological records. From the time of Vergil to the fifth century AD the proud Romans used to refer to the Celtic peoples as living 'beyond our World', 'on the edge of the habitable globe'. They meant that the Celtic peoples were beyond the limits of the civilization of Greece and Rome. The Classical civilization was a world to itself, a civilization raised to great heights in an incredibly short time by the introduction and spread of the art of writing. Already by the fifth century AD the Roman system of education had spread to Britain, and boys were being sent to school as a matter of course to learn writing. But under this Classical civilization with its written texts there lay another civilization rich and brilliant. Its stories and poems, and all its accumulated native tradition were carried on by word of mouth. This was the intellectual life of the Iron Age, dating from the seventh century BC or earlier. In the Mediterranean countries it gave way to Classical culture; but in Gaul, this earlier native Celtic culture persisted throughout the Roman period, and formed a remarkably interesting combination, Gallo-Roman culture.

Beyond Roman Gaul, however, the ancient Celtic culture of the Iron Age remained in cold storage, virtually untouched by Roman influence. This is the ancient native civilization of Ireland with her traditions intact from the Iron Age, like an unwritten manuscript of the ancient Celtic world. Ireland is the only Celtic country which has preserved a great wealth of ancient mythological stories.

Irish mythology is a great contrast to Greek mythology because the gods were not organized in early times by the poets into a great heavenly community like the gods of Olympus. They never live in the sky or on the mountain tops. They live individually either underground or on the earth, often across the seas or on distant islands.

The ancient mythological stories of Ireland may be divided into four chief groups. We do not include here stories of local cults of springs and rivers and lakes, such as are prominent in Gaulish religion. These are not prominent as independent cults in Ireland, and occur chiefly – and not even very commonly – in connexion with important gods, such as the *Dagda*, whose home was Bruig na Bóinne, close to the Boyne.[25]

Group 1 is of the older Celtic gods, who are known from early times in Gaul, and also, perhaps later, from Britain.

Group 2, a much larger group, the native Irish gods of underground, whose homes are in the *síd*-mounds, the great barrows of the dead. This is the group of whom the majority of our most picturesque stories are told. They are by far the best known to modern scholars.

Group 3, the gods of re-birth, also known from sources outside Ireland, and not originally, or at least obviously, associated with the *síd*-mounds, but with the sea.

Group 4. Stories of the supernatural world – *Tír Tairngiri*, 'the land of Promise'; *Tír na nÓc*, 'the land of the Young'; *Mag Mell*; and stories of mortals who visit it. These are commonly referred to as *echtrai*, 'adventures' and *baili*, 'visions, ecstasies'.

It is natural to suppose that the earliest gods are those who belonged originally to the ancient Celts of Gaul. Perhaps the chief was the god Lug who has already been discussed (p. 28 above). His name, as we have seen, has survived in many place-names in Gaul and possibly Britain. Various stories have survived as to how he came to Ireland; but his foreign origin is recognized by early allusions, for he is said in one story to come from overseas, and he is referred to as a *scál balb*, a 'stammering spirit', doubtless with reference to his foreign tongue. In Wales his name is cognate with that of *Lleu Llaw Gyffes* who is a prominent hero in the *Mabinogi* of *Math fab Mathonwy*. But he has been integrated with the Irish pantheon, being claimed as the originator of the Fair of Teltown, held a fortnight before the Festival of Lugnasad on the first of August and a fortnight after it, resembling the Olympic games. He was fostered and trained by the wife of one of the *Tuatha Dé Danann* till he was fit to bear arms. This training in martial accomplishments by a woman is an interesting allusion to an early Celtic traditional custom, to which we shall refer later.

The triad of the ancient Gaulish divinities, the *matronae* (L. *matres*) (cf. pp. 28–9 above) has also survived in the three mother goddesses of war in Ireland – the Mórrígan ('great queen') and Macha and Bodb, the essential goddess of battle – perhaps also in three Brigits. Mórrígan, is one of the early pan-Celtic divinities, and is also apparently the forerunner of Morgan la fée of the Arthurian cycle, and is said to have had a union with the Dagda a year before the battle of Moytura (cf. p. 188 below). She is an unpleasant person. The *Annals of Tigernach* have preserved s.a. 622 an ancient fragment of an elegy of a Leinster prince who was drowned in his little curach:

The deep clear depths of the sea and the sand on the sea-bed have covered them. They have hurled themselves over Conaing in his frail little curach. The woman has flung her white mane against Conaing in his curach. Hateful is the laugh which she laughs today.

The white-haired woman with her hateful laugh is the Mórrígan,[26] who has drowned the prince with the white breakers. We may think of the *Coire Brecain* referred to in *Cormac's Glossary*, 'the Cauldron of the Old Woman', the well-known whirlpool, the Corry-vreckan, between the northern end of Jura and the Isle of Scarba in the Inner Hebrides.

Another goddess attested by inscriptions both in Gaul and Britain is the goddess Brigit (cf. the name of the *Brigantes* in N. England). The late Irish text, the *Lebor Gabála*, represents her as the daughter of the Dagda, greatest of the Irish native gods. According to the story in *Cormac's Glossary* she is the patron of poets while her two sisters are goddesses of smiths and of laws. She appears to have been Christianized as St Brigit, whose shrine is at Kildare, where her sacred fire was kept burning.[27]

The earliest native Irish gods, those included in Group 2 above, live underground, occasionally in caves, more often in the prehistoric tombs of the ancient dead chieftains. The most famous of these is *Bruig na Bóinne*, one of three great beehive-shaped tombs, like the so-called 'Treasury of Atreus' in Greece. It is now called New Grange and is lit by electric light, so that it is possible to see from inside the impressive corbelled dome. These gods of the underworld are called *aes síde* (sing. *síd*), and their homes, the burial-mounds, are *síde*. The most interesting of these is *Brí Léith*, near Ardagh in Co. Longford, the home of the god Midir (cf. p. 190 below), who had been the fosterer of the god Oengus mac Óc, son of the Dagda and Boann.

The Dagda is the most prominent of the older chthonic gods. His name means literally 'the good god'; but the epithet does not imply that he is 'good' in the moral sense. 'The good god' is not a name, but an appellation, an epithet. When the Dagda's turn comes to state his qualifications in the council of war before the battle of Moytura he declares:

184

'All that you promise to do I will do, myself alone.'

'It is you who are the *good god*,' they say. And from this day he is called the Dagda, i.e. 'good for everything' – a leading magician, a redoubtable warrior, an artisan – all powerful, omniscient. He is *Ruad Ro-fhessa*, 'Lord of Great Knowledge'.[28]

One of our earliest Irish prose stories tells of the *Dagda* and his son the *Mac Óc*, and his mother *Boann* the goddess of the Boyne. By her union with the Dagda, Boann became the mother of Oengus of the Bruig. The common source of both the Boyne and the Shannon is traditionally in the spring of Segais, the supernatural source of all knowledge, situated in the Land of Promise. It was surrounded by hazel trees, the nuts of which fell into the well producing bubbles of inspiration, or, according to an alternative tradition, were eaten by the salmon of knowledge which dwelt in the spring. Both versions are constantly alluded to in Irish literature as telling the source of wisdom.[29]

Oengus mac Óc lives in the great *síd* Bruig na Bóinne, where at night he is visited by visions of a beautiful maiden in his sleep, and he falls into a wasting sickness for love of her. His parents are sent for, and after much enquiry they find that the girl is Caer from *Síd Uamain* in Connacht, the province ruled in the Heroic Age by Ailill and Medb. Hither comes the Mac Óc and finds Caer and her maidens in the form of white swans wearing silver chains, on Loch Bél Drecon at Crot Cliach in Mag Femin. He calls her to him, and they go to his home in the Bruig. The text of this story is thought to date probably from the eighth century.[30]

One of the most fascinating of the stories of the Underworld is another Connacht tale, *Echtra Nerai* ('*The Adventure of Nera*'). Here the Underworld is entered through a 'cave' (*uaim*) in the rock near the court of Ailill and Medb at Cruachain in Connacht. As the court are celebrating the feast of *Samain* (cf. p. 141 above), Nera goes outside and cuts down a corpse from the gallows who complains of thirst, and after giving him a drink Nera replaces him on the gallows. On returning to the court he finds that the *síd*-hosts have come and burnt it, and left a heap of heads of his people cut off – in fact a typical piece of Celtic raiding.

Nera at once sets off in pursuit, and follows the retreating procession of the *síde*, who are clearly dead men, for each remarks to his neighbour that there mut be a living man in the procession because it has become heavier. When they enter the *síd* (cave) of Cruachain the severed heads are displayed as trophies to the king; and the king finds a home and a wife for Nera, and his daily task is to supply the king with firewood.

Then in a vision his wife warns him that at the next *Samain* the *síde* will again destroy the court unless he goes and warns the king. He takes wild garlic and primroses and fern to prove that he comes from the Underworld, and he goes to the court of Ailill and Medb and warns them. They destroy the *síd*, but Nera was left 'inside and has not come out until now, nor will he come till Doom'. From the time that he joined the procession of the *síde* and entered the Underworld he had become one of the dead.[31]

The storytellers of ancient Ireland by whom these tales were handed down spoke of the gods and people of the spirit world as *áes síde*, or *sluag síde*, 'the host of the *síde*'. But by the time the stories came to be recorded they had long ago ceased to have any religious or cult significance. The gods are no longer thought of as spirits living unseen in our midst, but as beings of the far past. The scribes who wrote down the stories were Christian monks. To one version of the text of the *Táin Bó Cualnge* the following colophon is added by a monk or clerk: 'I who have written out this history, or more properly fiction, do not accept as matter of belief certain things in this history, or rather fiction; for some things are diabolical impositions, some are poetical inventions, some have a semblance of truth, some have not, and some are meant to be the entertainment of fools.' Although the clerks have lovingly preserved these traditions of an age long past, they have humanized the gods, even sophisticated them. They have deprived them of their original prestige as objects of cult, and relegated them to an artificial setting fitting them to a scheme of pseudo-history which was quite foreign to their origin. We may compare the way in which our Teutonic god *Othinn (Woden)* is made the ancestor of the earliest Anglo-Saxon kings in our own early records.

The writers of the later legends in Ireland made no distinction between the native Irish gods of the Underworld, the ancient Celtic gods of Gaul who also survived in Irish mythology, and the gods of the supernatural world – *Tír Tairngiri*, 'The Land of Promise'; *Tír na nÓc*, 'The Land of the Young'; *Mag Mell*, 'The Delightful Plain'. They call all the gods alike by the common name of the *Tuatha Dé Danann*, 'Tribes of the goddess *Danann*', or simply the *Tuatha Dé*,

'The Tribes of the goddess'. The *Tuatha Dé Danann* imply a goddess *Danann*,[32] but little is known of her from Irish mythology beyond her name. In some texts she is referred to as the mother of the three mythical brothers Brian, Iucharba and Iuchar. She doubtless corresponds to *Dôn*, in the Welsh *Mabinogi* of *Math, son of Mathonwy* (cf. pp. 348 f. below). Math's sister is Dôn, the mother of Math's nephews Gilfaethwy and Gwydion. In Welsh tradition Dôn's brother and nephews are human beings, not gods; but they are great magicians, and their expertise in magic seems like a late echo of their divinity. Indeed in Wales the gods of the *Tuatha Dé Danann* have been transformed into heroes in the medieval stories of the *Mabinogion*, while the learned and sophisticated treatment which in medieval times has adapted the gods to a chronological scheme is found in Wales in the early chapters of the *Historia Brittonum* of Nennius already by the early ninth century.[33]

The later Irish writers had a good idea that in prehistoric times Ireland had been populated by a series of immigrations and invasions; and they believed that the Goidels were the ruling population of Ireland at the beginning of the historical period. The gods must therefore be earlier. They pictured them as entering Ireland from overseas, just like the later human conquerors of Ireland. The account of the immigration in the Book of Invasions (p. 19) refers to them all as *Tuatha Dé Danann*. The inhabitants of Ireland whom they found in possession of the land were the *Fir Bolg*, who are pictured as agriculturalists, in contrast to the *Tuatha Dé Danann* who possessed magic and all arts and knowledge and handicrafts. The earliest form of the story, however, is the one given by Nennius in the *Historia Brittonum*, cap. 3.

The traditional Irish account of the invasion of Ireland by the conquering gods represents them as coming from overseas by way of Norway and northern Scotland, led by their druids in a magical mist. Their king was Nuada and they conquered the Fir Bolg, the older inhabitants, by their magical skill and arts, in the first *Battle of Moytura*, fought near Lough Arrow, Co. Sligo, but Nuada lost an arm in the battle. The Fir Bolg took refuge among the *Fomoiri* (literally 'under (-sea) phantoms'[34]) in the Hebrides and Isle of Man. The *Tuatha Dé Danann* now settled in Ireland as the conquering gods, and made an alliance with the *Fomoiri* from overseas. The *Fomoiri* are represented as half human, half monster, with one hand, one leg and three rows of teeth. Their leader Balor had one eye in the middle of his forehead and was grandfather to Lug. Their king, Bres, was related to the *Tuatha Dé*, and he ruled Ireland as regent after Nuada had lost his arm in the Battle of Moytura. However the exactions of the *Fomoiri* were intolerable to the people of Ireland. Moreover they were stingy of their victuals, and when the chiefs of the *Tuatha Dé* went to the feasts of Bres, king of the *Fomoiri* and regent of Ireland, 'their knives were not greased by them' and however often they visited him 'their breath did not smell of ale', and he did not patronize their poets or their horn-blowers, and altogether he behaved very unhandsomely. At last they turned him out. Nuada was reinstated with a fine new silver jointed hand, made for him by the divine physician Dian Cécht and the divine smith Creidne.

We are now on the eve of the greatest of all the stories of the Irish gods. It is very synthetic. The *Fomoiri* in their turn staged a great invasion, and were defeated by the Irish gods in the second *Battle of Moytura*. Here the storyteller has brought all the Irish gods together, both native and those from overseas, by a brilliant device in a kind of divine United States and divine Celtic War of Independence, in opposition to the tyrants and oppressors, the *Fomoiri* from overseas. This skilful device of describing the council of war before the battle has left us a full-length inventory and portrait of all the gods, as well as a view of them in action.

As Nuada has lost an arm he is disqualified from leading the battle. While the gods are in their fortress preparing for the battle, Lug arrives from overseas and claims that he has skill to help. He is not one of the *Tuatha Dé*. The gate-keeper hesitates to admit him, demanding to know what his skills are; but for every accomplishment that Lug claims, the gate-keeper names a member of the *Tuatha Dé* who is supreme in this same skill. There is Dian Cécht the physician, who heals the wounded by plunging them in a magic bath-tub, and who had supplied Nuada with a fully jointed all-purpose silver hand when he had lost his own in the battle against the Fir Bolg. Moreover Dian Cécht's skill was such, as we learn from another story, that when a man lost an eye he could replace it by a cat's eye. But, as the storyteller remarks, 'There was advantage and disadvantage to him in that, for by day it was always asleep when it should have been on the alert; and at night it would start at every rustle of the reeds and every squeak of a mouse.'

One of the most important gods assembled for the battle is Goibniu the smith, who makes and repairs the weapons. Another is Luchtine the wright, who makes the shafts for the spears; and there is Creidne who makes the nails. Such is their skill that when Goibniu cast the spear-heads so that they stuck in the jamb of the door, Luchtine used to fling the spear-shafts after them, and it was enough to fasten them, and Creidne used to cast the nails from the jaws of the tongs, and it was enough to drive them in. Goibniu also appears as the smith Gofannon in the medieval Welsh story of *Culhwch and Olwen* (p. 349).

Finally Lug claims that he himself possesses all the arts (he is *samildánach*), and is at once admitted and leads the battle, wearing his famous armour from the Land of Promise where he had been fostered, and winning victory for the gods.[35]

But the whole grand body of the gods are assembled and help him. His strong champion was Ogma, who is the god of eloquence, and is probably to be identified with the Gaulish god *Ogmios* (cf. p. 29 above).

During the battle Lug was heartening the men of Ireland, 'that they should fight the battle fervently so that they should not be any longer in bondage. For it was better for them to find death in protecting their fatherland than to bide under bondage and tribute as they had been.' The words of Lug still ring down through the ages. They might have been spoken yesterday. Then the Mórrígan came and was heartening the *Tuatha Dé* to fight the battle fiercely and fervently, and the *Fomoiri* were beaten to the sea.

Now Lug and the Dagda and Ogma pursued the *Fomoiri* for they had carried off the Dagda's harper. When they reached the banqueting-hall of the Fomorian king Bres, there hung the harp on the wall. That is the harp on which the Dagda had sounded the melodies, so that they would only sing out by his command; and the harp left the wall and came to him. And he played to them three melodies – the wailing-strain, so that women wept; and the smile-strain, so that their women and children laughed; and the sleep-strain and the host fell asleep. And through that strain the three gods escaped unhurt from the murderous host of the *Fomoiri*. And after the battle was won the Mórrígan and Bodb proclaimed the battle and the mighty victory which had taken place, to the royal heights of Ireland and to its *síd*-hosts, and its chief waters and its river mouths; and Bodb described the high deeds which had been done, and prophesied the degeneration of future years.

189

The story of the god Midir of Brí Léith really links the gods of the *síd*-mounds with a different group, the gods of rebirth, who do not seem to be primarily associated with the old pre-historic burial mounds, but with journeys overseas. Both groups of gods, however, have their home in the supernatural regions.

The home of Midir is in the Land of Promise and is localized in the *síd*-mound of *Brí Léith*, west of Ardagh in Co. Longford. He claims that Étaín in her former existence was his wife, but that she has been separated from him by the magic of a jealous rival. When Étaín in her later existence becomes the wife of Eochaid, king of Tara, Midir comes to reclaim her. Midir and Eochaid play at chess for high stakes. At first Midir allows Eochaid to win, and Eochaid lays the forfeit on Midir that he and his supernatural host are to build a great causeway across the bog of central Meath. When it is finished Midir again comes to play, and this time he wins, and demands a kiss from Étaín as his prize. A month later he returns to claim it. While the king and his court are feasting, and all the entrances are barred, Midir appears in their midst in all his supernatural beauty and splendour, and carries off Étaín through the smoke-hole in the roof, and they are seen as two birds circling in the sky above the hall.

In this story, or rather cycle of stories, Étaín lives in at least three generations, perhaps more, re-born each time, not just living on to old age. In each rebirth she keeps her own name, though her husband's name differs in every case. First she is Étaín wife of the god Midir in the *síd*-mound. Then she is Étaín wife of Eochaid, king of Tara. Then she is reborn as Étaín, her own daughter, indistinguishable from herself; for the Irish women were the vehicles by which the dead were reborn in generation after generation. The human husband has no spiritual rôle.

We shall see that this story of Midir and Étaín has a close parallel in the story of the god Manannán mac Lir, the spiritual father of the historical seventh century king Mongán. The only fundamental difference is that Midir belongs to the *síd*-mounds, the barrows of the dead, while Manannán seems to live by the sea.

The Irish mythological traditions which are distinct in origin from those of the gods of the Underworld, are those of Lug and Manannán, both of whom are directly associated with rebirth. We have seen traces of the ancient Celtic cult of Lug on the Continent, but not of Manannán. In Irish mythology Manannán is king of the Land of

Promise, or Mag Mell. According to Irish tradition he had fostered Lug in the Land of Promise and bestowed on him his famous armour – his helmet of invisibility, and his shield, which later Finn mac Umaill had. Welsh prose tradition (the *Mabinogi* of *Manawydan*) has preserved his family connexions better than the Irish. Here he is Manawydan, son of Llyr, and brother of Bran the Blessed. One of the earliest Irish stories, *The Voyage of Bran*, pictures them meeting in mid-ocean while Manannán is on his way to Ireland from the Land of Promise; and by his magic he transforms the sea and fish into the flowery plain with its flocks from the Land of Promise. The lyrics in which Manannán sings of the Land of Promise contain some of the loveliest imagery in Irish mythological tradition. And here it must be emphasized that the Land of Promise is sometimes identified as a supernatural region in the *síd*-mounds, the great barrows of the dead; sometimes as approached over the sea or a lake. It is a land where there is naught but truth; without death or decay, or sadness, or envy, or jealousy, or hate, or gloom, or pride, a land of plenty, of flocks and herds, of the ever-young, of flowers and fruit. It is *Mag Mell*, 'the Delightful Plain', *Tír na nÓc*, 'the Land of the Young'; '*Tír Tairngire*', the 'Land of Promise'.

It is natural that Manannán and Bran should meet like this in mid-ocean, for the family is closely connected with the sea. In the Welsh story of *Branwen, daughter of Llyr*, the family seat is on the rock of Harlech above Cardigan Bay. *Cormac's Glossary* describes Manannán as a famous sailor and weather expert of the Isle of Man. This is the passage in the Glossary where the god has been euhemerized as a human being: '*Manannán mac Lir*, a renowned trader who dwelt in the Isle of Man. He was the best pilot in the western world. Through acquaintance with the sky he knew how long there would be fair weather and foul weather, and when each of these seasons would change. Hence the Scots and Britons called him a god of the sea, and hence they said he was son of the sea, i.e. *mac lir* ('son of the sea').'[35]

The family to which Manannán belonged are not native to any one Celtic country but to the Irish Sea, and all its surrounding coasts, with its nucleus in the Isle of Man. This is, no doubt, why in Irish stories Manannán, like his fosterling Lug, is commonly shown to us as arriving from overseas.[36]

The most interesting gifts of Manannán are his magical powers of creating illusion, and his connexion with the belief in rebirth. Indeed his power of illusion is unlimited. He is a great shape-changer himself, and by this means he is able to control reincarnation, rebirth. He appears to be himself an avatar of Lug. He is a great begetter of children, a soul-conveyor, a *psychopompos*. He has no normal family life, no local habitation, no direct affinities with the ancient cult centres; but by his sudden appearances and disappearances and his power of shape-changing he can become the father of children of other men's wives. They are not his own children. He is a supernatural father.

The most astonishing story of Manannán's fatherhood is the birth of the historical King Mongán († 615) who ruled at Moylinny on Lough Neagh in the north of Ireland, a kingdom known as that of the Cruithni (cf. p. 20 above). The story relates that the king, Fiachna Lurgan, goes to Alba (Scotland) to help his ally, Aedán mac Gabráin (St Columba's king) against the Saxons. He leaves his wife in the royal rath at Moylinny, where a noble-looking man appears to her and tells her that her husband will be killed in battle next day unless she will consent to bear a son by himself, who will be the famous Mongán. To save her husband's life the woman consents, and next day this noble-looking man appears in Alba before the armies of Aedán and Fiachna and vanquishes Fiachna's opponent. When Fiachna returns home and his wife tells him all that has occurred, Fiachna thanks her for what she has done for him, and the story concludes:

So this Mongán is a son of Manannán mac Lir, though he is called Mongán son of Fiachna. For when he [i.e. Manannán] went from her in the morning he left a quatrain with Mongán's mother, saying:
'I go home,
The pale pure morning draws near:
Manannán son of Lir
Is the name of him who has come to thee.'

But the strange thing is that Mongán inherits the capacities of Manannán. For when he was three nights old Manannán came for him and took him away and fostered him in the Land of Promise, till he was twelve or perhaps sixteen years old. A counter-claim is made in another story that Mongán was Finn mac Cumaill reborn, but he would not let it be known. It was, however, announced publicly in the rath of Moylinny by Caílte, Finn's foster-son, who came to the rath from the land of the dead. As Mongán was commonly regarded as the son of Fiachna the Fair, it is just conceivable that the notion that he was a rebirth of Finn may be secondary.

The strangest thing about these stories of Mongán is that he lived in a Christian period. A poem attributed to the poet Mael Muru of Fahan in Donegal claims that Mongán came from 'the flock-abounding Land of Promise' to converse with Colum Cille; and that he managed to get into heaven by having his head under Colum Cille's cowl. Is it possible that there had been a heathen reaction among the Cruithni under Fiachna, and that they were re-converted under Mongán, possibly under the influence of Colum Cille? Good relations between Fiachna, king of the Cruithni, and Aedán mac Gabráin, Columba's king in Irish Dál Riata, which are clearly implied in the story of the conception of Mongán, give some colour to such a suggestion.

The Irish traditional belief in rebirth again takes us back once more to Continental records. Certain Classical authors relate that the Gaulish druids teach that souls do not die, but live again *in alio orbe*. Gaulish traditions have retained few traces of a belief in rebirth or of the function of a god as a *psychopompos*, a divine father of children claiming a human father, like Mongán. St Augustine, however, has a curious passage in which he asserts 'on unimpeachable authority' that 'unclean spirits – *Silvanos et Panes*, popularly called *incubi* – frequently assail women impudently; and certain *daemones*, whom the Gauls call *Dusii* are in the habit of both attempting and effecting this foul act.' Is it possible that St Augustine has known and naturally misunderstood stories such as we associate with Manannán, and that he is viewing them through the refracted medium of a Christian lens?

It would be hazardous to assume that the cult of Manannán mac Lir has always been confined to the Irish Sea or even that it originated in this area. Early Icelandic and Norse literature has recorded traditions which have close affinities with Manannán and the cult of re-birth and the Land of Promise. Mythological traditions relate to a certain Guthmundr of Glasisvellir who ruled a supernatural region resembling Tír Tairngire and whose subjects are said not to die, but to live from generation to generation, and his realm is called *Ódainsakr*, 'the field of the not dead', and *Land lifanda manna*, 'the land of living men'. The stories imply that it was a land of rebirth, a land of youth and of immortality. The Hebrides are a possible centre of distribution in the northern seas. The early Norse poem *Rígsthula* certainly originated in an Irish milieu, and here the Norse hero *Rígr* (Irish *rí*, 'king') is a begetter of human offspring, and perhaps associated with the sea.[38] In Norse sagas also, and in the Norse Helgi poems of the *Older Edda*, the rebirth of the dead is effected by the visit of a mortal to the land of the dead and to the barrows in which the dead are buried.

The spiritual rôle assigned to women in this cult of rebirth is a lofty one. In this phase of Irish mythology the woman, not the man, is the spiritual vehicle who conveys the soul of the dead to rebirth in a later generation. Indeed it may be said that speaking generally the high prestige of women is a feature characteristic of early Celtic civilization and especially of Celtic mythology. We have found the *matronae, matres* among the oldest figures of Gaulish mythology. In Ireland the native gods, the *Tuatha Dé Danann*, are thought of as 'Tribes of the goddess Danann'. The Mórrígan is the 'great queen'.

History and tradition alike echo the high prestige of women of Celtic mythology. Roman history has recorded no male enemies in Celtic Britain of the stature of Boudicca and Cartimandua. In the Heroic Age of Ireland Medb, Queen of Connacht, is the reigning sovereign. Ailill, her husband, is never more than her consort, and Medb is the greatest personality of any royal line of the Heroic Age.

In Irish and Welsh stories of Celtic Britain the great heroes are taught not only wisdom but also feats of arms by women. In the Irish saga known as 'The Wooing of Emer' Cú Chulainn is trained in all warrior feats by two warlike queens – Scáthach, who is also a *fáith*, i.e. 'a prophetess', an expert in supernatural wisdom – and Aífe. In the Welsh story of *Peredur* (later Percival) the hero is trained by the nine *gwiddonod* of Gloucester, who seem to be women of a similar profession. They wear helmets and armour, and they instruct Peredur in chivalry and feats of arms, and supply him with horse and armour. These women also train other young men, and they live with their parents in a settled home, a 'llys' or court. The establishment seems to have been of the nature of a military training school.

This high prestige of women is something very old in the British Isles. Among the ancient Picts matrilinear succession was the rule till the ninth century. Bede tells us that even in his own day whenever the royal succession among the Picts came in question their ruler was chosen by succession from the female line. Does it go back to the Continental Gauls? Prowess in arms at least seems not to have been lacking among Gaulish women. Ammianus Marcellinus, who wrote during the fourth century AD, has left us (XV, xii) an unforgettable picture of the Gaulish women warriors:

> Nearly all the Gauls are of a lofty stature, fair, and of ruddy complexion; terrible from the sternness of their eyes, very quarrelsome, and of great pride and insolence. A whole troop of foreigners would not be able to withstand a single Gaul if he called his wife to his assistance, who is usually very strong, and with blue eyes; especially when, swelling her neck, gnashing her teeth, and brandishing her sallow arms of enormous size, she begins to strike blows mingled with kicks, as if they were so many missiles sent from the string of a catapult. (Yonge's transl.)

It has been suggested above that the Irish gods fall naturally into three main groups, of whom the first, who are also found in Gaul, are possibly the oldest. The second are associated with the prehistoric grave-mounds, and would seem to be chthonic. The third are gods of 'rebirth'. There is a tendency among leading modern scholars to recognize a fourth class, consisting of certain men and women, heroes and heroines, who appear in Irish literary and historical traditions as human, but who are now generally believed to have been originally gods and goddesses. This relatively recent habit of thought is not confined to Irish scholars. It began among German students of folklore and mythology early last century and has affected mythological studies widely, both ancient Greek and modern Slavonic no less than Teutonic and Celtic. The subject cannot be discussed here, but a few instances may be mentioned of this new category of Irish 'gods'. This recent tendency forms an interesting contrast to the euhemerizing activities of the early medieval historians who represented the Irish gods as human invaders taking possession of Ireland by force of arms (cf. p. 187 above).

It has been thought that Cú Roí mac Dáiri, the ruler of Munster in the *Táin Bó Cualnge*, was a god because of certain magical attributes which he is said to have possessed, and certain ritual functions which he fulfilled in his own person. Yet in the heroic stories he is always represented as a human hero. In a scholarly and detailed discussion

Professor Gerard Murphy has argued for a divine origin for Finn mac Umaill, whose milieu is in Leinster and Connacht and who figures in the surviving stories as a human hero. The late Professor O'Rahilly declared categorically that Cormac mac Airt (cf. p. 54 above) was in reality, not a king but a god. An overwhelming majority of recent Irish scholars insist that Medb, Queen of Connacht in the *Táin Bó Cualnge*, was a goddess. The evidence is partly philological – her name denoting 'intoxication' – partly the long list of husbands attributed to her, partly her ritual marriage (p. 125). In Irish tradition, however, as in Greek, characters of the Heroic Age are never represented as gods, and literary traditions consistently represent them as human. The tradition may be accepted as it stands.

In an illuminating article Professor Binchy has recently set the ceremonial with which Medb is traditionally invested in a wider context, demonstrating its archaic character and its relationship to royal investiture of other Irish kings, and to kings in other parts of the world which imbued them with divine powers.[39] It may be added here that the ceremonial marriage of the reigning queen may be compared with the traditional ancient marriage customs of the Picts. For the evidence of investing a human ruler with a ceremonial which endowed him with divine powers reference may be made to certain ceremonies of 'rebirth' on the island of Bali in Indonesia, by which those who perform it become *dvija*, 'twice born', like the upper castes of India, and like them become 'gods'. Reference may also be made to a custom formerly practised in Travancore in south-west India, where the rulers are drawn from the *kṣatriya* caste, and the descent is through the female line. Here nevertheless before the rajah can mount the throne he is subjected to a ritual by which he exchanges his *kṣatriya* caste for that of a Brahmin, a 'god', one of the 'god-people'. The ceremonial symbolizes the double birth of the *dvija*, as man and god. The *kṣatriya* is, in fact, reborn.

The Irish gods are always pictured as beautiful in appearance and gloriously dressed. Lug has a golden helmet and golden armour and his shield is famous. An early poem uses the figure 'Lug of the shield, a fair *scál*', i.e. a fair phantom, or spirit (p. 282), and the late saga of the 'Fate of the Children of Tuireann' represents him as wearing the magical armour of his fosterer Manannán from the Land of Promise. Manannán himself is thus described at his first meeting with Fiachna Find:

He wore a green cloak of one colour, and a brooch of white silver in the cloak over his breast, and a satin shirt next his white skin. A circlet of gold around his hair, and two sandals of gold under his feet.

And again we recall the Gauls as described by Ammianus Marcellinus (XV, xii):

They are all exceedingly careful of cleanliness and neatness, nor in all the country ... could any man or woman, however poor, be seen either ragged or dirty.

On no occasion are we ever privileged to see the gods assembled as a community in Tír Tairngire or Tír na nÓc; but on more than one occasion we are privileged visitors with a king of Tara who is conducted there on a temporary visit, a kind of mystery. One of the early Irish tales with the title *Baile in Scáil* tells how the prehistoric king Conn Cétchathach was suddenly enveloped in a magical mist as he was on the royal ramparts of Tara with his three druids and his three poets. A horseman came riding through the mist who took them with him to his house in a rath with a golden tree beside the door. In the house was the god Lug, of great stature and beauty, and there beside a silver kieve full of ale sat a beautiful maiden, the 'Sovereignty of Ireland'. From a golden vessel she ladled out many drinks for Conn; and with every drink Lug, standing by, named one of Conn's descendants who would succeed him in the sovereignty, and Conn wrote down their names in *Ogam* on a piece of wood. Finally the mist dispersed and Conn and his companions found themselves back in Tara.[40] This story symbolizes the claim of the Goidelic rulers of Tara to their divine right – possibly also a claim that this divine right is derived from a cult introduced from overseas, and superseding the ancient native gods. A similar adventure – a mystery we may call it – befell Conn's grandson, Cormac mac Airt, but here instead of Lug, the god presiding over the rath in the Land of Promise is Manannán mac Lir. On this occasion Manannán has stolen Cormac's wife and son and daughter and taken them to his home in the Land of Promise; but when he restores them to Cormac he declares:

'I make my declaration to thee, O Cormac, that until today neither thy wife nor thy daughter has seen the face of a man since

197

they were taken from thee out of Tara, and that thy son has not seen a woman's face. Take thy family then,' says the warrior. 'I am Manannán mac Lir, king of the Land of Promise, and to see the Land of Promise was the reason I brought thee here.'[41]

This is a mystery in the Greek sense – a pre-view of the Land of Promise. In a way it is also Manannán's *apologia pro vita sua*, but it leaves all the important things unsaid. Manannán is the one early Irish god who has never been convincingly humanized by the literary tradition. He is a spiritual being to the last.

It is a strange story, or series of stories. To the modern mind Manannán is the most remote of all the Irish gods from the ideas of our own world. Is it the last outer ripple of Pythagorean continuity of personality transmitted from the late Mediterranean world through Gaul? We know that the Druids are credited with having taught such a philosophy in Gaul; and we have seen that Irish mythology has many links, not only with the mythology of the Celts of Gaul, but also with that of Wales and even Scotland. It is no isolated mythology, but the fine flower of the whole ancient Celtic world.

Irish mythology demonstrates as clearly as Greek mythology the wide gulf which separates *mythology* and *religion*. In both Greek and Irish religions, cults must at some remote period have given rise to the mythology; but the mythologies have travelled far in time, and sometimes in place from their original cult centres. They have reached us, not as religion, but as literary themes. There is neither awe nor reverence for the oldest gods, and gradually, as the gulf widens and religion and belief wanes, a spirit of light humour, even crude horseplay, colours the pictures of these gods. In the second *Battle of Moytura*, the Dagda, once regarded as *Ruad Ro-fhessa*, the 'lord of great knowledge' (cf. p. 185 above), has become a grotesque and cumbersome old man, 'so fat and unwieldy that men laughed when he attempted to move about'. He has a cauldron which holds 80 gallons of milk, and as much meat and fat – whole goats and sheep and swine. All this goes to the making of the Dagda's porridge. His ladle is big enough to hold a man and woman. Yet strangely enough this deterioration does not touch Lug or Manannán. They are in a class apart. Why, one wonders? Their beauty and their dignity never tarnish, nor the splendour of their appearance.

In the great battle which establishes the independence of the gods

198

against the *Fomoiri* it is Lug, the stranger from across the sea, Lug of all the arts (*Samildánach*), who leads the gods to victory; even though the Dagda, representative of the older native gods, who had also possessed all the arts and all knowledge, is present. Can we suppose that the cult of rebirth has superseded the ancient cult of the dead in the *síd*-mounds, and an even older more wide-spread cult – the nature religion of the cult of rivers and springs, so widely attested in Gaul? Perhaps the wide gulf which separates Irish mythology from religious cult is one reason why the Christian monks have felt no inhibition in recording the mythological stories in their books. On the other hand no scruples prevented them from recording the magical practices implied in the mythological stories. The use of the mysterious practice of imposing magical prohibitions known as *gessa* is constantly referred to, and it was the violation of the personal *gessa* imposed on Conaire Mór, the prehistoric king of Ireland, that brought about his destruction in the story of the Destruction of Dá Derga's Hostel. Clairvoyance is widely recognized and its incidence is usually preceded by the verb *adciu* 'see' – i.e. with my eye of inner vision: 'I see red, I see very red.'[42] Charms and incantations are freely used. The technique for obtaining a supernatural vision is recorded verbatim in one Irish text, and is known as *Imbas forosnai*, 'Inspiration which enlightens', and the names of other charms are recorded with their appropriate poetical formulae.

Irish mythology is a strange world of the imagination. Well might the ancient people of Mediterranean lands speak of the Celtic peoples, even those of Gaul, as 'beyond the setting sun, remote from our world'. Yet they are even more remote from the world of the Middle Ages. The Irish gods are neither 'little people' nor 'fairies', but tall and beautiful and fair; in all their physical strength and power and fairness of countenance, and even dress, they are superior to human men and women. They recall rather the descriptions of the Gauls which we find in Classical writers. There are no witches or devils, no puerile miracles or mere vulgar displays of magical power. The supernatural and the marvellous are invested with restraint and dignity. No question of guilt, or punishment or judgement in an after life ever disturbs the serenity of what Gerard Murphy has called the 'strange loveliness' of Celtic mythology. It is this 'strange loveliness' of 'the otherworld atmosphere which gives its special beauty to the Irish mythological cycle'.

NOTES

1 *Chorographia III*, vi, 8. For variant readings of the word see Dottin, *Manual*, p. 383, n. 5.
2 Plutarch, *Moralia De Defectu Oraculorum*, cap. 18.
3 *Moralia* XII, *De Facie quae in orbe lunae apparet*, cap. 26.
4 On Demetrius see Rhys Roberts, *Demetrius* (London, 1927), 273.
5 Procopius, *Gothic War* VIIIXX, 45–49.
6 Cyril Fox, *F.E.I.A.*
7 I. A. Richmond, *R.B.* 196. For a fuller account of the site see J. C. Bruce, *The Hand-Book to the Roman Wall* (7th edition, Newcastle-upon-Tyne, 1914) pp. 119 f.; 126 ff. See further n. 8 below.
8 For an inventory of the inscribed stones on this site see Collingwood and Wright, *R.I.B.* pp. 485–98 (nrs. 1520–62).
9 H. Usener, *Scholia in Lucanem* (Leipzig, 1869), p. 33. The manuscript of the *Scholia* is tenth century.
10 LXII, vi, 7. On the form of the name see Dottin, *Manuel*, 313.
11 *Annals*, XIV, 30.
12 Loth, *Chrestomathie* 222.
13 Reference may be made to Woodhenge, Sutton Hoo, Yeavering, and now Dunbar – all in Britain; and to sites in Gaul referred to in ch. XII below.
14 I. A. Richmond, *R.B.*, 192; Powell, *Celts*, 145 f.
15 I. A. Richmond, *R.B.*, 192 ff.
16 Suetonius, *Caesar*, 54.
17 *Ibid.*, 136 f., 194.
18 *Ibid.*, 142 f.
19 See R. E. M. Wheeler, *Lydney*; see especially Appendix I, pp. 132 ff. by J. R. R. Tolkien.
20 Lucian, *Heracles* 1 ff. See F. Benoit, Ogam V (1953), 33 ff.
21 See S. B. Platner, *Topographical Dictionary of Ancient Rome* (Oxford, 1929), s.v. Hercules Musarum, 255.
22 Kuno Meyer, S.C., no. 141.
23 Ed. E. Windisch (Leipzig, 1905), p. 797, l. 5524.
24 *Herodian* VIII, 3, 8. (Zwicker, *Fontes* I, p. 91).
25 *EIHM* 516.
26 O'Rahilly prefers this form *EIHM* 314, but Thurneysen gives *Morrígain* as the earlier form, which he explains as 'queen of phantoms' ('Maren-Königin'), *Heldensage* 63.
27 Giraldus Cambrensis, *Top. Hib.* II xxxiv-xxxvi.
28 *EIHM* 318.
29 *Ib.* 322.
30 *Heldensage* 300; ZCP XXII 3.
31 *Heldensage* 311.
32 *EIHM* 308–15.
33 See *Heldensage* 63; *EIHM* 475 f.
34 *Heldensage* 64.

35 Murphy, *Saga and Myth* 21.
36 *SC* 896.
37 For a curious passage on Manannán see *Heldensage* 516f.
38 See *GL* I 420.
39 See *Ériu* XVIII 134f.
40 *EIHM* 283.
41 *EIL* 110f.
42 C. O'Rahilly (ed.), *Táin Bó Cúalnge*, p. 143.

8

Celtic Christianity and its Literature

The introduction of Christianity into Gaul was a slow and gradual process. Of the beginning of the conversion we have no information whatever, but from the second century we have contemporary records of Christians in Lyons and Vienne. The community of Lyons was presided over by Bishop Pothinus, and the priest Irenaeus, who ultimately succeeded him in the see. In 177 a persecution of incredible severity descended upon the little community, and a number were subjected to imprisonment, followed by hideous tortures and death. Among the martyrs was the bishop Pothinus. As he was ninety years of age at the time, his original appointment to the see is hardly likely to have been very recent, and we are therefore perhaps justified in surmising that the Christian community of Lyons was not new at this time, despite the reference by Eusebius (*Ecclesiastical History* V.13) to 'those through whom our affairs had been established', and the statement by Sulpicius Severus that the Gospel had been slow to cross the Alps into Gaul.

Our information about this persecution and its sufferings is derived from an Epistle indited from the Gallican Churches to the Churches of Asia and Phrygia extracted by Eusebius, bishop of Caesarea (*c.* 260–*c.* 340), from a number of accounts of Gallican martyrdoms and letters. The Epistle is 'the first piece of the archives of the Church of Gaul, and is essentially reliable'.[1] It was incorporated by Eusebius in his Collection of Martyrdoms. This is now lost, but he has included portions of it in his *Ecclesiastical History* (V.1–3),[2] which is our fullest and most reliable source of information about the situation in Lyons and about the individual martyrs and their sufferings. Additional information is recorded by Gregory, bishop of Tours (*c.* 540–94), who had access to some sources of information, perhaps at Lyons, now no longer available, and who has recorded it chiefly in his work, *De Gloria Martyrum*, cap. 48.

The epistle itself claims to be written by the 'servants of Christ at Vienne and Lyons to the brethren throughout Asia and Phrygia', as well as to Eleutherius, the bishop of Rome. Eusebius, who seems to have had their letter before him, tells us (V.3,4) that it was taken to Rome by the priest Irenaeus: 'We have charged Irenaeus, our brother and our companion, to deliver this letter to you,' they wrote to the Pope, 'and we beg you to hold him in esteem as a zealot of Christ's testament.' (V.4) According to the testimony of St Jerome[3] Irenaeus fulfilled his mission, and we have no reason to doubt it. His absence from Lyons would best account for his not being involved in the persecutions. Later testimony speaks of his own martyrdom, but this is uncertain, and the date and manner of his death are unknown.

According to Gregory of Tours[4] Pothinus was probably the first bishop of Lyons. Of the personal history of Irenaeus himself (*c.* 130– *c.* 200) little is known. Gregory of Tours states that he had been 'directed' (*directus*) to Lyons by St Polycarp, who was bishop of Smyrna. Eusebius quotes from a letter purporting to have been written by Irenaeus to a friend, in which Irenaeus claims to have listened as a boy in Smyrna to St Polycarp (*c.* 69–*c.* 155), the martyred bishop of Smyrna, and to have heard him tell of his intercourse with St John and the other disciples who had seen the Lord.[5] Irenaeus was very possibly in Rome when St Polycarp came there to discuss with Anicetus the Easter controversy, and Eusebius refers to the friendly terms of the two bishops.[6]

We have no reason to doubt these early experiences of Irenaeus with the Greek teachers of Asia Minor and Rome, and indeed his own distinguished reputation as a scholar is fully consistent with such a preparation. He evidently wrote much, and though much of his writing has perished, enough has survived in translations into Latin, Syriac, and Armenian to demonstrate that he must have done much to establish the Chruch of Lyons as an important link between the Churches of the East and West. He was in fact the first great Catholic theologian, and apart from a recently discovered Armenian translation of 'The Demonstration of the Apostolic Teaching', his theological works are concerned with Christian apologetics in defence of orthodoxy. His principal work was the *Adversus Omnes Haereses* which was a direct attack on Gnosticism, and though written and partly preserved in Greek, it survives as a whole in an early Latin translation. Greek was still the principal language of the Church, but Lyons was a Latin city, and Irenaeus apologizes for what he regards as the deficiencies of his Greek style, on the ground that he is resident among the Keltae and for the most using 'a barbarous dialect'.[7]

The most interesting fact known of his actual function in his office as bishop is his intervention *c.* 190 in the famous Eastern controversy, which figures so prominently in the following centuries. A divergence between the various European churches and those of Asia had been in existence since apostolic times regarding both the date and the manner of celebrating Easter. The Asiatics, relying on an ancient local tradition, regarded Easter as the anniversary of the Saviour's death, and treated it as a fast, on whatever day of the week it fell, even if it fell on a Sunday; and even in Rome they continued to follow their traditional practice, declaring that they could not renounce the custom derived from the great luminaries of the Church who had died in Asia, in particular the apostle John. In 189 Pope Victor was inclined to cut off and excommunicate the Asiatics; but the bishops urged peace, and among them Irenaeus wrote in the name of the brethren whom he governed in Gaul, emphasizing that the point at issue was not only the question of date, but also the manner of fasting, and that their differences had arisen gradually over a long period of time; and he reminded Victor of the more conciliatory attitude of his predecessor Anicetus and his successors. Victor had the good sense to accept his counsels of conciliation.

Irenaeus mentions churches in Germania[8] and also in Celtic countries, and it seems that Christianity had already spread to some extent in Gaul, possibly with Lyons as a kind of mother-church, a radiating centre.[9] No other bishopric is named in the second century. After the death of Irenaeus the first Gaulish bishop mentioned in the documents is Saturninus of Toulouse, whose *Passio* fixes the beginning of his episcopate in 250; and contemporary documents show that by this time Gaul had a recognized episcopal organization, especially in the south, in the urban areas. Progress in the Christianization of northern Gaul was slower, however, for here the ancient Gaulish agricultural estates, in contrast to the Rhône valley, offered fewer natural opportunities for the development of the organization of the new religion.

The fourth century brought a new era to Christianity in Gaul and in the West generally with the reign of Constantine the Great (274–337), who became senior Augustus in 313, and who, the same year, together with his brother-in-law Licinius, issued the famous Edict of Milan which granted regulations in favour of the Christians. In 323 he became sole Emperor of East and West and although he did not become a professing Christian till officially baptized on his death-bed, he gave both legal and political help and encouragement to the Church. The persecutions were a thing of the past. Full liberty of conscience was established throughout the Empire.

By substituting Christianity for the official cult of the emperor as a state religion, Constantine created a unifying principle of government guided by the religious sanctions of a popular religion. In the hope of promoting unity within the Church he devoted special care to the suppression of schism and heresy. The Donatist schism, especially fierce in the Christian Church in Africa, called for his early attention, and in 314 he called a council of the bishops of the western provinces to meet at Arles, attended by the bishops of Spain, Italy, Africa and even Great Britain,[10] to discuss various questions touching Church discipline, among them the Easter question.

The Donatist schism had been a local matter within the Western Church. Far more momentous was the Arian question which divided the whole Christian world. The conflict had begun in Alexandria early in the fourth century, occasioned immediately by the priest Arius, who, following the teaching of Lucian of Antioch, denied the true divinity of Christ. The point at issue was, of course, a fundamental one, and aroused a fierce and widespread controversy. In the hope of promoting unity between the two halves of his Empire, and the Churches of East and West, Constantine called the Council of Nicaea in 325. More than three hundred bishops attended the Council, the majority from the Churches associated with Alexandria and Antioch; Britain was not represented, and Gaul by only one modest signature.

In Gaul itself the most outstanding force in the Church, and the protagonist in the Arian controversy, was St Hilary, who became bishop of Poitiers shortly after 350. His brilliant writings were the

205

chief contribution of Gaul to the questions which rent the Church in his day, and together with the writings of St Athanasius, laid the foundations of the Catholicism of the Western Church. During Hilary's exile in Phrygia from $c.$ 356–$c.$ 360, as a result of his unbending opposition to Arianism, he became the strongest pillar of the Western Church, all the more influential for the intimate knowledge of the Eastern Church which his exile had forced upon him. As a result of the leisure which his freedom from episcopal duties granted him, he had been enabled to compose his greatest work, the *De Trinitate*. Meanwhile shortly after Hilary's return to Gaul in 360 the Gaulish bishops sent a letter in which they paid homage to Hilary and reiterated their adherence to the formula of Nicaea. The letter marks the end of the Arian crisis in the Church of Gaul, and Sulpicius Severus claims that Hilary was universally recognized to have effected the return of the Church to its former state.[11] Both his eloquence and his learning were greatly appreciated by his contemporaries.[12] He died $c.$ 367. In the history of the Church of Gaul his is the first great name which we meet among the masters of thought since Irenaeus. His principal achievement had been the consolidation of Western Catholicism. On the foundations laid during the fourth century Christianity gradually established itself as the national Church of Gaul, and created the system of ecclesiastical organization naturally forming an integral part of the Roman civil administration within which it had arisen, and by which it had been made financially stable.

During the reign of Constantine many churches had received wide powers to establish themselves within the city walls. The bishop, now an official, was naturally installed within the city itself, and the ecclesiastical organization everywhere modelled itself on that of the civil service of the Empire. Towards the close of the fourth century almost every city had its bishop. On the death of Theodosius in 395 the Church of Gaul was already organized into its framework of dioceses and its episcopal hierarchy. During this period Christianity was spreading widely in Gaul. The nobility were joining the Church, not only in the cities, but also in the suburbs, the *vici*, which came to form the nucleus of the 'parish' endowed with a church and a priest, such as the church alluded to by St Paulinus of Nola in the neighbourhood of Bordeaux.[13] Such urban parishes were visited by the bishop on his episcopal visitations, and are pictured for us by Sulpicius Severus in his *Life of St Martin*, cap. 11 ff. With the spread of the Faith among the Christian landed gentry, privately owned Churches sprang up, built at the expense of the landowners on their own estates. One of the most charming subjects in the personal correspondence between Sulpicius Severus and St Paulinus of Nola is the recurrent theme of their pride and pleasure in the building and adornment of their own churches.

The term, the 'Church of Gaul', is a loose one, and more exactly denotes the Churches of the Gaulish provinces. There was no authoritative ecclesiastical centre, no primacy of Gaul. The Church was organized within the civil provinces which exercised authority superior to that of the bishops for important affairs, such as the ordination of bishops and the creation of new churches. Gradually the provincial council arose, presided over by the bishop of the civil metropolis. In 392 St Ambrose refers to the numerous councils of the Gaulish bishop. As late as 404 Pope Innocent 1, in a letter to Victricius, bishop of Rouen, forbade the bishops to submit their differences to the bishops of other provinces, urging them to settle their own affairs save only by recourse to the Apostolic Seat.[14]

The traditional Roman political framework in which the Church developed could hardly fail to have some influence on the nature of Christian worship. The poet Ausonius of Bordeaux, himself a professing and practising Christian, evidently regarded his attendance at early morning prayers in his private church as obligatory; but they took their assigned place in his 'daily round', and when he deems, as he naïvely tells us, that 'God has been prayed to enough' he turns as a matter of course to give the routine orders to his cook Sosias. Even during the late fifth century the letters and poems of Sidonius Apollinaris, bishop of Auvergne, charming and personal and intimate as they are, convey rather the impression of an official ecclesiastic than of a man with a deep inner religious life and vision. Yet we must not allow ourselves to be swayed by Salvian into the belief that the Gaulish bishops were without due care for their flocks. During the corn-famine the bishops gave generously of their own personal stores, transporting their stocks at their own expense to the districts which were most in need, going far beyond their official routine duties. Indeed all our evidence testifies to the care with which they discharged the responsibilities of their calling.

In this period of official Christian organization and personal security and conformity a new light broke into Gaul from the Eastern Mediterranean, suffusing the new religion with a more intense spiritual life. From the third century AD asceticism had spread among Christian communities from Egypt to Syria and far Mesopotamain lands, inducing them to abandon all worldly cares and responsibilities, and to retreat into the desert where they could devote themselves to a life of solitude and spiritual contemplation. In Egypt from the third century two areas were distinguished by the practical conduct of their religious life. In the deserts of Nitria, Skete and Climax to the west of the Nile Delta lived numbers of Christian ascetics, some in almost total solitude and simplicity and austerity of life, following their own individual rules, with no common discipline, and assembling for the eucharist only on Saturdays and Sundays. In Upper Egypt community life was developed early in the fourth century under Pachomius, whose military training in early life was probably in part responsible for the success of his organization of the cenobitic life and common rule in his monastery of Tabennesi.

Both these forms of asceticism spread to Western Europe in the fourth century and may be said to have transformed the official religion. Tidings of the intense religious life of the Desert Fathers may have first reached Gaul through St Athanasius, who was in exile in Trier from his bishopric in Alexandria during the year 336. Between 356 and 362 he wrote the *Life of St Antony* who had lived for thirty-five years in solitude in a ruinous Roman fort in the mountain of Pispir between the Nile and the Dead Sea, and this brilliantly written biography could not fail to have its effect on the more spiritual of the Christians of the West. Gradually the ideal of eremitism spread from the solitaries of Lower Egypt and reached Gaul, partly by the accounts of travellers who had visited them, as we learn from the *Dialogues* of Sulpicius Severus; partly by knowledge of small communities such as those on the islands fringing the Italian coast, of whom we read in the poem, *De Reditu Suo*, by Rutilius Namatianus, which relates his return voyage from Italy to Gaul, and refers incidentally to small communities on the islands of Gorgon and Capraria.

Early in the fifth century the eremitical ideal inspired St Honoratus, whose education had been in Greece, to found a monastic community on the island of Lerina off the coast of Provence. The learning and devotion of its monks rapidly gained for the little community a prestige almost equivalent to that of a western university. Shortly after the foundation of this island community cenobitic monasteries arose in southern Provence, the most famous being that of St Victor near Marseilles. The influence of both these monasteries was widespread and permanent, largely due to their intellectual activity. Among the future bishops nursed in Lerina Honoratus himself, Eucherius of Lyons, Faustus of Riez, Caesarius of Arles, are among the most impressive ecclesiastical names of the fifth century in Gaul, while the *Institutes* and the *Conferences*, the writings of John Cassian, abbot of the neighbouring cenobitic monastery of St Victor near Marseilles, are the most important writings on monastic discipline in the Western Church before the Rule of St Benedict.

Simultaneously with these famous monastic foundations a humbler and less formal monastic habit was gaining ground in Gaul, perhaps as a natural corollary to the privately owned and endowed Churches. St Jerome refers to a domestic monastery, 'a Choir of the blessed'[15] at Aquileia, in which he used to meet Rufinius. St Augustine tells of a community outside the walls of Milan, with St Ambrose at its head, and of another at Trier in which he had found a book containing a *Life of St Antony*,[16] and we may perhaps compare the community described by St Victricius, Bishop of Rouen, in his *De Laude Sanctorum*.[17] We have seen how Sulpicius Severus in Gaul, and his lifelong friend and correspondent St Paulinus at Nola in Italy, vied with one another in building and beautifying each his own church for the use of the community. Sulpicius Severus speaks of himself as surrounded by a *turba monachorum*, and in his *Dialogues* he represents his friend Posthumianus, recently returned from his sojourn with a solitary ascetic in the North African desert, as narrating his experiences to an eager listening audience. To St Paulinus the new vision of Christianity, born of the mysticism and asceticism of the East, had come as a revelation of blinding glory, an imperative call to renounce the world and devote his wealth and his vast estates – his *regna*, as Ausonius calls them – to Christ, founding a private monastery where he lived at Nola in the Campania with his Spanish wife Therasia, henceforth in the relationship of brother and sister. He refers to their establishment as a *monasterium*,[18] and its few select occupants as a *fraternitas monacha*.[19] His correspondence with his old friend and teacher Ausonius is our most eloquent testimony to the irresistible force with which this new ascetic ideal flooded the quiet officialism of Gaulish Christianity.

The great pioneer of the monastic movement in the West was St Martin, bishop of Tours. [20] He was probably born in 316, and died in 397. In early life he had been a soldier in the Roman army in Pannonia – now Hungary – near the Danube, but having been converted to Christianity he sought and obtained his release from the military authorities while the army was at Worms; but the exact date is uncertain. He spent a brief period as a solitary in a cell at Milan; but it was during the period when the Arian controversy was at its height, and Martin had evidently already developed a profound admiration for Hilary of Poitiers, whose intellectual life, like his own, had been largely formed in the atmosphere of the Greek Church. On Hilary's return from exile Martin sought him out, and after an unsuccessful attempt to find him in Rome, followed him to Gaul. Here he settled under Hilary's auspices, first living ascetically with a few monks in caves and wooden cells at Ligugé, and later founding his *magnum monasterium*, his 'great monastery', Marmoutier, in the neighbourhood of Tours. *C.* 370 he was consecrated bishop of Tours. Ligugé was the first monastery in Gaul, and Martin the earliest of the monastic bishops, who became a special characteristic of the 'Celtic Church' for several centuries.

In his career and personality Martin combined the practical organizer and the mystic, and these gifts, and the episcopal patronage of the great bishop Hilary, combined to make him the traditional founder of Western monasticism. Hilary was undoubtedly the chief influence in his life, and there can be no doubt whatever that Martin's work, and his prestige during his life-time, were inspired and guided by Hilary personally. How far Martin's early prestige, first in Gaul and later in Britain, is due to his disciple, Sulpicius Severus, who devoted much of his life and literary career to the creation of our picture of the saint, it is difficult to say. Martin has left us no writings of his own, but the charm of the writings of Severus, and the intimate picture which he has bequeathed to us, are inseparable from the saint who has inspired them.

It is a remarkable thing that western monasticism, inspired and supported by Hilary, the pillar of Western Catholicism, should have been a subject of active disapproval by the Gaulish bishops, but there can be no doubt of the fact. It is constantly referred to in the correspondence between Sulpicius Severus and St Paulinus of Nola. The democratic system which prevailed, and has always prevailed, in the monastic communities, was quite alien to the ecclesiastical hierarchy based on the Roman civil administrative system. This growing hostility between the episcopal and the monastic elements in Gaul became more pronounced in the early years of the fifth century, and episcopal disapproval was especially bitter against monastic appointments to vacant bishoprics. This disapproval was expressed unequivocally from the papal chair, and is voiced emphatically in a famous letter, the *Cuperemus quidem*, addressed in 428 by Celestine, bishop of Rome, to the bishops of Vienne and Narbonne on the occasion of the election of a bishop to the vacant see of Arles. The pope protests against the election of 'wanderers and strangers' (*peregrini et extranei*) to episcopal seats over the heads of the local clergy, who were known to their flocks and had a right to preferment in the districts in which they had laboured. He expresses his dislike of monastic bishop in no equivocal terms.

They who have not grown up in the Church act contrary to the Church's usages, . . . coming from other customs they have brought their traditional ways with them . . . clad in a cloak and with a girdle round their loins . . . Such a practice may perhaps be followed . . . by those who dwell in remote places and pass their lives far from their fellow men. But why should they dress in this way in the churches of God, changing the usage of so many years, of such great prelates, for another habit?[21]

I have dwelt on the early Christianity of Gaul because contemporary records are comparatively full and authentic. For the history of the early Church in Britain[22] we have no contemporary local records apart from a few stone inscriptions in the West. Local literary records in Britain do not begin before the sixth century, and in Ireland, where writing was introduced in all probability in the fifth century, in the time of St Patrick, his own writings are our only genuine documents of so early a date. We are therefore chiefly dependent on contemporary continental writers for our knowledge of the earliest Christianity in Britain, and for this purpose our fullest sources of information come from Gaul.

Our earliest direct references to Christianity in Britain, however, come from two north African sources. Tertullian, writing *c.* 200, states that the Gospel had already reached parts of Britain beyond the

Romanized areas (*Britannorum inaccessa Romanis loca Christo vero subdita*);[23] and Origen, writing *c.* 240, refers to Christianity as a force which was unifying the Britons (*quando enim terra Britanniae ante adventum Christi in unius dei consensit religionem?*).[24] Well-attested traditions relate three early martyrdoms in Britain – that of St Alban at Verulamium[25] and of Aaron and Julius at Carlisle or Chester, or possibly at Caerleon. An acrostic scratched on red wall-plaster from a Roman house at Cirencester has been credibly interpreted as a cross composed of the words *Pater noster*, together with the *alpha* and *omega*, the whole forming a Christian cryptogram, suggesting that it was used as a Christian symbol in Britain already before the Peace of the Church under Constantine in 312.

We have no records of the conversion of Britain, or of the source from which Christianity was first introduced; but it was evidently already well established comparatively early in Roman times, and the attendance of three British bishops at the Councils of Arles in 314[26] and Rimini[27] in 359 imply that it was already an organized institution.[28] It was evidently in full communication and sympathy with the Church of Gaul throughout the fourth century, for St Athanasius refers to the Church in Britain as having accepted the definitions established at the Council of Nicaea in 325,[29] and both Hilary of Poitiers[30] and Athanasius[31] mention the British bishops as well as those of Gaul as among their supporters. In Constantine's circular letter to all parts of the Empire inculcating unity in the observance of Easter the Britons are included among the countries to whom it is addressed.[32] The letters of St Jerome habitually specify Britain as among the nations who worship Christ.

In recent years archaeology has added to our knowledge of Christianity in Britain during the Roman period. A small building excavated at Silchester has been generally accepted since 1893 as a Christian church on account of its plan, but though it has been recently re-excavated the results have not yet been published and the Christian purpose of the building is not certainly proved. In the Roman city of Caerwent a small building was inserted in the ruins of the Roman public baths, with a plan and orientation strongly suggestive of a Christian Church[33] which might suggest a survival of Romano-British Christianity into post-Roman times; but again proof is lacking. Bede speaks of a church at Verulamium on the scene of St Alban's martyrdom as still surviving in his own day, and of others at Canterbury restored by the Saxon king Ethelbert of Kent, of which one, just outside the city, was assigned to his queen Bertha and her Frankish chaplain Liudhard, and others were also used by Augustine and his monks and their converts.

The most important excavation of a Roman Christian site in Britain is that of the villa of Lullingstone in Kent in 1949.[34] Between the years 364 and 370 the owner of the villa and his family became Christians. At least two of its upper rooms seem to have been transformed for use as a Christian chapel, and on one of the walls fragments of painted wall-plaster have been reconstructed and respresent six human figures with arms extended laterally, in the *orante* attitude of early Christian prayer; and in addition a large *Chi-Rho* monogram in a floral wreath was painted beside the praying figures. Another *Chi-Rho* monogram encircled by a wreath was painted on the wall of the ante-chamber. Evidently the occupants of the villa were Christians during the second half of the fourth century, and it is probable, though again not proved, that they had arranged this part of the house as a domestic oratory or a multi-cellular house-church, such as preceded the independent basilicas, and Christian worship evidently continued into the fifth century. Already before the close of the Roman Occupation, and undoubtedly as the result of the peace of the Church under Constantine, Christianity had become the official religion in Britain.

Even after the withdrawal of the Romans, communication between the British and the continental Churches continued. The barbarian pirates, already rendering the North Sea and the English Channel difficult and dangerous, were no absolute deterrent to the voyages of ecclesiastics and even private travellers to and from the Continent. Strangely enough it was at precisely this period that Rome is first recorded to have taken an active interest in affairs in Britain. At this time a certain Pelagius, a monk of Celtic birth, probably a Briton, was prominent in the spread of certain views on the continent which were regarded as heretical, and we learn from Prosper of Aquitaine, whose authority in this matter is entirely trustworthy, that Britain was regarded as a stronghold of the heresy.[35]

The views of Pelagius[36] are nowhere set forth by himself *in extenso*, and we are chiefly dependent on the reports of his opponents. The heresy attributed to him was the denial of original sin, and the claim that man is able to avoid sin by his own efforts without the necessity of aid by divine grace. Whether Pelagius developed the views attributed to him before he left Britain for the Continent is unknown, but the long and bitter controversy which ensued, commonly referred to as 'Grace and Free Will', probably had the effect of bringing Britain into closer touch with the continental Church than she had been before.

Accordingly in 429 Pope Celestine sent Germanus, bishop of Auxerre, as his own representative (*vice sua*) to Britain to uproot the evil.[37] We have a detailed account of this visit from Constantius,[38] apparently a presbyter of Lyons, who wrote before the close of the century, probably at the request of the bishop of Lyons. Constantius also records a second visit by St Germanus, probably *c.* 445, but for this second visit we have no supporting evidence. The nature of the narrative of Constantius indicates that it was composed primarily for edification, rather than as a historical document, and the author himself is at pains to disclaim complete responsibility for the authenticity of his facts. His literary conscience still adheres to the critical standards inculcated in the Roman high-schools of Gaul.[39]

Even Britain was still benefiting from the education of the schools founded by the Romans in this country, still taking an active part in continental thought, and Britishers were still able to travel freely to and from the Continent. This we learn from a collection of anonymous letters,[40] perhaps Pelagian in tone and certainly liberal, even democratic, in outlook, which are believed to date from this period. One delightfully personal letter in the series purports to have been written by a Briton travelling abroad to his father, probably a bishop, as his son addresses him as '*honorificentia tua*' and '*parens delectissime*'. The writer of this particular letter is taking his little daughter with him for training as a religious devotee in Sicily, and begs his father not to grieve on her account, but to think of her as he would if she were a boy 'who for his education must be separated for the time being from those who love him'.[41]

In all probability Christianity had an unbroken history in Britain. In eastern Britain the invasions of the heathen Saxons made communication with the Continental Church increasingly difficult, and from the fifth century onwards our continental sources cease, and we are dependent on British records, archaeological, epigraphical and literary, supplemented from Irish (Latin) sources in all these disciplines. The picture which they present is of the continuous spread of

214

Christianity westwards in our islands beyond the borders of the Roman Empire.

In the British (Celtic) kingdom of Strathclyde remains of two early Christian cemeteries have been traced by the inscriptions on the famous Catstone at Kirkliston some six miles west of Edinburgh,[42] standing *in situ* in the midst of the graves; and by the even more famous tombstone of Yarrowkirk near Selkirk, which also once stood in a large Christian cemetery.[43] In the south-western peninsula of Galloway is an extensive concentration of early inscribed stones.[44] The oldest is believed to be the *Latinus* stone at Whithorn of fifth or early sixth century date. The most interesting of the Kirkmadrine stones, a memorial to three priests, also probably dates from the fifth century.[45] Three of the Kirkmadrine stones, and two at Whithorn commemorate Christians, and must have stood on ancient church sites. Excavations are bringing to light early churches in the neighbourhood, notably those at the traditional site of St Ninian's chapel on the Isle of Whithorn, at Whithorn itself,[46] and on Ardwell Island.[47] An eighth century tradition recorded by Bede (*H.E.* III. 4) states that St Ninian[48] converted the Southern Picts 'long before' St Columba converted the Northern Picts. St Columba died in 597. Bede adds that Ninian's *locus* (monastic site) was known as *Candida Casa* ('the white house') 'because he there built a church of stone which was unusual among the British'.[49]

We have no records of the conversion of the Isle of Man, Wales, or Cornwall, but in Wales continuity from Roman time is indicated, though not actually proved. One stone from Pentrefoelas in Denbighshire, of the fifth or early sixth century, is very possibly connected with an early Christian cemetery on the site where the stone was found.[50] Perhaps the most cogent evidence for the early date of the Christian Church in Wales is the existence in Irish of a series of Christian Latin loan-words which would appear to have been introduced into Ireland by British missionaries before the date of the coming of Palladius to Ireland in 431 (cf. p. 218 below). This religious vocabulary, with some Irish additions, was just enough to provide a skeleton service of Christian terminology for a community with an organization still elementary.[51] The earliest Welsh saint of native tradition is St Dubricius (Welsh *Dyfrig*), but the earliest *Life* of a Welsh saint is probably that of St Samson of Dol in Brittany, which is not earlier than the seventh century.

It is probable that in the days of the early Church the countries on the shores of the Solway Firth, Morecambe Bay, and the Irish Sea, were in close touch, and in this, as in other matters, shared a common culture. The Manx language is believed to have its closest affinities in the Gaelic spoken at this time in Galloway,[52] and it is probable that Manx Christianity[53] would be introduced at an early period from the flourishing Christian Church of that region. However that may be, tradition and archaeology alike suggest that the conversion of the Isle of Man probably goes back to the fifth century, the period of the saint to whom the Cathedral of St Germans on Peel Island is dedicated. Dedications to St Patrick are likely to be later, and the early pre-Norse crosses do not reveal special Irish affinities. Of the six early Christian memorial stones one from Knoc y Doone in Andreas, inscribed in both ogams and Latin letters, is ascribed to the fifth century. Of the three most interesting inscribed monuments, the oldest is the so-called 'marigold' pillar with the inscription recording Bishop Inreit, which is ascribed to the seventh century.

Early records are entirely wanting, but the archaeological remains suggest that the Manx church corresponded closely to the early institutions of the Celtic Church everywhere in the British Isles, being monastic in organization, and consisting of a principal monastic foundation corresponding to the Welsh *clas* churches and a number of subordinate churches, known in Wales as *llan*. The only pre-Norse monastic foundation in Man, corresponding to the *clas* churches in Wales, is at Maughold, where a rich collection of crosses has survived, and where the important stele of Inreit suggests that Maughold was the seat of early bishops. Here, as elsewhere in Ireland and Scotland, we find in solitary places small hermitages, whether single, or grouped in an enclosure and containing a small oratory, such as at *Cronk na Irree Laa* a few miles south of Peel. A special feature of Man is the number of small oratories enclosed in an earthen bank, often enclosing early graves. These are widespread throughout the island, the remains of four being enclosed within the churchyard of Maughold alone. Within the enclosure small stone-built sanctuaries, more or less rectangular, are generally found, known as *keills*. Precise dating is at present impossible, but this grouping in relation to the church at Maughold is comparable with the numerous chapels associated with important Irish monasteries such as Clonmacnoise, where they are still to be seen.

216

1 and 2. Interior panels from the 'Gundestrup Bowl'. This magnificent silver cauldron is 42 cms high and 69 cms across, and weighs nearly 9 kg. It was discovered in a peat-bog in Denmark, but is believed to be of Celtic manufacture, and to date from the first or second century BC.

3. (left) This spectacular early La Tène type of helmet was found at Amfreville (Eire). It is made of bronze, with two iro hoops. The whole was covered with gold foil, and enamel studs were mounted around the lower edge. The large ornaments have been lost from the sides. The height is 6¼ inches.

4. Right: This beautiful bronze flagon is one of the chief treasures of Gaulish art. The handle is in the form of a predatory animal, while two smaller animals surmount the lid, and all are stalking the unsuspecting little duck on the spout.

5 Below: Small bronze cult charist from Merida, Spain. A mounted Iberian and his dog are pursuing a wild boar. The group is depicted on a wheeled vehicle or platform, and a curious feature is the series of little bells suspended from the rear. The modelling and proportion of the figures are of a high quality.

6 This beautiful work of art, now in the British Museum, is generally known as the 'Battersea Shield' because it was found in the River Thames at Battersea. It dates from c. 75 BC. and is a late example of the Gallo-British tradition of Celtic art.

7 A Gaulish warrior, characteristically depicted leaning on his long shield of La Tène type, which resembles the Battersea Shield. This is a Roman statue of the Augustan age from Mondragon (Vaucluse).

8 (above) Air view of a number of earthworks on the Hill of Tara, Co. Meath. The two ring forts in the foreground are enclosed in the earthwork known as Rath na Ríogh.

9 Dún Oengusa, Aran Islands, Co. Galway. This magnificent prehistoric fortress stands precariously on the edge of the cliff facing the Atlantic on Aranmore.

10 Grianán Ailech, Co. Donegal, a strong hill fort on a hill some 800 feet high, a few miles west of Londonderry. This stronghold of the Northern Uí Néill is the chief fortress of early northern Ireland. This photograph of the interior of the fort's intramural corridor shows the building technique which is of special interest.

11 The Aylesford Bucket was part of an elaborate internment in a circle of pit burials at Aylesford, Kent, constituting a Belgic cemetery of about the period of Caesar's invasion.

12 Gold torc from Snettisham, Norfolk. This is one of a series of torcs found during ploughing operations at Ken Hill, Snettisham in 1948-50.

13 Original door-frame of the Celto-Ligurian sanctuary of Roquepertuse (Bouches-du-Rhône). Three vertical pillars are furnished with niches for human skulls. Above the doorway is a gigantic bird. The pillars retain traces of paintings of fish and foliage. The height is $2\frac{1}{2}$ metres and the date third century BC.

15 The water-goddess Coventina. This is a recessed and gabled dedication tablet, found in the well sacred to the goddess Coventina at Barrowburgh (Brocolita) on Hadrian's Wall, Northumberland.

14 The Monster of Moves (Bouches-du-Rhône). A seated anthropophagous monster rests its forepaws on two bearded, severed human heads, their eyes closed in death. A human arm with bracelet protrudes from the monster's mouth, and its back is covered with scales. The group is of native stone and is 1 m. 12 cms high. The date is pre-Roman, probably La Tène II.

16 Brug na Bóinne, or 'New Grange', Co. Meath, a heathen sanctuary, is a superb megalithic tumulus of uncertain date, perhaps as early as 3000 BC.

17 The interior of the tumulus of Brug na Bóinne, showing the corbelled dome, some 20 feet high.

18 Inishmurray, Co. Sligo. This is the most fully preserved cashel wall of the early Christian island sanctuaries. Internal steps lead up to the summit and the cashel wall itself has an interior chamber entered from the doorway on the right. The sanctuary is on the edge of the sea, which is visible in the background, and the Sligo coast lies beyond.

19 The famous sixth or seventh-century Gallarus Oratory near Kilmalkedar (Co. Derry).

20 The Seven Churches of Aranmore, Co. Galway. In the early Celtic Church, important ecclesiastical sites were characterised by a number of small churches before the development of large structures was introduced under later foreign influence.

21 The Rock of Cashel, Co. Tipperary. This magnificent site was the fortress and ancient capital of Munster. In the foreground are the ruins of the cathedral, founded in 1169, and a perfect round tower, over 90 feet high, probably of tenth-century date. In the background is a plain rectangular castle of three storeys, and beyond the rock on low ground, Hoare Abbey, built soon after 1272, occupied by monks from Mellifont.

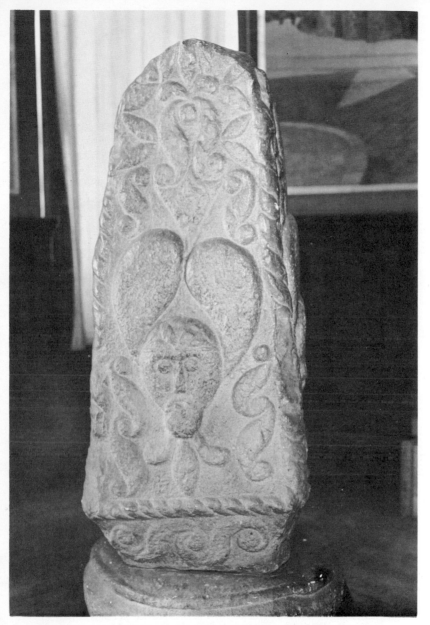

22 The famous stone pyramid carved in relief from Pfalzfeld, found at St Goar in the Hunsrück. It is one of the earliest and most typically Celtic of our carved monuments, measuring 148 cms high.

23 Head of a hero or chieftain from Mšecké Žehrovice, Bohemia, carved in local limestone. This is regarded as one of the finest examples of the stylisation of the human face produced by Celtic art. The hair and features are essentially Celtic. The prominent eyes, unformed ears, the triangular nose and slit-like mouth, the backward swept ridged fringe and the torc are all characteristic, as are also the flourishes of the moustache and eyebrows. Height 24 cms, c. 100 BC.

24–27 Gallo-Roman wooden sculpture from the sanctuary, doubtless therapeutic, at the source of the Seine, some 35 kms to the north-east of Dijon.

24 and 25 Carved wooden heads: the head on the right shows a considerable advance in modelling of structure and features, over that on the left.

26 Figure dressed in cloak and hood, possibly representing a traveller or pilgrim to the sanctuary.

27 The figure of a woman.

28 The eighth-century 'Tara Brooch' was found in a wooden box with a number of Viking objects at Bettystown, Co. Meath, near the River Boyne. It is made of bronze, penannular in form, and the chain attached indicates that it was one of a pair which probably fastened a cloak. It is richly decorated with gold thread, amber and enamel.

29 The Ardagh Chalice, a superb treasure of Irish ecclesiastical art and technique, dating from the eighth century. The two-handled cup is made of silver and decorated with gold, gilt bronze and enamel. The decoration has much in common with the 'Tara Brooch', notably in the interlacing filigree beasts of gold wire in the upper band of ornament, and in the blue and red enamel and gold in the studs.

30 The Book of Durrow. This superb Irish illuminated manuscript
dates from the seventh century. It is a small volume of the Gospels
($9\frac{1}{2}$ inches x $6\frac{1}{2}$ inches) and is known to have been in the possession
of the Columban monastery of Durrow, near Tullamore, Co. Offaly.

31 Glamis Cross, in the garden of the manse at Glamis, Angus.
The crucifixion is never represented on the Pictish stones,
but the cross occurs frequently. Here it is carved in high
relief, the surface entirely covered with conventional Celtic
design, chiefly knotwork. The background panels depict
Pictish motifs of human figures and symbols.

32 The 'Cross of the Scriptures', west side, Clonmacnois,
Co. Offaly. It bears an inscription requesting a
prayer for Flann, King of Munster, who died
in 904. This is one of the finest of the high crosses,
with an advanced scriptural iconography.

The Christianity of Cornwall probably shared with Wales a continuous history from Roman times, for although we have no actual record so early, there were no land barriers, and it has been shown (p. 78 above) that the Severn Sea united South Wales and Cornwall in a common culture. We have nine memorial stones which can be dated by their Roman lettering to the fifth or sixth century, and two bearing an early form of the *Chi-Rho* monogram.[54]

It was the Romans who first taught the British to cut stone, and it is no doubt ultimately to this Roman technique that the Britons owe their wealth of early stone inscriptions. The Britons moreover had Roman stone inscriptions constantly before their eyes in all parts of the country. On the other hand all the British (Latin) inscriptions are funeral monuments, whereas most of the Roman monuments are official and military. Moreover the British inscriptions of the fifth century are almost entirely personal and Christian, for which we lack precedent among the early Christians of Roman Britain, who do not seem to have erected tombstones. The British inscriptions from the fifth to the seventh centuries are closely comparable to those of Christian Gaul, not only in the institution of commemorating the dead in this way, but also in the formulae used and in the type of lettering. Although in general there is a slight time-lag in Britain in the phraseology and epigraphy, the conclusion is unavoidable that the epigraphy of the earliest British memorial stones is derived from Gaul in the first half of the fifth century. This important Christian Gaulish influence evidently reached the western shores of Britain by sea.[55]

One important inscription in Anglesey is of special interest in this respect. We have already referred to the inscribed memorial tablet in the church of Llangadwaladr commemorating the 'renowned king Catamanus', i.e. king Cadfan of North Wales, who died in 625. The lettering of the inscription is in almost pure manuscript half-uncials, and represents the latest fashion in the continental manuscript lettering of the time. Two other Anglesey inscriptions (CIIC nos. 968, 971) have similar lettering. The son of Cadfan was the great Cadwallon, who slew King Edwin of Northumbria, and the church was evidently founded by his grandson Cadwaladr who died in 664. The dynasty had just cause to commemorate its founder in the laudatory terms reminiscent of bardic panegyric, and under their auspices the court of Anglesey and North Wales may well have opened cultural communications with some Gaulish court of which we find later echoes in the early ninth century.

We have seen that the Saxon raids on eastern and south-eastern Britain did not cut off the British Isles from communication with the Continent, and though these raids must have been a serious hindrance to ecclesiastical communication they certainly did not preclude it. It is on recorded that St Victricius,[56] bishop of Rouen from c. 380 to c. 408, with whom both St Martin and St Paulinus of Nola were acquainted, visited Britain c. 395; and the history of Pelagianism, the anonymous letters referred to above, and the visit of St Germanus to Britain in 429 suggest uninterrupted relations with Britain throughout the fifth century. The history of the colonization of Brittany confirms this, and in the sixth century we have seen that a regular sea-route must have united the countries surrounding the Irish Sea with Gaul. This was, in fact, the period in which Christianity was established in Ireland from overseas.

How did Christianity first reach Ireland? The conversion is generally believed to have been in the fifth century, probably early in the century, and perhaps from two directions. Our earliest reliable notice is contained in Prosper's *Chronicle* s.a. 431, according to which a certain Palladius was ordained by Celestine, and sent as first bishop to the Irish 'believing in Christ' (*in Christum credentes*). The reliability of Prosper's testimony is beyond doubt, and implies that already before 431 there were communities of Christians in Ireland already sufficiently organized to justify Rome in sending a bishop to minister to their needs and to include them in the Roman obedience. So far our direct continental evidence gives us no hint as to the source of the initial conversion, but makes it clear that the earliest Christian organization was from Rome.

From now onwards we must rely on Latin records made in Ireland. Early and continuous Irish tradition (in Latin works) claims that Christianity was first introduced into Ireland by St Patrick[57] about the same time as the mission of Palladius, or shortly after. Writing is known to have been first introduced into Ireland in the fifth century. The *Annals of Ulster* (s.a. 431), doubtless relying on Prosper, record Palladius as having been sent by the bishop of Rome, Celestine, as first bishop of the Scots (Irish). In the following year the same annals record s.a. 432 the arrival of Patrick in Ireland. We really know nothing further about the mission of Palladius. The *Annals of Ulster* have a number of further entries recording the death of Patrick at various dates, e.g. 457 where he is referred to as *senex Patricius* (*Quies senis Patricii ut alii libri dicunt*); 461 (*Hic alii quietem Patrici dicunt*), and again in 492. These discrepancies have been very variously explained,[58] and are possibly in part due to the composite nature of the annals; but for our purpose the important fact is that the earliest Irish historical tradition believed that Christianity was effectively introduced into Ireland in the fifth century.

Our earliest and indeed our only reliable historical documents for the mission of Patrick and the foundation of his Church are two Latin letters believed on internal evidence to date from this period, and claiming categorically to have been written by the saint himself. These are the *Confession* and the *Letter to the Soldiers of Coroticus*. Both are brief, but both are of great importance. The former claims that Patrick was a member of a Romanized British family, that he had been carried off to Ireland as a slave at the age of sixteen, that he had spent six years there, and then escaped, and that in response to a vision he returned to Ireland and founded a Church, 'in the ends of the earth', '*ad exteras partes ubi nemo ultra erat*' (*Confessio*, 51), '*in ultimis terrae*' (ibid. 58). These expressions have no geographical significance, but are an ancient traditional form of reference to the British Isles, still current, but no longer intended to be interpreted literally. It is thus that St Columbanus, as late as the early seventh century, refers to Ireland in his letter to Pope Boniface IV: (AD 612–13) 'We, all the Irish, dwellers at the ends of the earth'.[59]

No *acta* of the saint have survived; and no early *vitae* and few early traditions of his disciples. Almost all the early documents claiming to be from his hand or those of his disciples have been shown to be spurious.[60] The biographical narratives of Muirchu and Tirechán, composed in the late seventh century, claim, probably with justice, to have incorporated traditions of at least a generation earlier, and are consistent with other surviving traditions incorporated in later works. These early documents present us with a consistent picture of a Church founded by Patrick in the fifth century, completely Roman in origin, tradition, character, and episcopal organization. In this respect they are consistent with the *Confession*, in which he leaves us in no doubt that he regards both himself and his fellow-countrymen in Britain as Roman citizens.

We may leave aside the difficult and controversial question of the authenticity and bias of the Patrician documents as a whole, for his own writings give us a clear indication of his mission and of a Church which he claimed to have founded, and these fifth-century writings are certainly our earliest evidence for Christianity in our islands from the time that direct Continental evidence ceases. It is a fact generally accepted that all these early documents imply the existence of a Church of Ireland from the fifth century, organized in all essential respects on lines comparable with that of the contemporary episcopal church in Gaul. This Gaulish Church we have already seen to have been essentially an urban Church, reflecting the official legal and administrative system of the Roman civil service. This was probably the organization of the early Church in Britain also, and the one with which Patrick would be familiar. The later traditions of his sojourn in Lérina and his contact with St Martin of Tours, indeed with any Continental Church, are entirely without foundation.

Yet in admitting the establishment of an Irish episcopal Church by Patrick we are confronted by a serious problem. In our traditional picture of the Irish Church in the sixth century the Patrician Church plays relatively little part. The organization is partly episcopal but largely monastic. Nothing authentic is known of Patrick's immediate successors, and the great ecclesiastical establishments which are traditionally reported to have sprung up throughout Ireland at this period never claim to have been established by him, or by Palladius, or by any of their disciples. This Irish Church in the sixth century comes before us as organized and governed increasingly on monastic lines. There is, however, no central organization with authority over all the monasteries. Each large monastery is independent and governed by an abbot with full rights and responsibilities over its lands and finances, though often in more or less close relationship with great secular authorities, on whose patronage they seem to have been in some measure dependent for their establishment and survival.

Each of these large independent monasteries was entirely self-governing. They each had their own rules, and their own ascetic discipline. They correspond in form and prestige to the Welsh *clas* churches, the 'mother' churches of Wales, sometimes forming centres of subordinate ecclesiastical establishments, and from time to time even founding or giving their protection and blessing, and extending their benefits and their discipline to anchorite retreats (cf. p. 223 below). Among the great Irish monastic establishments claiming their foundation from saints traditionally ascribed to the sixth century were Clonmacnoise in the west from St Kieran, which developed as an important religious and educational establishment; Bangor in Co. Down in the north-east from St Comgall, which became a great centre of historical studies; Clonard in the east from St Finnian, proverbial for the number of saints traditionally fostered there; Lismore in the south, founded by Mo-Chuta, which developed interesting intellectual contacts with the Continent. Other important early foundations are Ardmore in Co. Waterford, traditionally founded by St Declan, the chief saint of the Dési, and still today a quiet retreat which has hardly undergone any change since the erection of its round tower; and Imblech Ibair (Emly), the chief church of the Eóganacht of ancient Munster, about fifty miles inland from Ardmore, founded by St Ailbe. These Munster churches claimed by tradition to have been founded before the coming of St Patrick, and in this they may indeed by right.

We do not know precisely how or when the monastic system entered Ireland. It is in some respects comparable with that introduced by St Martin into Gaul, and it spread rapidly throughout the country, and with it the new spirit of mysticism, a new and stricter way of life, a more intense devotion and ascetic discipline. This movement had its origin, as we have seen, in the ascetics of the eastern deserts, Egypt, Syria and Mesopotamia. In accordance with their retirement from the world these ascetics also renounced worldly rank and abandoned their relatives and even their personal names. Eugippius tells us in his *Life of St Severinus*, the apostle to the Danube tribes in Noricum (in modern Austria), that to the end of his life the saint never revealed his name. This practical democracy, which has always been, and still is, a fundamental principle of monasticism, was doubtless one of the principal elements in its rapid success in the West. We have also seen that it is one of the features in the new monastic movement in Gaul which gave serious offence to Pope Celestine (cf. p. 211 above).

In fact this new movement in Gaul had had a harder battle to fight where the episcopal system of Church government was deeply rooted in the system of Roman local government. In Ireland no initial difficulty or organization existed. It was a pastoral country, with no towns, and had never been under Roman administration. The monasteries served as an admirable centre for the religious needs and the civilizing amenities of the surrounding tribes. There was therefore no clash between the episcopal and monastic rights, such as occurred in Gaul. Independent of one another as the great monastic organizations were, the chief clash was one which occasionally arose between one monastery and another. The annals record several instances in which such hostilities even amounted to armed conflicts in later times. In general, however, the Ireland of the seventh century presents us with a map of great monastic foundations, independent, deeply religious, eagerly cultivating education and scholarship, and the arts of civilization.

It is important to emphasize that here, as in Gaul, the difference between the diocesan and the monastic churches is simply one of Church government and ecclesiastical practice, not of doctrine. The monastic church was never heretical or schismatic. It adhered in all respects to the established hierarchy of the Catholic Church with the bishop at the head, and the presbyter, deacon and subordinate clergy below him. The bishop was responsible for the consecration of churches and of other bishops. He often lived within the monastery, and sometimes bishop and abbot were the same person. There was no cleavage, and although this monastic development has come to be habitually designated 'The Celtic Church' the term is not strictly accurate, for the Church was in all essentials Catholic. Nevertheless during the period when the barbarian invasions made travel difficult, and the Church in the Celtic countries was relatively debarred from close regular participation in the developments of the continental Church as these took place from time to time, the Church in Ireland grew conservative and in some respects out of date in its practices, and the term 'Celtic Church' has come to denote this conservative form of Church practice. In Ireland the monasteries were so powerful and numerous that the 'Celtic' and the 'Irish Church' have come to be practically interchangeable terms.

We do not know by what route the monastic movements entered the British Isles. Various indications suggest the south of Ireland, possibly by way of Ardmore; but whether from Gaul direct, by way of Aquitaine, or from northern Spain, or direct from the Eastern Mediterranean is unknown. All three have been suggested. Moreover in close relationship with the monastic development there appeared in all the Western Celtic churches a movement of greater asceticism, commonly referred to as the 'anchorite reform'; but the term is perhaps misleading, for the 'anchorites' not rarely formed a body within an actual monastery, or within its obedience, while at other times the more ascetic anchorites lived as solitaries, or in very small groups in remote islands in the sea, or in solitary places. The Scottish place-name *Dysert*, Irish *dísert* (L. *desertum*) still recalls these early retreats, and the ruins of their beehive-shaped buildings (*clochán*) still survive on the island of Inishmurray off the coast of Sligo and the little settlement like an eagle's eyrie at the top of some 600 steps on the rock of Skellig Michael eight miles out in the Atlantic off the Kerry coast; in islands in the Inner Hebrides of Scotland, and on North Rona[61] with its oratory and graveyard sixty miles north of the Butt of Lewis, and Sula-Sker[62] ten miles out from Rona, with chapel and bee-hive huts. It was in search of just such a solitary place in the Ocean that Cormac úa Liatháin, abbot of Durrow and also a bishop and an anchorite, found himself astray in the Arctic regions, and eventually arrived in Iona.[63] The most interesting of these voyages is the historical voyage of St Colman who is related by Bede (H.F. IV, 4) to have retired with his followers after the Synod of Whitby in 663 to the island of Inishbofin off the west coast of Mayo.

The isolation of the anchorites' retreats has ensured their preservation, whether wholly or partially intact, and the simplicity of their architecture may easily mislead us in regard to the building technique of the early Irish Church. In the remoter islands only the local stone could be used, and such as could be easily flaked, since available tools precluded elaborate quarrying. The technique is in general surprisingly competent, the rude stone slabs or flakes being carefully corbelled to form a vault and so laid as to slope slightly outwards to carry off the rain. The *clocháin* excavated by F. Henry on Inishkea North[64] off the west coast of Co. Mayo are elaborate little structures, and those of Skellig Michael reveal by the prominent stones which protrude at easy stages cork-screw fashion up the external face of the *clochán* the native substitute for scaffolding in construction.[65] All the *clocháin* are bone-dry inside, and the largest could comfortably accommodate more than a dozen persons.

On the other hand Professor O'Kelly has recently brilliantly demonstrated[66] that in the more easily accessible Church Island close inshore on the Kerry coast near Valencia, where the local cooperation of a congregation could be counted on for transport and labour, suitable building stone was brought by sea, and a more advanced building erected. Few of the early churches on the mainland have survived destruction, but among a few survivals partially preserved, the little Church of Kilmalkedar, and the so-called Gallerus oratory – the latter still perfect – illustrate the builders' skill in a more ambitious form of construction.[67] These churches are not round but quadrilateral, with rounded angles only. The walls of Gallerus are so constructed by their internal batter as to reduce the span required by the corbelled roof. The inclination of the jambs of the door and the internal splay of the tiny windows also serve a structural purpose. Again the stones are so laid as to carry off the rain externally, and leave the structure bone-dry inside.

The technique of all early Irish church buildings precluded the possibility of large structures. These Irish churches, all small, whether single or in groups, thus conform naturally to the tradition of the early Armenian churches as a number of small buildings. In Ireland this grouping can be traced in the monastic settlement of Inishmurray off the Sligo coast, in the settlement of Skellig Michael, in the group of later buildings known as the 'Seven Churches' on Inishmore in the Aran Islands in Galway Bay, and survived in the monastic settlements of Ardmore and Clonmacnoise. With the Norman Conquest and the introduction of the Cistercian Order into Ireland (cf. p. 250 below) all this was changed. The archaic building conception of Irish tradition passed almost in a night, transformed into the impressive Norman church of Cashel and to the lovely abbeys of Mellifont, Jerpoint and Boyle.

The Anchorites[68] are often identified with the Culdees, with whom they had much in common; but the exact nature of the Culdees is still obscure. The name seems to mean 'companion of God' (cf. Latin *comes*) and comes to be used in the sense of 'client', 'dependent', perhaps on the analogy of the legal relationship.[69] Such organization as the term implies is vague and seems to have varied locally, and in Scotland at least it suggests a comparatively late development. The early Rule of the Anchorites, which is commonly known as the *Rule of Columcille*, enjoins them to be alone in a desert place in the neighbourhood of a chief monastery; but the so-called 'Anchorite reform' has no technical significance beyond that certain documents, such as the *Rule of Tallaght*,[70] give evidence that from time to time certain

224

monasteries formulated their rule under an abbot of a strict persuasion.[71]

An Irish document known as the *Catalogus Sanctorum*, claiming to be contemporary with our ascetics, but in reality of the ninth or even the tenth century,[72] divides the saints of Ireland into three orders, placing St Patrick in the first order, the great monastic founding saints in the second, and the third order, we are informed, are 'those who dwell in desert places and live on herbs, and water, and alms, and have nothing of their own'. In reality there is no chronological order. These ascetics and anchorites are contemporary with the great saints of the sixth century,[73] and the term 'anchorite reform' is somewhat misleading. They represent a widespread influence from Eastern asceticism, which is found in Gaul where solitaries in the forest of La Perche and elsewhere were known to Gregory of Tours; and in Brittany in the little archipelago off the Paimpol Peninsula in the north[74] and even in the province of Galicia in northern Spain; but it is above all in the Celtic Church of the west that the life of silent contemplation is most deeply rooted, and eventually inspired a class of hermit poetry unique in the purity and simplicity of its personal devotion and its love of all the little things of nature (p. 289).

It was inevitable that a struggle for supremacy should arise between the diocesan church system of the Patrician tradition[75] and the 'federation of monastic communities',[76] the monastic system of the so-called 'Celtic Church' – the former based on long-established usage and the highest prestige in the Continental Church, the latter an innovation, but in Ireland firmly established. Of the early phase of the struggle we know little, largely owing to the fact that no external authority makes any reference to St Patrick. Neither Gildas nor Bede mention him. Adamnán has no word of Patrick or his Church, nor yet has Columbanus. Yet in the seventh century we have the Life of Patrick by Muirchu emphasizing the rise of Armagh as the church founded by him; and the *Memoir* by Tirechán defining the extent of his *paruchia* and virtually claiming it as coterminous with Ireland itself. A struggle for supremacy in the Church in Ireland was already under way, and by the ninth century the prestige of Patrick and the Church of Armagh was supreme. The Age of the Saints was a memory. It was long cherished and of infinite value in the spiritual history of the Irish people at home and in their intellectual influence abroad. But it was no longer paramount in official circles.

The outcome of the struggle turned on the principle of unity. The absence of any form of central organization in the Celtic Church, as in the early Irish political system, rendered it vulnerable, and certain to be superseded by any strong centralized authority. This occurred with the conquest of Ulster, the most powerful kingdom of Ireland at this period, by the dynasties of the Uí Néill (cf. p. 85 f. above), all owing a nominal allegiance[77] to their over-king at Tara. Hitherto there had been no central paramount dynasty in Ireland. It appears from the Irish Laws that the highest type of kingship in Ireland in the early period is the king of a province.[78] The so-called 'high-king' (the *ard-rí*) of Ireland is a pure fiction, created later as propaganda in support of the Tara dynasty. The task was not a difficult one, for with the conquest of the Ulaid the Uí Néill had also possessed themselves of Emain Macha, the ancient Ulidian capital two miles from Armagh. The inherited oral culture of Emain and the new Latin culture, including the art of writing, sedulously cultivated at Armagh, were henceforth wholly at the service of the Uí Néill. The cult of St Patrick and the earliest written documents became their chief strength, creating an ancient fictitious high-kingship of Ireland and supporting it with all the strength of a powerful church.

Meanwhile we have seen (cf. p. 86 above) that the Northern branch of the Uí Néill dynasty, situated in the north-west of Ireland, in their advance eastwards, had conquered Oriel and threatened the little northern kingdom of Dál Riata. We have also seen that in the fifth century a branch of the Dalriadic dynasty expanded across the sea and founded a dynasty in south-western Scotland, and a Scottish kingdom of Dál Riata, later known as the kingdom of Argyll. The territory must have been hitherto under Pictish rule, but tradition records no opposition, and for all we know to the contrary the new kingdom may have been the result of a peaceful penetration with Pictish acquiescence. The Northern Uí Néill, who had apparently shared originally in alternate succession with the Tara branch as head of the Uí Néill dynasties, must have been fully aware that the conquest of the Ulaid, and the establishment of the Church of Armagh would inevitably result in the establishment of the Tara branch of Southern Uí Néill as the dominant rulers of all northern and central Ireland. Accordingly they sought expansion overseas, uniting with the Dalriadic dynasty in Argyll (*Airer Goídel*, 'the country of the Irish').

226

The prince of the Northern Uí Néill who represented the dynasty in Argyll was St Columba. As a potential heir to the kingship of Tara, his personal prestige was high. He adopted the surest way to establish the power of the new kingdom by uniting his political prestige with that of Dál Riata, and by establishing a new centre for the Celtic form of the Irish Church at Iona, which should be, like Armagh itself, under royal prerogative. It was here that he inaugurated Aedán king of the new kingdom of Dál Riata in Scotland. It was from here that he negotiated a peaceful settlement with Brude mac Maelchon, king of the Northern Picts, the *rex potentissimus*, of Bede, and with this double royal support established his powerful monastic sanctuary on Iona to be henceforth the head of the Celtic Church. The constructive statesmanship and the spiritual and intellectual integrity of Columba resulted in the peaceful creation of what was to become politically the kingdom of Scotland, and ecclesiastically the head of the Celtic Church in Ireland, Scotland and England.

The spiritual life of Columba has come down to us chiefly through the work of the panegyric poets of his native land, and the prose biography of Adamnán. Of the poems and literary works attributed to him and his contemporaries all are of later date, with the possible exception of the *Amra Choluimb Chille*, a composition of highly artificial alliterative verse,[79] attributed to the Irish bard Dallán Forgaill, which is now believed to be a genuine sixth century document. This *amra* ('Eulogy') is an encomium on the saint by the bard Dallán, prompted traditionally by gratitude for Columba's support of the poets of Ireland, who were threatened with banishment on account of their extravagant claims in payment for their works. The large number of scattered survivals of later bardic poetry purporting to be contemporary panegyrics on the saint, no less than the later literary activity which tradition has attributed to Columba himself, are the grateful tribute of later ages to the most illustrious member of a dynasty always famous for its patronage of both the early poets and the later Latin learning.

The institutions of the monastery of Iona were typical of the monastic Celtic Church. Columba was a priest and an abbot, but never a bishop, and he always deferred to a bishop in the celebration of the Mass. Bede (H.E. III, 4) mentions it as a peculiarity of the Columban Church that its head was always a priest. The successors of Columba in the abbacy followed the traditional Irish pattern of the coarbship, that is to say, the abbot was commonly a member (a *com-orba*, 'co-heir') of the family of the original founder. The Columban Church was essentially Irish. Its greatest abbot, the saint's biographer Adamnán, was a great-grandson of the first cousin of Columba, and himself a member of the *Cenél Conaill* of the Northern Uí Néill. It is striking testimony to the early prestige of Iona that it rapidly became the head of the 'Celtic' confederation of churches, that is to say of the 'Columban' communities in Ireland, and almost achieved for them the unity which might have established them as a permanent institution. The Viking raids sapped the strength of Iona. It was pillaged in 795, 802, and 806, and in 825 the community were massacred. The relics and the jurisdiction of the Columban churches seem to have been divided about this time between Dunkeld in the safer inland region on the Upper Tay, and Kells in Ireland, and Kells henceforward became the centre of the 'Celtic Church'.

There were other and more fundamental reasons for the decline of the prestige of the Columban Church, as we shall see. During the sixth century the cult of St Patrick and the importance of Armagh as his principal sanctuary gradually became paramount in Ireland with the expansion and consolidation of the power of the kings of Tara. The biography of the saint by Muirchu, and the Memoir by Tirechán, both written in the interests of Armagh, did much to support the cult of Patrick, while Muirchu's emphasis on the saint's observance of the Easter festival at Tara had underlined the importance of Catholic unity in conformity with Roman usage. Numerous writings, now regarded as post-Patrician forgeries, but purporting to be contemporary documents, attest the tradition of a strong movement, sponsored by the Irish monastic scriptoria, towards furthering the saint who had come to Ireland, not as a monastic founder, but as a direct emissary from the episcopal Church sponsored by Rome and Gaul, and already established in Britain.

The difference of organization and of the principle of government which we have traced in the early Church in Gaul and in Ireland was not confined to these countries. It prevailed throughout the Celtic countries, insular and continental. This difference gave rise during the seventh century to a controversy commonly referred to as the 'Easter Controversy' because the dating of Easter formed the terms of reference on which the dispute turned. The Catholic Church had officially adopted the practice of the dating of Easter as fixed in 457 by Victorius of Aquitaine. The Celtic Church, on the other hand, justly proud of its long and honourable record, preferred to adhere to the traditions handed down by its *seniores*. In reality, however, the long and hard-fought controversy which ensued was not one of superficial details. The issue lay much deeper, and was nothing less than the struggle of the Church of Rome on the one hand to establish unity and supremacy which alone would safeguard the survival of Catholic Christianity in the West; the struggle of the Celtic Church, on the other hand, to maintain its spiritual independence and right to adhere to its own ancient and honourable traditional usages.

In our island the issue was disputed separately in the different countries. It is highly significant that the south of Ireland, always in direct touch with continental developments, was the first to accept the Roman Order. A letter from Cummian, who was probably abbot of Durrow, to Segéne, bishop of Iona (623–52), suggests that already by 629 most of the south-east of Ireland had celebrated Easter according to Roman practice. The letter is still extant, [80] though the text is much corrupted, and this is the only surviving controversial document written in Ireland on the paschal controversy. To defeat opponents the pro-Roman party sent to Rome for guidance – note again the apparently easy communication – and in 636 the south of Ireland joined the 'new Order which had lately come from Rome'. It is interesting to observe that in this they were ahead of the Celtic Church in Britain. Moreover it was nearly sixty years before the north of Ireland conformed.

The church in Northumbria had had a chequered career. Edwin, the Anglian king of united Bernicia and Deira, had been converted by St Paulinus from Canterbury in 627. On his death he was succeeded by Oswald who had spent his exile during Edwin's reign in Scotland, and on his accession had introduced the saintly Aidan from Iona and established the Columban Church in Northumbria. Oswald was succeeded by his brother Oswiu who had shared his northern exile; but Oswiu had married a daughter of Edwin, who naturally adhered to the Roman form of Christianity in which she had been instructed by Paulinus. The co-existence of the two usages at the Northumbrian court created an impossible situation, and was resolved at the Synod of Whitby in 663 by King Oswiu giving the prerogative to the Roman Order.

St Paulinus had been sent to Canterbury direct from Rome, and after the Synod of Whitby it was only to be expected that the Northumbrian Church would make efforts to bring the whole of the Columban churches into the Roman obedience. Bede tells us that the Northumbrian monk Ecgberht had striven long and unsuccessfully to this end in Ireland, and it is probable that the revival, towards the close of the seventh century, of the bishopric of Whithorn in Galloway, which now lay in Anglian territory, was intended to form a centre for pressure on Ireland to this end. Its first bishop was Pecthelm, a pupil of Aldhelm of Malmesbury and correspondent of Bede. During 686 and the two following years Adamnán, the abbot of Iona, had been at the court of his *amicus*, his royal *alumnus*, King Aldfrith, now ruling in Northumbria, and had now transferred his adherence to the Roman rule. As a result he joined his efforts to those of the monk Ecgberht in Ireland and as Bede tells us, 'he brought almost all that were not under the domination of Iona into Catholic unity'. The victory of the Roman party in Ireland was probably ratified at the Synod of Birr, *c*. 697, at which Adamnán himself presided. Adamnán and Ecgberht then went to Iona where Adamnán died shortly afterwards (704), but in 716 Iona celebrated Easter by the Roman dating. In the same year the king of the southern Picts, after consultation with the Northumbrian abbot Ceolfrith of Jarrow, expelled the Columban clergy from his kingdom. The supremacy of Iona as head of the Irish Church now passed to Armagh. The victory of the Church of St Patrick and of the see of Armagh was complete.

In Wales and the continental Celtic Churches conformity came later. Bede had told us nothing of the conversion of Wales to Christianity, but he devotes a long narrative to the efforts of St Augustine of Canterbury to win their obedience. Bede pictures Augustine making two journeys to the west to interview a number of the British bishops, and to adjure them to preserve Catholic unity 'with him' (*secum*) and 'jointly with him' (*una nobiscum*) to preach the Gospel to the heathen (*gentibus*), i.e. doubtless the Saxons. On their refusal he leaves them with a prophecy, tantamount to a curse, that they will suffer vengeance from the hands of their enemy – a prophecy which Bede evidently regards as fulfilled in the Battle of Chester in 616. Bede is our only authority for this story, which he relates in the style of a saga in three episodes, and he has evidently derived the whole narrative from oral tradition. In fact the Welsh did not accept the authority of Rome in the person of the Archbishop of Canterbury till more than a generation after Bede's death, and in Cornwall not till the tenth century. The Continent naturally accepted the reformed Easter earlier than Britain – Spanish Galicia as early as 633, and in the Celtic monastic foundations of central Europe the reform had largely been accepted by the eighth century; but the changes were very gradual and ancient usages died hard. In 818 the great abbey of Landévennec in Brittany under its abbot Matmonoc accepted the behest of Louis the Pious to abandon Celtic practices and adopt the Roman tonsure and the Rule of St Benedict, and the other Breton monasteries followed in due course.

It is one of the most impressive facts of the Celtic Church that there were no martyrs. Even the Easter controversy had been a worthy and dignified one on both sides. It had, moreover, given birth to a corpus of literature by the adherents of both parties which are our principal basis for the spiritual history of the period. In the documents which had their origin in the so-called 'Roman' party we detect the first influences of contemporary continental literary discipline – the beginning of chronology and of historical records in local annalistic chronicles, and of a sense of the importance of precision in documentation. The most important Irish compilation of records of councils and of canon law was the *Collectio Canonum Hibernensis* which had appeared in Gaul in the eighth century, and which was known and copied early in Brittany. In Ireland a compendium was made, and copies and versions were multiplied early in the eighth century by members of the 'Roman' party.[81] The documents of the Irish party were undoubtedly inspired by a desire to formulate the traditions, the rules, the ideals which had been handed down to them by their *seniores*, and to which they still clung. Theirs is not a literature of trained theologians or of speculative thought; but in the Rules, such as that of Tallaght, the so-called Rule of Columcille by Columbanus of Bobbio, and in the Penitentials, there breathes the spirit of unworldliness of the early Celtic Church, which earnestly inculcates and formulates the austere form of its discipline.

The most influential development in the literature of the controversy was the recording of the *vitae* of the Celtic saints, their *acta*, the manner of their birth and death, their miracles – without which in this uncritical age no cult could be established, no saint or sanctuary gain popularity. The *vita* had a history on the continent as old as

Christianity itself. The earliest form is perhaps the *Acta* of the Apostles in the New Testament. A later development is the funeral sermon, a natural transference to Christian purposes of the heroic panegyric and elegiac orations of heathen Classical times. Famous Christian examples are the funeral oration of the Christian rhetor, Pacatus, for St Paulinus of Nola († 431), and in the West the commemorative sermon of St Hilary of Arles for St Honoratus, founder of the monastery of Lérina early in the fifth century.[82] Already between 356 and 362 St Athanasius had adopted the narrative form made popular by late Greek romances, and adapted it with brilliant success to his *Life of St Antony*, and the permanent place of the *vita* in hagiography in the West had been ensured by Sulpicius Severus in his *Life of St Martin*.

Our earliest extant *vita* of St Patrick was written by Muirchu (cf. p. 228 above), who claims in his Preface to be composing in a new form, such as had been introduced by his 'father' Cogitosus. This is probably a reference to the *Life of St Brigit* composed by Cogitosus earlier in the seventh century.[83] In view of the narrative form of Muirchu's *Life of St Patrick*, the author's reference to the 'new style' suggests that the narrative style had already reached Ireland and superseded the older form of *acta*. The School of Armagh to which Muirchu adhered was already *en rapport* with the latest literary fashions.

The Classic *vita* of the 'Celtic' party is the *Life of St Columba*[84] by Adamnán, his collateral descendant and coarb in the abbacy. This is not, strictly speaking, a biography, and is not composed in a unified narrative form. It is divided into three parts, of which the first consists of the saint's prophecies, the second of his miracles, the third of his visions. By the time it was written, probably between 685 and 689,[85] this form of literary framework was already old-fashioned, having been superseded by the narrative models made popular by Athanasius and Sulpicius Severus. But Adamnán was not unaware of the later narrative form of hagiography, for the *Life of St Germanus* by Constantius was already known in Ireland, and is actually cited by Adamnán himself in the *Vita* (ii, 34). Indeed Adamnán was both well informed and intellectually advanced by the standards of his time. He was well read in the literature current on the Continent.[86] In another work by him, *De Locis Sanctis*,[87] he relates what he had learned from a Gaulish bishop Arculf, who had come to land in Iona while forced out of his course during a voyage from the eastern

232

Mediterranean, where he had visited Jerusalem and many other 'holy places'. Bede knew the work, which Adamnán presented to King Aldfrith of Northumbria, and evidently esteemed it highly, for he relates the circumstances of its composition (H.E. v 15), and gives some details of its contents, adding that the king had the work circulated, and the writer was sent back to his own land enriched with many gifts. The whole incident and its record are significant of the newly awakening interest felt in Celtic lands regarding the geography of the modern world to which the travels of the *peregrini* must have greatly contributed, as the narratives of Arculf by Adamnán and of Fidelis by Dicuil (cf. p. 235 below) prove.

Adamnán's *Life of St Columba* is a historical work of high value. Like all hagiographers of the period he wrote primarily for edification, rather than for historical purposes. Yet his references to historical persons and events have a precision and actuality rare for his time, and despite much that is vague and inadmissible, he gives us on the whole our most illuminating picture of the life of the early Church in Britain before the work of Bede.[88] It is, in fact, the most distinguished record that we possess of the old Celtic monastic Church of Ireland.

The most illustrious and influential of the adherents to the Celtic Order was St Columbanus. He was the first to carry the controversy beyond the borders of the Insular Celts and to plead the cause of the Celtic Order before the Holy See in a series of letters to Popes Gregory I and Boniface IV,[89] which are a unique source for the Irish attitude in the Easter controversy. He is also the most famous of the early *peregrini*, men who, like St Colman of Lindisfarne, left their country with a group of adherents for the sake of a religious ideal, and founded religious communities of the stricter discipline in distant regions. He was a Leinster-man by birth, a member of the community of St Comgall of Bangor in Co. Down, but *c.* 590 he set out with twelve disciples as a *peregrinus* to the Continent, passing through Western Gaul to Burgundy. Here he settled in a retreat in the forest of Annegray, and later established two other religious foundations at Luxeuil and Fontaine, the former of which became a famous school of learning; but his attitude in the Easter controversy, and his outspoken views on the necessity for the stricter discipline, rendered him unpopular with the court and bishops of Burgundy, and he was forced to leave the country, passing to the courts of Neustria and Austrasia and thence to Switzerland.

In the neighbourhood of Bregenz he made a stay of some duration in the company of his Irish friend and disciple, St Gall, who had followed him throughout his wanderings from the monastery at Bangor. Eventually St Gall decided to settle permanently in Switzerland, and at his tomb a monastery developed into the famous school of learning which still bears his name, and houses one of the most precious libraries in Europe.[90] Columbanus himself, however, passed over the Alps into Lombardy, where he was welcomed by the king and queen, who granted him a valley in the Appennines in which to settle. Here his long saintly Odyssey found its final consummation in his foundation of the monastery of Bobbio, no less famous as a school of learning than St Gall. Both monasteries became important gathering places for Irish *peregrini* travelling to Rome. A valuable *Life of St Columbanus* was written by the monk Jonas who had entered Bobbio in 618 and who must have known many of the saint's companions.[91]

The influence of Columbanus on the civilization of Western Europe has been held comparable with that of St Columba.[92] In particular his influence through his continental monastic foundations has been a major factor in the development of the intellectual life of the early Middle Ages. Moreover, the impetus which his foundations gave to learning and to books, and to the realization of the potential revolution in the intellectual life inherent in the art of writing, extends far beyond his personal literary achievement. He was the last and greatest founder of Celtic monasticism in its most rigorous form, including the insistence on the abbatial control of monastic administration.

Columbanus was not an original thinker or a profound scholar, and his influence, like that of his great namesake Columba, is to be measured rather by his immediate permanent practical achievement than by his literary work. Yet he was not deficient by the standard of Latin education of his day, and his style still retains its power to impress us by its vigorous and direct rhetoric. The *Rule of St Columbanus*[93] is undoubtedly in the main the work of his hand and is the earliest surviving rule of Irish origin. Although written on the Continent it is completely representative of the Irish Church, and probably reproduces the Rule of St Comgall's famous monastery at Bangor in which Columbanus had been trained. It is intended especially for the guidance of the spiritual life of cenobitic communities,

234

inculcating absolute obedience, constant toil, and ceaseless austerities and devotional exercises. The *Penitential* which passes under his name is also based in the main on earlier Irish penitential tradition,[94] but lays special emphasis on the importance of the frequent practice of private confession.

The ancient and much traversed route to Rome over the Alps, the old Roman road known later as the *via barbaresca*, became the chief pilgrims' route in the Age of the Saints; and on the way there were special inns for the pilgrims.[95] The Abbey of St Gall was close to this route, and the *Life of St Gall* and other documents have preserved for us details of the distinctive pilgrims' habit and behaviour. As in all caravan journeys, ancient and modern, the travellers moved in large parties, and Walafrid Strabo, writing in the early ninth century, tells us that the habit of wandering had become almost a second nature to the Scots (i.e. the Irish). They could not presumably carry books with them in any quantity, but it is significant that writing-tablets were known in Germany as *'pugilares Scotorum'* ('the writing tablets of the Irish').

The devotion of Irish monks to learning was already well known outside Ireland in the eighth century. In one of his most remarkable passages Bede tells us (H.E. iii 27) of the devotion of the Irish monasteries to learning, and of their generosity to English students, 'nobles and others', who came to them either to pursue religious studies or to live a life of stricter discipline. Some of these embraced the monastic life, while others preferred to pursue their studies, visiting the cells of various teachers. The Irish welcomed them, dispensing free hospitality and supplying them with books for their reading and instruction free of charge. Even on the Continent we gather from Notker Balbulus (*c.* 840–912)[96] that two Irishmen arrived in Gaul incomparably well versed in sacred and profane learning, which they offered for sale as vociferously as others do their wares. They were honourably received by Charlemagne from whom they asked no payment for their teaching save a habitation and their food and clothing. For one of them he established a school in Gaul for noble and humble alike, while the other was established as a teacher on equally liberal lines in Pavia.[97]

One of the earliest of these Irish scholars who frequented the Carolingian court and became a teacher in the palace school was Dicuil,[98] whose learning and literary work are of great interest, and remarkable for their time. He was probably a monk of Iona perhaps

235

taught by Suibne, the abbot who died in 772. In Iona he had been present during the visit of a *peregrinus* to the Holy Land before 767, and he had known Irish anchorites in the Northern Isles, apparently the *papar* (Irish anchorites) in *Thile* (Iceland) and the Faeroe Islands, who had been obliged to abandon their settlements by the Vikings (cf. p. 158 above). It seems probable that he himself had also visited the Faeroes, and it has been conjectured that his settlement on the Continent may have been the result of the sack of Iona in 806. His chief literary works are a treatise on astronomy and computistical matter, written in a mixture of prose and rhythmical verse, and *De Mensura Orbis*. The latter is the earliest geographical survey of its kind compiled in the Frankish Empire, and although based in the main on Roman geography, especially the work of Pliny, the author has too lively a mind to resist inserting some delightful reminiscences of his own – the elephant sent by Harun al Rashid to Charlemagne in 804; the account which he had himself heard of the pilgrimage of the monk Fidelis to the Holy Land; and an account of Iceland and the Faeroes. His geographical work anticipates King Alfred's translation of Orosius by inserting contemporary matter significant of the expanding interest in geography in the West in the ninth century.

By the middle of the ninth century, at a time when the barbarian invasions were threatening the traditional Classical learning on the continent, new life was breathed into both scholarship and independent speculative thought in Western Europe from the British Isles by both Anglo-Saxon and Celtic, especially Irish scholars. The Irish in particular have left a deep and abiding influence on the European culture of the ninth and following centuries. Of remarkable interest are the circles of learned Irishmen centred at Laon, north east of Paris, and Liège, east of Brussels, who about the middle of the ninth century, settled for at least a decade in these continental centres. About this time we have record of a number of individual Irishmen who had come on a mission to the court of King Charles the Bald at Liège from Maelsechlainn, the Irish king, announcing a victory over the Norsemen, and begging a free passage as *peregrini*, that is to say as pilgrims, to Rome. About the same time, and perhaps as a member of the same mission we also find at Liège Sedulius Scottus, or Scottigena, poet, scholar, scribe, theologian, and courtier, one of the most learned men of his time. He is closely associated with a little group of scholars who, like himself, have probably sojourned on their way to

236

Liège at the court of Merfyn Vrych, king of North Wales, which seems to have had a claim to some culture (cf. p. 150 above). The evidence indeed suggests that the court of Merfyn in North Wales was at this time a recognized halt and centre of culture on the regular route of *peregrini* from Ireland to the court of Charles the Bald at Liège, and that Irish, and perhaps Welsh scholars also were honoured at Liège for their learning and courtly polish.

Of the Irish scholars attached to the court at Liège the central figure was undoubtedly Sedulius Scottus.[99] The precise place of his origin and education are unknown, though indications in his writings suggest that some at least of his literary sources were of Irish provenance. In the words of Laistner, 'Like some uncharted comet the Irishman Sedulius appeared at Liège about the middle of the ninth century (845–58) to vanish again as mysteriously as he had come.'[100] His work is no less remarkable for its wide range than for the precision and facility of his Latin scholarship, especially his command of an extensive variety of Latin metres. His good taste in Latin prose style is shown by the value that he set on Cicero. In his collection of extracts from Latin authors which he assembled in the *Collectaneum*[101] he refers to no less than seven of the works of Cicero, while the majority of his contemporaries are limited to one or two. That he possessed some knowledge of Greek, probably not very profound, is generally acknowledged. A colophon in Greek characters to a manuscript of the Greek Psalter, now in Paris, runs: 'Sidulios Skottos ego egrapsa' ('I, Sedulius Scottus wrote it').[102]

The writings of Sedulius reveal him as in the full current of the literary fashions of his time. In the *Collectaneum*, which has been called his commonplace book, he assembled extracts of outstanding merit from Classical authors, and at a time when books and libraries were comparatively rare such collections had a practical value. The form reached its classic development in the *Adages* of Erasmus. His *Liber de Rectoribus Christianis*,[103] written in prose interspersed with verse, which chiefly summarizes the preceding prose passages, is an early example of the series of studies in political theory, and more especially in regard to the duties of rulers, which gained such wide currency throughout Europe from Russia to Iceland, in the Middle Ages, and which are commonly referred to as 'Mirrors of Princes'. It is significant that Sedulius was evidently influenced in this work by the chapter on the Unjust King in an anonymous Irish treatise *De Duodecim abusivis*

237

saeculi, written early in the preceding century. He shared the lively interest of his time in grammatical treatises, and wrote commentaries on Eutyches, Priscian, and Donatus, and he made contributions to the current literature of Biblical exegesis with a *Collectaneum in Matthaeum* and a *Collectaneum in omnes beati Pauli Epistolas*. The latter has a special interest for us in that it forms one of a group of Pauline commentaries almost all of which are of direct Irish origin. This, as Kenney points out,[104] makes it probable that Sedulius either wrote his Collectaneum in Ireland, or used books brought from Ireland.

Today we remember Sedulius with most pleasure for his poems,[105] eighty-three in number; for he carried his learning with the ease and grace of his countrymen, and while he is unique in his period for the variety and correctness of his lyric metres, he possessed the lightness of touch which characterizes the well-educated mind. It is in this brightness of spirit that he composed poems to Hartgar, bishop of Liège (840–54), begging to be admitted into his school, and begging, both seriously and humorously, for benefits for himself and his fellow scholars – for wine, and meat, and honey, and for better lodgings. The same facility and tact which enabled him to beg from Hartgar without giving offence, enabled him also to greet his successor, Bishop Franco. Indeed like a modern poet laureate Sedulius was a master of occasional verse, and a large proportion of his poems deal in a dignified style with contemporary public events, such as the death of Bishop Hartgar (no. XVII), and the accession of his successor Franco (XVIII, XIX, LXVI). Many are addressed to royalty – to King Charles the Bald himself, to the Emperor Lothair, his Empress Ermengarde, and their sons Louis and Charles (XII–XXVII *et alia*). Three of his poems on contemporary events (XLV–XLVII) link him again in all probability with the court of North Wales. One of these, which bears the title *De Strage Normannorum* (XLV) is virtually a hymn of thanksgiving for a victory over the Norsemen – that '*gens inimica*', '*homines viles*' – and was probably inspired by the battle in which their leader Gormr was killed (cf. p. 153 above). Another poem (XLVII) appears to refer to an 'altar' set up by King Roricus, doubtless Rhodri Mawr of North Wales. It is not impossible that these three poems were composed before Sedulius came to the Continent; but Charles was so seriously harassed by the Norsemen at this time that the death of their leader would certainly be an occasion for rejoicing at Liège, and it would be natural for Sedulius to celebrate this great event.

It is perhaps in his gayer occasional trifles that the humour of Sedulius marks him off from the more sombre cast of thought of the Middle Ages. It is thus that he addresses his friend Robert by the grammatical declension of his name (LVIII).

> Bonus vir est Robertus,
> Laudes gliscunt Roberti.
> Christe, fave Roberto,
> Longaevum fac Robertum. . . .

His gift of light humour is seen in its most engaging form in a mock heroic poem of 140 lines on the death of a ram torn to pieces by a dog (XLI). The poem is complete with a formal epitaph. The ram at bay cows the attacking dogs – all but one – by a heroic ten-line speech in the grand manner, and after this heroic death Sedulius, with daring levity, pronounces a formal eulogy in the exalted manner of Classical epic:

Without blemish was he, and spake not empty words, Báá or Béé were the mystic sounds he used to utter. As a lamb enthroned on high to redeem sinners the Son of God Himself tasted bitter death. Going the road of death, torn by cruel hounds, thus good bell-wether thou dost perish for the unrepentent thief. As a ram was made a sacrificial offering for Isaac, so thou art a pleasing victim for a poor wretch.[106]

The poetical quality of the art of Sedulius expresses itself most fully in his treatment of serious themes – religious festivals, national disasters, of the gentler aspects of nature symbolized in Spring. In a passage of the *Liber de Rectoribus* he passes by a natural transition from the horrors of war to a vigorous passage on a storm in the natural universe:

When the east wind's gusty gale rages boisterously, thundering down from the high mountains, the white hail falls in clouds, and straightway forests totter, and the ocean tide is upheaved, and the wind hurls threats at the stars as the lightning crackles, then fear strikes the heart of trembling mortals, lest heaven-sent wrath lay low the race of earthly men.[107]

In contrast to the vigour of this threat of nature in tumult he reflects her gentler mood in Spring in the little verses on Easter, when

The earth makes flower-bearing bulbs to swell with blossom and rejoices to have a painted robe of flowers. Now bright-plumed birds soothe the air with song, from their young beaks they pour a song of lofty triumph. The skies exult, the earth is glad, and now re-echoes an hundredfold its notes of Halleluia. Now the church choir, singing in chant of Sion, lifts up its hosanna to the sky's poles above.[108]

Among the most charming of the lighter poems of Sedulius is the little eclogue *De Rosae Lilique Certamine* (LXXXI), an idyllic dialogue in which the lily and the rose each claims superiority – the rose for her bright colour as the sister of the dawn, beloved of Phoebus; the lily with her pallor as symbol of virginity, beloved of Apollo. The dispute is brought to a conclusion by Spring, who is pictured as a youth reclining on the grass, who reminds them that they are both twin sisters, daughters of the earth, their mother.

Contemporary with the little group of scholars and poets gathered around Sedulius at Liège is the most outstanding intellectual Irishman on the continent in the ninth century, Johannes Scottus Eriugena, 'John the Irishman',[109] of whom it has been justly said that, with the exception of Columbanus, he was the most important individual whom Ireland gave to the continent in the Middle Ages.[110] The two men are however immeasurably different. Columbanus was essentially a practical participator in the struggle for the survival of the Irish Church of his native tradition, an upholder of its ideals and a practical guide to those who were its members. John was above all a scholar and a thinker, partly theologian, partly philosopher; but his independence and originality of thought defies facile classification. His origin and early life are unknown; but he appears *c*. 850 as the outstanding personality of another group of Irish scholars in the sphere of Charles the Bald centred at Laon and Rheims. He seems to have been a member of the palace school, at least from 845 to 870, and though his knowledge of both Latin and Greek are outstanding we have no evidence that he was an ecclesiastic, and little knowledge of his personal life.

From the point of view of Irish scholarship the greatest interest of the Irish scholars in these centres west of the Rhine is the study of Greek. Indeed all knowledge of Greek under the Franks at this time seems to have been an Irish monopoly, shared in very varying degrees by a number of their members, among them Martin of Laon and Sedulius himself. We have a Greek Psalter at the close of which is a Greek colophon: 'I, Sedulius Scottus, wrote it.' But the Greek knowledge of John was unique among his contemporary continental scholars, and was on a level of scholarship which enabled him to interpret correctly even difficult Greek texts, and was justly valued by Charles the Bald, who commissioned him to undertake the translation of the Pseudo-Dionysus, a particularly difficult author, and of the *Ambigua* by Maximus Confessor († 662). He also translated other texts from the Greek fathers. His great work, however, is a highly original treatise incorporating his philosophical and theological views on the Creator and the Universe, written in Latin between 862 and 866 with a Greek title, and a Latin sub-title, *On the Division of the Universe*. But John was centuries ahead of his time, and his original work carries us beyond the Celtic world into the Europe of the Middle Ages.

The learning of the Irish ecclesiastics had made astonishing strides in our period. We have seen, however, that it is no new development. We have Bede's frank acknowledgment of the devotion of Ireland to learning which was no new thing in his day. Moreover it is hardly sufficiently realized even yet how independent this intellectual development was from the art of writing. Writing was merely incidental to the long history of Irish, as of all Celtic, learning. The history of the Celtic literature preserved from pagan Ireland, and only at a comparatively late date incorporated in written texts, proves beyond any doubt that the literature of the Christian Church and Latin learning among Irish scholars was only the final flowering of centuries of the high cultivation, first in Gaul and later in the Western Celtic countries, of oral tradition, which had been made possible by the high and honourable status accorded to the *filid*, the class of intellectual men responsible for its formulation and faithful transmission.

The idealism and asceticism of the Age of the Saints, which found its most remarkable expression in the voyages of the *peregrini* to seek a life of solitude in the ocean, has inspired a special group of Irish stories, which are among the most delightful in the literature, known as *Immrama* (sing. *immram*), which will be discussed more fully in chap. 10 (p. 328). They are not in origin fictitious. They are in part a reflection of voyages such as those of Cormac ua Liatháin seeking a solitude in the ocean, as related to us by Adamnán (cf. p. 223 above), and of the three Irishmen who are related in the Anglo-Saxon Chronicle to have visited King Alfred in 891. But we have seen (pp. 174 f. and 183) that stories of such voyages were already fully developed in the Irish literary traditions of the heathen period, and are closely related to the *echtrai* ('adventures'). The two stories of St Brendan's voyages to be considered later are in fact a direct reflection of the *peregrinatio*, the voluntary exile which was one of the characteristic ascetic practices of the Age of the Saints. Perhaps the chief difference between the *echtrai* and the *immrama* lies in the fact that in the *echtrai* the interest is concentrated on the scene in the Otherworld, while the journey, which may be over the sea in a coracle or underground, is merely a subordinate framework. In the *immrama*, the Otherworld is definitely located on islands in the western ocean, and the story is the narrative of the voyage and the adventures which befall the travellers in their search for this 'promised land' from the time of their setting out till their return.

Of the Christian *immrama* the oldest is *Immram Curaig Maíle Dúin*, 'The Voyage of Mael Dúin's Boat', which in its present form dates from the tenth century, but is probably based on an eighth century original,[111] and which will be discussed on p. 328 below. It may be said here briefly that the story of Mael Dúin and his foster-brothers relates their voyage over an endless ocean, visiting fantastically magical islands, and monsters reminiscent of medieval bestiaries and late Classical wonder tales. Two other Christian *immrama* listed in the *Book of Leinster* are also preserved. One of these is *Immram Snédgosa ocus Maic Riagla*, 'The Voyage of Snédgus and Mac Riagla', a saga of the ninth or tenth century, of which the original version is a poem of seventy-six stanzas.[112] An interesting reference in the poem to the Norse raids, introduced as a cautionary element, suggests the tenth century as its most probable date. The story is of two *peregrini* from Iona who voyage in the Western Ocean, visiting eight islands. The incidents are indebted to the *Immram Maele Dúin*, 'Voyage of Mael Dúin', and to the visionary literature to be discussed below, and contain much Biblical matter. The third *immram* referred to in the *Book of Leinster* list is the *Immram Curaig Úa Corra* ('The Voyage of the Boat of Uí Corra') preserved in late manuscripts. The text as we have it is also late, but it contains older material already found in the *Immram Maele Dúin* and that of Brendan (see below), and the tale is possibly based on an early, even eighth century original.[113]

242

By *c.* 800 tales of the pilgrimages of the Irish saints across the sea were already current in Irish monastic circles. Of these the most famous were the stories of the voyages of St Brendan of Clonfert,[114] both the account contained in the *Vita Brendani* – of which there are two distinct versions and many variants – and the more famous account in the *Navigatio Brendani*. The evidence suggests that the ocean voyage, which figures so prominently in the *Vita* as we have it, was not a part of the original *Vita*, which may have included only the saint's journey to Britain. On the other hand the ocean voyage forms the subject of the far more famous and developed form of the Brendan story, the *Navigatio Brendani*, which would seem to be a composition of at latest the tenth century, very probably of the first half of the century.[115] Allusions to the Brendan story in the earliest *Lives* of St Malo suggest that if they were part of the original texts the Brendan legend might date from the early ninth century.[116]

The relationship of the various Brendan legends to one another are, in fact, somewhat confusing, and it is very possible that the great voyage of Brendan of Clonfert may have been originally attached to his older contemporary, Saint Brendan of Birr. The *Martyrology of Tallaght*, perhaps of ninth century date, commemorates on 22 March the 'going forth of the family of Brendan',[117] where the reference is to Brendan of Birr. The *Voyage of Mael Dúin*, which is believed to be older than the *Navigatio* legend, speaks of a solitary survivor of fifteen disciples of Brendan of Birr who had found a hermitage in the Western Ocean,[118] and in the *Martyrology of Oengus the Culdee* (at 29 November) which is believed to be earlier than AD 800, there appears to be an obscure allusion to the sea in connexion with his name. The *Litany of the Pilgrim Saints*,[119] contained in the *Book of Leinster*, alludes to the pilgrimage of Brendan, but without further specification.

During the late ninth or early tenth century the *Navigatio Brendani* was composed on the model of such works as the *Voyage of Mael Dúin*. It is a Latin prose work and has been preserved practically intact, and the manuscript evidence shows it cannot be later than the first half of the tenth century, and derived from an earlier copy. The hero is St Brendan the Navigator who is related in the *Annals of Ulster*, s.a. 557 (recte 558) or 563 (recte 564) to have founded the monastery of Clonfert in Co. Galway, and to have died in 564 (recte 565). The earliest reference to the saint, however, is in Adamnán's *Life of St*

Columba (I, 26; III, 19), and Adamnán's reference and the *Vita* suggest that his origin was in Kerry. The *Navigatio*, as its name would suggest, relates, not to the life of the saint, but to his voyage only, which within its supernatural framework presents us with a veiled picture of the ideal monastic life. Great emphasis is laid on Brendan's precepts and on the observances of the monastic routine, and the author was undoubtedly a monk.

The *Navigatio*[120] opens with a visit to Brendan one evening by a certain father Barinthus who had just returned from a visit to Mernoc. Mernoc had once been a member of his own community, but had fled away to embrace a solitary life, and now had many monks in his charge on the Island of Delights. Mernoc's community is pictured much like the Desert communities of Egypt, each monk living in his own cell and meeting in church for divine office, their food being of the simplest vegetables and fruits. Barinthus relates that he and Mernoc had entered a small boat together and sailed westward to the island called the 'Land of Promise of the Saints', where they landed and spent fifteen days, experiencing all the delights of the flowers and fruits of this supernatural realm, but were not allowed to penetrate into more than half the island, after which they returned to Mernoc's community in the Island of Delights, and forty days later Barinthus left to return to his own cell, spending the night with St Brendan and his brethren on his way.

After a fast of forty days, however, Brendan and fourteen monks set out to the west in a curragh to seek the Land of Promise of the Saints, of which Barinthus had spoken, and the narrative relates with much picturesque detail their visits to many islands and their supernatural adventures. They first visited St Enda's monastery on Aran Mór, after which the narrative relates their supernatural adventures in many islands of the Western Ocean. On one island were many flocks of sheep larger than oxen; on another was a 'Paradise of birds'. The island of St Ailbe offers a detailed picture of the routine of a silent community of Christian monks, and the voyage thereafter offers marvels such as we find in the lost-Classical *Liber monstrorum*. Brendan and his brethren are supernaturally nourished and safely guided and protected throughout by a supernatural youth who directs their course and their religious observances as a kind of spiritual mentor. The monks celebrate each Easter by camping on what they take to be a large island, but which is in reality a whale Jasconius (Irish *iasc*,

244

'fish'). They are nourished by supernatural fish and fruits, and escape the perils of a volcanic island. They visit Judas Iscariot sitting on a rock in brief respite from the torments of Hell. They also visit the cave in which dwells the hermit Paul; and finally they reach the Land of Promise of the Saints. They are not allowed to penetrate to the interior, however, and after receiving the blessing of their angelic guide they travel to the Island of Delights, and after three days there they return to Brendan's own monastery.

The *Navigatio* is the most charming of all the *immrama*, and even today has lost nothing of its appeal, partly on account of the simplicity and intimacy of its gifted narrative, even more for the gentle and affectionate relations between Brendan and his monks. The structure also is interesting and unusual, for we have here, in fact, three *immrama* in one – the brief opening account of the initial voyage of Barinthus to visit the monastery of his former monk, Mernoc, on the 'Island of Delights'; the more fully related but still summary account of the joint subsequent voyage of Barinthus and Mernoc to the island 'Land of Promise of the Saints', and the final voyage of St Brendan and his followers to the island 'Land of Promise', and their final return to Brendan's own monastery, which is related *in extenso*, and to which the two former brief voyages serve as *remscéla*, 'preliminary stories'. It is a fine literary work, and it became deservedly popular throughout Europe in the Middle Ages, and was translated into many languages.[121]

Throughout the narrative great emphasis is laid on Brendan's precepts to his monks and on the careful observance of the monastic routine, and the author was undoubtedly a monk. Nevertheless the tale is not written from the point of view of Brendan's community, or even exclusively from the point of view of the Irish Church. 'Its tone is more cosmopolitan than that of any other Irish hagiographical document.'[122] The objective of Brendan's voyage in the *Navigatio* is not an island retreat in which to live as an anchorite, but *Tír Tairngiri*, the 'Land of Promise' in the full Christian interpretation of the term, the spiritual 'promised land' of the saints in that early conception of Paradise – peaceful, genial, care-free, abundant, reached after many perils and temptations, but without any Purgatory or emphasis on the medieval conception of Hell. The *Navigatio* has been justly described as an epic, indeed the 'Odyssey of the Old Irish Church'.[123]

245

The *Vita Brendani* has perhaps been influenced by the *Navigatio* which is believed to have left traces in the manuscripts. The briefer account of Brendan's voyage is included in the *Vita*, from whatever source, and we thus possess two apparently independent accounts of the saint's *immram*. Unlike the *Navigatio*, however, the *Vita* has been very imperfectly transmitted, and we possess only a number of conflate versions. Two Latin *vitae* are extant, both published by Plummer,[124] in a number of Latin variant texts, the first the *Vita Sancti Abbatis de Cluainferta* i, and the *Vita Brendani Secunda*, the latter in a single manuscript dating from the end of the twelfth century. This *Vita* II is described by Plummer as really a quite peculiar recension of the *Navigatio* and need not detain us. There are also three Irish versions[125] of the *Vita*, of which the one contained in the *Book of Lismore*,[126] a manuscript of the latter half of the fifteenth century,[127] is probably based on a Latin version, though some elements which it contains are not found in any of our extant Latin versions, and this Irish version is not taken directly from any of them, and is not conflated with the *Navigatio*, though not uncontaminated by it.[128] In both the Latin and the Irish versions of the *Vita* two voyages are ascribed to Brendan, the first unsuccessful, the second successful. He is said to have been born in Munster, the son of a certain Finnlug, and in the time of Aengus mac Natfroich, and to have been taken by Bishop Eirc to St Ita who fostered him for five years. After he had eventually received Holy Orders from Bishop Eirc he received a message from an angel from Heaven –

Arise, O Brendan, for God has given thee what thou soughtest, even the Land of Promise.

Accordingly Brendan and his followers, ninety in all, set sail over the western seas in three curraghs, passing many marvellous islands for a space of years, variously given as five and seven, and every year they landed to celebrate Easter on the back of a whale. After many adventures and encounters with the devil and a vision of Hell they reached a certain beautiful island, with a Church and men's voices praising the Lord, and there they received a divine message on a wood tablet bidding them return home:

The island which ye seek ye will find, and this is not it.

On his return home Brendan consulted St Ita as to his voyaging and she ascribed his failure to his having sailed in curraghs covered with skins of dead animals, whereupon he and his *familia* had a large wooden vessel built in Connacht, and having first visited Aranmore sailed westward into the Ocean. Many and various were the enchanted islands – including an island of mice as big as 'sea-cats', another where dwelt a monstrous sea-cat, and here also dwelt an ancient hermit who directed them to the island they were seeking. The Irish version breaks off with their reception there by a holy old man, naked save for a covering of white feathers like a dove, and a voice like an angel, from whom they received spiritual instruction. At this point the Irish *Life* breaks off, but the Latin versions tell of Brendan's return; of a subsequent voyage to Britain and of his visit to Gildas; of the many monasteries which he founded in Ireland, including the most famous of them all, Clonfert, and finally his death – believed to be in 577 – and his burial in Clonfert.

The emphasis in the *Vita* is perhaps rather on the saint's *imtheacht* than on his *immram*. He had set out on pilgrimage in response to a heavenly vision to seek a retreat in the Ocean, the spiritual goal of his vision; but he was not permitted to remain and returned to teach the way of salvation to the Irish. The account of his death in the arms of his sister Bryg is beautifully described:

On the Lord's day, after offering the Holy Sacrifice of the altar, St Brendan said to those about him:

'Commend to God in your prayers my departure from this life.' Whereupon his sister Bryg said to him:

'Dear Father, what have you to fear?'

'I fear,' said he, 'as I pass away all alone and as the journey is darksome; I fear the unknown region, the presence of the King, the sentence of the Judge.'[129]

But the compiler of the *Martyrology of Oengus the Culdee* entertained no misgivings for Brendan. He enters his festival on 16 May with the words:

The summons of Brendan of Cluain (i.e. Clonfert)
Into the victorious eternal life.

247

An extensive literature related to that of the *echtrai* and the *immrama* is that of the 'Vision', which is a natural development of the fulfilment of the purpose of the two former. The three together may be regarded as constituting a kind of spiritual trilogy. The vision, like the *echtra* and the *immram*, had its precursor already in heathen literature, where it was known as a *baile* (cf. p. 183 above). In its Christian development it was known in Latin as a *visio*, in Irish by its derivative, *fís*, or more commonly *aislinge*; but the terms *baile* and *aislinge* are not always rigidly distinguished. The *aislinge* was a literary form widespread in the international literature of the Middle Ages, and is one of the commonest conventions in the Lives of saints. In the seventh century the Visions of St Columba form one of the three divisions into which Adamnán divides his Life of the saint (cf. p. 232 above). This literary genre is introduced incidentally with the vision of Dryhthelm related in Bede's *Ecclesiastical History* (V. 12). The culmination of this noble and dignified theme is Dante's *Divine Comedy*.

The Irish visions tell us much of what was read and studied in the early centuries of Christianity in the Irish world. The earliest account is that of Fursa.[130] The Irish version is preserved in a manuscript of the seventeenth century, but the text may be of thirteenth or fourteenth century date, and is a fairly close version of Bede's account (*H.E.*, III, 19). Two Latin versions of Fursa's *Life* exist, the first of which, the *Vita Prima*, which probably dates from the seventh century, is very close to Bede's own narrative and is probably derived from the 'little book' which Bede refers to three times as his own source.[131]

According to Bede's account (*H.E.*, III, 19) Fursa was an Irish monk who desired to spend his life as a pilgrim for love of God, and accordingly crossed to Britain and settled in the territory of King Sigeberht of East Anglia where he founded a monastery in Cnobheresburh, identified with Burgh Castle.[132] Apparently he had already, before leaving Ireland, had an illness in which, during a state of trance, he had seen a heavenly vision and received divine admonition to persist in the holy life.[133] In his Anglian monastery he fell sick, and one night in a trance his soul left his body and was granted a blessed vision of choirs of angels singing in Heaven. At cock-crow his soul returned to his body but three days later his soul again left his body, and was granted a vision of the blessed. Though evil spirits strenuously sought by their accusations to prevent his heavenly journey they were defeated by his angel guardians; but the contest is

248

here represented as a spiritual one, unlike the fantastic horrors of the ordeals in Tundale's vision about to be considered. Moreover when Fursa reached a great height he saw the world below as a dark valley between great fires; but again the ordeal is a moral and spiritual one, and he was saved from the fire and the accusations of the devils by the angelic hosts and by the holy men of his own nation who gave the spiritual aid which proved his salvation. Eventually his soul was returned to his body.

Bede goes on to inform us that Fursa subsequently made over the care of the monastery to others, and resolved to adopt the life of an anchorite; but finally under the threat of the heathen (i.e. Saxon) invasions he sailed to France, where he was well received at the court of the Frankish king Clovis, 'or by the patrician Erconwald', and, after founding a monastery near Paris, died and was interred at Péronne. The accounts of the life of Fursa are of exceptional interest in view of the validity of much of the historical milieu.

One of the earliest and best of the visions is composed in the vernacular, and is known as the *Fís Adamnán* ('The Vision of Adamnán').[134] The work will be discussed more fully below (p. 323 f.). Here it will be enough to mention that the work belongs to the literary genre which we are here discussing and purports to be a vision of the great abbot of Iona, but is probably a work of the tenth century as it stands. The theme of the narrative, like most of the Latin vision literature with which we are here more directly concerned, is a vision which appears to the saint in which his soul was parted from his body and made a journey, under the guidance of its guardian angel, to Heaven and Purgatory, and to Hell.[135]

The *Vision of Tundale*[136] is a Latin work on a theme similar to that of the Irish *Fís Adamnán* and the Latin *Vision of Fursa*. The hero, however, is not an ecclesiastic but a sinner and a layman, a knight of Cashel, one who had been a formidable enemy of the Church until in a trance his soul suddenly left his body and was unable to make its return, being welcomed by a horde of tormenting demons. On Tundale's calling upon God now for the first time, his guardian angel banished the demons, and promised him mercy, but only after he should have first suffered trial. The scenes through which Tundale passes in succession, especially those of purgatory and Hell, are of the crudest material characteristic of the cosmopolitan teaching of the time, redeemed only by a genuine sympathy for the poor and respect for the Church, especially the ascetic devotees and saints whose 'countenance was like the sun at midday'. The charitable and devout dwell in the outer Heaven, surrounded by a wall of silver, the saints, the angels and God himself within the circuit of a wall of gold, and in a setting reminiscent of the 'Land of Promise'.

The author was a monk named Marcus, probably of the Irish monastery of Ratisbon in southern Germany. The allusions in the narrative suggest that the vision has its setting in 1148, and that it was written in 1149. The author was evidently a Munster man and an upholder of the reform of St Malachi, abbot of Bangor in Co. Down († 1148), who introduced the Cistercian Order into Ireland, and whom Tundale pictures in his vision of Heaven alongside St Patrick. With them are several bishops, four of whom Tundale had known in person. Indeed throughout the whole fantastic setting the author, like Dante, achieves some sense of actuality by relating Tundale's encounters in his vision with many well-known historical contemporaries.

The setting and the milieu are Irish and local, and the eschatology resembles that of the earlier Irish visionary literature; but there are also many traces of the apocryphal literature still circulating in Ireland in the twelfth century. The gentle humanity and the spirituality of the Irish vision literature in the native tradition, whether vernacular or Latin, has disappeared, and the crude symbolism of the medieval horrors of Hell and Purgatory have taken their place, redeemed only by the music and radiant light of the vision of Heaven. The images throughout are concrete, the experiences physical, and the Vision would seem to reflect eastern ecclesiastical art but without its dignity and its exaltation. The change in the spiritual climate from the Age of the Saints to the medieval Church is perhaps reflected in the fact that, with the exception of the *Navigatio Brendani*, the *Vision of Tundale* became the most widely popular of all stories of medieval Ireland, and was translated throughout Europe.

NOTES

1 Élie Griffe, *G.C.T.*, 13.
2 Migne, *P.G.* XX, col. 407 ff.; English translation by T. H. Bindley, *The Epistle of the Gallican Churches* (London, 1900).
3 *De Viris Illustribus*, XXXV; P.L. XXIII, col. 649.

4 *Historia Francorum* V, I. 29.
5 *H.E.* V, 20; cf. Irenaeus, *Adversus omnes Haereses*, III. 3. 4.
6 *H.E.* V, 24.
7 *Adversus omnes Haereses*, Preface.
8 *Adv. Haeres.* I. X. 2. Tertullian. *Adv. Judaeos* VII.
9 Cf. Duchesne, *E.H.C.* I, 185.
10 Eusebius, *Hist. Eccles.* X, v.
11 *Chronica*, II, 45.
12 St Jerome, *Commentarius ad Galatas* II, Preface; Sulpicius Severus, *Chronica* II. 42.
13 *Epistolae* XII; cf. XX, 3.
14 Letter *Etsi tibi*, *P.L.* XX, col. 472, cap. III.
15 *Chron.* s.a. 379.
16 *Confessions* VIII. 6.
17 Migne, *P.L.* XX, col. 445.
18 *Ep.* 5, 15.
19 *Ep.* 23, 8.
20 For an account of St Martin see É. Griffe, *G.C.*, Ch. VI.
21 *Ep.* 4, Mansi. III, p. 264; Migne, *P.L.* I, col. 430.
22 See J. M. C. Toynbee, 'Christianity in Roman Britain', *J.B.A.* XVI (1953), 3 ff.; Hugh Williams, *C.R.B.*
23 *Carmen apologeticum adversus Judaeos* vii.
24 *Homily iv in Ezek. Hieron. interpr.*
25 See the late fifth-century *Life of St Germanus* by Constantius; the reference by the sixth-century poet Venantius Fortunatus (*M.G.H.* XI; *Poet.* IV, i); and Bede, *Hist. Eccles.* I, 7. Cf. W. Levison, *Antiquity* XV (1941), 337 ff.
26 Eusebius, *Hist. Eccles.* X. 5, 21 f.
27 Sulpicius Severus, *Chronica* II, 41.
28 See I. Richmond, *A.J.* CIII (1947), 64.
29 Athanasius, *Ad Jovianum imp.*
30 *De Synodis*; Migne, *P.L.*, *Hilarii Op.* ii, col. 479.
31 *Apol. Cont. Arian.*; *Hist. Arian ad Monach.* Prol. cap. 28.
32 Eusebius, *Vita Const.* III. 17.
33 V. E. Nash-Williams, *Archaeologia* LXXX (1930), p. 235, fig. 1; B.B.C.S. XV, ii (1953), p. 165 ff.
34 G. W. Meates, *L.R.V.*; *ibid.*, Ministry of Works Guide-book (London, 1962).
35 *Prosperi Tironis Epitoma Chronicon*, s.a. 429 ed. Mommsen, *Chronica Minora* I (Berlin, 1892), p. 341 ff.
36 For recent works on Pelagius see G. de Plinval, *Pélage* (1943); J. Ferguson, *Pelagius* (1950).
37 Prosper, *Epitoma Chronicon*, s.a. 429.
38 A critical discussion of the person of Constantius and his account of St Germanus is given by N. K. Chadwick, *P.L.E.C.G.*, ch. IX, and references, especially those to the works of the late W. Levison.

39 For an account of these see Haarhoff, *The Schools of Gaul* (Oxford, 1920).
40 See C. P. Caspari, *Briefe* (Christiania, 1890).
41 *Briefe*, p. 15.
42 J. Anderson, *S.E.C.T.*, 247 f.
43 *Ibid.*, 351; K. Jackson, *Antiquity* XXIX (1955).
44 For a brief official note on the subject see C. A. Radford & G. Donaldson, *Whithorn and Kirkmadrine*; also S. Cruden, *E.C.P.M.S.*, and the short bibliography *ad fin* (both Ministry of Works illustrated guides, published at Edinburgh, 1957). See especially C. A. Ralegh Radford, *Antiquity* XVI (1942), p. 1 ff.
45 *Whithorn and Kirkmadrine*, p. 46, and plate opposite p. 40.
46 *Ibid.*, loc. cit.
47 Charles Thomas, *Excavations on Ardwell Island*, etc. 1964. Preliminary Reports, Edinburgh 1964, 1965.
48 For a valuable study of the documents relating to Ninian see W. Levison, *Antiquity* XIV (1940), p. 280. For some recent studies see N. K. Chadwick, *T.D.G.N.H.A.S.* XXVII (1959), 9; John MacQueen, *St Nynia*.
49 The name undoubtedly refers to the exceptional building technique of dressed stone, in contrast to the wooden buildings which were usual in Britain at that period. Cf. Belgrade (*Beograd*, 'The white city'). The word is common in Yugoslavia with this significance. See A. B. Lord, *The Singer of Tales* (Harvard, 1960), p. 35. Russian oral epics habitually speak of *bélokammenaya Moskra*, 'Moscow of the white stone walls', with reference to the rusticated masonry of the Kremlin.
50 V. E. Nash-Williams, *E.C.M.W.*, no. 183.
51 Binchy, S. H., no. 2, p. 166.
52 K. Jackson, 'Common Gaelic', P.B.A., XXXVII (1951), p. 77 f.
53 For a brief account of Manx Christianity see Anne Ashley, *C.I.M.*
54 H. O'Neill Hencken, *A.C.S.*, 121 ff.
55 On the origin and nature of these inscriptions see K. Jackson, *L.H.E.B.*, 157 ff.; and for a detailed critical inventory see Nash-Williams, *E.C.I.W. passim*.
56 See Kenney, *Sources*, p. 159, n. 7.
57 For St Patrick see D. A. Binchy, 'Patrick and his Biographers', *S.H.* no. 2, p. 7 ff.
58 For some discussion see D. A. Binchy, S. H., no. 2, p. 111 ff.; T. F. O'Rahilly, *T.P.* Cf. also for the chronological question James Carney, *S.I.L.H.* ch. ix.
59 *Toti Iberi, ultimi habitatores mundi*, G. S. M. Walker, *Sancti Columbani Opera* (Dublin, 1957), 38.23.
60 D. A. Binchy, S.H. no. 2, p. 42 ff.

61 See Joseph Anderson, *S.E.C.T.*, I, 116; Stewart, *Ronay* (Oxford, 1937); Nisbet and Gaile, *A.J.*, CXVI (1961), 88.

62 Joseph Anderson, *S.E.C.T.*, 114.

63 Adamnán, *Vita Columbae*, V, 6; II, 40. Cormac's three voyages perhaps formed the subject of a saga cycle. We may compare the voyage of Brendan and other *immrama* discussed on p. 242 below.

64 J.R.S.A.I. (1945), 127 ff.

65 We are indebted to Dr Harold Taylor who demonstrated the structural necessity and competence of these protruding stones for indicating the ascent of a *clochán* on Skellig by their means.

66 'Church Island', *P.R.I.A.*, LIX (1957–9) Section C, p. 57 ff.

67 For a general account and plans of all these early *clocháin* and oratories, see H. G. Leask, *Irish Churches and Monastic Buildings*, Vol. I (Dundalk, 1955), p. 25 ff.

68 A valuable study of the anchorites and culdees was contributed by R. Flower, 'The Two Eyes of Ireland', to the *Church of Ireland Conference, A.D.* 432–1932 (Dublin, 1932), p. 66 ff.

69 We are indebted to Professor D. A. Binchy for this suggestion.

70 Ed. E. Gwynn, *Hermathena* XLIV, 2nd suppl. vol. (Dublin, 1927), p. 31.

71 Some discussion of the interesting views of the late Robin Flower on this question is given by N. K. Chadwick in *A.S.*, 88 f.

72 The text is printed by Haddan & Stubbs, *Councils* II. ii, p. 292 f. See the important study by Paul Grosjean, S. J. Bollandist, A.B. LXXIII (1955), 197 ff.

73 See Father John Ryan, *I.M.*, 260.

74 Pierre Barbier, 'Les Vestiges monastiques des Iles de l'embouchure du Trieux: l'ile Saint-Maudez et l'ile-verte', *S.E.C.* (LXXX, 1951), 5 ff.; cf. *ibid.*, *Le Trégor Historique et Monumental* (Saint-Brieuc, 1960), pp. 48f.; 104; 247 f., and figures 19, 20.

75 See Binchy, *S.H.* ii, 169.

76 *Ibid.*, loc. cit.

77 As Professor Binchy has emphasized, 'Patrick and his Biographers', S.H. no. 2, p. 149 ff.

78 *Ibid.*, p. 63.

79 For an account of the manuscripts and subject matter, together with an English translation, see Whitley Stokes, R.C. XX (1899), p. 30 ff. For a discussion of the metre see Calvert Watkins, *Celtica* VI, 219, 228, 237, 243.

80 The text is translated by Kenney, *Sources*, p. 220 f.

81 See Kenney, *Sources*, p. 247 ff.

82 English translation by F. R. Hoare, *W.F.*, 247 ff.

83 Kenney, *Sources*, p. 432.

84 The edition by Bishop William Reeves (Dublin, 1857) is still the classic work on the subject. The best modern edition and trans-

lation is by A. O. and M. O. Anderson (Edinburgh and London 1961).

85 Kenney, *Sources*, p. 432.

86 For the literary works used by Adamnán see the study by Gertrud Brüning, ZCP XI (1917), 217 ff.; D. A. Bullough, SHR xliv (1965), 23 ff.

87 Edited and translated by Denis Meehan (Dublin, 1958).

88 See D. Binchy, S.H. no. 2, 57.

89 For the letters see G. S. M. Walker, *Sancti Columbani Opera* (Dublin, 1957), p. 36 ff.

90 See J. M. Clark, *A.St.G.*, *passim*; and more recently Hans Reinhardt, *Der St Galler Klosterplan* (St Gallen, 1952).

91 Kenney, *Sources*, p 203 f.

92 *Ibid.*, p. 187.

93 *Ibid.*, p. 197 f.

94 *Ibid.*, pp. 200, 240 ff.

95 For the following information and references to these Irishmen on the Continent see J. M. Clark, *A.St.G.*, p. 26 ff.

96 *Gesta Caroli Magni: Mon. Germ. Hist., Script.* (ed. Pertz) II, 731.

97 This aspect of Irish intellectual activity has been brilliantly demonstrated by Nigra, Traube, Manitius, and in more recent work, by Gougaud, J. M. Clark, Derolez and others. Cf. further *S.E.B.C.* by Chadwick, Hughes, Brooke and Jackson, 101 ff. For a valuable recent study see K. Hughes, 'Irish Monks and Learning', in *Los Monjes y los Estudios* (Abadia de Poblet, 1963).

98 For Dicuil see Kenney, *Sources*, p. 545 ff.: J. J. Tierney (ed.), *Dicuili Liber de Mensura Orbis Terrae* (Dublin, 1966).

99 For Sedulius and his circle see Kenney, *Sources*, p. 563 ff.; M. L. W. Laistner, *T.L.*, 251; cf. a study by N. K. Chadwick, *S.E.B.C.*, 93 ff., and the references there cited.

100 *T.L.*, 251.

101 Edited by S. Hellmann, *Sedulius*.

102 Manitius, *G.L.L.M.* I, p. 318. See however, Hellmann, *Sedulius*, p. 95, n. 2.

103 Edited by Hellmann, *Sedulius*.

104 *Sources*, p. 565, n. 2.

105 Edited by Traube, *M.G.H. Poet. Lat. Aevi Carol.* III (1886), pp. 151–237.

106 Hellmann, *Sedulius*, 204; *M.G.H., Poet.* III, p. 219; Laistner's translation, *T.L.*, 394.

107 Hellmann, *Sedulius*, p. 71; *M.G.H., Poet.* III, p. 612. Laistner's translation, *T.L.*, 394.

108 *M.G.H., Poet.* III, p. 219, *De Pascha* III; Laistner's translation, *T.L.*, p. 394.

109 A valuable account of John Scottus is that of Laistner, *T.L.*, see especially 244 ff.; 323 ff.; Kenney, *Sources*, p. 569 ff.

110 Kenney, *Sources*, p. 571.

111 See M. Dillon, *E.I.L.*, 125 ff. and the references there cited; Kenney, *Sources*, p. 410, n. 140; translation by P. W. Joyce, *O.C.R.*, 112 ff.

112 Dillon, *E.I.L.*, 130; Kenney, *Sources*, p. 447 f.; edited and translated by Whitley Stokes, R.C. IX, 14 ff.

113 Kenney, *Sources*, p. 741; edited and translated by Whitley Stokes, R.C. XIV (1893), 22 ff.; also translated by P. W. Joyce, *O.C.R.*, 130.

114 Kenney, *Sources*, pp. 406 ff.; Plummer, *L.I.S.*, Vol. I, Introduction, p. xvi ff.; Text of the Irish *Vita*, Vol. I, p. 44 ff.; Translation Vol. II, p. 44 ff.

115 Kenney, *Sources*, p. 414 ff.

116 *Ibid.*, p. 410.

117 *Ibid.*, p. 410, n. 140.

118 *Ibid.*, loc. cit.

119 *Ibid.*, p. 728.

120 For the *Navigatio*, see Kenney, *Sources*, more especially pp. 411 ff.; 414 ff.; C. Selmer, *Navigatio Sancti Brendani Abbatis* (Notre Dame, 1959).

121 For a discussion of the possible routes by which the Brendan legend reached the Continent, see C. Selmer, 'The Beginnings of the Brendan Legend', *The Catholic Historical Review* XXIX (1943), 169.

122 Kenney, *Sources*, p. 411.

123 *Ibid.* p. 415.

124 The Latin texts of the *Vitae* are edited by C. Plummer, *V.S.H.*, *Vita Prima*, Vol. I, p. 98; *Vita Secunda*, Vol. II, Appendix I, p. 270. For an account of the texts see Vol. I, Introduction, xxxvi ff. The Irish Life is edited by C. Plummer, *L.I.S.*, Vol. I, p. 44 ff.; translation, Vol. II, p. 44 ff. See also Vol. I, Introduction, xvi ff. Texts of the Latin *Vita* and the *Navigatio* were published in a useful form by Bishop Moran, *Acta Sancti Brendani* (Dublin, 1872); and an English translation by D. O'Donoghue, *Brendaniana* (Dublin, 1893).

125 Cf. note 122 above.

126 Edited and translated by Whitley Stokes in *Lives of Saints from the Book of Lismore* (Oxford, 1890).

127 *Ibid.*, p.v.

128 Plummer, *V.S.H.* I, p. xxxix.

129 The text is that of the *Codex Salmanticensis*. See D. O'Donoghue, *Brendaniana*, p. 263; translation by O'Donoghue, loc. cit.

130 For particulars of manuscripts and editions see Kenney, *Sources*, p. 501 f.; Plummer, *Bede* II, 169 f.

131 Kenney, *Sources*, p. 502. For a summary and brief account see Boswell, *I.P.D.*, 166 ff.

132 See Plummer, *Bede* II, p. 440.

133 The order of events in Bede's narrative is confused and Plummer

255

appears to regard the first illness, trance and vision as taking place in Ireland in early life, the second as occurring in East Anglia (see *Bede*, II, p. 169 f.). It is to be suspected, however, that some form of duplication has taken place.

134 Kenney, *Sources*, p. 444 f.; Irish text in Dottin, *Manuel d'Irlandais Moyen* (Paris, 1913), II, p. 101 ff.

135 *Fís Adamnán* is translated by Boswell, *I.P.D.*, 28 f.

136 See Kenney, *Sources*, p. 741 f. The Irish text is edited under the title *Aisling Tundail* (with a brief introduction by Kuno Meyer) in V.-H. Friedel and Kuno Meyer, *La Vision de Tondale* (Tnudgal) (Paris, 1907), p. 89 ff.; M. Dillon, *E.I.L.*, 132. The story is discussed and summarized by C. S. Boswell, *I.P.D.*, 212 ff.

9

The Celtic Languages and the Beginnings of Literature

(i)

In discovering the Celts and tracing their early movements, we are guided by the names of settlements they founded, of men who led them, of the gods they honoured, that is to say, by features of language. The Celtic languages deserve a place in any discussion of the Celtic past, because they are one of the less known groups of the Indo-European family and in some respects one of the most interesting. Surviving in the historic period only on the north-western fringes of Europe, they show the archaic character that the study of linguistic geography has taught us to expect. In grammar and syntax, in the subordination of the word to the sentence as a unit, and even in some details of vocabulary, Old Irish resembles Sanskrit.

Something has been said already (p. 16f.) about the documents in Gaulish that remain to us, place-names, personal names and inscriptions. These ancient sources tell us little about the grammar of Gaulish, but they do give us the characteristics of the Celtic sound-system as distinguished from that of Latin or Greek or Gothic or Sanskrit. We know from them that where Latin or Sanskrit has p, a Celtic language will have none; where Latin or Greek has $\bar{e}$, a Celtic language will have $\bar{\imath}$; where Latin or Greek has $\bar{o}$, Celtic will have $\bar{a}$. Thus uer- in Gaulish *Uercingetorix* is cognate with Latin *super*, Greek ὕπερ, and -rix is cognate with Latin *rex*; in the name *Eposognātus*, which means 'familiar with horses', the Gaulish equivalent of ἱππόδαμος, -gnātus is cognate with Latin *gnōtus*, Greek γνωτός.

The later forms of Celtic have a long history and are rich in literary sources, so that we can study their development for an

257

unbroken period of more than twelve centuries. They fall into two groups, Brythonic and Goidelic, sometimes called P-Celtic and Q-Celtic because in Brythonic an original q^u- appears as p, whereas in Goidelic it remains as q in the earliest period and later becomes k (written 'c').[1] Familiar examples are the numeral 'four' (*Latin quattuor*) and the pronoun 'who' (Latin *quī*[2]) which appear in Welsh as *pedwar* and *pwy*, in Irish as *cethir* and *cia* respectively.[3]

The earliest Irish documents we have are inscriptions in a curious alphabet called *Ogam*, the key to which is given in a tract in the Book of Ballymote.[4] The older form of Ogam consists of fifteen consonants, in three groups of five, and five vowels, the consonants written as strokes to the right or left of a stem-line or diagonally across the line, the vowels as notches in the line; and the line is usually the corner, or arris, of a pillar-stone. The alphabet is based on the Latin alphabet, and each letter is named from a tree or a plant having it as initial. Thus B is called *beith* 'birch', C is *coll* 'holly', D is *daur* 'oak', and so on. This nomenclature and the division into groups prompted the idea of an old connexion with the runic alphabet; but it seems more probable that Ogam was invented in Ireland when knowledge of writing first spread from Britain, but perhaps before Christianity was widely known. A curious fact is that the Middle Irish name for Q, *quert* agrees with Old English *cweorð*. The borrowing could be either way. The origin of Ogam is thus unknown, and the name itself is obscure. It can hardly be separated from Gaulish *Ogmios* (p. 180 f.), Irish *Ogma*, but the connexion is not clear. It was evidently a ceremonial script, for we find it only on memorial stones, and in the sagas it is associated either with funeral rites or with cryptic messages.[5]

Some of these inscriptions are perhaps pre-Christian, that is to say, as early as the fourth century. There is no means of dating them more exactly, but some are Christian, so that we have an approximate date;

and they are in a form of language still close to Latin, and quite different from the earliest manuscript form in which the original final syllables have been lost or reduced. As this manuscript form goes back to the sixth century, a lapse of time prior to the sixth century must be allowed. There are about three hundred inscriptions known, most of them in west Munster, Érainn territory, and forty in Wales. A few have been found in Scotland and in the Isle of Man.

A notion of the form of the Irish language of this period is given by these three examples here presented in transcription: CUNAGUSOS MAQI MUCOI VIRAGNI '[The stone of] Cunagussus descendant of Viragnos', CIIC no. 70; DALAGNI MAQI DALI '[The stone of] Dalagnos son of Dalos' ib. no. 119; DUMELI MAQ IGLASICONAS NIOTTA COBRANOR[IGA] '[The stone of] Dumelos son of Glasicu sister's son of Cobranorix' ib. no. 252.

In normal Old Irish of the eighth century the last would be: Dumil maicc Glaschon niad Cobarnríg.

The Goidelic dialects are Irish, Scottish Gaelic and Manx. But the last two have a separate history only since the sixteenth century. The Brythonic dialects are Welsh, Cornish and Breton. Cornish and Breton can already be distinguished from Welsh in the very few documents that remain from early times (from the eighth to the eleventh century);[6] but it is only much later that Breton and Cornish are represented in texts of any extent, and for our immediate purpose Irish may be equated with Goidelic and Welsh with Brythonic. Moreover, the Welsh language, even in the earliest texts, presents a more advanced stage of development in both grammar and syntax than Old Irish, so that Old Irish is our earliest extant source for the characteristics of the Celtic languages.

In both Ireland and Wales, literature was in the hands of a professional class of poets who used a conventional form of language, and in the early period there is no evidence of dialect. In Ireland we have short poems in praise of famous men from as early as the sixth century, and one longer poem, the famous eulogy of St Columba, which is believed to have been written at the time of his death (AD 597).[7] The oldest passages of the law-tracts, composed in an archaic form of verse, are probably as old as the sixth century. Those ancient tracts are the earliest surviving evidence of any extent for any Celtic language, for the inscriptions consist almost entirely of proper names.

They were probably preserved for centuries by oral tradition before they were first written, and they represent a very old inheritance of learning. The content of the law-tracts is in great part old Indo-European tradition, and the jurists who composed them were heirs to those learned men reported among the Celts of Gaul by Posidonius and Julius Caesar. A comparison with the Hindu *Mānavadharmaśāstra* suggests itself, and in fact there are notable points of resemblance (pp. 26 f., 132 f.).[8]

In Old Irish, as in Sanskrit, the verbs commonly form the various temporal and modal stems independently of each other, so that they cannot be arranged in 'conjugations', as they are in Latin. In this respect Irish has preserved the Indo-European system more faithfully than any other Western dialect. There are, however, two classes of 'weak' verbs, in -$\bar{a}$ and -$\bar{\imath}$ respectively, which correspond to the Latin first and fourth conjugations (*amāre, finīre*), and in the later language they gain ground, so that by the Modern Irish period (thirteenth century) the old 'strong' verbs have disappeared save for a few survivals which are classed as 'irregular'.

Another archaic feature of the verb is that when compounded with prepositions, it may have two, three or even four prepositions, of which the first is separable and may have a pronoun attached to it, as in Latin *ob vos sacro*. In the earliest period the first preverb, with or without a pronoun attached, may even stand at the head of the sentence with the verb at the end, as in Vedic; or the whole compound may be at the end without an infixed pronoun, the other normal Vedic type. Thus:

(a) Vedic: *prá tám mahyā raśanáyā nayanti*, 'they lead him with the great bridle'.

Irish: *ath márchathae fri crícha comnámat cuiretar*, 'great battalions are driven back towards the enemies' territories' (*ad-cuirethar*); *for-don itge Brigte bet*, 'May Brigit's prayers protect us!' (*for-bet*).

(b) Vedic: *mā no yajñād antargāta*, 'Do not exclude us from the sacrifice'.

Irish: *oen-chairde fón Eilg n-àragar*, 'one peace is established throughout Ireland' (*ad-regar*).[9]

In the classical Old Irish period (eighth and ninth centuries), the verb has become fixed in initial position, and this has been explained as a development from type (a), the main verb being attracted to initial position by the first preverb in compounds, and carrying the simple verb with it. In Early Welsh too the initial position of the verb is frequent, and in Modern Welsh it is the general rule. There is little doubt that originally the Welsh verbal system was like the Irish, and that initial position in Welsh is susceptible of the same explanation; but by the time that Welsh texts are plentiful, the language has reached the stage of Modern Irish, and the earlier system can be traced only in occasional forms that have survived.[10]

From an early time the professional poets were aware of language as something to be cultivated and preserved. In the monasteries this sentiment prompted the study of Priscian's grammar, and one of our principal collections of Old Irish glosses is from a manuscript of Priscian. In the lay-schools it led to the formation of a whole doctrine of grammar quite independent of the Latin tradition, such as is nowhere else to be found in Europe. The earliest form of this native tradition is embodied in *Auraicept na nÉces*, 'The Scholars' Primer', which, while partly based on Donatus and Isidore, contains much that is purely Irish in origin.[11] But centuries later, perhaps in the fifteenth or sixteenth century, one or other of the bardic schools compiled grammatical tracts for the instruction of apprentice poets, which prescribed a literary standard for Modern Irish verse and prose.[12] These tracts are Modern Irish, and are beyond the limits that we have set ourselves, but they deserve mention for their originality and for the linguistic sense that directs the unknown authors. They have not yet received from linguists the attention they deserve.

Within the Indo-European family of languages, Celtic is most closely akin to Italic, and, as we might expect from the geographic position of the Celts when they first appear, there are details of grammar and vocabulary connecting Celtic and Germanic. These three indeed form a group of west European languages to the exclusion of Greek and Slavonic.

Features common to the three western languages are first a number of words that are peculiar to them, and second the merging of the perfect and aorist of the verb in a simple preterite tense.

Latin *uerus*, 'true' appears in German as *wâr*, Irish *fír*, Welsh *gwir*. Latin *caecus* 'blind' is Gothic *haihs* and Irish *caech*. There are names of trees and animals[13] and of tools,[14] besides a few more important words such as Irish *treb* (W. *tref*) 'home, dwelling' which appears as *-thorp* in English place-names and in Oscan (the dialect of the Samnites) as *triíbúm* 'a building', and a word for the 'community', pre-

261

served not in Latin but again in Oscan *touto* and in Irish *tuath* (W. *tud*) and Gothic Þ*iuda*. The Latin word for an inspired poet, *uates*, occurs in Irish as *fáith* (W. *gwawd* 'poem') and in Germanic as Gothic *wods* 'mad, possessed'.

In these three languages, too, the old difference between aorist and perfect disappeared early, and the preterite formations which emerged in each of them present a mixture of aorist and perfect forms. The perfect disappeared as a distinct tense later on in Greek and in Sanskrit, but the mixed preterite of the western languages is characteristic. And the same may be said of the loss of the optative as a distinct mood, which leaves only the subjunctive as a potential in opposition to the indicative.

There are some words that Celtic shares only with Germanic, which point to a special relationship. Some of them can be shown to be loan-words from Celtic into Germanic, as having suffered a Celtic sound-change. For others there is a possibility that they belong to this group although no demonstration is possible. The rest are simply a common inheritance.

A clear example of borrowing is the word for 'kingdom'. We know that for Latin $\bar{e}$ and Celtic $\bar{\imath}$, Germanic regularly has $\bar{a}$. The Gothic word for kingdom is *reiki*, corresponding exactly to Old Irish *ríge*, and clearly a loan-word.

There are other words common to the two dialects that have legal or ritual values: Ir. *giall* 'hostage', OHG *gisal*; Ir. *rún* 'secret', Goth. *runa*; Ir. *dún* 'fort', 'enclosed dwelling', OE *tún*; Ir. *dligid* 'he owes', Goth. *dulgs* 'debt'; I-E *leiq^u-* in the sense 'to lend' (Germ. *leihen*, Ir. *airliciud*). And it has been suggested that these are also loans from Celtic and are evidence of a period of Celtic domination over German neighbours; but this opinion remains merely an opinion and seems incapable of proof. The Celts were in the early Iron Age doubtless culturally more advanced through contact with Mediterranean civilizations, and must have enjoyed a prestige sufficient to explain the borrowing; but these words may belong to the same category as the words for 'axe' (Ir. *biáil*, OHG *b hal*), 'club' (Ir. *lorg*, ON *lurkr*); 'lead' (Ir. *luaide*, MHG *lot*); 'wood' (Ir. *fid*, OHG *witu*); 'herb' (Ir. *luib*, Goth. *lubja-*); 'trousers' (Gaul. *braca*,[15] OE *broc*); 'horse' (Ir. *marc*, OHG *marah*). They are words which occur only in Germanic and Celtic and which may belong to some northern European language of pre-Indo-European age.

The kinship between Celtic and Italic is much closer. Many features of sound and form and vocabulary bear witness to a close association of the Celts with the Italic tribes in prehistoric times, perhaps early in the second millennium BC. Both groups have preserved the three-vowel system, e, o, a, whereas $e > i$ in Germanic. In both groups I-E q^u remains in one area and becomes p in another; and in both there is an assimilation of original p to a following q^u: Lat. *quinque*, Ir. *cóic* $<$ $*q^u onq^u e$; Osc. *pempe*, Welsh *pump*. Sanskrit *pañca* and Greek πέντε prove that $*penq^u e$ was the original Indo-European form. So also to Lat. *coquo* 'I cook' (Gk. πέσσω) there corresponds Welsh *pobaf*. The long vowel in Latin *grānum*, Ir. *grán*; Lat. *nātos* Gaul. *gnātos*; Lat. *plānus*, Ir. *lán* shows agreement in the treatment of r, $\bar{n}$, l.

But it is in the forms, the morphology of nouns and verbs, that the most impressive points of agreement are found. Just as Latin has a genitive singular of the second declension *domini*, so Gaulish has gen. *Segomari*, *Dannotali*, *Equi* (name of a month in the Coligny Calendar); and in Irish the Ogam inscriptions still show MAQI. But Germanic, Greek, and Sanskrit have quite different endings for the genitive of o-stems.

For the superlative degree of adjectives Italic and Celtic present a suffix -*sṃmo*- which has borrowed the -*s*- of such comparatives as *plus*, magis, in contrast to *optimus*, *summus*, which have the other form. Thus to Latin *maximus*, *facillimus* ($<$ $*faklisṃmos$) correspond Irish *nessam* 'nearest', Welsh *nessaf* (Osc. n.pl.f. *nessimas*), and similarly Irish *messam* 'worst', Osc. a.pl.f. *messimas*.

One striking feature of the verbal system is the formation of the subjunctive stem. Here Irish is more archaic than Latin, which has developed regular 'conjugations'. In Irish there are two possible ways of forming the subjunctive, by adding $\bar{a}$ to the root, or by adding -*s*-: *berid* 'he carries', subj. stem *berā*- (Lat. ferat); *rethid* 'runs', subj. stem *ress*- ($<$ *ret-s*-), (cf. W. *gwares* 'that he may help'). While the $\bar{a}$-subjunctive appears in three of the four Latin conjugations, it is formed from the present stem, not from the root, and only a few isolated examples, e.g. *advenat* (*advenio*), *tagat* (*tango*), preserve the older system. The *s*-subjunctive appears in *dixo*, *dixim*, *aspexo*, *aspexim*, *faxo*, *faxim*, and similar forms. It is clear that Irish and Latin here share a common past.

The most interesting correspondence is the formation of passive and deponent in r. Umbrian *ferar* and Irish *berir* 'is carried', Latin

263

sequitur and Irish *sechithir* 'follows', Latin *loquitur*, Irish -*tluchethar*, are impressive examples, although the deponent forms are not exactly equatable. These *r*-forms appear in Welsh and Breton too, and they appear at the opposite extreme of the Indo-European area, in Tokharian,[16] and also in Hittite. They are therefore a very old feature and their survival in Celtic and Italic is a strong link between the two groups.[17] Moreover, as the *r*-passive was a present tense, the preterite passive had to be managed otherwise, and in both groups the form is supplied by means of the participle in -*to*-: *actus (est)* in Latin, *ro acht* in Irish.

There is also a group of words that Celtic shares only with Italic, and which show no evidence of having been borrowed by either from the other: Ir. *fota* 'long', Lat. *uastus*; Ir. *moeth* 'soft', Lat. *mitis*; Ir. *bras* 'strong, vigorous', Lat. *grossus*. The word for 'earth, land'; Ir. *tír*, which is a neuter *s*-stem ($<$ *tersros*?) is cognate with *tírim* 'dry', and both Oscan *teerum* and Latin *terra* are from the same root. There are also some words for parts of the body: Ir. *cúl* 'back of the head', Lat. *culus*; Ir. *druim* 'back', Lat. *dorsum*; Ir. *sál* 'heel', Lat. *talus*; Ir. *ucht* 'breast', Lat. *pectus*. And other examples are *culpa*, Ir. *col*; *saeculum*, Welsh *hoedl*; *scūtum*, Ir. *sciath*, W. *ysgwyd*, though in the last instance the Italic and Celtic forms have different vowel grades. The prepositions *cum* and *de*, Ir. *con*- and *di*, are found only in Italic and Celtic.

Vendryes has observed too that both Italic and Celtic have lost the Indo-European words for 'son' and 'daughter', and while the innovations do not correspond,[18] the agreement of change points to some common change in the family system.

In recent years the tendency has been to deny that there was ever a period of Italo-Celtic unity, or to use the term Italo-Celtic simply as referring to common features of sound and form without implying anything more. Obviously the archaisms common to Irish and Sanskrit cannot mean close affinity, because the areas are at opposite extremes; but if two or three dialects in one continuous area show common survivals, a measure of affinity is implied. In this case the common innovations are impressive. In phonology there is the assimilation of p to a following q^u as in *quinque*; in morphology the genitive sg. m. in -*ī*, the superlative suffix of adjectives, the formation of the subjunctive, and of the preterite tense (shared with Germanic) and the preterite passive. In vocabulary only the new words for 'son' and 'daughter' are properly innovations, and they do not agree. The common words are presumably a shared inheritance from some neighbouring language. Added to all this, the survival of the passive and deponent in -*r* may fairly be allowed to count in the reckoning,[19] and I suggest that Pedersen was right when he inisted that a period of Italo-Celtic unity should be admitted, and that it should be dated much earlier, perhaps by a thousand years, than the Indo-Iranian period (*Groupement* 8; *Linguistic Science* 313, 318).

Some linguists will prefer to say merely that Italic and Celtic are closely akin. Those who hold that Oscan-Umbrian and British have their common features ($p < q^u, \bar{\imath} < \bar{u}$) by common inheritance rather than by chance, will think in terms of an original 'common' period. Linguistic geography has taught us to think always of groups of dialects in which isoglosses cross each other in great variety. Italo-Celtic, if the name is allowed, will have been a group of dialects spoken north of the Alps *c.* 2000 BC, having enough common features distinguishing them from Greek, on the one hand, and Germanic on the other, to mark them as one group. But it is a matter in which no certainty is attainable, and to some extent it is a matter of mere terminology. Professor Watkins has recently argued strongly against the notion that there was ever a period of Italo-Celtic unity, while conceding that Italic and Celtic are closely akin.[20] Pedersen insisted that Italo-Celtic as one language was a fact of prehistory, and more recently Kurylowicz discusses the 'Italo-Celtic' *r*-endings of the verb, and the 'Italo-Celtic' superlative adjective in -*is-amo-*.[21] Italic and Celtic are both archaic dialects of Indo-European, showing some common innovations and some interesting archaisms, geographically neighbours when their history begins. In our opinion the term Italo-Celtic is valid and corresponds to a reality, not that there was ever an Italo-Celtic nation, but that there was a group of dialects sufficiently akin to be so called.

If we suppose that the Celts emerge as a separate people about 2000 BC, Goidelic may be a very early form of Celtic, and Gaulish (with British) a later form;[22] and the first Celtic settlements of the British Isles may be dated to the early Bronze Age (*c.* 1800 BC), and even identified with the coming of the Beaker-Folk in the first half of the second millennium. This was suggested by Abercromby long ago (*Bronze Age Pottery* ii 99) and more recently by Crawford, Loth and Hubert. It would mean a lapse of time, a thousand years, between the first settlements and the Belgic invasions that Caesar mentions, quite long enough to explain the absence of any trace of Goidelic in Britain outside the areas of later Irish settlement. It would accord well with the archaic character of Irish tradition, and the survival in Ireland of Indo-European features of language and culture that recur only in India and Persia, and, for language, in Hittite or in the Tokharian dialects of Central Asia.

The discovery that fragments of manuscripts found in East Turkestan were in an Indo-European language was published by Sieg and Siegling in 1908. This was astonishing, but even more remarkable was the discovery that this Tokharian language was most closely akin to Celtic and Italic.[23] Then came the demonstration by Hronzy in 1915 that clay tablets in cuneiform script found at Boghazkoi in Asia Minor preserved the language of the Hittites, and that this language too is Indo-European. Again a special affinity with Celtic and Italic appeared. The connexion with Irish has since been shown to be of special interest.[24]

If the earliest Celtic settlements date from the Bronze Age, the question whether the invaders were Goidels or Brythons does not arise. Linguistic features that distinguish the Brythons may be much later, some of them innovations ($\bar{u} < \bar{\imath}$; $q^u_{\cdot\cdot} > p$) which spread from a centre on the Continent and never reached the 'lateral' areas of Ireland and Spain. Rhys suggested this long ago.[25]

(ii)

Whenever the Celts came, they brought with them ancient Indo-European institutions, and notably a tradition of bardic poetry which seems to correspond to the verse, lyric in form and heroic in content, celebrating famous men (κλέα ἀνδρῶν) which has been supposed for the Indo-European period.[26]

The learned class included priests, prophets and poets, if we adopt Caesar's classification, but there must have been jurists, historians and leeches as well. For by the time which Irish and Welsh documents become available, these three kinds of learning are prominent, and the pagan priests and prophets are only a memory. The traditional learning was handed down orally in law-tracts and genealogies, and the literature in poems and sagas which preserve very archaic literary forms.

In Wales the Four Ancient Books[27] contain a large collection of lyric verse on heroic themes, praise-poetry such as is described by Posidonius and Diodorus for the Gauls; but the earliest of these

266

poems are perhaps not earlier than the ninth century. They deal mainly with the Men of the North, *Gwyr y Gogledd*. Urbgen (Urien) of Rheged, Riderch (Rhydderch) of Strathclyde, Guallauc, and Morcant are four northern kings of the sixth century whose praises are sung in poems attributed to Taliesin or to Aneirin, themselves supposed to have lived at that time.

The most moving of the early Welsh poems is the *Gododdin*; and it is also the most interesting in various ways. Indeed there is a problem of identity, for what is known as 'the *Gododdin*' appears to be a collection of short poems of uncertain date. It is preserved in the Book of Aneirin (thirteenth cent.) and has for its main theme a battle between Mynyddawg, king of Manaw Gododdin, and the king of Deira. Gododdin was the territory between the Forth and the Tyne, west of Bernicia, and Catraeth is the Welsh form of Catterick in Yorkshire.[28] In the manuscript the title reads: *Hwn yw e Gododin. Aneirin ae cant.* 'This is the *Gododdin*. Aneirin composed it.' The poem is thus named from the place. It consists of one hundred and three stanzas (*awdlau*)[29] of varying length: the shortest has only three lines, the longest twenty-eight. The whole text makes more than 1200 lines, and a poem of this length would be unique of its kind; but the *Gododdin* seems to be a compilation of heroic poetry about the Men of the North. Sometimes several *awdlau* begin each with the same words, as is so common in Welsh gnomic verse, and these must belong together. Sometimes the theme is praise of a single hero or of a group of heroes, who are not identified. One part of the text, about a fifth according to Sir Ifor Williams, shows traces of ninth century spelling, which point to an exemplar of that date. There may have been a ninth century nucleus around which the collection of poems has gathered. One is reminded of the Irish *Bórama*, in which the long struggle between Leinster and the North is related, with many incidental poems. But there is no convincing reason for any earlier date. Sir Ifor Williams, indeed, proposed that some of the *Gododdin* poems were composed in the sixth century, and some of the poems attributed to Taliesin as well. Apart from poems attributed to Taliesin and Aneirin, we have no Welsh texts of the sixth century, and we can only judge the state of the language at that time from the evidence of British names in Latin inscriptions. Jackson has examined this evidence in great detail, and has come to the conclusion that 'the Welsh language, in the form of Primitive Welsh, had come into existence not by the first but at any rate by the second half of the sixth century, and that the poems of Taliesin and Aneirin could have been composed in Welsh, not British, towards the end of that century' (*LHEB* p. 693). But his conclusion is partly based upon acceptance of the arguments of Morris Jones and Sir Ifor Williams (*ibid.* p. 651), and these arguments are incomplete. The metrical system of these early poems is not exactly known. It appears to be syllabic, not rhythmical, but the use of rhyme is established. With only one manuscript, emendation is difficult, and Sir Ifor Williams had often to confess a doubt as to the true reading. A line of seven syllables is common, and it may end in a word of one, two or three syllables. End-rhyme is required almost without exception. The line may have only five syllables, as in the first stanza, but lines of eight, nine and ten syllables are frequent. Neither the syllabic length nor the cadence of the line is fixed. We may be faced by a very corrupt text, or by a tradition that has broken down. The general use of rhyme is important. Thurneysen showed, however, that a similar sort of verse, with rhyme but no fixed number of syllables appears in Irish in the sixth century (ZCP xix 206), so that the use of rhyme does not conflict with a sixth century date for the *Gododdin* poems. It is rather on grounds of language that one must hesitate to accept it. Jackson supposes that syncope and the loss of final syllables are not earlier than the first half of the sixth century, and the evidence of the inscriptions accords with this date. Can we suppose before the end of the century the emergence of a Welsh language not notably earlier than that of the ninth century? Plural inflexion of the adjective is already breaking down, and a singular verb may occur with a plural noun: *trychan meirch godrud| a gryssywes ganthud* 'three hundred fierce horses sped along with them' (CA 45 1136). The case is even more doubtful for Taliesin, as we shall see.

The more probable opinion is that the early songs of the *Gododdin* collection were composed in the ninth century on themes that were traditional, and attributed to Aneirin, just as so many Irish poems were attributed to St Columba that cannot, from the language, be as early as his time.

This early heroic poetry of Wales is court-poetry, lament for brave men fallen in battle, praise of famous princes, not the narrative of events. There is more warfare in the early Welsh poems than in the Irish, for the British were at war with the Anglo-Saxons already in the fifth century, whereas Ireland was free of foreign invasion until the

Vikings came. And what remains to us, obscure and apparently often corrupt as it is, is nobler perhaps and better sustained than the earliest surviving fragments of Irish heroic verse. I find it hard to believe that it is not also later in date.

The *Gododdin*, which is believed to be the oldest of all, begins with a lament for a young warrior whose name is not even mentioned:

> A man in courage but a boy in years
>> Brave in the din of battle
>> Swift horses with long manes
>> Under the graceful youth
>> A light broad shield
>> On the crupper of a swift horse.
>> Clean blue swords,
>> Fringes of fine gold.
>> Before his wedding-feast
>> His blood streamed to the ground.
>> Before we could bury him
>> He was food for ravens.

Several groups of stanzas (*awdlau*) begin with a formula: 'Men went to Catraeth'; 'He went down to battle'; 'Never hall was made'; 'It is a duty to sing'. For some stanzas two texts occur in the manuscript, and they vary so widely that one must suppose a long period of oral tradition. Sometimes three hundred are praised, of whom only one returned from the fight. More often the theme is praise of a single warrior, and it is not always clear that the battle of Catraeth is referred to.

Gwŷr a aeth Gatraeth oedd ffraeth eu llu;	Men went to Catraeth; they were ready for battle.
Glasfedd eu hancwyn, a gwenwyn fu.	Fresh mead was their feast, but it was poison.
Trichant trwy beiriant yn catau–	Three hundred by command in order of battle,
A gwedi elwch tawelwch fu.	And after the shouting there was silence.
Cyd elwynt i lannau i benydu,	Though they went to churches to do penance,
Dadl diau angau i eu treiddu.	True is the tale, death came to meet them.

• • •   • • •

269

Tri chan eurdorch a grysiasant	Three hundred wearing gold torques set out
Yn amwyn breithell, bu edrywant	To defend their land, sad was their fate.
Cyd ry lladded wy wy laddasant,	Though they were slain, they slew.
A hyd orffen byd edmyg fyddant.	They shall be honoured till the end of the world.
Ac o'r sawl a aethom o gydgarant	Of those of us kinsmen that set out,
Tru namyn un gwr nid enghysant.	Alas! only one returned.

In the manuscript as we have seen, the Gododdin poems are headed: *Hwn yw e Gododdin. Aneirin ae cant* 'This is the Gododdin. Aneirin composed it.' The heading seems to cover the twelve hundred and fifty-seven lines that follow, for we then have a new title: *Eman a dechreu Gorchan Tutvwlch* 'Here begins the Song of Tudfwlch.' But the attribution to Aneirin is probably a fiction. T. Gwynn Jones said long ago: 'The Gododdin, as known to us, at least, is not a connected poem. It is rather a series of detached lays or stanzas' (*Cymmrodor* xxxii 4).[30]

The two other famous poets of the seventh century are Taliesin and Llywarch Hen. Morris Jones in his great study of the Book of Taliesin[31] stated the case for accepting some of the poems as genuine, and attempted translations of seven of them. Sir Ifor Williams came to the conclusion that twelve historical poems may fairly be attributed to Taliesin, and he edited them in his *Canu Taliesin*. Nine of them had already been accepted by Morris Jones, and the argument for admitting the language of the poems to be as early as the sixth century was stated by him with great care. But it is not convincing. He cites Rhys, who said that the language is 'not much older, if at all, than the manuscript on which it is written';[32] and the manuscript was written late in the thirteenth century. Scholars are now agreed that British had been transformed into Welsh by the end of the sixth century,[33] but it is hard to believe that seven centuries could have produced so little change. The fragments of Old Welsh that survive are too meagre to provide a satisfactory criterion.[34]

The heroes celebrated in these poems are still heroes of the northern Britons. Urien, lord of Rheged, is the chief name, and Owein was his son. Rheged has been identified with the country around Carlisle. The poems are mostly in the *awdl* form, twenty-five to fifty lines in length, the basic line having nine syllables (*cyhydedd naw ban*); but lines of ten syllables, and a short line of five, six or seven syllables, also occur. Rhyme is required throughout. The 'Lament for Owein' is an *awdl* of heptasyllabic lines with the rhyme-scheme of Irish *rannaigecht*, final rhyme between the even lines and internal rhyme between the final of the odd lines and a word in the middle of the even (Irish *aicill*). It seems most unlikely that this fully developed system of rhymes should be as early as the sixth century.[35]

Here are two of the poems which Morris Jones and Sir Ifor Williams have claimed to be by Taliesin himself. Both of them have been translated by the two scholars,[36] and I rely upon them.

The Battle of Argoed Llwyfain

Bore duw Sadwrn cad fawr a fu	On Saturday morning there was a great battle
O'r pan ddwyre haul hyd pan gynnu.	From sunrise till sunset.
Dygryswys Fflamddwyn yn bedwar llu;	Fflamddwyn advanced with four companies;
Goddau a Rheged i ymddullu,	While the army of Goddau and Rheged was gathering.
Dyfyn o Argoed hyd Arfynydd.	Summoned from Argoed and as far as Arfynydd.
Ni cheffynt eirios hyd yr un dydd.	They shall not delay even for a day.
Atorelwis Fflamddwyn fawr drebystawd,	Fflamddwyn shouted with great boasting:
'A ddodynt yng ngwystlon? A ŷnt parawd?'	'Will they give me hostages? Are they ready?'
Ys atebwys Owain, dwyrain ffosawd,	Owein answered, the ravager of the east;
'Nis dodynt, nid oeddynt, nid ŷnt parawd;	'They will not give them. They were not, they are not ready;
A chenau Coel byddai cymwyawg	And a brave whelp of Coel's breed would be sore afflicted

271

Lew, cyn as talai o wystl nebawd.'	Before he gave a single hostage.'
Atorelwis Urien, udd Erechwydd,	Urien, lord of Yr Echwydd, shouted:
'O bydd ymgyfarfod am gerennydd,	'If there be talk of peace,
Dyrchafwn eidoedd odd uch mynydd,	Let us raise a rampart on the mountain.
Ac amborthwn wyneb odd uch ymyl,	Let us raise our faces over the top.
A dyrchafwn beleidr odd uch pen wŷr,	Let us raise our spears over our heads, men,
A chyrchwn Fflamddwyn yn ei luydd,	And charge Fflamddwyn in the midst of his host
A lladdwn ac ef a'i gyweithydd.'	And slay him and his companions.'
Rhag Argoed Llwyfain bu llawer celain,	By the Elm Wood there were many corpses.
Rhuddai frain rhag rhyfelwyr,	Ravens were blooded by the warriors
A gwerin a gryswys gan hynefydd.	And men rushed forward with their chief.
Armaaf flwyddyn nad wy cynnydd.	For a year I will sing a song to their victory!

A Lament for Owein

Enaid Owain ab Urien Gobwyllid Rheen o'i raid.	The soul of Owein ap Urien, May the Lord have regard to his need!
Rheged udd ae cudd tromlas,	The Prince of Rheged who lies under the heavy earth,
Nid oedd fas i gywyddaid.	It was no shallow task to praise him!
Isgell gŵr cerddglyd clodfawr,	The grave of a famous man renowned in song,
Esgyll gwawr gwaywawr llifaid,	His sharp spears like the rays of dawn,
Cany cheffir cystedlydd	For the equal will not be found

272

I udd Llwyfenydd llathraid.	Of the glorious prince of Llwyfenydd.
Medel galon, gefeilad,	Reaper of enemies, captor,
Eisylud ei dad a'i daid.	Like his father and grandfather.
Pan laddawdd Owain Fflamddwyn	When Owein slew Fflamddwyn,
Nid oedd fwy nogyd cysgaid.	It was no more than to fall asleep.
Cysgid Lloegr llydan nifer	The wide host of Lloegr sleeps
Â lleufer yn eu llygaid;	With the light in their eyes.
A rhai ni ffoynt haeach	And those that were loth to flee
A oeddynt hyach no rhaid.	Were bolder than was needed.
Owain a'u cosbes yn ddrud,	Owein punished them fiercely,
Mal cnud yn dylud defaid.	Like a pack of wolves chasing sheep.
Gŵr gwiw uch ei amliw seirch	A fine warrior in his many-coloured harness,
A roddai ferch i eirchiaid.	Who gave horses to suppliants.
Cyd as cronnai mal caled,	Though he would gather like a miser,
Rhy ranned rhag ei enaid.	It was given away for his soul's sake.
Enaid Owain ab Urien	The Soul of Owein ap Urien,
Gobwyllid Rheen o'i raid.	May the Lord have regard to his need!

As for Llywarch Hen, none of the poetry formerly attributed to him is now believed to be his. It appears rather that there was a saga, or a cycle of sagas, about Llywarch Hen and his twenty-four sons, of which only the verse speeches have been preserved, and these may belong to the ninth century. This theory, put forward by Sir Ifor Williams, is all the more attractive because it brings Welsh literary tradition into accord with Irish. The characteristic form of Irish saga is a prose narrative with dialogue in verse, and it has been shown that this is also the ancient Indian form, and probably therefore the earliest Indo-European form.[37] Now it has been discovered in Wales. But the Welsh record corresponds to the *saṃvāda* or dialogue hymns of the Rigveda, the verse dialogue without its framework of prose; and we may suppose that the prose narrative was left to the oral tradition of the *cyfarwydd*. The verse, being bound by metrical rules, was, so to speak, canonical, and was written down when the monks began to record native, as opposed to Latin, documents.

Llywarch Hen was a chieftain of the northern Britons in the sixth century, and a cousin of Urien, prince of Rheged. His sons were all killed in battle during his lifetime, and legend presents him as a desolate old man, alone with his memories. The attribution of poems to him is on a par with the attribution of Fenian ballads to Oisín, son of Finn, except that Llywarch is an historical figure. The fragments of verse that survive, without the prose context, even where the text is clear, do not make a coherent whole. The most quotable are the *englynion* in lament of old age. As so often in early Welsh and Irish poetry, there is an initial formula which links the stanzas in groups.

Cyn bum cein faglawg, bum hy,	Before my back was bent, I was brave.
Am cynwysid yng nghyfrdy	I was welcomed in the drinking hall
Powys, paradwys Gymru.	Of Powys, the paradise of Wales.
Cyn bum cein faglawg, bum eirian;	Before my back was bent, I was comely.
Oedd cynwaew fy mhâr, oedd cynwan,	My spear was the first in a charge.
Wyf cefngrwm, wyf trwm, wyf truan.	My back is bowed. I am weighed down and sad.
Baglan brenn, neud cynhacaf.	Little crutch of wood, it is Autumn.
Rhudd rhedyn; melyn calaf.	The bracken is brown, the stubble yellow.
Neur digereis a garaf.	I despised what now I love.
Baglan brenn, neud gaeaf hyn.	Little crutch of wood, it is Winter.
Yd fydd llafar gwŷr ar llynn.	Men talk much over their drink.
Neud diannerch fy erchwyn.	No one comes near my bedside.

Baglan brenn, neud gwaeannwyn.	Little crutch of wood, it is Springtime.
Rhudd cogeu; goleu i gwyn.	Cuckoos are brown. There is light at a feast.
Wyf digarad gan forwyn.	No maiden loves me.

The lament goes on: what most he loved is now hateful, a woman, a stranger, a young horse; what most he hated is now come upon him, coughing, old age, sickness and sorrow. At the end of this rather dismal complaint, he even longs for death.

Another group of *englynion* formerly associated with the name of Llywarch Hen has been shown by Sir Ifor Williams to belong to the lost saga of Cynddylan, lord of Pengwern near Shrewsbury, who lived early in the seventh century, and died fighting against the English. In fact there is no mention of Llywarch in these poems. They are speeches put into the mouth of Heledd, sister of Cynddylan, who laments her brother's death. One passage is famous, and worth quoting. It begins with a lament for the hall of Cynddylan:

Stafell Cynddylan

Stafell Gynddylan ys tywyll heno,	The hall of Cynddylan is dark tonight,
Heb dân, heb wely;	Without fire, without bed.
Wylaf wers, tawaf wedy.	I shall weep a while and then be silent.

Stafell Gynddylan ys tywyll heno,	The hall of Cynddylan is dark tonight,
Heb dân, heb gannwyll;	Without fire, without candle.
Namyn Duw pwy a'm dyry pwyll?	Who but God keeps me sane?

Stafell Gynddylan, neud athwyd heb wedd,	Hall of Cynddylan, thou hast lost thy beauty.
Mae ym medd dy ysgwyd;	Thy shield is in the grave;
Hyd tra fu ni bu dollglwyd.	While he lived, there was here no hurdle in a gap.

275

Stafell Gynddylan ys tywyll heno,	The hall of Cynddylan is dark tonight,
Heb dân, heb gerddau;	Without fire, without musicians
Dygystudd deurudd dagrau.	Tears furrow my cheeks.
Stafell Gynddylan, a'm gwân ei gweled	The hall of Cynddylan, it wounds me to see it,
Heb doed, heb dân;	Without roof, without fire;
Marw fy nglyw, byw fy hunan.	my lord is dead, and I live on.
Stafell Gynddylan, a'm erwan pob awr	The hall of Cynddylan grieves me always,
Gwedi mawr ymgyfrdan	after so many friendly meetings
A welais ar dy bentan.	that I saw around thy hearth.

Then Heledd describes the eagles as they scream over the bodies of the fallen:

Eryr Eli ban ei lef heno,	The eagle of Eli is screaming tonight.
Llewsai ef gwyar llyn,	He has feasted on blood,
Crau calon Cynddylan Wyn.	the heart's blood of Cynddylan the Fair.
Eryr Eli a glywaf heno,	The eagle of Eli, I hear him tonight.
Creulyd yw; nis beiddiaf.	Bloodstained is he. I dare not go near him.
Ef yng nghoed; trwm hoed arnaf.	He is in the forest. Heavy is my sorrow.
Eryr Pengwern pengarn llwyd, heno	The tufted grey eagle of Pengwern, tonight
Aruchel ei adlais,	His cry is loud,
Eiddig am gig a gerais.	greedy for the flesh of one I loved.
Eryr Pengwern pengarn llwyd, heno	The tufted grey eagle of Pengwern, tonight

Aruchel ei eban,	His clamour is loud,
Eiddig am gig Cynddylan.	greedy for the flesh of Cynddylan.

Eryr Pengwern pengarn llwyd, heno	The tufted grey eagle of Pengwern, tonight
Aruchel ei adaf,	His claw is raised,
Eiddig am gig a garaf.	greedy for the flesh of one I love.

Eryr Pengwern, pell galwawd heno,	The eagle of Pengwern will call afar tonight,
Ar waed gwŷr gwylawd;	He will feast(?) on the blood of men.
Rhy elwir Tren tref ddiffawd,	Tren shall be called an unlucky town.

Eryr Pengwern, pell gelwid heno	The eagle of Pengwern calls afar tonight
Ar waed gwŷr gwylid;	He feasts(?) on the blood of men.
Rhy elwir Tren tref lethrid.	Tren will be called a famous town.

There is another remarkable poem which introduces the fashion of prophecy so much practised in the later verse, *Armes Prydein* 'The Presage of Britain'. It was composed in the first half of the tenth century, and is a summons to the Britons to rise up and drive the Saxons from their country. Cynan and Cadwaladr, the last sovereign prince of Britain, who died in 682, will arise again to lead the victorious army, and the foreigners will be driven headlong into the sea, where they will wander with no place to land. The Men of Dublin and the Gaels of Ireland, together with Cornwall and Strathclyde, will join the Britons under the banner of Saint David in driving out the invader.

The poem is preserved in the Book of Taliesin (thirteenth century), and contains nine *awdlau*, 199 lines in all. It is the oldest and perhaps the best of the prophetic poems. Sir Ifor Williams, in the preface to his edition, argued successfully that *Armes Prydein* must be earlier than the

Norman Invasion, since the enemy is still the Saxon, and earlier than the Battle of Brunanburh (937) in which Athelstan extinguished the hope here expressed by the poet. On the other hand, the Men of Dublin are mentioned as a separate kingdom, which he thinks unlikely before the second half of the ninth century. Athelstan must be the English king referred to, and he came to the throne in 925. A date $c.$ 930 seems probable, perhaps after the humiliation of the council at Hereford, when Athelstan compelled the Welsh princes to submit, and to promise a yearly tribute, for the tribute is mentioned several times.[38]

Here is a passage to illustrate the form and content of the poem. The metre is syllabic, a line of nine syllables (sometimes ten) with end-rhyme throughout the *awdl*. Alliteration and internal rhyme are freely used, but end-rhyme is the only required ornament.

Ll. 127–146:

Dygorfu Cymry i beri cad, a llwyth lliaws gwlad a gynnullant,	The Cymry have been forced to battle and they will muster the kingdom's host
A lluman glan Dewi a ddrychafant	and raise aloft the gleaming banner of David
i dywyssaw Gwyddyl trwy lieingant.	to lead the Irish under its linen border,
A gynhon Dulyn genhyn y safant.	and the heathens of Dublin will stand beside us.
Pan ddyffont i'r gad nid ymwadant.	When they come to the battle they will not fail:
Gofynnant i'r Saeson py geisysant,	they will ask the Saxons what they wanted,
pwy meint eu dylyed o'r wlad a ddaliant,	what right they have to the land they hold,
cw mae eu herwi pan seiliasant,	where are the lands from which they set out,
cw mae eu cenedloedd, py fro pan ddoethant.	where are the kinsfolk, from what country are they come.
Yr amser Gwrtheyrn genhyn y sathrant.	Since the time of Gwrtheyrn they trample among us!

Ni cheffir o wir rantir an carant.	Not rightly is the patrimony of our kinsmen thus held.
Neu freint an seint pyr y sanghysant?	Why have they trod upon the sanctuaries of our saints?
Neu reitheu Dewi pyr y torrasant?	Why have they broken the laws of David?
Ymgedwynt Gymry pan ymwelant	The Cymry will take care when they meet
nid ahont allmyn o'r nen y safant,	that the foreigners shall not go from where they stand
hyd pan talhont seithweith gwerth digonsant	till they pay sevenfold for what they have done,
ac angau dihau yng ngwerth eu cam.	even to the doom of death for their crime.
Ef talhawr o anawr Garmawn garant	By the strength of the kinsmen of Garmon
y pedair blynedd a'r pedwar cant!	they shall pay for the four and four hundred years!

The tradition of the return of Cadwaladr to deliver the Cymry from their oppressors recurs in Geoffrey of Monmouth's *Historia Regum Britanniae*, and is a commonplace of the prophetic poems. Here it is foretold:

Yng nghoet ym maes [ym mro] ym mryn,	In wood and plain and hill and dale, like a torch in the darkness, Cynan will march with us in the van of every battle.
cannwyll yn nhywyll a gerdd genhyn	
Cynan yn rhagwan ym mhob discyn.	
Saeson rhag Brython gwae a genyn.	The English will cry woe as they flee before the Britons.
Cadwaladyr yn baladyr gan ei unbyn,	Cadwaladr with his chieftains will be a pillar of strength,
trwy synnwyr yn llwyr yn eu dichlyn.	hunting them down with cunning and persistence.

Pan syrthwynt eu clas dros eu herchwyn,	When their troops fall upon their beds, those foreigners will be in pain, with red blood on their cheeks.
yng nghustudd a chrau rhudd ar rudd allmyn.	
Yng ngorffen pob angraith anrhaith dengyn.	After each challenge, there will be great plunder. The English will flee headlong to Winchester as fast as they can.
Seis ar hynt hyt Gaer Wynt kynt pwy kynt techyn.	
Gwyn eu byd wy Gymry pan adroddynt	The Britons will rejoice when they announce that the Trinity has delivered us from our woe.
ry'n gwarawd y Drindawt o'n trallawd gynt.	

We have heard nothing of Arthurian tradition in the poems that have been mentioned, and in fact the King Arthur of Romance literature is a much more famous person than his Welsh original. There are a few early poems in which Arthur is mentioned, and two of them give him prominence.[39] One is a dialogue between him and his gatekeeper, in which Arthur names his companions and recounts their exploits. It is no. xxxi in the Black Book of Carmarthen, and breaks off unfinished. There are many references to episodes which must have been told in a heroic literature that is lost, and we are made to realize that what survives is merely the shadow of a vanished tradition. The other poem is *Preideu Annwfn* or 'The Spoils of Annwfn', no. xxx in the Book of Taliesin, which is an account of a journey to the Otherworld in quest of the magic cauldron. The poem is obscure and tells us very little about Arthur except that he led the expedition. Of three shiploads that set out, only seven men returned.

This early Welsh poetry is not widely known, on account of the difficulty of the language. It is of great interest, partly for this very reason, and also for the fragments of ancient tradition that it preserves.

The earliest Irish poetry that has been preserved dates from the sixth century. It is alliterative syllabic verse, lyric in form and heroic in content, in praise of famous men, or in lament for the death of a hero. The old prosody was syllabic and unrhymed. It was based upon a long line of seven syllables with trisyllabic cadence and caesura after the fourth, and a short line of five syllables. With a permitted extra syllable in initial position, and the possibility of acephaly and catalexis, there were lines of as many as eight syllables and as few as three. In the earliest period both quatrains and stanzas of irregular length occur, but later the quatrain is the normal form. Eighty-four metres are analysed in Murphy's *Early Irish Metrics*, and eighty of them are quatrains.

It has recently been shown successfully by Professor Calvert Watkins that this Irish heroic verse has a common origin with Greek and Vedic metres, and is an ancient Indo-European inheritance.[40] By the sixth century the use of end-rhyme appears. Later the number of syllables becomes more regular in each metre, and internal rhymes are introduced, so that the whole system is transformed. But the old heroic metre, based on a seven-syllable line with trisyllabic ending and no rhyme, survives as an epic form in the sagas into the early Modern Irish period.[41]

We have poems in praise of several kings of Leinster, Labraid Loingsech, Catháir Már, Énna Cennselach, and of other kings and warriors, legendary or historical, and the famous Eulogy of Saint Columba, in this ancient verse-form. In both form and content they answer well to the description of bardic poetry by Posidonius and Diodorus in their accounts of the Gaulish bards.

Luccreth mocu Iair (Chiara), Find Fili, Ferchertne Fili, Lugair Lánfili, Laidcenn mac Bairchedo, Torna Éces, Senchán Torpeist, and Dallán Forgaill are among the early poets whose names have come down to us. Colmán mac Lénéni, founder of the abbey of Cloyne, who died in 604, is another, and of his poetry several fragments survive. Only stray quatrains survive, as a rule, but the Eulogy of Saint Columba, attributed to Dallán, is a poem of some 150 lines; and four poems of the class called *fursundud* ('illumination') have 22, 54, 52, and 35 quatrains respectively. These latter are little more than lists of names, arranged in verse to aid the memory, and are hardly poetry. They are attributed to Luccreth mocu Chiara, Find Fili, and Laidcenn. Only the attribution of the *Amra* to Dallán Forgaill can be regarded as genuine; and the *Amra* is interesting more for its style and language than for its poetic quality.

Labraid Loingsech, a legendary king of Leinster, supposed to have reigned in the fourth century BC, is the hero of a saga, *The Destruction of Dinn Ríg*, which is the Origin-Tale of the Leinstermen (p. 311).

Labraid seems to have been greatly cherished by the poets, for we have several fragments in praise of him:[42]

Lug of the shield, bright phantom,[43] there was none under Heaven so terrible as the son of Áine. A man higher than the gods, firm acorn, clean tree of many branches, grandson of Loegaire Lorc.

Here is another, attributed to Ferchertne Fili:

Dinn Ríg, strong Tuaim Tenbai – thirty nobles died there in anguish. Labraid, the fierce champion, crushed and burned them, the warrior of Ireland, grandson of Loegaire Lorc.

There are many more of these rhetorical praise-poems, or fragments of poems, which bring us back to the heroic age. Here is one dedicated to Mes Delmann, a legendary king of the Domnainn of Leinster, supposed to have lived in the first century:

Mál ad-rualaid iathu *m*arb	A prince has gone to the lands of the dead,
*m*ac *s*oer *S*étnai;	the noble son of Sétne;
*s*elaig *s*rathu Fomoire	he laid waste the valleys of the Fomoire,
for *d*oíne *d*omnaib.	overcoming worlds of men.
*D*i óchtur *A*linne	From the summit of Ailenn
*o*irt *t*riunu *t*alman;	he slew the strong ones of the earth,
*t*rebann *t*rén *t*uath *m*ár	strong tribune of great tribes,
*M*ess *D*elmann *D*omnann.	Mes Delmann of the Domnainn.

There is a problem with regard to these poems. It is agreed that they are not earlier than the seventh century, though some of them are attributed to poets supposed to be contemporaries of the kings whose praise is sung. Why should court-poets write in praise of kings of so remote a past? Are the poems trial-pieces, written by apprentice-poets on set themes, or was the ancestor-cult so strong, or these ancestors so famous, that the poets found them worthy subjects of repeated praise? Labraid Loingsech of Leinster does seem to have enjoyed great fame, as did Conn of the Hundred Battles and his brother Catháir Már and his grandson Cormac mac Airt; and Niall of the

Nine Hostages in the north and Conall Corc in the south. Maybe the few stories that survive about these early kings are mere fragments of a lost literature.

Here are two quatrains which have both rhyme and alliteration, with a varying number of syllables in the line. The style and temper are the same as before:

The Four Sons of Cú Chorbb, king of Leinster

Nia Corbb, Corbmacc, Cairpre,
  caine airt, ara, oirt airgtib,

ocus Messin Corbb, coim eirr

  arachliched cairptib.
Cethir bráithir buirr bresta,
  fian, forraigtis forlond:

fri maccu ní gaibed
  Con Corbb comlond.

Nia Corbb, Corbmac, Cairpre,
a splendid warrior, charioteer
who slew by hundreds,
and Messin Corbb, a handsome chariot-fighter
who warded off chariots.
Four mighty warlike brothers,
a band who used to overcome a greater number;
no equal number could withstand the sons of Cú Chorbb.

And the following examples have rhyme, with a fixed number of syllables in the line:

Labraid Loingsech

Labraid luam na lergge,
  faglaid fri fuam fairgge,
glass gluairgrinn fri gente,

  blass buainbinn na bairddne.

Labraid, pilot of the battlefield,
plunderer where the sea roars,
bright stong bolt against the heathens,
ever a sweet taste for bardic song.

Bran Berba († 795)

Bran dond, dín sluaig, seol
ngairgge,
garg rind, recht rán, ruad
n-orbbai,

Bran the Brown, protection of the host, a fierce raider;
harsh spear, glorious one, strong by heredity;

283

orb gaeth, grian laech, lán fairgge,	heir to wisdom, sun of warriors, full tide;
fael crú, cú chuan nad chorbbai.	a bloody wolf, dog of the pack, who does no wrong.

Fedlimid mac Crimthainn (†847)

Is hé Feidilmith in rí diarbo opair oenlaithi	Fedlimid the king for whom it was the work of a single day
aithrígad Connacht cen chath ocus Mide do mannrad.	to leave Connacht kingless without a battle, and to lay Meath in ruins.

Poetry of this kind has an appeal only by its heroic temper and for the ancient tradition it preserves. This was probably the earliest kind of poetry in the Indo-European tradition, mere sequences of terms of praise cast in lyric form. We do not know whether the quatrains that survive are mere fragments of longer poems. It is quite probable. The poems were composed for the entertainment of princes and in their honour, and must have lasted some appreciable time in recitation. The later bardic poems of the classical period are rarely less than twenty quatrains, and often more than twice as long. But these early verses preserve a tradition more ancient than anything that Greek or Latin literature has to show, and are comparable to the poetry in some of the Gupta inscriptions of India. Such poetry was still being composed in the eleventh century, with richer ornament of internal rhyme, for we have two fragments in praise of Mael Sechlainn, king of Ireland, who died in 1022.

Mael Sechlainn

A Maíl Shechlainn, nít mess methchrainn airgfea Rechrainn rebthruinn ruaid;	Mael Sechlainn, you are no fruit of a dead tree, you shall plunder Rechru, that sportive stalwart island.
a chliath chorrga thromda thogda dorrga thogla Temra tuaid.	Phalanx of sharp spears, heavy and choice, angry javelin, destroyer from Tara in the north.

Mael Sechlaind mac *D*omnaill *dathgil*, dorn i *Tailtin tulgatánaig*; daig ná *d*aim *c*rannchur mo chara *anfad mara murbratánaig*.	Mael Sechlainn, son of fair Domnall, a strong hand over Tailtiu of the wattled breast-work. My friend is a fire-brand that will not suffer the casting of lots, a storm over the salmon-rich sea.

There was a tradition of satire in the early verse also, and here are some examples:

Ro cuala ní tabair eocha ar duana: dobeir aní as dúthaig dó bó.	I have heard that he gives no horses in reward for poems: he gives according to his nature – a cow!
Ní fuilet a maíne, nocho mó atá a maisse: nocho mór a gére, nocho déne acht braisse.	He has no wealth, nor has he beauty: his wit is feeble, prating is all he is good for.

Besides praise and satire, there are fragments of lament. A queen laments her dead husband, Aed mac Ainmirech († 598):

Batar inmuine in trí toíb frisná fresciu aithirrech, toibán, Temro, toíb Tailltcn, toíb Aeda maicc Ainmirech.	Beloved were the three sides that I shall never see again, the dear side of Tara, the side of Tailtiu, and the side of Aed son of Ainmire.

By the eighth century the old metrical system inherited from prehistoric times had given place to this new form based upon rhyme, with the quatrain as the normal measure. The new ornament of rhyme was quickly elaborated, while the old ornament of alliteration was retained and improved. Rhyme appears first in Latin hymns of the third and fourth centuries. Commodius was the first to use it.[44] Augustine has it in his *Psalm against the Donatists*. 'But Sedulius, in the fifth century, is the first hymn-writer to make any considerable use of rhyme', says Raby.[45] The use of rhyme was taught by Virgilius Maro Grammaticus, whose work was well known in Ireland, and some of the earliest Irish Latin hymns are rhymed. The *Altus Prosator* of Saint Columba († 597) is in rhymed couplets, and Saint Columbanus († 615) uses disyllabic and even trisyllabic rhyme in his *Carmen de Mundi Transitu*. The Irish monks seized upon rhyme and made it a regular ornament of poetry long before it became customary elsewhere.

Murphy[46] points out an elaboration of rhyme such as never appears in continental hymns, in the Irish hymn to Saint Martin by Oengus mac Tipraiti († 745):

> Martinus mirus *more*
> *ore* laudavit Deum:
> pure corde *cantavit*
> atque *laudavit* eum.

Here beside end-rhyme between the even lines there is internal rhyme between the finals of the odd lines and a word in each following line. And the native Irish ornament of alliteration is also used with effect. This combination of end-rhyme, internal rhyme and alliteration, of which we have just seen early examples, constitutes the 'new form' (*nua-chruth*), recognized by the Irish metrical tracts. It was doubtless the invention of monks who were heirs to the old metrical tradition, and acquired the new ornament of rhyme with their Latin learning; and it is the basis of the Irish system of *Dán Dírech* and of the Welsh system of *Cynghanedd*. The Irish genius for poetry was later to develop this new craft in the use of consonance, assonance and alliteration with wonderful success.

In addition to the new form, however, the monks brought a new voice into poetry, and from the eighth century onwards we have lyric poems in which love of Nature, love of solitude and love of holiness, love of God, are the source of inspiration. The old theme, praise of famous men, is still cultivated by the professional poets. That was their duty and their means of livelihood. But the finest poetry of the succeeding ages, until the breakdown of the old Columban monasticism with the Cistercian reform in the twelfth century, was written in the monasteries by the *nua-litridi* ('new writers'), as they were called.

The new metres specially honoured as of equal status with the old were *dian* and *sétnad*. For these a price was allowed by the jurists, as for the old metres;[47] and these two are based upon lines of seven or eight syllables. The Ambrosian hymns and hymns of Prudentius and

Venantius Fortunatus, iambic or trochaic tetrameters, had the same syllabic count, and it is probable that the monks claimed special recognition for metres with such precious associations. But it is too much to say that the new metres derive from Latin models, as Murphy has done, following Thurneysen.[48] Watkins has shown that the seven syllable line was the basic long line of a native tradition of poetry going back to Indo-European times.[49]

Two famous hymns may be cited to illustrate the Ambrosian metre. The first is by St Ambrose himself:

> Splendor paternae gloriae,
> de luce lucem proferens,
> lux lucis et fons luminis,
> diem dies inluminans.

The second is still sung at the Office of Compline:

> Te lucis ante terminum
> rerum creator poscimus
> ut solita clementia
> sis praesul ad custodiam.

And here are verses from the *Vexilla Regis* by Venantius Fortunatus, in which rhyme is frequent:

> Confixa clavis viscera
> tendens manus, vestigia
> redemptionis gratia
> hic immolata est hostia ...
>
> Salve ara, salve victima,
> de passionis gloria,
> qua vita mortem pertulit
> et morte vitam reddidit.

These were some of the models which gave prestige to the Irish quatrain based on lines of seven or eight syllables. It was the rhymed form of these metres which actually gàve a new form to Irish poetry.

In the monasteries, then, a new lyric poetry was born in which the theme is lyric as well as the form. 'These poems', says Kuno Meyer, 'occupy a unique position in the literature of the world. To seek out and watch and love Nature, in its tiniest phenomena as in its grandest, was given to no people so early and so fully as to the Celt.'[50]

Here are two quatrains which appear on the margin of a ninth century manuscript of Priscian, preserved at Saint Gall in Switzerland. Alliteration and rhyme are indicated as before by *italics*:[51]

Dom-*f*arcai *f*idbaide *f*ál
fom-chain *l*oíd *l*uin, *l*uad nad
cél.
Huas mo *l*ebrán, ind *l*ínech
fomchain tr*irech* inna n-*én.*

A hedge of trees surrounds me,
a blackbird's lay makes music
for me – I shall tell it. Above
my lined book the trilling of
the birds makes music.

Fom-*ch*ain *c*oí *m*enn *m*edair *m*ass
hi mbrott gla*s* de *d*indgnaib
doss
Dé bráth – nom *ch*oimmdiu
coíma! – caín-scríbaimm fo
roída ross.

The clear-voiced cuckoo sings
me a lovely chant, in her grey
cloak from bush to bush.
God's Doom, may the Lord
protect me! – happily I write
under the greenwood.

Another stray quatrain is in the same mood, and here the rhymes are richer still:

Och, a luin is b*uide* duit
cáit sa *m*uine i fuil do *n*et:
a *d*íthrebaig nad *clind cloc*,
is *bind boc* s*íthemail* t'*fet*.

Ah, blackbird, you are glad
wherever your nest is in the
thicket:
hermit that clinks no bell,
sweet, soft, peaceful is your note

The nimble bee:
Daith *b*ech *buide* a h*uaim* i
n-*uaim*
ní *suail* a *uide* la gr*éin*:
*f*ó for *f*uluth sa *mag m*ár
dag a *d*agchomal 'na ch*éir*.

Nimble is the yellow bee
from cup to cup,
he makes a great journey in the
sun, boldly flitting into the
great plain,
then safely joins his brethren
in the hive.

A rainstorm at night:
Uar ind adaig i *M*oín *M*óir
feraid *d*ertain, ní *d*er*óil*:
dorddán fris-tib in *g*aeth *gl*an
*g*éissid ós *ch*aille *cl*ith*ar*.

Cold is the night in Moín
Mór. The rain pours down in
flood: a deep roar, against
which the wind laughs high,
sounds over the sheltering wood.

288

Here there is no internal rhyme, but there is alliteration in each line. The end-rhymes are unrhythmical, and this fashion became most popular in later Irish and Welsh poetry. Watkins has shown that it may have begun in Irish when rhyme was introduced into the old metres, where the final syllable was anceps.[52]

Another example in the same metre and in the same mood may be given here. It cannot be earlier than the ninth century, for the warriors from Norway are mentioned:

> Is acher in gaíth inn*ocht*,
> fu-*f*uasna *f*airgge *f*ind-*folt*:
> ní ágor réimm *m*ora *mind*
> dond *l*aechraid *l*ainn ó *Lothl*ainn.[53]

This sudden awareness of nature comes as a delightful shock, and it is surely to be credited to the monks, who learned to love all created things as God's gifts to Man, and to seek happiness in the hermit's life. Robin Flower has explained the emergence of this personal poetry in Ireland as a result of the Culdee movement of the eighth century which flourished specially at Tallaght and Finglas, and gave a new impulse to religion and to literature. 'It was not only that these scribes and anchorites lived by the destiny of their dedication in an atmosphere of wood and sea; it was because they brought into that environment an eye washed miraculously clear by a continual spiritual exercise that they, first in Europe, had that strange vision of natural things in an almost unnatural purity.'[54]

Often, indeed, the note of holiness is clearly heard, and we are sure that the poet is a monk who is seeing Nature as a reflection of the divine beauty:

Dúthracar, a Maic Dé bí,	I wish, O Son of the living God,
a Rí suthain sen,	eternal ancient King, for a
bothnat deirrit díthraba	secret hut in the wilderness,
command sí mo threb.	that it might be my dwelling.
Uisce treglas tanaide	Shallow green water around it,
do buith ina taíb,	a clear pool to wash away sins
linn glan do nigi pectha	by the grace of the Holy Ghost.
tría rath Spirta Naíb.	

289

Fidbaid álainn immocus
   impe do cech leith,
fri altram n-én n-ilgothach,
   fri clithat dia cleith.

A lovely wood nearby, around
it on every side, to nurse the
singing birds, for shelter to hide
it.

Deisebar fri tesugud,
   sruthán dar a lainn,
talam togu co méit raith
   bad maith do cach clainn.

A southern aspect for warmth,
a stream across its glebe,
choice, prosperous land which
would be good for every plant.

.   .   .   .   .   .

Eclais aíbinn anartach,
   aitreb Dé do nim,
sutrulla soillsi iar sain
   úas Scriptúir glain gil.

A pleasant church, with linen
cloth, a dwelling for God from
heaven, and shining candles
above the pure white Scripture.

.   .   .   .   .   .

Mo lórtu bruit ocus bíd
   ónd Ríg as chaín clú,
mo bithse im ṡuidiu fri ré,
   guide Dé in nach dú.

Enough of food and clothing
from the King of fair fame, and
to be sitting for a while,
praying to God in any place.[55]

Can it be that the first impulse came from the canticle *Benedicite opera Domini Dominum* which was sung as part of the Office of Lauds in Ireland and so appears in the Antiphonary of Bangor?[56]

One of the best of these longer poems is put into the mouth of Marbán the hermit, a brother of Guaire, king of Connacht. Guaire reigned in the seventh century, but the poem is much later, perhaps of the tenth century. Marbán had retired into a hermitage, living simply and alone, and the king went to persuade his brother to leave his cell and return to the life of a warrior. Here is Marbán's answer:

Atá úarboth dam i caill;
   nís fitir acht mo Fhíada:
uinnius di-ṡíu, coll an-all,
   bile rátha, nosn-íada.

I have a shieling in the wood.
None knows it but my Lord:
an ash-tree on this side, a hazel
on that, a great tree by a rath
encloses it.

.   .   .   .

Mét mo boithe bec nád bec,
  baile sétae sognath:
canaid sian mbinn dia beinn
  ben a lleinn co londath.

The size of my shieling is rather
small, a homestead with familiar
paths: from its gable a she-bird
sings a sweet song in her thrush's
cloak.

. . .

. . .

Aball ubull (mára ratha)
  mbruidnech mbras;
barr dess dornach
collán cnóbec
  cróebach nglas.

A tree of apples as big as those
of fairyland, great bounty; a
pretty clustering crop from
green-branched hazels with
their tiny nuts.

Glére thiprat,
essa uisci
  (úais do dig);
bruinnit ilair
cáera ibair,
  fidait, fir.

An abundant well and falls of
water, delicious drink; berries
of yew, bird-cherry and privet
break forth in plenty.

. . .

. . .

Tecat caínfinn,
corra, faílinn;
  fos-cain cúan;
ní céol ndogra
cerca odra
  a fráech rúad.

Fair white birds come, herons,
seagulls – the sea sings to
them, no mournful music;
brown grouse from the russet
heather.

. . .

. . .

Fogur gaíthe
fri fid flescach,
  forglas néol;
essa aba;
esnad ala:
  álainn céol.

The sound of the wind against a
branching wood, grey cloud,
river-falls, the cry of the swan:
delightful music![57]

This song of praise is kept up for thirty-two quatrains, and Guaire
replies that he would give his kingdom and all his inheritance to share
such happiness.

The sensibility to form and colour and sound, the delight in detail, recur in songs of summer and winter which Kuno Meyer first made known.[58] His rendering of the Song of Summer, while not the most exact, is still the most successful, and some of it is borrowed here:

> May-Day, season supreme!
> Splendid is colour then.
> Blackbirds sing a full lay
> if there be a slender shaft of day.

> The hardy cuckoo calls aloud:
> Welcome, splendid summer!
> It calms the bitter storm
> which tears the branching wood.

>   •   •   •

> The corncrake, a strenuous bard, discourses;
> the high, cold waterfall
> sings joyfully from the warm pool,
> rustling of rushes has come.

>   •   •   •

> A timorous, tiny persistent little fellow
> sings at the top of his voice,
> the lark sings clear tidings:
> 'May-Day fair and peaceful!'

That was written in the ninth century. It has seemed right to quote freely from this Irish nature poetry, because it is unique in European literature and not well known to the Common Reader.

In Wales too this new voice comes into poetry, but the early examples have not been even approximately dated, as grammatical criteria are lacking, and scholars have to depend on features of spelling and of rhyme. The Welsh nature poems seem to me to have their inspiration from the Irish, and the nature theme was then adapted to serve in gnomic poetry where it lost its savour and declined into mere formula. One passage from a poem in the Black Book of Carmarthen (thirteenth century) echoes the opening of the Irish poem on May-Day so closely that borrowing seems likely:

Cyntefin ceinaf amser,	May-Day, the fairest season,
Dyar adar, glas calledd,	loud are the birds, fresh the young grass,
Ereidr yn rhych, ych yng ngwedd, Gwyrdd môr, brithotor tiredd.	ploughs in the furrow, oxen yoked, the sea is green, the fields are speckled.
Ban ganont gogau ar flaen gwŷdd gwiw,	When the cuckoos sing in lovely trees,
Handid mwy fy llawfrydedd,	I grow more sorrowful;
Tost mwg, amlwg anhunedd,	smoke stings, my grief is plain,
Can ethynt fy ngheraint yn adwedd.	for my kinsfolk are departed.
Ym mryn, yn nhyno, yn ynysedd môr,	On hill and plain and islands of the sea,
Ymhob, ffordd ydd eler	whatever road one travels,
Rhag Crist gwyn nid oes ynialedd.	there is no retreat from blessed Christ.

Another long sequence of *englynion* opens with lines describing winter:

Llym awel, llwm bryn, anodd caffael clyd,	Keen is the wind, bare the hill, it is not easy to find shelter; foul is
Llygrid rhyd, rhewid llyn,	the ford, the lake is frozen; a
Rhy saif gŵr ar un conyn.	man can stand on a single stalk.
Ton tra thon töid tu tir;	Wave over wave covers the
Goruchel gwaeddau rhag bron bannau bre;	shore; loud wails the wind against the mountain peaks;
Braidd allan orsefir.	one can hardly stand outside.
Oer lle llwch rhag brythwch gaeaf;	The lake is a cold place in the winter storm, dry are the reeds,
Crin cawn, calaf trwch,	the stalks are broken, fierce is the
Cedig awel, coed ym mlwch.	wind, there are logs in the chest.
Oer gwely pysgawd yng	The fish's bed is cold under the

nghysgawd iäen;
    Cul hydd, cawn barfawd;
    Byr diwedydd, gwŷdd
gwyrawd.

ice, the stag is lean, the reeds
are bearded; the evening is
short, trees bend.

But the verses that follow lapse into rather dreary gnomes, from which the quality of poetry is lacking. The making of these strings of *englynion* must have become a fashion, for several groups of them are linked by an initial formula: 'Snow falls', 'Mountain snow', and so on; and it marks a period of decline. The passage that I have quoted may be as early as the tenth century, and later poets may have added more and more *englynion* to make up the incoherent sequences as we find them in the manuscript. But Glyn Davies suggests, perhaps rightly, that these pages and others in the Black Book are a mere jumble of stanzas, a *débris* of poetry, recited to the scribe by one who could remember only fragments.[59]

By the time of the earliest extant Welsh poetry, the ornament of rhyme is well established, and we have nothing in Welsh to set beside the old unrhymed syllabic metres in Irish. But the origin of the *englyn* and of the later *cywydd* is probably to be found in the old Indo-European prosody, a line with a fixed number of syllables, subject to acephaly and catalexis, free as to quantity in the first part and with a fixed cadence after the caesura. This has been shown convincingly for the old Irish metres, and Ireland and Wales were heirs to a common Celtic heritage.

NOTES

1 Gaulish here agrees with Brythonic, and is P-Celtic.
2 In Latin this form serves as relative, in Welsh and Irish as interrogative.
3 In the earlier Irish of the Ogam inscriptions, however, *q* is distinguished from *c*, as in MAQI, the genitive singular of the word for 'son', which occurs in most of the inscriptions.
4 Ed. Calder, *Auraicept na nÉces* 272 ff. There is an unpublished text of it in B.M. Additional 4783.
5 For various opinions about the origin and name of Ogam, see MacNeill, PRIA xxvii (1909) C 329 ff.; Macalister, *The Secret Languages of Ireland* 20 ff.; Marstrander, NTS i 180 ff. (RC xlv 412); Thurneysen, *Beiträge zur Geschichte der deutschen Sprache u. Literatur*, lxi 188 ff.; Vendryes, *ÉC* iv 83 ff.; J. Kurylowicz, BSL

lvi 1 ff.; Richardson, *Hermathena* lxii (1943); O'Rahilly, EIHM 495; Jackson, LHEB 156; D. A. Binchy, *Studia Hibernica* 1, 8. O'Rahilly appears to think that Ogam was brought into Ireland from Gaul. Richardson stresses the importance of the special sign for *ng* (agma).

6 A complete account of the sources is given by Jackson, LHEB 42 ff.

7 See p. 227.

8 See Binchy, 'The Linguistic and historical Value of the Irish Law Tracts' 23, 27, 30 (PBA xxix, 1943); R. Thurneysen and others, *Studies in Early Irish Law*, pp. vi, 183, 223.

9 See Watkins, *Celtica* vi 32–37.

10 See Henry Lewis, 'The Sentence in Welsh' pp. 11 f. (PBA xxviii, 1942) where the divergent word-order of Middle Welsh is discussed.

11 G. Calder, *Auraicept na nÉces* (rev. Thurneysen, ZCP xvii 277; xix 128).

12 For the bardic schools, see O. Bergin, *Irish Bardic Poems*, Introd. Bergin edited the tracts in *Ériu*, viii–xiv. For the tracts see B. Ó Cuív, 'Linguistic Terminology in the Mediaeval Irish Bardic Tracts', TPS 1965 xx.

13 Lat. *corulus* 'hazel', Ir. *coll*; Lat. *salix* 'willow' (OHG *salaha*), Ir. *sail*; Lat. *flos*, 'bloom', Ir. *bláth*; Lat. *piscis* 'fish', Ir. *iasc* are examples.

14 *ueru* 'spit' (Goth. *qaìru* 'post'), Ir. *bir*; *cribrum* 'sieve' (OE *hrídder*), Ir. *criathar*.

15 This word seems to be a borrowing from Germanic, for the English *-c* implies original *-g*.

16 The *ā*-subjunctive is also a feature of Tokharian.

17 In terms of linguistic geography they appear as a common archaism. They are, however, historically a very early common innovation, as Pedersen has shown, *Groupement* pp. 14 ff.

18 *filius*, Ir. *mac*, W. *mab*; *filia*, Ir. *ingen*, W. *merch*.

19 For the importance of common survivals see J. Puhvel (ed.), *Ancient Indo-European Dialects* (Berkeley, 1966).

20 'Italo-Celtic Re-visited' in J. Puhvel *op. cit.*

21 *The Inflectional Categories of Indo-European* 64 ff., 238.

22 But the distinction must not be exaggerated. The isogloss separating *p* and *q* is the main one, and this was no great obstacle, as the *Uoteporigis* inscription shows. For its relative unimportance, see E. Hamp, *Lochlann* i 211.

23 H. Pedersen, *Tocharisch* pp. 2, 145, 152, 155.

24 C. Watkins, *Celtica* vi 13 f.

25 *EIHM* 436 n. 2. It could be true even if the change $q^u > p$ be of 'Italo-Celtic' date (p. 9 sup.), but Thurneysen pointed out that this may have happened in each language independently, ZCP xvi 287 n. 2.

26 See Theodor Bergk, *Opusc. Phil.* ii, 392–3, cited by Watkins, *Celtica* vi 199–200.
27 Skene, *Four Ancient Books of Wales*, published the contents of the White Book of Rhydderch, the Red Book of Hergest, the Book of Taliesin and the Book of Aneirin, now commonly known as the Four Ancient Books.
28 See I. Ll Foster and G. E. Daniel, *Prehistoric and Early Wales* 234.
29 The *awdl* is a stanza of verses bound together by end-rhyme, the verses having a varying number of syllables (see p. 271). When the end-rhyme changes, a new *awdl* begins.
30 'The Gododdin appears as a string of stanzas, evidently recovered from oral tradition, in which the sequence and relation of the parts had been lost', Morris Jones, *Cymmrodor* xxviii (1918), p. 7.
31 *Cymmrodor* xxviii.
32 Rhys, *Welsh Philology* pp. 138–9.
33 Jackson, *LHEB* 693.
34 The earliest manuscript evidence is the *Surexit Memorandum* in the book of St Chad, which probably dates from the eighth century, see *LHEB* 42 f. The earliest inscription in Welsh, as distinct from British, is the Cingen Stone, which was carved in the seventh century, see BBCS xi 92; *LHEB* 668.
35 See Parry, *Oxford Book of Welsh Verse*, p. 538. Morris Jones analysed the metres of the poems he edited (*op. cit.*).
36 *Cymmrodor*, xxviii 156; *Lectures on Early Welsh Poetry*, 63.
37 'The Archaism of Irish Tradition', PBA xxxiii (1947), pp. 9–11.
38 See also *Lectures on Early Welsh Poetry* 53 f.
39 See K. H. Jackson, *ALMA* 12–19. Loomis has stated the case for assuming a lost Arthurian cycle in Britain before Geoffrey of Monmouth, see 'The Arthurian Legend before 1139' in *Wales and the Arthurian Legend*, Cardiff, 1956. See also T. Jones, 'The Early Evolution of the Legend of Arthur', Nottingham Mediaeval Studies viii (1964).
40 'Indo-European Metrics and Archaic Irish Verse', *Celtica* vi 194 ff.
41 See G. Murphy, *Early Irish Metrics*, p. 19.
42 The heroic verse which follows was edited and translated by Kuno Meyer in *Äid* and *Bruchst*.
43 See N. K. Chadwick, SGS iv 1.
44 Rhyme occurs in metrical inscriptions, pagan and Christian, found in the Roman province of Africa, Raby, *Christian Latin Poetry*, p. 14.
45 *ibid.* p. 25.
46 Murphy, *Early Irish Metrics*, pp. 16–17.
47 Murphy, *ibid.* p. 12.
48 *ibid.* pp. 12, 25.
49 *Celtica* vi, 218 ff.
51 *Ancient Irish Poetry*, p. xii.
51 This is not all, for there is also a delicate correspondence called

uaithne 'consonance', between the final of the first line and the rhyming finals of second and fourth: the vowel corresponds in quantity, and the final consonant(s) in class and quality.

52 *Celtica*, vi, 225.
53 Translated on p. 169.
54 *The Irish Tradition*, p. 42.
55 For text and translation, see Murphy, *Early Irish Lyrics* 28.
56 Glyn Davies suggested long ago that the impulse may have come from some ancient book of devotions. *Cymmrodorion* 1912–13, p. 92. Professor MacEóin has shown that the *Canticum Trium Puerorum* is the source of the invocation of the elements in the Loricae, *Studia Hibernica* 2, 214.
57 See Murphy, *Early Irish Lyrics* 10.
58 *Four Old-Irish Songs of Summer and Winter*. London, 1903.
59 *Cymmrodorion* 1912–13, p. 84.

10

Irish Literature

When we think of Irish or of Welsh literature, it is poetry and legend that claim our attention. Drama, rhetoric, philosophy, history suggest famous names in Greek and Roman tradition, and there were famous dramatists and philosophers in ancient India; but in Ireland and Wales, as in Anglo-Saxon England, literature of entertainment and antiquarian lore are all that have come down to us. Not indeed that history was neglected. Far from it. The Irish delighted in remembering the past. But learning was one of the duties of the *filid*, and it consisted largely of myth supplemented by deliberate invention, and the cataloguing, commonly in verse, of kings and their battles during the historic period, a record which is the more reliable as the events are less remote. The preserving of genealogies of the great families was a great part of the historian's duty, and this was prompted by zeal for the honour of the patron's family rather than for historical truth. These historians had not been to school to Herodotus; their chief aim was to sing the praise of their princes and to increase the fame of the tribe, not to discover the sequence of events and establish and explain the facts of history.[1]

Moreover, the legendary tales of Ireland and Wales have their origins in oral tradition, and are in fact anonymous. There is no known author of *Táin Bó Cualnge* or of *Culhwch and Olwen*. The poetry is largely anonymous too, as we have seen already, although here we have the work of individual unknown authors, sometimes ascribed to famous men of the past, Saint Columba or Find Mac Cumaill in Ireland, Aneirin or Taliesin in Wales. A remarkable feature of early Irish tradition is the total absence of narrative poetry, and the same may be said of Wales. The earliest Irish poetry is by court poets, praise, satire or lament, and the tales are told in prose.

The Irish stories, in their form and in their content, are fascinating and delightful, and at the same time disappointing and often even wearisome. What we have in the great manuscript collections that survive in the Book of the Dun Cow, Rawlinson B 502 or the Yellow Book of Lecan, to name three of the most famous, are very imperfect written records of oral tradition. We can be grateful to the scribes (the early ones were monks) for having written these texts at all, but, as Gerard Murphy has well said, when we imagine the oral tale as immeasurably better than the surviving monastic record, we are not indulging mere fantasy, but restoring a soul to the corpse that is buried in a manuscript.[2]

Irish literature in the period that concerns us, from the eighth to the twelfth century, presents heroic and mythological tradition that is free of Greek or Roman influence. The heroic tales describe a barbarian world in which some of the customs reported by classical authors of the Celts of Gaul are still observed. Loyalty, bravery, honour and hospitality are the virtues most admired. It is an aristocratic society. The gods sometimes interfere in the affairs of men, and in the mythological tales the notion of magic, of an unseen Otherworld, is commonplace.

One grand motif, which is the great Irish contribution to European literature, is the notion of love, sudden, overwhelming, lasting until death, love that brings sorrow to the lovers. It is best known in the story of Tristan and Isolde, which derives from Irish sources.[3]

The tales fall into cycles, mythology, the Ulster cycle, the Cycle of the Kings, and Fenian tales; and with the mythology may be grouped the tales of the Otherworld (*echtrai* 'adventures', and *immrama* 'voyages'), in which the hero sets out on a journey and finds himself in fairyland. These last are of special interest as possible sources of the Arthurian romances. There is an old list of tales in the Book of Leinster in which they are grouped not in cycles, but by types, as Destructions, Cattle-Raids, Courtships, Battles, Apparitions, Voyages, Tragedies, Adventures, Banquets, Sieges, Plunderings, Elopements, Eruptions, Visions, Love-Stories, Hostings and Invasions. Many of the titles given are of stories now lost, and not all that survive are included. We see, at least, what a mass of literature was there.

Of the mythological cycle only a few tales have survived, but there are references in the literature to many that have been lost. The finest is *The Wooing of Étaín*, of which we have a ninth-century text. There are three stories, which form a sequence. In the first Étaín becomes the wife of a fairy king, Midir of Brí Léith. Then, after a thousand years, she is re-born as a human, and becomes the wife of Eochaid Airem, king of Tara; and in the third story she returns with Midir to the Otherworld. There is a strange beauty here which is perhaps unequalled in any other Irish story, the temper of love, the power of magic, and a happy ending. And the form is unique, for it is one tale in three episodes, as it were a comedy in three acts (p. 190f.).

The Battle of Moytura is our chief source for Irish, and indeed for Celtic mythology, for almost all the Irish gods appear there. The Irish gods are called *Tuatha Dé Danann* 'Peoples of the goddess Danu' and they fight against a race of giants called *Fomoiri*. This is an account of the battle. Nuadu is here the king, and the Dagda ('Good God'), also called *Ollathair* ('Great Father'), Lug of the Long Arm, Goibniu the smith, Dian Cécht the leech, Credne the metal-worker, Luchta the wright, Ogma the champion and the Mórrígan are among those who take part. But the narrative is rambling and formless, and its value is rather mythological than literary (p. 188 f.)

The magic of the Otherworld is brought closer in the Adventures and Voyages. This Otherworld is thought of as in the western sea. It is called 'Land of the Living', 'Delightful Plain', 'Land of the Young' or 'Promised Land', the last a translation of *terra repromissionis*. It is a country where there is no sickness nor age nor death, where happiness lasts for ever and to wish for something is to possess it, where a hundred years are as one day. It is the Elysium of the Greeks, the *Förd Lifanda Manna* of the Norse, and may represent ancient Indo-European tradition.

A beautiful girl approaches the hero and sings to him of this happy land. He follows her, and they sail away in a boat of glass and are seen no more. Or else he returns to find that all his companions are dead, for he has been away for hundreds of years. Sometimes the hero is on a journey, and a magic mist descends upon him. He finds himself before a fairy palace in which strange adventures befall him; and he returns having succeeded in his quest.

One of the oldest of the adventure-tales is the story of Bran son of Febal, who is lured away to the Land of Women, as it is called here, by a fairy visitor. She describes the beauty and pleasures of the Otherworld in a splendid poem of twenty-eight quatrains which sets the tone for many other such descriptions. There is an island supported by four pillars of gold. On a plain of silver games are held, with chariotraces and boat-races. Lovely colours shine on every side. Joy is constant. There is no sadness nor anger, neither sorrow nor sickness nor death. Music sounds always in the air. The sea washes the wave against the land, so that tresses of crystal fall on the shore. The chariots are of gold and silver and bronze, the horses golden chestnut, roan, even blue as the sky. The sun-god is described:

A fair-haired man comes at sun-rise to light up the level lands. He rides over the white plain against which the ocean murmurs. He stirs the sea into blood.

Bran sets out upon the sea with twenty-seven companions. After two days and two nights he sees a man approaching, who drives his chariot over the water. It is the god Manannán, and he sings a lay in which the peculiar magic of these descriptions of the Otherworld again finds expression. Bran thinks that he is rowing upon the sea, but for Manannán it is a flowery plain. The waves that Bran sees are flowering shrubs. The leaping salmon are calves and frisking lambs. His boat is floating over an orchard of fruit-trees.

After some adventures Bran reaches the Island of Women, but he is afraid to land. The leader of the women throws him a ball of thread which sticks to his hand, and she draws his boat ashore.[4] They go into a great hall where there is a bed and a wife for every man. The food that they eat does not diminish. They thought they were there a year, but it was many years.

When Bran returned to Ireland, the people who had gathered on the shore asked him who he was, and he said: 'I am Bran son of Febal.' 'We know him not,' they said, 'but the Voyage of Bran is one of our ancient stories.' One man was put ashore, and he turned to ashes at once, as though he had been in the grave for hundreds of years. Bran told his adventures to the people and bade them farewell; and from that time forward his adventures are not known.

This tale is in the pagan tradition, and happiness is imagined as consisting of the pleasures of food and love as they are found in the Otherworld. The same is true of several other *echtrai*, and one must admire the fidelity with which Christian monks preserved them for us. *Echtrae Conli, Echtrae Loegairi, Echtrae Cormaic, Echtrae Airt meic Cuinn* and *Serglige Con Culainn* are other such tales, all of them infused with the same magic quality, which is echoed after four hundred years in the Arthurian romances.

In the *Adventure of Loegaire*, when the hero returns from his quest, the Connachtmen leap forward to welcome him home. 'Do not come near us,' said Loegaire, 'for we have come to say farewell.' His father, Crimthann Cass, king of Connacht, begs him to stay: 'Do not leave me! I will give you the kingdom of the Three Connachts, with their gold and silver, their steeds and bridles, and their fair women; but do not leave me!' Loegaire answers in a poem praising the joys of the Otherworld. They travel on the mist, leading a mighty army. There is delightful music, and the happiness of love:

Delightful fairy music, travel from one kingdom to another, drinking mead from bright vessels, talking with one you love.

We play with men of yellow gold on golden chessboards: we drink clear mead in the company of a proud armed warrior.

Der Gréine, daughter of Fiachna, is my wife; and, to tell all, there is a wife for each of my fifty men.

After that he went from them into the fairy mound again, and he shares the kingdom of the fairy mound with Fiachna mac Rétach in the fortress of Mag Mell, and Fiachna's daughter is with him, and he has not come out yet.

Here the Otherworld is identified with a fairy mound (*síd*). There are, indeed, two notions of the Otherworld. It can be reached either by a journey over the western sea, or by entering one of the mounds into which the *Tuatha Dé Danann* were believed to have fled when they were defeated by the sons of Míl. *Bruig na Bóinne*, now identified with the great Bronze Age burial-mound of New Grange in Co. Louth, was the dwelling of Oengus, who won it from the Dagda by a ruse. It was a wonderful place where fruit-trees were always in fruit. There was a roast pig and also a vat of fine liquor which never diminished when consumed. Brí Léith, a hill near Ardagh, Co. Longford, was the home of Midir; Bodb Derg, son of the Dagda, was the lord of Síd ar Femen, which is Slievenamon, Co. Tipperary; Síd Clettig on the Boyne was the home of Elcmar, and Síd Finnachaid that of Aillén mac Midgna, or of Lir. Nuadu dwelt in Síd Alman, the Hill of Allen, Co. Kildare, Siugmall, brother of Elcmar, was lord of Síd Nenta on Lough Ree. And the five (sometimes six) *bruidne* of Ireland, which had no local habitation, were also Otherworld dwellings. Each of them, we are told, had an inexhaustible cauldron, like the Dagda's cauldron, from which no company went away unsatisfied.

But there were also the islands of the Otherworld, and the gods associated with them seem to be distinguished from the *Tuatha Dé Danann*. Manannán mac Lir is the principal figure among them. He drives his chariot over the sea, and was said by Cormac mac Cuilennáin, the ninth century glossator, to have lived in the Isle of Man; but his true home was Emain Ablach, the Avalon of Arthurian tradition. With him are associated other deities who do not appear among the *Tuatha Dé Danann*; Labraid Swift-Hand-on-Sword and his wife Lí Ban; Eogan Inbir and his wife Bé Cuma; Eochaid Iuil and his wife Fand, who invites Cú Chulainn to be her lover, and several others. These 'nobles of the Land of Promise' may have belonged originally to a different cult, for there were several ethnic groups among the Celtic invaders of pre-history, Cruithin, Érainn, Goídil (Féni), and perhaps others as well (pp. 183–94).

The tales commonly known as the Ulster Cycle are so called because most of them are about warriors of the Ulaid, the dominant people in the province of Ulster (*Cóiced Ulad*) in pre-historic times. But Ailill and Medb, king and queen of Cruachain in Connacht, and some famous warriors of the Connacht-men are often in the story. Here the 'Celtic magic' of the Otherworld is forgotten, and we are in an Heroic Age as Chadwick has defined it. These are not tales of mystery and imagination, but stories that are meant to be historical, and that have at least some history behind them. The weapons and war-chariots, the feasts and assemblies, the social order portrayed in the Ulster Cycle correspond closely to the accounts of the Celts of Gaul and Britain given us by ancient writers.[5]

The central story of the cycle is the Cattle-Raid of Cooley, *Táin Bó Cualnge*; and the hero of the story, and of the whole cycle, is Cú Chulainn ('Culann's Hound'), brave, generous, handsome, beloved of women, who chose fame and an early death rather than a long life without honour. In the *Táin* Cú Chulainn stands alone defending Ulster against a whole army throughout the winter, while the Ulstermen lie stricken by a mysterious sickness. The climax of a series of single combats that he fights is his meeting with Fer Diad, his friend and fosterbrother, whom he slays after three days of fighting. The story ends with the coming of the Ulstermen and the rout of the Connacht army.

Many of the shorter sagas are linked to the *Táin* as prefatory tales (*rem-scéla*) which explain some episode in the great battle, and of these deservedly the most famous is the Exile of the Sons of Uisliu, *Longes Mac nUislenn*.[6] It explains why Fer Diad and others of the Ulster warriors were in the Connacht camp, fighting against Ulster; but that is not the real motif of the story. This saga is the earliest example in European literature of tragic love.

LONGES MAC N-UISLENN

The Exile of the Sons of Uisliu

The Ulaid were feasting one day in the house of Fedlimid, the story-teller of King Conchobar, and while they were there a girl-child was born to the wife of Fedlimid, and a druid prophesied about her future. The prophecy is in verse. The girl's name is to be Derdriu, and she will grow to be a woman of wonderful beauty and will cause enmity and trouble and will depart out of the kingdom. Many will die on account of her.

The Ulaid proposed to kill the child at once and so avoid the curse. But Conchobar ordered that she be spared and reared apart, hidden from men's eyes; and he said that he himself would take her for his wife. So Derdriu was entrusted to foster-parents and was reared in a dwelling apart. A wise woman, Leborcham, was the only other person allowed to see her.

Once the girl's foster-father was flaying a calf outside in the snow in winter to cook it for her; and she saw a raven drinking the blood in the snow. Then she said to Leborcham: 'Fair would be a man upon whom those three colours should be: his hair like the raven, and his cheek like the blood, and his body like the snow.' 'Grace and prosperity to you!' said Leborcham. 'He is not far from you, inside close by: Noísi the son of Usnech.'[7] 'I shall not be well,' said she, 'until I see him.'

Once that same Noísi was on the rampart of the fort sounding his cry. And sweet was the cry of the sons of Usnech. Every cow and every beast that would hear it used to give two-thirds excess of milk. For every man who heard it, it was enough of peace and entertainment. Good was their valour too. Though the whole province of the Ulaid should be around them in one place, if the three of them stood back to back, they would not overcome them, for the ex-

304

cellence of their defence. They were as swift as hounds at the hunt. They used to kill deer by their speed.

When Noísi was there outside, soon she went out to him, as though to go past him, and he did not recognize her. 'Fair is the heifer that goes past me,' said he. 'Heifers must grow big where there are no bulls,' said she. 'You have the bull of the province,' said he, 'the king of the Ulaid.' 'I would choose between you,' said she, 'and I would take a young bull like you.' 'No!' said he. Then she sprang towards him and caught his ears. 'Here are two ears of shame(?) and mockery,' said she, 'unless you take me with you.'

Noísi sounded his cry, and the Ulstermen sprang up as they heard it, and the sons of Usnech, his two brothers, went out to restrain and warn him. But his honour was challenged. 'We shall go into another country,' said he. 'There is not a king in Ireland that will not make us welcome.' That night they set out with one hundred and fifty warriors and one hundred and fifty women and one hundred and fifty hounds, and Derdriu was with them.

They fled to Scotland, and took service with the king. But Derdriu's beauty excited his envy, and the sons of Usnech had to flee and take refuge on an island in the sea.

Then Conchobar invited them back and sent Fergus, Dubthach and his son, Cormac, as sureties; but Noísi and his followers were killed when they came to Emain, and Derdriu was brought to Conchobar, and her hands were bound behind her back.

When the sureties heard of this treachery, they came and avenged the crime: three hundred of the Ulaid were killed, and women were killed, and Emain was burnt by Fergus. And Fergus, Dubthach and Cormac went to the court of Ailill and Medb, and for sixteen years the Ulaid had no peace.

Derdriu was for a year with Conchobar, and she never smiled or raised her head from her knee.

And when the musicians came to her, she used to say:

'Though you think the eager warriors fair, who march proudly over Emain, more proudly used they to march to their house, the brave sons of Usnech. . . .

Sweet to Conchobar, your king, are the pipers and horn-blowers, sweeter to me the cry of the sons of Uisliu. . . .

305

Dear was the grey eye which women loved. It was fierce against an enemy. After a visit to the woods, noble course, delightful was his cry through the black forest.

I do not sleep; and I put no purple on my nails. Joy comes not into my mind, since the sons of Usnech do not come. . . .

Joy is not for me in the assembly of Emain which nobles fill, nor peace nor happiness nor comfort, nor a big house nor fair ornament.'

And when Conchobar was comforting her she used to say:

'Conchobar, what are you doing? You have caused me sorrow and tears. As long as I live, I shall not love you.

What was dearest to me under heaven, and what was most beloved, you have taken him from me, – a great wrong – so that I shall not see him till I die. . . .

Two bright cheeks, red lips, eyebrows black as a chafer, pearly teeth bright with the noble colour of snow. . . .

Do not break my heart. Soon I shall die. Grief is stronger than the sea, if you could understand it, Conchobar.'

'What do you hate most of what you see?' said Conchobar. 'You,' she said, 'and Eogan son of Durthacht.' 'You shall be a year with Eogan,' said Conchobar. He gave her to Eogan. They went next day to the assembly of Macha. She was behind Eogan in the chariot. She had prophesied that she would not see two husbands on earth together. 'Well, Derdriu,' said Conchobar. 'You look like a sheep between two rams, between Eogan and me.' There was a big rock in front of her. She thrust her head against the rock, so that it shattered her head, and she died.
That is the exile of the Sons of Usnech, and the exile of Fergus and the Tragic Death of the sons of Usnech and of Derdriu.

This story is preserved in several manuscript versions and in modern folklore. The version presented here, from the Book of Leinster, is the oldest, and may be as early as the eighth century.

Next to *Táin Bó Cualnge* in length, and perhaps in importance too, is the story of Bricriu's Feast, *Fled Bricrenn*, in which the chief motif is the *curad-mír* or Hero's Portion, for which Cú Chulainn and two other warriors contend, just as Gaulish warriors did according to Posidonius. A second theme is the Champion's Ordeal, when Cú Chulainn and his two rivals are challenged to cut off the head of a giant on condition that they allow him to cut off their heads on his return. It has been used again by the author of *Sir Gawayne and the Green Knight*.

The first of these themes is best presented in one of the liveliest and most entertaining of all the Irish sagas, *The Story of Mac Da Thó's Pig*. Here one warrior after another claims the right to carve the pig at a feast, and each in turn has to yield to a rival who establishes a better claim. The boasting of each claimant, and the scornful abuse that is then showered upon him, provide excellent dialogue. At last, when the Connacht champion, Cet mac Mágach, has put several Ulstermen to shame and is about to carve the pig, Conall Cernach enters the hall.

The Ulstermen gave Conall a great welcome. Conchobar took off his hood and waved it about. 'We would like to get our supper,' said Conall. 'Who is carving for you?' 'It has been conceded to the man who is carving,' said Conchobar, 'Cet mac Mágach.' 'Is it true, Cet,' said Conall, 'that you are carving the pig?' Then Cet said:

> Welcome to Conall
> heart of stone
> fierce energy of the lynx
> glitter of ice
> red strength of anger
> in a warrior's breast
> a wounder, a conqueror!
> Son of Findchoem, you are a match for me!

And Conall said:

> Welcome to Cet
> Cet son of Mágu
> warrior's dwelling
> heart of ice

307

plumage (?) of a swan
chariot-fighter strong in combat
angry sea
handsome fierce bull
Cet son of Mágu!

'Go away from the pig!' said Conall. 'What should bring you to it?' said Cet. 'Truly,' said Conall, 'that is to challenge me to a contest! I will contest with you for once, Cet,' said Conall. 'I swear the oath of my tribe, since first I took a spear in my hand I have not passed a single day without killing a Connachtman, nor a night without setting fire, and I have never slept without a Connachtman's head under my knee.' 'It is true,' said Cet, 'you are a better warrior than I. If it were Ánluan who were in the house, he would contest with you. It is bad for us that he is not in the house.' 'But he is!' said Conall, taking Ánluan's head from his belt. And he hurled it at Cet's chest so that blood flowed from his mouth. He went away from the pig, and Conall sat down by it.

Conall proceeds to take the best part for himself, and to the Connachtmen he gives only the fore-legs of the pig. Enraged by this, they rise from their places and the Ulstermen rise to oppose them, so that soon corpses are heaped upon the floor and blood is flowing through the doorways.

This admirable tale from the ninth century describes the very scene that Posidonius must have witnessed, or heard described, in Gaul a thousand years before. One could not have better evidence for the archaism of Irish tradition.

When Cú Chulainn was in the east, learning feats of arms from Scáthach so that he might win the hand of Emer, he fought against another woman-warrior, Aífe, an enemy of Scáthach; and he overcame her and had a son by her. All this is told in a long saga called 'The Wooing of Emer'. The boy is to come to Ireland when he grows to manhood, and he is not to tell his name on the demand of a single warrior. 'The Tragic Death of Aífe's Only Son' tells of the boy's coming to Ireland and of his death by the hand of his own father. It is the story of Sohrab and Rustum, the theme also of the Hildebrandslied, evidently an ancient Indo-European motif. It is of the ninth century in the form in which we have it. The simplicity and the restrained emotion of the story make it memorable.

AIDED OENFIR AÍFE

The Tragic Death of Aífe's Only Son

The men of Ulster were assembled at Trácht Éisi, when they saw a boy coming on the sea in a boat of bronze with gilded oars. He was performing strange feats, bringing down birds alive with his sling, and then releasing them. He would scatter them out of sight by a trick of his hands, and then sing to them so that they flew back to him. The Ulstermen were alarmed and sent a champion to meet him and prevent his landing, or discover his name. Condere goes first, but the boy defies him. Then the mighty Conall Cernach goes down. The boy hurls a stone from his sling, and Conall falls. The boy binds his arms with the strap of his own shield. 'Let someone else oppose him!' says Conall Cernach.

Cú Chulainn was practising his feats as he approached the youth, and the arm of Emer daughter of Forgall was around his neck. 'Do not go down!' said she. 'It is a son of yours that is down there. Do not kill your only son! Refrain, O eager son of Soailte. It is not brave or wise to oppose your valiant son. . . . Turn towards me. Listen. My advice is good. Let Cú Chulainn hear! I know what name he will tell, if the boy down there is Conla, Aífe's only son.'

Then Cú Chulainn said: 'Forbear, woman! I heed not a woman's advice. . . . Make not your womanish talk of gentle conduct. . . . The good spear drinks good liquor. Though it were he, indeed, woman,' said he, 'I would kill him for the honour of Ulster.'

Then he went down himself. 'You play well, boy,' said he. 'But your play is cruel,' said the little boy, 'that two of you do not come, so that I might tell my name to them.' 'Should I then have taken a child along with me?' said Cú Chulainn. 'You shall die, if you do not tell your name.' 'Be it so,' said the lad.

The boy came towards him. They smote each other. The boy shaved his head with his sword by a measured stroke. 'This is enough of insolence,' said Cú Chulainn. 'Let us wrestle then!' 'I shall not be able to reach up to your belt,' said the boy. The boy got upon two stones, and he thrust Cú Chulainn between the stones three times. And the boy did not move either of his feet from the stones, and his feet went into the stones up to his ankles. The mark of his feet is there still. Hence is named the Strand of the Track in Ulster.

Then they went into the sea to drown each other, and the boy put him under twice. He went against the boy in the shallow water and played him false with the *gae bolga*. For Scáthach had taught the use of that weapon to none but Cú Chulainn alone. He cast it at the boy through the water so that his entrails were about his feet. 'That is what Scáthach did not teach me!' said he. 'Woe to you who have wounded me!'

'It is true,' said Cú Chulainn. He took the boy in his arms and bore him away, and he carried him up and cast him before the Ulstermen. 'Here is my son for you, men of Ulster!' said he.

Another saga tells why the hero, Froech son of Fidach, took part in the Táin. It is a love-story, the wooing of Findabair, daughter of Medb and Ailill, by Froech. One passage shows well the sensitivity to form and colour that so often delights us in both verse and prose. Froech has been sent across a river to fetch a branch from a rowan tree:

Froech went then and broke off a branch from the tree, and brought it back over the water. Findabair used afterwards to say of anything beautiful she saw, that she thought it more beautiful to see Froech coming across a dark pool, the white body, the lovely hair, the shapely face, the grey eye, the gentle youth without fault or blemish, his face narrow below and broad above, his body straight and perfect, the branch with the red berries between his throat and his fair face. Findabair used to say that she had never seen anything half or a third as beautiful as he.

Something of the same incandescent quality shines out in the description of Étaín as she bathes at a spring. This Étaín was a daughter's daughter of Étaín, the wife of Midir (p. 299), and was a mortal. At the beginning of a saga, 'The Destruction of Ua Derga's Hostel', the king discovers her:

He saw a woman at the edge of a well, and she had a silver comb with gold ornament. She was washing in a silver basin on which were four birds of gold, and bright little gems of purple carbuncle on the chasing of the basin. She wore a purple cloak of good fleece, held with silver brooches chased with gold, and a smock of green silk with gold embroidery. There were wonderful ornaments of animal design in gold and silver on her breast and shoulders. The sun shone upon her, so that the men saw the gold gleaming in the sunshine against the green silk. There were two golden tresses on her head, plaited in four, with a ball at the end of every lock. The colour of her hair was like the flower of the iris in summer or like pure gold after it has been polished. She was undoing her hair to wash it, so that her arms were out from beneath her dress. White as the snow of one night were her hands, and her lovely cheeks were soft and even, red as the mountain foxglove. Her eyebrows were as black as a beetle's back. Her teeth were like a shower of pearls. Her eyes were as blue as the hyacinth, her lips as red as Parthian leather. High, smooth, soft, and white were her shoulders, clear white her long fingers. Her hands were long. White as the foam of a wave was her side, long and slender, yielding, smooth, soft as wool. Her thighs were warm and smooth and white; her knees small and round and hard and bright. Her shins were short and bright and straight. Her heels were even and lovely. If a rule had been laid upon her feet it would hardly have shown any imperfections in them, unless it should crease the flesh or the skin. The blushing light of the moon was in her noble face, a lofty pride in her smooth brow. The radiance of love was in her eyes; the flush of pleasure on her cheeks, now red as a calf's blood and changing again to snowy whiteness. There was gentle dignity in her voice. Her step was firm and graceful. She had the walk of a queen. She was the fairest, loveliest, finest that men's eyes had seen of all the women of the world. They thought she was of the fairies. Of her it was said: 'All are lovely till compared with Étaín. All are fair till compared with Étaín.'

The Cycle of the Kings begins with a group of Origin-Tales which represent very old tradition. They are of the same *genre* as the Roman story of Romulus and Remus, or the Greek story of Athene and Poseidon at the founding of Athens. One of them specially deserves mention because it contains the motif of the Iron House, which, as we shall see, was borrowed into the Welsh story of Branwen (p. 344 inf.). It is called 'The Destruction of Dinn Ríg', and tells the story of Labraid Loingsech, ancestor-god of the Lagin, or Leinstermen. It is a tale of vengeance, and dates from the ninth century in its present form.

Cobthach Coel, king of Brega, killed his brother, Loegaire Lorc, king of Ireland and his brother's son, Ailill Áine, who was king of Leinster. Ailill's son, Labraid, was sent into exile. Later he returned with an army of Munstermen, captured Dinn Ríg, and became king of Leinster in his turn.

Labraid was at peace with Cobthach. He invited Cobthach to visit him, and a house was built for his entertainment. That house was strong, for it was made of iron, walls and floor and doors. The Leinster-men were a full year building it, and father spoke not to son, nor mother to daughter, as the proverb says: 'Every Leinsterman has his secret.' Cobthach came with thirty kings in his train, and all were burned in the iron house.

Many of the sagas are about kings of the historical period, and one of the best of them is 'The Tragic Death of Mael Fothartaig son of Rónán'. The text as we have it dates perhaps from the tenth century. It is the story of Phaedra and Hippolytus in an Irish setting, and is well told. In the first dialogue the tragic theme is brought in, and it is repeated at once when the boy meets the queen. The tension is never relaxed.

Rónán was king of Leinster in the seventh century, and died *c.* AD 624. In the saga his son Mael Fothartaig is the most famous boy in Leinster. It was around him that men gathered at assemblies and games. He was the darling of the girls and the lover of the young women. His mother died, and his father was for a long time without a wife.

'Why do you not marry?' said his son. 'You would be better off with a wife.' 'I am told,' said Rónán, 'that Echaid has a handsome daughter.' 'You are no husband for a girl,' said the lad. 'Will you not marry a settled woman? I would rather that for you than a skittish girl.'

But the old man married the girl, and she at once fell in love with his son, and sent her maid to persuade him. As the boy refused her love, she accused him falsely. 'A curse on your lips, wicked woman!' said Rónán. 'You lie!'

Mael Fothartaig came in, and was drying his legs at the fire. He spoke two lines of verse, and the girl was able to match them. 'It is true then,' said Rónán. And he told one of his men to kill the boy with a spear-thrust. When Mael Fothartaig was dying, he told his father the truth. There is a fine lament by the old king over his son's body towards the end. He praises Mael Fothartaig and his companions, and bids the servants feed the two dogs who mourn for their master:

> 'Doiléne has served me well:
> her head is in the lap of everyone in turn
> seeking one whom she will not find.

> .   .   .   .

> My son Mael Fothartaig
> was the leader of the pack:
> the tall, fair champion who shone abroad
> has found a cold dwelling-place.'

Another important saga of the Cycle is 'The Story of Cano son of Gartnán'. It is more attractive for its matter than for its form in the only manuscript that preserves it, The Yellow Book of Lecan, for it is somewhat incoherent, and there are some obscure passages. The story is pure invention, for though the characters are historical, they are not contemporaries, and moreover it is plainly woven from several old motifs. One of these is the motif of Tristan, so that this tale ranks with the story of Deirdre as one of the early Celtic sources of the Tristan legend. The parallel here rests upon the love-theme, the fact that Créd is the young wife of an old king, whose name is Marcán (diminutive of Marc), and the final episode in which Cano approaches the coast in a ship, Créd dies before he reaches land, and he dies soon afterwards.[8] Another motif that occurs is the love of the unseen one, *adṛṣṭakāma* in Sanskrit tradition, which in Irish is called *grád écmaise* 'love of one known only by repute'; and there is also the motif of the external soul.

Cano was the son of a Scottish king. His death is recorded in the Annals in 688. In the story he comes to Ireland as an exile, and is received with honour by king Diarmait, whose daughter was already in love with him before she had seen him. She saves him from danger, and he goes away to visit Guaire, king of Connacht. He comes first to the house of Marcán, whose wife Créd was a daughter of Guaire. She too was already in love with him. Marcán had a son, Colcu, apparently a stepson of Créd. Later, when Cano was with Guaire, Créd and Marcán came to a feast, and also Colcu. Créd asked that she be allowed to pour the wine that night, and she gave a sleep-potion to all save herself and Cano. Then she entreated him, but he refused to be her lover while he was a mere adventurer, and promised to make her his queen when he should be king of Scotland. He gave her as a pledge a stone which contained his life.

Cano was recalled to Scotland and became king, and every year he used to make a tryst with Créd at Inber Colptha (the mouth of the Boyne), but Colcu was always there with a hundred men to prevent their meeting. At last they made a tryst at Loch Créde in the north. Créd came, bringing with her the magic stone. Cano approached from the east, so that they were within sight of each other, when Colcu appeared again and drove him off. Créd dashed her head against a rock, and the stone broke as she fell. Cano died three days after he had gone back to Scotland.

Even this bald summary shows the peculiar interest of the story, an historical figure being presented as the hero of a Tristan romance, with the extra distinction of an external soul. The manuscript text has not much style about it, but we have seen that a finer oral form is to be imagined (p. 299).

The Fenian Cycle was the latest to take shape as a separate tradition in the literature. Recent research by Gerard Murphy and by O'Rahilly has shown that Find, the central figure of the Fenian Cycle, is identical in origin with the great god of the Celts, Lug of the Long Arm. Find is a warrior-hunter god, who slays a one-eyed god of fire, a burner. There are early references to Find, but they are fragmentary; and the old list of sagas (p. 299) contains only a few Fenian titles. It is clear that even by the twelfth century, Find and the *fiana* were only on the way to becoming famous in literature. It may be said that one of the titles in the list is *Aithed Gráinne re Diarmait*, 'The Elopement of Gráinne with Diarmait', and we know from other evidence that the famous love-story of Diarmaid and Gráinne was known in the tenth century, although the only surviving text of it is of the Modern Irish period (15th century?). It is a variant of the Deirdre story (p. 304), and Gertrude Schoepperle showed long ago that these two stories represent the Celtic source of the romance of Tristan and Isolde.

The twelfth century was a period of recovery and reform in Ireland as elsewhere in Europe, and there was a great revival of literature and of learning. The Book of the Dun Cow, the so-called Book of Leinster, and the famous Rawlinson manuscript were all written at that time; and it was then too that the great classical themes of the Siege of Troy,

314

the Aeneid, and the Destruction of Thebes were introduced into Irish. It was in this time of transition that there came the sudden flowering of the Fenian Cycle. It coincided with the first appearance in Ireland of ballad poetry, and the Fenian ballad appears as a new literary form.

One of the earliest of these Fenian ballads is the Sleep-Song for Diarmaid, supposed to be sung by Gráinne, as she watches over her lover asleep:

Codail beagán, beagán beag,	Sleep a little, just a little, for
óir ní heagail duit a bheag,	there is no danger in a little
a ghiolla dia dtardus seirc,	sleep, boy to whom I have
a mheic Í Dhuibhne, a	given my love, Diarmaid, son
Dhiarmaid.	of Ó Duibhne.
Codail-se sunn go sáimh,	Sleep soundly here, noble
a Í Dhuibhne, a Dhiarmaid áin;	Diarmaid Ó Duibhne; I shall
do-dhéan-sa t'fhoraire dhe,	watch over you, handsome son
a mheic Í dhealbhdha	of Ó Duibhne.
Dhuibhne	

She thinks of other lovers who eloped and slept in safety, and then she thinks of danger, and of the animals of the forest who seem to be afraid:

The stag in the east does not sleep; he does not cease to call:
even though he is in the forest, he has no thought of sleep.

The lively music does not cease in the curved branches of the trees;
they are noisy there, even the thrush is not asleep.

Tonight the grouse does not sleep in the deep rough heather;
shrill is the note of his clear voice; among the streams he does not
    sleep.

Fenian ballads became very popular, and the big collection known as *Duanaire Finn* has been made the subject of a special study by Gerard Murphy.[9] Many of them are in the form of a dialogue between Oisín, son of Finn (MacPherson's 'Ossian'), and Saint Patrick, in which Oisín tells the saint stories about the adventures of the *fiana*, or Fenians. Most of these ballads are of the Modern Irish period, but the dialogue tradition goes back to a famous prose text which ushers in the Fenian Cycle in the twelfth century, *Acallam na Senórach*, 'The Colloquy of the Ancient Men.' It is a frame-story which tells how Saint Patrick meets the Fenian warriors Oisín and Caílte, and journeys through Ireland with one or other of them. The warriors tell the saint more than two hundred anecdotes, many of them attached to the places they visit on their way.

One conversation between Saint Patrick and Caílte begins well:

'Was he not a good lord with whom you were, Find mac Cumaill that is to say?' Upon which Caílte uttered this little tribute of priase:

'Were but the brown leaf which wood sheds from it gold, were but the white wave silver, Finn would have given it all away.'

'Who or what was it that maintained you so in your life?' Patrick asked. And Caílte answered: 'Truth that was in our hearts, and strength in our arms, and fulfilment in our tongues.'

As they wander through Munster, they come to a place from which the Fenians had formerly set out to fight the battle of Ventry. Caílte tells the story of Cael who had seen a beautiful girl named Créd in a dream, and who wooed and won her on the way to the battle. Cael was drowned at Ventry, and his body was washed up from the sea; and Créd lay beside his body and lamented his death:

The haven roars over the angry surf of Rinn Dá
Bárc: the wave against the shore laments the
drowning of the warrior of Loch Dá Chonn.

Plaintful is the crane from the marsh of Druim
Dá Thrén: she cannot protect her loved ones,
the fox of Dá Lí pursues her nestlings.

Sad is the note of the thrush in Dromkeen, and
sad the music of the blackbird in Letterlee.

Sad is the cry of the stag in Druim Dá Léis: the
doe of Druim Síleann is dead, and the stag of
Díleann laments her . . .

The *Acallam* is one of the most successful works of Middle Irish literature, and could serve as a happy introduction to Modern Irish. Gerard Murphy has suggested that it may be a deliberate literary composition by an individual author, the scribe of the original manuscript, unlike the heroic sagas which clearly derive from oral tradition.[10] It would then present an interesting comparison with the Welsh *Mabinogion*.

In tracing the beginnings of Irish literature we saw the 'new forms' of poetry which the monks evolved, and the nature poetry and hermit poetry which was their special contribution. These new forms soon spread to the secular poetry, and from the ninth to the twelfth century there is a rich tradition. The hermit's voice is still heard, but there is humour and passion as well.

One famous manuscript, written perhaps at the Irish abbey of Reichenau on Lake Constance, has found its way to the Austrian abbey of Sankt Paul in Carinthia, where it is known as *das irische Schulheft*, 'the Irish Copybook'. It is, indeed, a student's note-book, notes on Virgil and on the Greek declensions, quotations from Horace, Saint Jerome and Saint Augustine; and among them are four Irish poems. One is a heroic poem in praise of Aed son of Diarmaid, and it is in the new form, showing the adoption by the professional poets of the rhymed quatrain for their panegyrics:

Aed oll fri *a*ndud n-*á*ne,	Aed who is great in kindling brilliance,
Aed *fonn* fri *f*uilted *féle*,	Aed who is a support in dispensing hospitality,
in *d*eil *d*elgnaide as ch*óemem*	conspicuous pillar, dearest of the chieftains
di dindgnaib *Roerenn réde*	of level Roeriu.
Mac *Diarmata d*il *d*amsa,	Son of Diarmaid, dear to me,
cid *iarfachta* ní *insa*;	if it be asked, it is not difficult
a *m*olad maissiu *máenib*	to tell; his praise more precious
l*ú*aidfidir *láedib limmsa*	than wealth will be sung in lays by me.

There are eight quatrains, and end-rhyme and internal rhyme are freely used, as well as the old ornament of alliteration.

The other three poems are monastic, and in one of them the poet with delicate humour compares the zeal of his cat in catching mice with his own efforts in learning:

Messe ocus Pangur bán
cechtar nathar fria šaindán:
bíth a menmasam fri seilgg,
mu menma céin im šaincheirdd.

Pangur Bán and I, each of us
at his special art: his mind is
set upon hunting, and mine
upon my proper craft.

Caraimse fos, ferr cach clú,
oc mu lebrán, léir ingnu;
ní foirmtech frimm Pangur bán:
caraid cesin a maccdán.

I love to stay – it is better than
fame – at my book, eagerly
pursuing knowledge. Pangur
Bán does not envy me:
he loves his childish art.

Ó ru biam, scél cen scís,
innar tegdais, ar n-oendís,
táithiunn, díchríchide clius,
ní fris tarddam ar n-áthius.

When we are alone together,
content in our house, we have
something to which we can
apply our skill, an endless sport.

Gnáth, huaraib, ar gressaib gal
glenaid luch inna línsam;
os mé, du-fuit im lín chéin
dliged ndoraid cu ndronchéill.

Often at times with feats of
valour, he catches a mouse in
his net; and I, there falls into
my net a difficult rule of hard
meaning.

Fuachaidsem fri frega fál
a rosc, a nglése comlán;
fuachimm chéin fri fégi fis
mu rosc réil, cesu imdis.

He directs his full bright eye
towards the wall; I direct my
clear though feeble eye towards
keenness of knowledge.

Faelidsem cu ndéne dul
hi nglen luch inna gérchrub;
hi tucu cheist ndoraid ndil
os mé chene am faelid.

He rejoices with swift action
when a mouse is caught in his
sharp claw; when I grasp a
difficult matter, I too am
joyful.

Cia beimmi amin nach ré
ní derban cách a chéle:

Though we be thus any time,
neither disturbs the other; each

| maith la cechtar nár a dán; | of us likes his own art, alone in |
| subaigthius a oenurán. | his pleasure. |

Hé fesin as choimsid dáu	He is his own master at the
in muid du-ngní cach oenláu;	task he follows every day; I
du thabairt doraid du glé	ply my separate task, bringing
for mu mud céin am messe.	what is dark into the light.

That poem was written early in the ninth century. From the same early time comes another which tells the sorrow of old age, and memories of youth, beauty and love. It is the 'Lament of the Old Woman of Beare':

Ebb-tide has come to me, as to the sea; old age makes me yellow; though I may grieve thereat, it comes happily to feed on me.

I am Buí, the hag of Beare. I used to wear a new smock always: today I am so forlorn that I do not even wear an old one.

It is wealth that you love, not people; in our day it was people that we loved.

Beloved were those over whose lands we rode: we fared well among them, and they made little of it.

Today you ask for plenty, and give little away: and although you bestow little, you make a great boast.

Swift chariots, and horses that won the prize, there was once a flood of them. Blessed be the King who gave them!

When my arms are seen, long and thin – pleasant was the art they practised: they used to be about glorious kings.

When my arms are seen, long and thin, they are not fit, I declare, to put around comely youths.

The girls are glad when May-Day comes: grief suits me better, for I am a wretched old woman.

I speak no honied words; no sheep are killed for my wedding; my hair is scant and grey; a mean veil is no shame to it.

I care not that a white veil be on my head: many a bright scarf was on my head when I drank good ale.

The wave of the great sea is noisy: winter has aroused it. I expect neither noble nor slave's son to visit me today.

I enjoyed the summer of youth while it lasted, and even the autumn; the winter of age, which overwhelms everyone, has begun to overtake me.

I had my day with kings, drinking mead and wine: today I drink whey and water with shrivelled hags.

The flood-wave and the swift ebb-wave: what the flood-wave brings you, the ebb-wave takes out of your hand.

The flood-wave and the ebb in turn have both come upon me so that I know them.

It is well for the islands of the wide sea: flood comes to them after ebb. I have no hope that flood after ebb will come to me.

There is an old story which tells of a sorrowful love, and recalls the tragic history of Abélard and Héloise. This too belongs to the ninth century. Liadan and Cuirithir were lovers, and Liadan entered a convent. Her lover pursued her, and they placed themselves under the guidance of Saint Cummine the Tall. At first he allowed them to converse, but not to look upon each other. Later he permitted them to sleep together, with a child between them lest they should do wrong. It is an instance of *mulieris consortium,* which was a recognized form of asceticism in early Ireland and elsewhere. They failed in this test, and Cuirithir was sent to a monastery and later went into exile across the sea. Here is the lament of Liadan:

Cen áinius
in gním í dorigénus
an ro carus ro cráidius

Joyless what I have done! I
have grieved the man I loved.

Ba mire
nád dernad a airer-som
mainbed omun ríg nime

It was madness not to do his
will, but for the fear of heaven's
King.

Níbu amlos
dosom an dál dúthracair
ascnam sech phéin i Pardos.

No misfortune was the lot that
he desired, to seek Paradise
without punishment.

320

Bec mbríge	It was a small thing that turned
ro chráidi friumm Cuirithir;	Cuirithir against me; I was
frissium ba mór mo míne.	gentle towards him.
Mé Liadan;	I am Liadan; I loved Cuirithir;
ro carussa Cuirithir;	it is as true a word as ever
is fírithir adfiadar.	spoken.
Gair bása	Only a short time I was with
i comaitecht Chuirithir;	Cuirithir; my companionship
frissium ba maith mo gnássa.	was good for him.
Céol caille	The music of the forest sang to
fom-chanad la Cuirithir,	Cuirithir and me, and the
la fogur fairge flainne.	sound of the raging sea.
Do-ménainn	I should have thought that
ní cráidfed frimm Cuirithir	nothing I would do would
do dálaib cacha dénainn.	turn Cuirithir against me.
Ní chela	Conceal it not, he was my
ba hésium mo chridc-ṡcrc,	heart's love, whoever else I
cia no carainn cách chena.	may have loved.
Deilm ndega	A roaring flame has dissolved
ro thethainn mo chridese;	this heart of mine; without
ro fes nicon bía cena.[11]	him for certain it cannot live.

One more example of personal poetry may be quoted for its humorous and moving comment on the human predicament. Here it is a monk who complains of distractions at prayer:

It is a shame how my thoughts wander! I fear great danger on the Day of Judgement.

During the psalms they stray on to a wrong path: they run, they distract me, they are sinful in the presence of the great God.

Through lively meetings, through crowds of foolish women, through woods and cities, they are swifter than the wind,

Now through pleasant paths, and again through unseemly wilderness.

Without a boat they can travel on the sea; with one swift leap they go from earth to heaven.

They run their foolish course, and after naughty roaming come back home again.

Though one try to bind or fetter them, they have no constancy, no mind for rest.

Neither knife nor scourge restrains them; they slip from my grasp like an eel's tail.

Neither lock nor vaulted prison nor any bond, fortress or sea or bare fastness, can stop their course.

O chaste Christ beloved, to whom every verdict is clear, may the grace of the sevenfold Spirit come to keep and check them!

O powerful God, Creator, rule this heart of mine, that Thou mayst be my love, that I may do Thy will!

O Christ, may I be united to Thee: may we be together! Thou art not fickle and inconstant: Thou art not as I am.

Latin was, of course, the first literary language of the monks, and the earliest writings we have are in Latin, beginning with the writings of Saint Patrick himself, the works of Saint Columbanus and Adamnán's *Vita Columbae*, which have been discussed already (pp. 219, 233 f.). Gradually the vernacular came to be used in prose as well as verse, at first perhaps merely to write glosses on a Latin text, as in the famous glossed codices of Würzburg, Milan and St Gall; but from the beginning of the eighth century there are prose tracts written in Irish.[12] The earliest is a homily on the Mass, preserved in a manuscript at Cambrai, which was written at the end of the seventh century. The Book of Armagh contains long notes in Irish of the early eighth century, and the author apologizes for using Irish on this occasion: 'Finiunt haec pauca per scotticam inperfecté scripta non quod ego non potuissem romana condere lingua sed quod uix in sua scotica hae fabulae agnosci possunt. Sin autem alias per latinam degestae fuissent non tam incertus fuisset aliquis in eis quam imperitus quid legisset aut quam linguam sonasset pro habundantia scotaicorum nominum non habentium qualitatem.' In the Tripartite Life of Saint Patrick (*c.* 900) we have a sustained narrative in Irish prose.

A fine example of vernacular prose in the monastic tradition is *Fís Adamnán*, 'The Vision of Adamnán'. It belongs to a group of texts which derive from Jewish and Christian sources and describe visions of Heaven and Hell experienced by holy men. These visions provide interesting evidence of what was read and studied in Ireland in the eighth and ninth centuries, and it appears that apocryphal writings, condemned elsewhere, continued in favour among the Irish.

Saint Adamnán, author of the *Vita Columbae,* a beautiful Latin life of Saint Colmcille, was abbot of Iona (679–704), tenth in succession to Colmcille, its founder. He is credited with a vision of Heaven and Hell, the account of which is as early as the tenth century in it sextant form. C. H. Boswell goes so far as to say that the unknown author excels all other precursors of Dante, and Seymour is of a like opinion.[13] The Vision of Adamnán is eloquent and simple: in style and structure it is probably the best that we have in Irish prose down to the twelfth century.

The soul of Adamnán went forth from his body, and was brought by his guardian angel to Heaven and to Hell. The host of Heaven is described: the apostles and the Blessed Virgin are around Christ. On Mary's right hand are holy virgins 'and no great space between them'.

Though the brightness and light in the land of the saints are great and wonderful, as we have said, more wonderful a thousand times is the brilliance in the plain of the heavenly host around the throne of the Lord himself. That throne is a well-wrought chair, supported by four pillars of precious stone. Though one should hear no other music but the fair harmony of those four pillars, it would be enough of happiness. Three stately birds are perched on the chair in the King's presence, and their task is to keep their minds ever intent upon their Creator. They sing the eight Hours, praising and glorifying the Lord, and a choir of archangels accompanies them. The birds and angels begin the music, and the whole host of Heaven responds, both saints and holy virgins.

Above the Glorious One seated on His throne, there is a mighty arch like a wrought helmet or a royal diadem. If human eyes should see it, they would melt away at once. There are three Zones around it, and what they are cannot be told. Six thousand thousands in the form of horses and of birds surround the fiery chair which blazes eternally.

To describe the mighty Lord who is on that throne is not possible for anyone save Him alone, unless He should tell it to the heavenly orders; for none shall tell His ardour and energy, His glow and gleam, His dignity and beauty, His constancy and firmness, the number of angels and archangels that sing their chant before Him . . . Though one should gaze around, east and west and north and south, he will find on every side the noble face seven times as bright as the sun. He will see no human form, neither head nor feet, but a mass of fire blazing throughout the world, and all in fear and trembling in its presence.

After the description of the citadel, we are told of those who are outside the gate, awaiting the last judgment. A curtain of fire and a curtain of ice hang in the gateway and strike against each other with a sound terrible to the ears of sinners. To the host of Heaven within it is heard as sweet faint music.

There are seven heavens and six gates through which the souls must pass. When Adamnán has seen all this, he is brought to Hell over a bridge which leads across a valley of fire into the Land of Torment. The various torments suffered by those guilty of particular sins are described, as in the *Inferno*. After they have been shown to Adamnán, his soul is brought back to Heaven in the twinkling of an eye; but when it thinks to stay there, the voice of his guardian angel bids it return into the body it has left, and tell in assemblies and congregations, lay and cleric, the rewards of Heaven and the pains of Hell, as the angel has revealed them.

The Otherworld motif and the Christian Vision literature are parodied in an excellent satire called The Vision of Mac Con Glinne[14] which was composed in the twelfth century by some disillusioned scholar, whose wit and vigour invite comparison with Brian Merriman's 'Midnight Court'. The genealogical lore of the *filid*, the poetical descriptions of *Mag Mell*, visits to mortal heroes by fairy maidens, even the Bible itself is mocked by this nameless satirist who seems to be following the fashion of the troubadours.

Cathal, king of Munster, was possessed by a demon of gluttony, so

324

that he ate immense quantities of food. There was at the time a scholar named Ainiér Mac Con Glinne who was famous for his gifts of satire and eulogy. One Saturday evening, as he was pursuing his reading at Roscommon, a longing came upon him to give up learning for poetry. He decided to go as a poet to the court of Cathal, in the hope of getting plenty to eat there, for he loved good food. On the morrow he set out for Cork, and by nightfall he arrived at the guest-house of the monastery. He found the door open, in spite of wind and rain, and no one in attendance. The blanket was full of lice and fleas. The bath had not been emptied since the previous night, nor even the heating-stones taken out.

Since no one came to wash his feet, the scholar washed them himself in the dirty bath and lay down to sleep. But the lice and fleas were as many as the sands of the sea or as sparks of fire or the dewdrops on a May morning or the stars of heaven, and he could not rest. He took out his psalter and began to sing the psalms, 'and the learned and the books of Cork relate that the sound of the scholar's voice was heard a thousand paces beyond the city, singing his psalms, through spiritual mysteries, in dia-psalms and syn-psalms and decades, with *paters* and canticles and hymns at the end of each fifty'.

The abbot, Manchín, sends a servant with the guest's ration, which consists of a cup of whey-water. Mac Con Glinne satirizes this meagre fare and declines it. His conduct is reported to the abbot, who orders him to be stripped, beaten, and thrown into the river Lee, and left to sleep naked in the guesthouse. In the morning he shall be judged by the abbot and monks of Cork and shall be crucified for the honour of the abbot himself, of St Finnbarr, and of the church. The first part of this sentence is carried out, and next morning the monks assemble in the guesthouse. The abbot will have him crucified at once, but he asks for a trial; and, though they plead against him with much wisdom and learning, they cannot find anything in his sayings for which he deserves crucifixion. He is led out to his doom without the sanction of law, but he asks leave to eat his viaticum before he dies, and binds the abbot with sureties and pledges.

His satchel is brought to him, and he takes out two wheaten loaves and a piece of bacon. He takes tithes of the bread and meat and considers paying them to the clergy or bestowing them in alms, but he decides that none has greater need than himself, and, as for the monks of Cork, they are curs, thieves, and dung-hounds, and he will not

325

have the devil accuse him, when he crosses the line, of paying tithes to them. So the first morsel he eats is the tithe. He finishes eating and is led away, but he continues to delay his execution by insisting on drinking water drop by drop from the pin of his brooch. At last he agrees to go in humility. An axe is given him, and he is made to cut his passion-tree and bear it on his back to the green of Cork.

As the monks are about to crucify him, Mac Con Glinne asks a boon of Manchín, namely, that he may have a last feast and fine raiment before going to his death. Manchín denies him this and says that, as the evening is far advanced, he shall be stripped of the scant clothing he wears and tied to a pillar, as a first punishment before the great punishment of the morrow. The monks bind him to the pillar and retire to supper, leaving him to fast. At midnight an angel appears to him and reveals a vision.

In the morning, when Manchín and his monks arrive, Mac Con Glinne begs leave to relate the vision. Manchín refuses, but the monks will hear it, and he proceeds to relate it. The prelude is a rhymed genealogy of Manchín in terms of food:

'Bless us, O cleric, famous pillar of learning,
Son of mead, son of juice, son of lard,
Son of stirabout, son of pottage, son of fair radiant fruit,
Son of smooth, clustering cream, son of buttermilk, son of curds,
Son of beer, glory of liquors, son of pleasant bragget,
Son of twisted leek, son of bacon, son of butter,
Son of full-fat sausage,' and so forth.

The vision which follows is a verse parody upon the Voyage-Tales. He sets out in a boat of lard on a lake of new milk.

The fort we reached was fair, with earthworks of thick custard, beyond the lake. Its bridge was of butter, its wall of wheat, the palisade was of bacon.

. . . . .

Smooth pillars of old cheese, beams of juicy bacon, in due order, fine rafters of thick cream, with laths of curds supported the house.

. . . . .

Behind was a spring of wine, rivers of beer and bragget, every full

326

pool had a flavour. A flood of smooth malt over a bubbling spring spreads over the floor.

. . . .

I saw the chieftain in a mantle of beef-fat with his fair noble wife. I saw the server at the cauldron's mouth, his flesh-fork on his shoulder.

We are told that there was much more in the vision than the text relates; and when Mac Con Glinne had finished, Manchín announced that it had been revealed to him that this vision would cure the king of his disease, and that the scholar must go to king Cathal at once. Mac Con Glinne claims a reward. 'Are not thy body and soul reward enough?' says Manchín. And the scholar answers that he cares not for his life, for Heaven awaits him with its nine orders, the Cherubim and Seraphim, and all the faithful chanting in expectation of his soul. He must have as a reward the abbot's cloak. Manchín refuses, but the monks insist, and the cloak is placed in the custody of the bishop of Cork, pending the successful cure of Cathal.

It would be too long to follow here the excellent humour of the story of the cure. Mac Con Glinne contrives to oblige the unhappy king to fast for two nights. He then orders a feast and has Cathal tied to the wall and brings in the luscious food. As he proceeds to eat it himself, the king roars and bellows and orders his death. Now Mac Con Glinne recites his vision in two poems which are fresh compositions on the same theme, new parodies of the *echtrae* motif. To these he adds a fable, again in parody, of the visits to mortals by persons of the Tuatha Dé Danann; but here, too, food is the theme. This fable is an excellent piece of humour and eloquence. In prose and verse the author mocks at the heroic and mythological sagas, the wonders of the Otherworld, and the fair maidens whose anatomy they describe in such detail. Even the scribes who recorded the tales are satirized, for the author solemnly retails conflicting versions of various episodes, the learned giving one, the books of Cork another, in mockery of the variants frequently given in the sagas. The satire is sustained at great length with unfailing merriment and with gluttonous descriptions of the food-paradise to which the scholar has journeyed. Meanwhile, we are left to imagine the distress of the hungry king.

'At the pleasure of the recital and the enumeration of the many and various delicious foods in the presence of the king, the lawless beast that lay in the entrails of Cathal son of Fínguine came up so that it

327

was licking its lips outside his mouth.' The scholar was now bringing each tempting morsel to the lips of the king, and at last the demon of gluttony darted from his mouth, seized one of the morsels, and hid under the cooking-pot. The pot turned over and caught it. 'Thanks be to God and St Brigid!' said Mac Con Glinne, putting his right hand over his mouth and his left over the mouth of Cathal. Linen sheets were put around Cathal's head, and he was borne away. The house was then cleared and burnt to the ground, but the demon escaped and perched upon a neighbouring house. Mac Con Glinne called upon him to do reverence. The demon replied that he must, although he would not. If he had been suffered to remain three half-years longer in Cathal's mouth, he would have ruined all Ireland. If it were not for the wisdom of the monks of Cork and for the multitude of their bishops and confessors (this is a last thrust), if it had not been for the righteousness and honour of the king and the virtue, wisdom, and learning of Mac Con Glinne himself, he would have leaped into that scholar's throat, so that he would have been driven through Ireland with whips and scourges, until he was taken off by hunger. Mac Con Glinne made the Sign of the Cross against the demon with his gospel-book, and the demon flew into the air to join the host of Hell. Cathal rewarded Mac Con Glinne with cows and cloaks and rings and horses and sheep, and the abbot's cloak to boot.

The Otherworld motif which inspired the *echtrai* (p. 183) is also the matter of the *immrama* ('voyages), and of these the most successful is the 'Voyage of Mael Dúin', which is supposed to be the source of the famous *Navigatio Brendani*. It is ascribed in one manuscript to Aed Finn, 'chief scholar of Ireland'; but he has not been identified. The tale is not later than the tenth century.

Mael Dúin was a love-child and was fostered by the queen, who was a friend of his mother, and reared as one of her own children. Like Oengus in 'The Wooing of Étaín', he discovered from the taunt of a companion that he was not her son; and he then learned that his father, Ailill Ochair Ága, had been murdered by marauders from Leix. He asked the way to Leix, and wise men told him he must go by sea, so he went to Corcomroe (in the present County Clare) to consult a druid, who appointed the day on which he should begin to build his boat and the number of men he should take, namely, seventeen. However, after he had set sail, his three foster-brothers

328

swam out after the boat and were taken aboard in violation of the druid's counsel.

They voyaged all day until midnight, when they reached two small islands from which there came a great noise of intoxication and boasting; and they heard one man cry out that he was the better warrior, for he had slain Ailill Ochair Ága, and none of Ailill's kindred had avenged the crime upon him. Mael Dúin's people rejoiced at having come straight to the house of the murderer; but, while they spoke together about it, a storm arose, and their boat was carried away to sea. When morning broke they saw no land. Mael Dúin reproached his foster-brothers for having brought this misfortune upon them by causing them to disobey the druid's instruction. They left their boat to sail wherever God might guide it, and so their wonderful voyage began.

The boat travels over the endless ocean and brings them to many marvellous islands, thirty-one in all. On the islands and in the open sea they encounter prodigies the account of which displays considerable power of imagination and a nice sense of humour.

On the first island they see a swarm of ants, each as big as a foal, which seek to devour them; so they flee. On another they find only great birds and take some of them for food; on another a wild beast like a horse with sharp nails on his hooves, and they flee in terror. The next island is occupied by demons who are having a horse-race. Sometimes they find food and drink made ready for them. A branch plucked by Mael Dúin bears three apples after three days, and they all eat of these apples for forty days and are satisfied.

They found another island surrounded by a stone wall. When they came near, a great beast arose and ran around the island. Mael Dúin thought it faster than the wind. It went to the summit of the island and stretched itself on the ground with its feet in the air. It would turn in its skin, the flesh and bones revolving and the skin unmoved; or at another time the skin turning like a mill, the bones and the flesh quite still.

They fled in haste, and the beast came down to the shore and hurled stones after them, one of which pierced Mael Dúin's shield and lodged in the boat's keel.

On one island there are apple-trees with golden apples. Red swine devour the apples by day and disappear underground at night. Then the sea-birds come and eat the apples. Mael Dúin says that it can

329

fare no worse with them than with the birds, and they go ashore. The earth is hot so that they can hardly stay, for the swine are blazing hot. They fill the boat with apples and escape.

On the next island they find a feast prepared, and they eat and drink. There is a wealth of treasure guarded by a cat. One of the foster-brothers seizes a gold bracelet, and the cat jumps right through him and burns him to ashes. Later they come to an island inhabited by a hideous miller, who tells them that he grinds half the corn of Ireland in his mill, all that is ever begrudged. On another there are people whose bodies and clothes are black. They wail unceasingly. The lot falls on one of the two remaining foster-brothers who goes ashore; and at once he turns black and wails like the others. Two are sent to rescue him and suffer the same fate. Four more go and succeed in bringing back the last two, but not the foster-brother.

After other adventures they reach an island where they find an old man whose clothing is his hair. He tells them he is of the Men of Ireland. He is a pilgrim and has come out floating on a sod of earth which the Lord established in that place. The sod grew miraculously year by year to be an island, and the souls of his children and his kindred in the form of birds have settled in the trees there. All are fed by the ministry of angels. He prophesies that Mael Dúin and his companions will return home safely, all save one man. After three days they depart.

At one time the sea is like green glass, transparent and beautiful; at another it is like a cloud, so that they fear it will not support them. Below them now is a wonderful country with great strongholds. A fearsome beast in a tree seizes an ox and devours it. In terror they sail over this region and escape. A stream of water flows through the air like a rainbow, and they pass below it and spear salmon from the water over their heads. From Sunday evening until Monday morning the stream subsides and does not flow. They fill their boat with salmon and go on their way. They behold a pillar of silver rising out of the sea to which a great silver net is attached. The boat passes through a mesh of the net. Diurán brings with him a piece of the net and vows to lay it on the altar at Armagh.

At last they reach an island, which is plainly the Land of Women of the *echtrai*. Seventeen girls are there preparing a bath for them. One of the girls comes to welcome them and announces that the queen invites them into the fort. A feast is served, and, when they have finished

330

eating and drinking, each of Mael Dúin's men takes a wife, and Mael Dúin sleeps with the queen. In the morning she bids them abide there. Age will not come upon them, and they will live forever and enjoy the pleasures they have known there every night without any toil. One of Mael Dúin's companions grows weary and wishes to go home (as in *Echtrae Brain*), but Mael Dúin wishes to stay. The others prevail upon him, and one day, while the queen is away, they set sail. She rides down to the beach and throws a ball of thread to Mael Dúin. He catches it, and she draws the boat back to land (as in *Echtrae Brain*). Three times she treats them so, and at last Mael Dúin says that someone else must attend to the ball of thread. They set out again, and when the queen throws her ball of thread another man takes it and it clings to his hand, but Diurán cuts off his arm,[15] and they sail away.

Now comes an episode which Zimmer rightly held to be the occasion of the later attribution of a marvellous voyage to St Brendan of Clonfert.[16] They land on a large island, one half of which is wooded with yews and oaks, while the other is an open plain grazed by a great flock of sheep. They see a little church and a fort, and in the church they find an old monk. His hair covers him completely. He is one of the fifteen disciples of St Brendan of Birr who set out on a pilgrimage and landed there. All are dead save him alone. He bids them eat of the sheep, and they stay there for a while. (St Brendan of Birr died AD 565, St Brendan of Clonfert, AD 576. And it is not here said that the former made the voyage himself, merely that fifteen of his monks did so. The latter, however, was known to have made other voyages and easily became the subject of a regular *immram*.)

On the same island they see a huge bird which eats the fruit of a branch which it carries in its claws. It is visited by two eagles, which pick the lice from its head and body and remove the old feathers. Then they pick some of the fruit and cast it into a lake, so that the foam of the water becomes red. The great bird descends into the lake and washes himself. Afterward his flight is swifter and stronger than before. They understand that he has undergone the renewal of youth according to the word of the prophet who says: *renovabitur ut aquilae iuventus tua* (Ps. ciii. 5). Diurán bathed in the lake, and he never lost a tooth or a hair of his head, nor did he suffer weakness or disease from that time forth.

On the next island the third of the foster-brothers meets his doom. It

331

is inhabited by people who play and laugh unceasingly. The lot falls upon him to go ashore, and he at once begins to play and laugh like the others. His companions wait a long time, and then abandon him.

Then they saw another island which was not large, with a wall of fire all around it; and that wall revolved about the island. There was an open doorway in the side of the wall, and each time the doorway came in front of them they saw the whole island and all that was on it with all its inhabitants, many handsome people in lovely garments with golden cups in their hands as they feasted. And they heard their ale-music. And they were for a long time watching the wonder which they saw, and they found it delightful.

Two more islands are visited, on one of which they meet a hermit who bids them return home and foretells that they will find the slayer of Mael Dúin's father but that they must spare him because God has saved them from many dangers. At last they see an Irish falcon flying to the south-east. They follow the course of its flight, and at nightfall they come to the first island, from which the wind had borne them out to sea. They are made welcome, and they relate all the wonders that God has shown them according to the word of the 'prophet' who says: *haec olim meminisse invabit.*

Mael Dúin returns to his own country. Diurán lays the silver on the altar of Armagh. They relate their adventures from beginning to end, and the dangers and perils which they had experienced on sea and land.

The Adventures and the Voyages have to do with the Otherworld, and so we are led back to where we started. The Fenian Cycle too has its origin in myth. The Ulster Cycle and the Cycle of the Kings are heroic in temper. If one were to attempt a history of early Irish literature, there would be nothing in it of the history of ideas, nor would there be an account of great writers, for the prose tales are anonymous, and of the poets whose names we know, none are outstanding. The best of the poetry is anonymous too. Indeed there would not be much history at all in the sense of development or progress, but merely a sequence of literary events in some degree of chronological order. The compass of Irish literature is not wide: the incandescent imagination that glows in the description of Étaín washing at a spring, or Froech swimming across a river, or of the sound and movement of the sea in several poems; the motif of the doomed lovers, the heroic figure of Cú Chulainn, the tragic fate of a son slain by his own father, the vivid account of feasting in a heroic society that we get in 'Bricriu's Feast' and 'The Story of Mac Da Thó's Pig', the wonderful nature poetry and hermit poetry; these are the elements that make up the claim of Irish literature to recognition. And then one must reckon in for credit the early time at which they appear.

NOTES

1 Cf. Winternitz's account of the Indian historians, *Geschichte der indischen Literatur*, iii, 81–82.
2 *SM*, p. 11.
3 G. Schoepperle, *Tristan and Isolt* (London, 1913).
4 Cf. inf. p. 331.
5 See K. H. Jackson, *The Oldest Irish Tradition*, Cambridge, 1964.
6 Ed. with transl., V. Hull, New York, 1949.
7 Uisnech and Uisliu are alternative forms of the name.
8 Professor Binchy, who has edited this tale, finds little resemblance to the Tristan story, see *Scéla Cano meic Gartnáin*, p. xvii.
9 *DF* II and III, Dublin, 1933, 1953.
10 *The Ossianic Love and Romantic Tales of Medieval Ireland* (Dublin, 1961), p. 25.
11 Murphy, *Early Irish Lyrics* 82.
12 The language of the oldest law-tracts is earlier, but it is not certain when they were first committed to writing (p. 259).
13 *IPD*; St John D. Seymour, *Irish Visions of the Otherworld*, 98 f.
14 ed. K. Meyer, London, Nutt, 1892.
15 Meyer has pointed out that this motif is borrowed from the story of the Argonauts, ZCP x 360.
16 ZfdA xxxiii 295 f.

11

Welsh Literature

From what we have seen of the earliest Welsh poetry it is clear that only fragments have survived, half-remembered traditions of the Gododdin, poems attributed to Taliesin, among others the fine lament for Owein ap Urien, dialogue poems from lost sagas of Llywarch Hen and Cynddylan, and a few nature poems and gnomic verses. The great period of Welsh poetry was still to come, with the rise of the Court poets (*Gogynfeirdd*) in the twelfth century and the later glory of Dafydd ap Gwilym. In the meantime there is less evidence of poetic inspiration in Wales than in Ireland, although the contact between the two countries was close.

One legendary figure, Myrddin, is enshrined in traditions that link him with the Irish king Suibne Geilt, 'Sweeney the Mad'. Suibne, king of Dál nAraidi, fought in the battle of Moira in 637, and is supposed to have lost his reason in the din of battle. *Buile Suibne*, 'The Frenzy of Sweeney', is the story of his life in the wilderness, with some fine poems in which the mad king laments his misery and describes the forest and the animals that roam there.

Myrddin was supposed to have lived in the sixth century, and to have fought on the losing side in the battle of Arfderydd (Arthuret, near Carlisle) in 573. He too went mad and fled into the forest of Celyddon (Caledonia). 'There he lived for half a century, with no company but the trees and the wild beasts, mourning for the slaying of Gwenddolau and afraid lest Rhydderch should come against him. In this frenzied condition Myrddin acquired the gift of prophecy.'[1]

In fact the name was invented by means of a false analysis of Caerfyrddin (Carmarthen), of which the second element is derived from *moridūnon* 'sea-fort'. In one poem he is addressed as *Llallawc* and *Llallogan Vyrdin*, and his name is Laloicen in Joceline's Life of St Kentigern, and Lailoken in two other tales, forms plainly adapted

334

from the Welsh epithet.[2] And the story of Myrddin and the Suibne story present a Celtic variant of the Wild Man theme.[3] The earliest reference to Myrddin is in the tenth century poem, *Armes Prydain*, and some verses attributed to him may be as old, for exact dating of anonymous Welsh poetry is difficult. *Buile Suibne*, on the other hand, is hardly earlier than the twelfth century. Either side may have borrowed from the other, and the territory of Dál Riata, which lay partly in east Ulster and partly in Scotland, must have been a centre of exchange. It is geographically close to the scene in each case.

Like the Irish hermit, Marbán in *Tromdám Guaire*, Myrddin had a pet boar, and in one of the poems attributed to him he addresses it:

Afallen beren a phren melyn	A sweet yellow apple-tree
A dyf yn halar heb âr yn ei chylchyn;	grows on the bare headland.
A mi ddysgoganaf gad ym Mhrydyn	And I foretell a battle in Britain in defence of its land
Yn amwyn eu terfyn â gwŷr Dulyn.	against the men of Dublin.
Seithlong y deuant dros lydan lyn,	With seven ships they shall come over the wide water,
A saith cant dros fôr i oresgyn.	seven hundred men from across the sea for conquest.
O'r sawl y deuant nid ânt i gennyn	Of them who come, only seven shall escape from us,
Namyn saith lledwag gwedi eu lletgyn.	empty-handed after their defeat.
Afallen beren a dyf tra Rhun	A sweet apple-tree grows beyond the Rhun.
Cywaethlyswn yn ei bôn er bodd i fun,	I strove beneath it to please a girl,
A'm ysgwyd ar fy ysgwydd a'm cledd ar fy nghlun,	With my shield on my shoulder and my sword at my side,
Ac yng Nghoed Celyddon y cysgais fy hun.	and in Coed Celyddon I slept my sleep.
Oian a barchellan, pyr bwyllud hun?	Hark, little pig! Why did you think of sleep?
Andaw di adar dyfr ny ymeiddun.	Listen to the waterfowl at their mating!

335

Tëyrnedd dros fôr a ddaw ddyw Llun.	Lords from across the sea will come on a Monday.
Gwyn eu byd hwy Gymry o'r arofun.	The Welsh may rejoice at their plan![4]

This is vague stuff, partly recalling the saga of Myrddin, partly prophetic; and Professor Parry suggests that original poems about Myrddin may have been swamped by the prophecies. Prophecy was a literary fashion in Wales down to the fifteenth century, rather in the spirit of the Jacobite *aisling* in Ireland. It was prophecy born of defeat, foretelling a hero, Arthur, Cadwaladr, Owain, who would arise again to deliver his people; and many of these prophetic poems were attributed to Taliesin or to the legendary Myrddin.[5] The address to his pet pig quoted above may have prompted a sequence of stanzas beginning: 'Hark, little pig', which would be later than the others, for one of them refers to the Norman invasion of Ireland:

Oian a barchellan, oedd rhaid gweddi	Hark little pig! We must pray for fear of the five chiefs from
Rhag ofn pum pennaeth o Norddmandi;	Normandy. And one of the five will cross the
A'r pumed yn myned dros fôr heli	salt sea
I oresgyn Iwerddon dirion drefi.	to conquer Ireland of the kindly homesteads.
Ef gwnahawd ryfel a dyfysgi	He shall make war and tumult
Ac arfau coch ac och ynddi.	and there shall be bloody weapons, and lamentation there.
Ac wyntwy yn ddiau a ddoant oheni	And they will come from there and do reverence at Saint
Ac a wnânt enrhydedd ar fedd Dewi.	David's tomb.
A mi ddysgoganaf fyd dyfysgi	And I foretell that there shall be tumult,
O ymladd mab a thad; gwlad a'i gwybi.	son fighting against father – the whole country shall know it.
A myned i Loegrwys ddiffwys drefi,	And they shall go into desert England.

Ac na bo gwared byth i
Norddmandi.

May there be no help for
Normandy for ever![6]

The prophecies of Myrddin have an antiquarian interest, as this sort
of vaticination is characteristic; and the verse-form is important for
the history of Welsh poetry. End-rhyme is still the only requirement.[7]
It divides the poem into stanzas of eight or twelve lines. Alliteration
and internal rhyme are frequent, but not required, so that we are still
far from the *cynghanedd* system.

With the twelfth century the great period of Welsh poetry begins,
and it may be significant that its beginning coincides with the rise of
the bardic schools in Ireland, and follows upon the reign of Gruffudd
ap Cynan, king of Gwynedd, whose mother was the daughter of a
Norse king of Dublin. He spent his youth in Ireland, and it has been
suggested that he brought back poets and musicians to Wales.[8] We
know nothing of what occasioned the event in Ireland, but it is a fact
that from the beginning of the twelfth century the craft of poetry was
studied and practised in a stricter form than before, and that there
emerged the great families of hereditary bards, O'Daly, O'Higgins,
O'Hussey, Macaward and others, who cultivated a classical form of
language and diction which remained unchanged for five hundred
years. It may have been a result of the revival of learning under Brian
Boru. In Wales the rise of the *Gogynfeirdd* may have been due to the
national recovery in the reign of Gruffud. But it can hardly be doubted
that there is a connexion between the appearance at about the same
time in both countries of schools of poetry, and of the strict forms of
cynghanedd in Wales and *dán dírech* in Ireland.[9]

There had been native schools in Ireland from the remote past.
The metrical tracts of the tenth century prescribe the metres and
the heroic literature that were to be studied in each year of a twelve-
year course of apprenticeship, and it is safe to assume that there was a
long tradition behind them.[10] But these were apparently new schools,
in the hands of new men who took over the discipline of poetry after
the old order of *filid* had disappeared. Something similar must have
happened in Wales.

Bardic poetry in Wales and in Ireland was a highly technical craft,
bound by strict metrical rules, and conventions of form and diction.
As Parry says, the sound is as important as the sense. Its normal theme,
and its chief purpose, was praise of a patron. His courage in battle, his

generosity and the glory of his ancestors are the subjects of praise; and with this convention established, the poetic achievement becomes one of craftsmanship.

The earliest of the court poets whose work has survived is Meilyr (fl. 1100–37), who composed an elegy on Gruffudd ap Cynan. His son, Gwalchmai, praised Owain Gwynedd, son of Gruffudd, for his prowess against the Normans:

Ar gad gad greudde, ar gryd gryd graendde,	For battle a bloodier battle, for terror greater terror
Ac am Dâl Moelfre mil fanieri;	and a thousand banners around Tal Moelfre;
Ar lath lath lachar, ar bâr beri,	a flashing spear against each spear, lances to meet a lance,
Ar ffwyr ffwyr ffyrfgawdd, ar fawdd foddi;	fierce fury to meet fury, drowning those who sought to drown him.
A Menai heb drai o drallanw gwaedryar,	And the Menai without ebb from the flowing of blood,
A lliw gwyar gwŷr yn heli.	and the colour of men's blood was on the sea.

Here already the torrent of alliteration and rhyme amounts to *cynghanedd* in its effect, although the strict rules of *cynghanedd* are not yet binding.

The princes themselves sometimes took to poetry, and there are poems by Hywel ab Owain Gwynedd, a grandson of Gruffudd ap Cynan, which are livelier verse, and have more magic in them, than the more formal work of the professional bards. In one of these, *Gorhoffedd Hywel ab Owain* ('Hywel ab Owain's Delight'), he praises Gwynedd, his father's kingdom:

Ton wen orewyn a orwlych bedd,	The foaming white wave washes over a grave,
Gwyddfa Rhufawn Befr, ben tëyrnedd.	the tomb of Rhufawn Pefr, prince of rulers
Caraf, drachas Lloegr, leudir gogledd heddiw,	I love today what the English hate, the bright land of the North,

Ac yn amgant Lliw lliaws calledd.	and the clustering reeds by the Lliw.
Caraf a'm rhoddes rybuched medd	I love those who gave me mead in plenty
Myn y dyhaedd mŷr, maith gyfrysedd.	where the seas reach in long contention.
Caraf ei theulu a'i thew annedd ynddi,	I love its household and its strong dwelling,
Ac wrth fodd ei rhi rhwyfaw dyhedd.	and to go to war at the king's pleasure
Caraf ei morfa a'i mynyddedd	I love its fens and its mountains,
a'i chaer ger ei choed a'i chain diredd,	its castle near the woods and its fair herds.
A dolydd ei dwfr a'i dyffrynnedd,	its river-meadows and its valleys,
A'i gwylain gwynion a'i gwymp wragedd.	its white seagulls and its lovely women.
Caraf ei milwyr a'i meirch hywedd,	I love its soldiers and its trained stallions,
A'i choed a'i chedyrn a'i chyfannedd.	its forest, its fastnesses and its farms.
Caraf ei meysydd a'i mân feillion arnaw	I love its fields with their little clover
Myn yd gafas ffaw ffyrf orfoledd.	Where I found a lord strong in triumph.
Caraf ei brooedd, braint hyüredd,	I love its lands, birthright of the brave,
A'i diffaith mawrfaith a'i marannedd . . .	its wide wilderness and its wealth.

Another poem is about a girl:

Fy newis i, rhiain firain feindeg, Hirwen, yn ei llen lliw ehöeg.	My choice, a slim, fair bright girl tall, lovely in her heather-coloured gown;
A'm dewis synnwyr, synio ar wreigaidd, Pen ddywaid o fraidd weddaidd wofeg.	My chosen joy to watch the maid When she whispers gentle words.

339

A'm dewis gydran, cyhydreg â bun, A bod yn gyfrin am rin, am reg.	My chosen part to be with a girl, to be alone with her secret and her gift.
Dewis yw gennyf i, harddliw gwaneg, Y ddoeth i'th gyfoeth, dy goeth Gymraeg.	My choice, foam-coloured one, wise among women, is your fine Welsh.
Dewis gennyf di; beth yw gennyd di fi?	You are my choice. What am I to you?
Beth a dewi di, deg ei gosteg?	Why are you silent, sweet silence?
Dewisais i fun fal nad atreg gennyf; Iawn yw dewisaw dewisdyn teg.	I have chosen a girl and have no regret; it is right to choose a fair girl of choice.

There is joy and simplicity in these poems that sets them apart from the praise-poetry of the professional bards, who cultivated obscurity of diction and an archaic vocabulary. Metrically they are quite strict: nine syllables in the line, the first line of the couplet sometimes having ten or eleven; end-rhyme throughout, save in a few lines where there is compensation by internal rhyme in the next line. The metre is an *awdl* of *cyhydedd naw ban* (a couplet with nine syllables in each line), *cyhydedd hir* (a couplet of ten and nine), and *toddaid* (eleven and nine, with internal rhyme), with rich ornament of alliteration and internal rhyme, bringing us close to the fully developed *cynghanedd*.[11]

Another prince-poet is Owain Cyfeiliog, who was prince of Powys from 1149 to 1195, and of whose work only one poem survives. It is called *Hirlas Owain* 'Owain's Tall Blue Horn', and the theme is a banquet at the prince's court, where he calls on the cup-bearer to fill the horn for the warriors in turn.

Dywallaw, fenestr, na fynn angeu, Corn can anrhydedd yng nghyfeddeu,	Fill, cup-bearer, as thou wouldst live, the horn held in honour at the banquet,
Hirlas buelin uchel freinieu, Ariant a'i gortho, nid gortheneu;	the long blue horn, high in renown, ringed with rich silver,

340

A dyddwg Dudur, eryr aereu,	and bring to Tudur, eagle of
Gwirawd gysefin o'r gwin	battle, the first draught of
gwineu;	ruddy wine.
Oni ddaw i mewn o'r medd	If there come not in a draught
goreu	of the best mead
Gwirawd ran o ban, dy ben	from the bowl, thy head shall
faddeu!	pay for it!
Ar llaw Foreiddig, llochiad	Bear to Moreiddig, protector
cerddeu,	of poets, whose praise the
Cyrdd cenynt ei glod, cyn oer	minstrels would sing, before
adneu.	the chilly grave.
Dierchyr frodyr, fryd uchel	Two fearless brothers they,
ddeu	lofty of mind,
Diarchar arial, a dan daleu,	of vigour that knows no fear
	and noble brows,
Cedwyr a'm gorug	warriors that did me service . . .;
gwasanaetheu . . .	Praise is their portion, these I
Moliant yw eu rhan, y rhei	spake of –
gynneu, –	
Marwnad bid, neud bu newid	nay, 'tis the death-song is their
y ddeu!	portion; they are dead both!
Och Grist! mor wyf drist o'r	O Christ, how sad am I for
anaeleu	the pain of his loss,
O goll Moreiddig, mawr ei	Moreiddig, how great the need
eisieu!	of him.[12]

Perhaps the grandest poem of this period of the *Gogynfeirdd* is that which marks its close, the famous lament for Llywelyn ap Gruffudd, the last of the Welsh princes, by Gruffudd ap yr Ynad Coch. Llywelyn was killed in an attack on the castle of Builth in 1282, and his death put an end to the hope of freedom in Wales. The same despair did not settle upon Ireland until the flight of the earls in 1607. In Wales, as in Ireland later, the poets realized the disaster that had befallen their country, and the traditions of courtly life on which they so much depended; and they proclaimed their sorrow. In this poem grief somehow lends the poet wings, and he soars beyond the bonds of professional praise-poetry. It says for Wales what was so finely said again for Ireland by Owen Roe Macaward in his lament for the Earls of Tyrone and Tyrconnell.

Oer calon dan fron o fraw – allwynin	My heart is cold within my breast from fear
Am frenin, dderwin ddôr, Aberffraw.	And pity for the king of Aberffraw, an oaken door.
Aur dilyfn a dalai o'i law,	He gave fine gold with a free hand;
Aur dalaith oedd deilwng iddaw. . . .	the golden chaplet was his due. . . .
Gwae fi am arglwydd, gwalch diwaradwydd;	Alas for my lord, the hawk unrivalled!
Gwae fi o'r aflwydd ei dramgwyddaw.	Alas for the sorrow of his fall!
Gwae fi o'r golled, gwae fi o'r dynged,	Alas for the loss, alas for the fate,
Gwae fi o'r clywed fod clwyf arnaw.	Alas for the news that he is stricken!

The lament reaches its climax in lines that are famous among Welshmen, and are indeed a grand expression of mourning. The music of the verse, with its elaborate ornament, is here no mere substitute for poetry. Here sound and sense combine in a flood of eloquence inspired by anger and sorrow:

Poni welwch-chwi hynt y gwynt a'r glaw?	See ye not the wind's rush and the rain?
Poni welwch-chwi'r deri'n ymdaraw?	See ye not how the oaks beat together?
Poni welwch-chwi'r môr yn merwinaw – 'r tir?	See ye not the sea, how it lashes the land?
Poni welwch-chwi'r gwir yn ymgyweiriaw?	See ye not the truth in its travail?
Poni welwch-chwi'r haul yn hwylaw – 'r awyr?	See ye not the sun, how he hurries through heaven?
Poni welwch-chwi'r sŷr wedi r'syr-thiaw?	See ye not the stars, how they are fallen?
Poni chredwch-chwi i Dduw, ddyniadon ynfyd?	Will ye not believe in God, fond menfolk?
Poni welwch-chwi'r byd wedi r'bydiaw.	See ye not the world in its peril?

Och hyd atat-ti, Dduw, na ddaw – môr dros dir!	Oh, that to Thee, O God, it might come, the sea flooding the land!
Pa beth y'n gedir i ohiriaw?	What thing is left us that we linger here?
Nid oes le y cyrcher rhag carchar braw;	There is no place to flee to from the prison of fear,
Nid oes le y triger; och o'r trigaw!	there is no place to abide in; alas, the abiding!
Nid oes na chyngor na chlo nac agor,	There is no counsel nor key nor open way
Unffordd i esgor brwyn gyngor braw.	to cast from our souls the sad conflict of fear.[13]

The rich patterns of alliteration and rhyme that are known as *cynghanedd* have not reached their full development, but the effect here is almost as though they had.[14] It would be worth the reader's while to hear this passage read in Welsh in order to have a right impression of the achievement.

The poems of the *gogynfeirdd* were recited in the hall by the *pencerdd* or the *bardd teulu*, and another entertainment was provided by the *cyfarwydd*, the story-teller. Of the tales that were told only a few have been preserved, and they are commonly known as *Mabinogion*, since the famous translation by Lady Charlotte Guest became popular. But the title belongs properly to four tales, which in the manuscripts arc described as 'branches of the *Mabinogion*', so that we speak commonly of 'the four branches'.

The Four Branches of the *Mabinogion* are a sort of miracle inasmuch as they came in the eleventh century, anonymous and unheralded by any earlier prose of their kind, yet written by a master of prose style, simple, eloquent and beautiful. The style is far above the content of the tales, for the narrative is not always cohèrent nor clearly motivated, nor is there a sequence of the four stories. The story of Manawydan is a sequel to that of Branwen, and Pryderi appears in all four; the marriage of Pwyll and Rhiannon is referred to in *Math*. But the four stories are independent. *Pwyll* and *Math* stand by themselves. Yet the Four Branches of the *Mabinogion* are clearly the work of one redactor, someone who had gathered together fragments of a vanish-

343

ing tradition and possessed a gift for composition and a sense of style. The two that have most appeal are *Branwen* and *Math*.

Matthew Arnold first said of the *Mabinogion*: 'The mediaeval story-teller is pillaging an antiquity of which he does not fully possess the secret.' Gruffydd in his study of *Math fab Mathonwy* showed how much can be won from contemporary Irish and Scottish folklore to throw light on the composition of the *Mabinogion*, and incidentally he established the connexion in Irish tradition between the god Lug and the hero Finn mac Cumaill. His suggestion that the Four Branches were originally a sequence of tales with Pryderi as the central hero is, however, not convincing. Jackson in his Gregynog Lectures[15] has brought more light on the matter, and has shown convincingly that the stories were compiled by literary antiquarians after the tradition of the *cyfarwydd*, the professional storyteller, had been lost, and that they derive from various sources, international folk-lore motifs, old Celtic mythology, and borrowings from Irish sagas. The redaction that we have is the work of a single and singularly gifted author.

The tale of Branwen daughter of Llyr has much to do with Ireland. Matholwch, king of Ireland comes to ask for Branwen, sister of Bran the Blessed, king of Britain. After she has been received as queen in Ireland, she is made to suffer cruel punishment in vengeance for an insult offered to Matholwch while he was in Britain. Bran hears of it and comes with an army to rescue her. The armies of both sides are destroyed in the ensuing battle. The seven Welsh survivors bring the head of Bran back with them, and finally they bury it in London.

Some episodes of the story introduce motifs that recur in Irish sagas. Mac Cana has made a careful and well balanced study of the tale in which he points to several episodes that seem to be simply borrowed.[16] One that has long been recognized as of Irish origin is that of the Iron House.[17]

In the story of Branwen, Bran the Blessed has given Matholwch a wonderful cauldron which restores the dead to life. Here is the passage describing how he came to possess it:

One day I was hunting in Ireland, on the summit of a hill above a lake in Ireland called the Lake of the Cauldron; and I saw a tall fair-haired man coming from the lake with a cauldron on his back. And he was a huge, tall, evil-looking man; and there was a woman

344

following him, and if he was tall, she was twice as tall. And they came towards me and greeted me. 'Well,' said I, 'what is your errand?' 'This is my errand, Lord,' said he. 'This woman will bear a child in six weeks, and the son that will be born of that pregnancy in six weeks will be a fully armed warrior.' I undertook to support them: they were with me for a year. For that year I kept them without hindrance: after that there was objection. And by the end of the fourth month they were making themselves hated and were wanton throughout the land, outraging and molesting and vexing both men and women. Thereupon my country rose up against me and demanded that I part with them, and gave me a choice between my country and them. I put it to the counsel of my people what should be done with them. They would not go willingly: they could not be made to go unwillingly by force of battle. And in this extremity, they caused a room to be built all of iron. And when the room was ready, they summoned all the smiths in Ireland, and all who possessed tongs and hammers, and they made them heap charcoal up to the height of the room. And food and drink in abundance were served to them, to the woman and the man and their children. And when it was known that they were drunk, fire was put to the coal all round the room, and the bellows that had been placed around the house were blown, a man to every two bellows; and they began to blow the bellows until the house was white-hot around them. Then they took counsel on the floor of the room; and he waited till the iron wall was white, and with the great heat he came against the wall with his shoulder and broke out through it, and his wife followed him. And none escaped from there save him and his wife. 'And then, I suppose, Lord,' said Matholwch to Bran the Blessed, 'he came over to you.' 'Then, indeed,' said he, 'he came here, and he gave me the cauldron.'

In several Irish sagas the τειχοσκοπία technique is employed to identify approaching strangers. A watcher describes what he sees, and from his description someone who knows them tells who they are. This is sometimes used to good effect as one group comes after another, more and more splendid, with a climax at the arrival of Cú Chulainn himself, as in *Bricriu's Feast*, or in Mac Roth's description of the approaching warriors to Fergus in *Táin Bó Cualnge*.[18] *The Destruction of Da Derga's Hostel* introduces this motif to describe the company at

345

the Hostel. Ingcél tells what he sees, and Fer Rogain recognizes the warriors from his description. In the course of this long account, there is one passage which closely resembles an episode in Branwen:

'I was almost overcome with terror as I beheld those three. There is nothing stranger than the two bald heads one on each side of a man with hair, two lakes one on each side of a mountain, two hides one on each side of an oak, two boats full of thorns on a round board, and a little stream of water, as it seemed, on which the sun shines as it flows down, and a hide arranged behind it, and the pillar of a palace like a great lance above it. The shaft would make a full load for a yoke of oxen. Find a likeness for that, Fer Rogain.' 'I can find it. That is Mac Cécht son of Snaide Teiched, champion of Conaire son of Eterscél. Mac Cécht is a good warrior. He was lying asleep on his couch when you saw him. The bald heads on each side of the man with hair that you saw are his knees on each side of his head. The lakes on each side of a mountain that you saw are his eyes on each side of his nose. The hides on each side of an oak that you saw are his ears on each side of his head. The two boats on a round board that you saw are his shoes upon his shield. The slender stream of water that you saw on which the sun shines as it flows down is the flickering of his sword. The hide arranged behind it is the scabbard of his sword. The pillar of a palace that you saw is his spear, and he brandishes that spear till the two ends come together. And he makes a cast of it as and when he likes. Mac Cécht is a good warrior.'

In *Branwen* the Men of the Island of the Mighty are seen by the king's swineherds, coming to avenge the wrong done to the queen. The swineherds come to tell what they have seen:

'Hail to Your Lordship!' said they. 'We have seen a forest on the ocean, where we never before saw a single tree.' 'That is a strange thing,' said he. 'Do you see aught else?' 'Lord,' said they, 'we see a great mountain beside the forest, and it is moving; and a high ridge on the mountain with a lake on each side of the ridge; and the forest and the mountain and the rest are all in motion.' 'Well,' said he, 'there is no-one here who knows anything of that unless Branwen knows it. Ask her.'

Messengers went to Branwen. 'Lady,' said they, 'what do you think this is?' 'Though I am not a Lady,' said she, 'I know what this

346

is. The men of the Island of the Mighty are coming over, for they have heard of my being punished and dishonoured.' 'What is the forest which they saw on the sea?' said they. 'The masts and spars of ships,' said she. 'And what was the mountain which they saw beside the ships?' 'That was my brother, Bran the Blessed,' she said, 'wading through the shallows. There was no ship that could carry him.' 'What was the high ridge with a lake on each side?' 'That was he, looking upon this island,' said she, 'for he is angry. His eyes on each side of his nose are the two lakes on each side of the ridge.'

Mac Cana has shown convincingly that the author of *Branwen* has borrowed from the Irish saga, and from several other Irish stories; and that he has woven the old themes into a new texture which is not altogether coherent, but which succeeds all the same by virtue of its graceful style and the air of magic that pervades it.

These qualities appear again to good effect in the final episode of *Branwen*, when the survivors of the great battle in Ireland have returned to Wales with the severed head of Bran, and abide at Gwales[19] in Penfro. In origin it is an account of the happiness of the pagan Otherworld, but the monkish author seems not to realize this. The exuberant fancy of the Irish description of the Otherworld in the *Voyage of Bran* and the *Wasting Sickness of Cú Chulainn* are here exchanged for a tranquil simplicity. The heroes have been told that they shall enjoy this happiness for eighty years until they open the door looking out upon Aber Henvelen towards Cornwall:

There they found a fair royal site above the sea. And there was a great hall, and to the hall they went. And they saw two open doors, but the third door, on the Cornwall side, was shut. 'Behold, said Manawydan, 'the door that we are not to open.' And they spent that night there content and happy; and of all the sorrow that they had witnessed, or that they themselves had suffered, they remembered nothing, neither of that nor of any other grief.

And there they spent the four score years, and knew that they had never passed a happier or more delightful time than that. It was no less agreeable than when they first came, nor could they tell from one another that they had been there so long. It was no less pleasant to have the head there with them than when Bran the

347

Blessed had been alive among them. And from those four score years was named the Feasting of the Noble Head.

The grace and gladness of this prose is what charms the reader of the Mabinogion. *Branwen*, indeed, is fairly successful as a story, but *Math fab Mathonwy* is a medly of themes that are hard to disentangle, as Gruffydd has shown, and it is those qualities of form that outweigh the lack of purpose and construction.

Math is lord of Gwynedd. Gwydion son of Don tells him that Pryderi, a prince in the south, has wonderful swine, and promises to obtain them. He does so by magic, turning toadstools into horses, hounds and shields, which he barters for the precious swine. The enchantment lasts only for a day, and Gwydion escapes with his prize while the magic lasts. Pryderi comes in pursuit and is killed fighting against Math.

While Math is absent, Gwydion and his brother rape the maiden who has been Math's footholder.[20] In punishment Math turns them into deer, swine, wolves, in successive years till their crime is expiated.

Gwydion tells Math to take Arianrhod daughter of Don, his sister's daughter, as footholder, for the footholder must be a virgin. But she proves to be no maid. The child that she bears is adopted by Gwydion, and in four years he is as big as a boy of eight.

One day Gwydion brought the boy to visit his mother. She was angry at this reminder of her shame, and laid a curse on the child that he should have no name until she gave him one. Gwydion disguised himself and the boy as shoemakers, and Arianrhod was tricked into naming the boy Lleu Llawgyffes ('Bright One of the Dexterous Hand').[21] She then laid a curse on him that he should never take arms till she should give them to him. Gwydion created a hostile fleet by magic, and came with Lleu in disguise to defend Caer Arianrhod. Arianrhod gave them weapons to defend her, whereupon the ships vanished. Tricked again, she laid a curse on her son that he should never have a wife until she gave him one.

Math and Gwydion made a wife for Lleu out of flowers, and named her Blodeuwedd ('Flowerface'). One day, when Lleu was away at court, Gronw Pebyr came to Ardudwy on a hunting expedition. He and Blodeuwedd fell in love at once, and slept together for three nights. He told her to discover how Lleu could be killed.

Like Delilah in the Bible story, Blodeuwedd persuaded Lleu to tell

348

her his secret. He had the gift of magic invulnerability: he could not be killed either in a house nor out of a house, neither on horse-back nor on foot. He said that he could be killed only by a spear that was worked on for a year only at Mass-time on Sundays. The only way in which he could be killed would be when standing with one foot on the back of a he-goat and the other on the edge of a bath-tub, and then only by the unique spear. Here three familiar folk-motifs are combined: the faithless wife discovering her husband's secret (ST. K 2213.4.1); the paradoxical tasks (ST. H 1050); unique invulnerability (ST. Z 310). Jackson observes that the combination of the two last seems to be archaic, and points to the parallel with Vritra in the *Mahābhārata*, who can be killed neither by day nor by night, neither by stone nor by wood and so on.[21]

After a year Blodeuwedd contrived the required conditions, and Gronw Pebyr wounded Lleu with the venemous spear. He flew away in the form of an eagle.

Gwydion set out in search of Lleu, and found him by following a sow that fed on the maggots that fell from the dying eagle's flesh, as he roosted in a tree. Gwydion restored him to human form and healed him of his wound. Blodeuwedd was changed into an owl, and Gronw Pebyr was slain by Lleu.

Math is not successful as a story. There is no hero, unless it be Lleu Llawgyffes. His adventures are the main interest, but Gwydion is more of a champion than he. Lleu can be killed in a certain way, but the author seems to forget himself, for he is not killed, only changed into an eagle; and he later recovers and takes revenge. Yet Gwydion is at first a villain and suffers shameful punishment. Least of all is Pryderi the hero. He is merely cheated of his swine, and then killed in trying to recover them. The birth and youthful exploits of Lleu lead us to expect a heroic sequel, but all we are given is folk-lore. The name of the great god of the Celts is here a mere borrowing.

The story is, nevertheless, good entertainment, folk-tale and fairytale, in which men are changed into beasts, a fleet of ships or a wife can be made by magic, crimes are punished and virtue rewarded.

CULHWCH AND OLWEN

Culhwch and Olwen is in some respects the most interesting of the Welsh sagas. It contains a great amount of legendary material in which

349

reference is made to persons and traditions that were once familiar to a Welsh audience, and some famous figures of Irish mythology and heroic legend are here included among Arthur's warriors, Cnychwr son of Nes, Cubert (= Cú Roí?) son of Daere and Fercos son of Roch. Manawydan son of Llŷr, who is the Irish Manannán, is also in the list of names. Moreover, Arthur and his court are here in the centre of the story, whereas they are not even mentioned in the Four Branches.

The story is more folk-tale than heroic saga, and indeed there is a general resemblance to modern Irish folktales about the King of Ireland's Son: the widowed king who marries again, the jealous stepmother who imposes on the king's son a quest to a giant's fortress, the helpers, the ordeals, the successful issue of the quest and a happy ending, with no exact geographical setting.

Goleuddydd, wife of Cilydd, bears a son at a place where a swine-herd is keeping a herd of swine. Through terror of the swine, the child is born, [23] and he is put out to nurse.

The boy's mother soon died, and after seven years the king married again. When the queen discovered that the king had a son, she asked that he hide him no longer, and the lad was summoned to court. The queen swore a destiny upon him that he would never marry till he should win Olwen daughter of Ysbaddaden Chief Giant; and the king's son was at once filled with love for Olwen 'though he had never seen her'. [24] His father sent him to Arthur's court to ask for Olwen as a gift, for Arthur was his cousin.

Culhwch's arrival at the court of Arthur echoes the arrival of Lug of the Long Arm at the court of Nuadu in the Irish *Battle of Moytura*. At first he is refused admission, and then Arthur orders that he be admitted, and makes him welcome. Culhwch demands that Arthur get him Olwen, and invokes the names of Arthur's warriors. The list of more than two hundred and fifty names includes some, such as Manawydan son of Llyr, who cannot have been thought of as warriors at Arthur's court, and ends with the names of twenty women. It is plainly a mere catalogue of names, and to some of them brief notes of explanation are attached.

Then the great quest begins. When the warriors arrive at the fort of Ysbaddaden, a shepherd warns them that none who came on that quest before had come away alive. They force their way into the fort and salute the giant. His eyelids are raised up with forks, so that he

350

may see them, and he hurls a poisoned spear at them.[25] Bedwyr catches the spear and hurls it back, wounding the giant in the knee.

After he has hurled three poisoned spears in vain, and himself received three wounds, the giant addresses Culhwch and imposes on him a series of impossible tasks which must be performed in order to win his daughter, Olwen. This list of tasks is again a collection of legendary motifs in which a great deal of lost tradition seems to be evoked. It makes tedious reading, but in delivery by a good story-teller, it might be entertaining. Forty tasks are recited, and to each Culhwch replies: 'It is easy for me to get that, though you think it is not easy.' The twenty-first task is to get the comb and scissors that are between the two ears of Twrch Trwyth son of Taredd Wledig, to dress the giant's hair; and nearly all the subsequent tasks are ancillary to this, a hound to hunt the boar, a leash for the hound, a collar for the leash, a huntsman to hold the leash, a horse for the huntsman, and so on.

The earlier tasks include references to legendary or mythological figures, Amaethon son of Don, Mabon son of Modron, the birds of Rhiannon, the cauldron of Diwrnach the Irishman, pointing to a lost hoard of tradition.

Now the greater quest begins under the leadership of Arthur himself. In the sequel many of the tasks are performed and many are simply forgotten. The search for Mabon son of Modron is well told. The warriors go to consult the Ouzel of Cilgwri, who sends them to a stag, who sends them to an owl, who sends them to an eagle, who sends them to a salmon; and the salmon guides them to Caer Loyw (Gloucester) where Mabon is held captive. (Here the folk motif of The Oldest Animals is artlessly introduced.)

Some passages of the story are incoherent, as when Gwythyr saves an ant-hill from fire, and we are told that the grateful ants later brought flax seed for the performance of one of the tasks. The actual performance is never related. Later there is a digression about the rivalry of Gwythyr son of Greidawl and Gwyn son of Nudd for the hand of Creiddylad daughter of Lludd, and we are told that when they had been reconciled, Arthur obtained the steed and the leash that the giant had demanded.

After the performance of sundry tasks, Arthur gathered together the warriors of the Island of Britain and its three adjacent islands, and of France and Brittany and Normandy and the Summer Country; and he went to Ireland to hunt Twrch Trwyth. The rest of the saga is an account of the hunt. The magic boar crosses into Britain and is hunted across the Severn into Cornwall. The scissors and comb are captured, and the boar escapes into the sea.

One other task is performed, making rather an anti-climax to the story, and Culhwch returns in triumph with all his trophies to the giant's court. The giant was beheaded, 'and that night Culhwch slept with Olwen, and she was his only wife so long as he lived. And the hosts of Arthur dispersed, every one to his country.'

Of the five Welsh tales in which Arthur is prominent, *Culhwch and Olwen* is the most interesting. Here it is Arthur who receives the hero and who leads the hunt for Twrch Trwyth. The warriors who perform the other quests are men in his service. He appears not merely as king of Britain, but as ruler of France, Brittany and Normandy; and one of the principal passages in the story is the long and tedious list of his warriors. But he is not in the centre of the action. Culhwch and Yspaddaden are the central figures, and we are not told much about Arthur himself. His sword, *Caledfwlch*, his shield and spear, and his ship, *Prydwen* (which is also mentioned in the old *Preideu Annwfn*) are already famous.

Another Arthurian tale is *Rhonabwy's Dream*, a strange and incoherent story in which Arthur cuts a rather poor figure. He is splashed with water by a horse crossing a ford, and one of his men strikes the horse. He then engages in a board-game with Owein, who denies his requests, and treats him as an equal. But even here he is the great emperor, and the armies of the Norsemen are in his service. When Rhonabwy asks whether the army will flee, he is told: 'The Emperor Arthur has never fled, and if you were heard saying that, you would be a lost man.' Moreover, all this happens in a dream, as Rhonabwy sleeps on a yellow ox-hide.

The other three Arthurian tales, *Gereint*, *Owein* and *Peredur* are strongly influenced by Norman-French literary convention. The relationship between them and the French romances, Erec, Yvain and Perceval, of Chrétien de Troyes has not been clearly established. They are not mere translations from the French, but they are believed to be adaptations of French romances which themselves derived from earlier Welsh sources.[26] A discussion of them is beyond our purpose.

These prose romances are the end of a tradition, and have no sequel in the literature. In Wales as in Ireland it was originally an oral

352

tradition, and the tales were recited at the king's court, or the noble-man's house, by the *cyfarwydd*, and told in a ruder form no doubt by humbler storytellers beside the fire in the house of every man. In both countries Norman influence introduced new fashions in literature, and the future lay with translations, first from Latin and later from French. The Siege of Troy, the Aeneid, the Thebaid, and the Story of Alexander, Charlemagne, Marco Polo and Sir John Mandeville are the sort of entertainment that became fashionable among the great; and the native traditions survived mainly as folktales, told in the country cottages, as they are still told in parts of Ireland even now. It was poetry that flourished in Wales later on, and that has con-tinued to flourish in a wonderful way.

NOTES

1 *HWL* 27.
2 Jarman, *The Legend of Merlin*, Cardiff 1960.
3 Stith Thompson, *Motif Index* F 567.
4 This may refer to the return of Rhys ap Tewdwr and Gruffudd ap Cynan, see Griffith, *Early Vaticination* 88.
5 *HWL* 26, 30.
6 The reference is to Henry II, who visited St David's on his return from Ireland, and was later at war with his son, see *HWL* 32–33.
7 Cf. sup. p. 268.
8 See Arthur Jones, *The History of Gruffydd ap Cynon* 180 n. 4; *HWL* 45.
9 The 'classical' period of bardic poetry is commonly said to begin *c.* 1250, but an historical poem which O'Brien dated *c.* 1120 shows conformity to strict rules for alliteration and rhyme, see *Ériu* xvi 157 ff. The full development of strict *cynghanedd* came in the fourteenth century.
10 R. Thurneysen, Mittelirische Verslehren, *Irische Texte* ii.
11 Lloyd-Jones, *Court Poets* 26, PBA XXXIV (1949).
12 transl. Bell.
13 trans. Bell in *HWL*, p. 54.
14 *Cynghanedd* was not fully developed till the fourteenth century, see *HWL* 122.
15 K. Jackson, *The International Popular Tale in Early Welsh Tradition*, Cardiff, 1961.
16 P. Mac Cana, *Branwen Daughter of Llŷr*, Cardiff, 1958.
17 See C. O'Rahilly, *Ireland and Wales* 106 ff.
18 W. Faraday, *The Cattle-Raid of Cualnge*, pp. 117 ff.
19 Probably the island of Grassholm in Pembrokeshire, see *Pedeir Keinc* 214–15.

20 The king's footholder is an officer of the court according to Welsh law.
21 Here there seems to be a survival of old tradition, for the dedication *Lugovibus* at Osma in Spain (*CIL* II 2818) is by shoemakers, so that the god Lugus would seem to have been their patron; and *Lleu* is the Welsh form of his name. See pp. 28, 183.
22 W. J. Gruffydd, *Math*, pp. 31, 301 ff.; Jackson, *The International Popular Tale and Early Welsh Tradition* 106 ff.
23 The famous Irish king Cormac was born in the forest during a thunderstorm, and was suckled by a wolf-bitch (see *CK* 24).
24 Cf. the Irish *grád écmaise*, p. 313.
25 Balor, in the Irish *Battle of Moytura*, has the poison in his eye, the lid of which was raised by four men, when he wished to destroy an enemy (*RC* xii 100).
26 See Jones and Jones, *The Mabinogion*, pp. xxviii ff.; Parry, *HWL* 87.

12

Celtic Art

The preceding chapters will have made it clear that from the middle of the first millennium BC the Celts were the most powerful and the most impressive peoples in Europe beyond the frontiers of the Mediterranean lands. These Celtic tribes, originally widely dispersed throughout central Europe, gradually concentrated in the west into the more homogeneous political nation of the Gauls. While they have left only sparse records of themselves in written form, chiefly in inscriptions (pp. 16–17, 257 above), we have a considerable amount of information about their history and their institutions from the writings of the Classical peoples with whom they were in contact. In addition, we have an ever increasing source of information on their material culture and way of life from archaeology. We know something of how they lived and died; how they fought and what weapons they used; we know something of their religion and mythology, but owing to the absence of a fully literate society we have no written record from the Gauls themselves of their spiritual or their personal life.

We have, however, a direct contact with them through their art. From the earliest times, until its last fine flowering in the peripheral island countries of the West in the early Christian centuries, Celtic art is a rich and highly individual development, influenced and modified by Eastern and Southern influences, but never superseded, or even transformed by them. It is distinguished by a fundamental individuality which is essentially Celtic, and which remains constant throughout its history wherever the Celtic peoples are found. We can trace its early roots already in the period of Hallstatt culture in the first half of the first millennium BC; but the art which we would define as distinctively Celtic coincides with the Second Iron Age and is that of the La Tène period of about 500 BC to AD 100. This is the art

355

of Gaul at the height of her power, before the Roman Conquest. The flowering of this art is in no way diminished in the insular Celtic countries during the early centuries of the Christian era. In the peripheral countries it survived the Roman Conquest, and in Ireland, where no Roman Conquest took place, this original Celtic art continued to flourish and develop until the Middle Ages, only partially modified by new motifs in the Viking Age. Our leading authority on Continental Celtic art, the late Professor Jacobsthal, summarizes his impression at the close of his book on *Early Celtic Art* with the words: 'In my opinion the whole of Celtic art is a unit. It is the creation of one race, the Celts.'[1]

Celtic art has been justly called the first great contribution by the Barbarians to European Art (Jacobsthal, p. 163). Its origin is unknown, although it has been thought until recent times that it must have developed in the earliest phase from a single School; but where, when, how? What was the initial inspiration? The answer to these questions is hidden from us. Recent opinion[2] is less precise in this matter, interpreting it as a slow composite development under varying conditions and in varying localities. Yet it is a distinct national art. The salient features of Celtic art are quite different from those of other national arts, such as the art of the Phoenicians and the Iberians, the Etruscans, the Greeks. Yet Celtic art is no isolated development, and its history is eloquent of many foreign contacts. These have played a large part in its growth from different quarters and at different periods, and enable us to gain something of a chronology in its history over the centuries.

What, then, are the basic qualities which we recognize in Celtic art wherever it is found? Perhaps the most fundamental is its originality, the choice and combination of the motifs, chiefly from the world of nature, the animal and vegetable world, with only occasional and incidental human elements, the whole forming a fantastic creation of the imagination, remote from reality. An invariable element in these creations is the refinement of mind which inspires the compositions. There is a total absence of coarseness of conception or of treatment. This refinement expresses itself everywhere in delicacy of line, an unerring artistic taste in the use of flowing curves and their purpose in a given design.

The artistic result is the achievement of abstract perfection and grace. The Celtic artists had an instinctive realization of the value of

356

the flowing line and sureness of touch in its delineation. They had a love of pattern. To them nature supplied the inspiration of an artistic motif, expressed at a remove from the sensory perceptions, not – we would insist – as a symbol, but as controlled by artistic instinct and technique. Celtic artists had a keen sense of the value of ornament and of its adaptation to a given material object, combined with an unerring sense of form, which is especially noticeable in their coins. Their rich and even redundant wealth of design, amounting almost to a *horror vacui*, spent itself in a generous application of conscious artistic effort to make the most of its opportunities and of its material. This art is essentially imaginative rather than representational. It is rarely possible to distinguish the species of foliage in their designs. In both the plant and animal world the result is a stylization rather than a direct reproduction, and the blending of various species results in fantasies which remind us of the late Classical bestiaries. This phase of Celtic art has given its stamp and characteristic features to its whole long history, and persists through the migrations and wars of the people and the period of the great Gaulish nation before the Roman conquest until we trace the lost grammar of native Celtic ornament in the beautiful curvilinear stylized floreate designs on the Marne pottery [line drawings], preserved, for example, in the Museum of St Brieuc in Brittany, and in the art, many centuries later, of the ornamental marginal figures in Irish manuscripts, and per- haps – though here the intermediate stages are less certain – in the Pictish grave slabs.

This basic form of Celtic art reached its highest development in the period of the Empire. The Celtic art rooted in the Hallstatt phase in the first half of the first millennium BC had not been in any sense a national development, but was a part of the contemporary inter- national art of Eurasia, and shared in the corresponding phase of the Greek 'geometrical period'. Its common features are the stylization of all natural representations into linear, and especially angular, geometrical forms and repetitions. Typical motifs are superimposed bands of identical wooden-looking horses in procession, and an end- less repetition of rows of aquatic birds. It is a 'wholesale' art, such identical bands being easy to apply to metal-work and pottery, and cheap to reproduce.

By the eighth century a more advanced phase of art had developed in Greece and Italy, transformed by richer and more varied influences

357

from the East, and known to Classical archaeologists as the Orientalizing period. Three centuries later a similar fashion developed in Gaul, involving a complete transformation from the older geometrical style to the richer, fuller, and freer play of the imagination in the artistic expression of the world of nature, a curvilinear, a more crowded, and essentially fantastic style, combined in such a way as to produce a totally new and very individual art. The cultural development of Gaul, in company with that of North Europe in general, lagged behind that of the Eastern Mediterranean countries, and in the Gaulish development of this new art the fresher and richer inspiration did not come directly from the East but tardily, by an indirect route, in part through Greece to Italy, and from Italy to Central Europe, perhaps also through the Caucasus; but the ultimate source was still the East.

This period of the art which we define as specifically Celtic, shows itself fully developed in fantastic combinations of animals and foliage, bizarre and unnatural images of natural objects, the flora and fauna of the East, lotuses, palms, lions, and the wild beasts of the desert, divorced from their realistic images and recombined in alien settings, sometimes wholly, sometimes only partially. The amazing thing about this new style of the La Tène period which succeeded to that of the Hallstatt is that it has no obvious beginnings, no gradual evolution. Like Pictish art in Scotland it is a mature and finished product when it first appears. Some new and powerful external stimulus could alone account for it, introducing foreign motifs into Celtic ateliers, such as the animals of the desert, the vegetation of the tropics. But how these Oriental elements came to the Northern Celts remains mysterious. Direct contacts are ruled out by the absence of evidence for direct political or trade relations, either across the Steppes or from Greece by sea. They would seem to have filtered through by intermediaries, especially and earliest through Etruria.

Many of the most fantastic motifs which characterize Celtic art are combined in the repoussé decoration of its greatest masterpiece, the large silver cauldron, commonly called the Gundestrup bowl. It was found in 1891 in separated sections in a peat-bog in Denmark, but it is of Celtic manufacture, and is generally thought to date from the first or second century BC. The presence of Oriental elements, such as the elephant, and other features in the design have suggested the middle Danube as its possible origin. The Scordistae tribe of that region are reported by Athenaeus to value silver above gold,[3] and the remarkable size of the cauldron – 42 cm. high, 69 cm. across and its weight of almost 9 kilogrammes[4] are unique in silver objects among the Celts. Even more remarkable are the lively and spectacular scenes depicted on the surface inside and out – the horned god Cernunnos, and other divine beings; human masks; snakes; animals, natural and imaginary; birds; armed warriors in procession; and ritual scenes such as the drowning of a human being, held head downwards by the legs in a tub.

Although we cannot establish the beginning of Celtic art as we have characterized it above, its native spiritual growth may be limited to the La Tène phase of culture in Europe. Its later developments were more splendid, but not, in general, different in kind. Celtic art has been called an art of ornament, of masks, of foliage, and beasts in a wholly imaginative combination, and these are certainly elements in which their art excels, and which separate it from the Greek world of natural man and his environment. It is the art of a people intensely aware of their environment in the world of nature before the first elements of scientific classification had begun. If it lacks the humanity of the Greek world it also lacks the arrogance which has dominated European art since Classical times – since the Greek red figure vases and the Greek masterpieces of sculpture first revealed to man his own dignity and supremacy in the world of creation.

The Gaulish artist crowded his canvas, aiming at effect by richness of fancy rather than by impressive economy. He never learnt the positive value of blank space to enhance the effect of a subject and form a major part of an artistic composition. This was the great discovery of Greeks of the period of the red figure vases which never reached the Gaulish artists, but we shall find it in the art of the insular Celts of Ireland. The affinities of the Gaulish artists remained with the Cycladic artists who loved to fill in the spaces around the main figures of their pottery with rosettes, shells, and little whorls faintly reminiscent of lower marine life. Characteristics of the earlier phases of Greek painters persisted in Celtic art, heavily sur-charged and enriched, especially in the Irish manuscripts. We can trace them especially in the illuminations of the Gospels in the *Book of Kells*. Here too the angular human figures, comparable to those of the early Slavonic ikons, are reminiscent of the human form on Greek black figure vases rather than of the natural human forms on the red figure.

359

One of the most striking, and perhaps the most revolutionary, features of La Tène art is the introduction of polychrome. This came into Gaul simultaneously with other Oriental fashions. In the early polychrome phase the element of colour was chiefly introduced by coral inlay; but in the second phase coral gives place largely to red enamel, which is much more richly and profusely used. Its origin is unknown, but it was probably in Central Asia – perhaps Persia. In Britain red enamel was used as a splendid ornament of jewelry, horse trappings, chariot mounts, and arms, among the most splendid example being the Battersea shield of La Tène II. With the height and proportions of this shield it is interesting to compare the stone sculpture of the Gaulish warrior of the Augustan era from Mondragon, now at Avignon. This statue shows that the shield of La Tène II must have been still in use at the time of the Roman Conquest, and indeed most of the shield bosses found in the trenches at Alesia are of this type.

The developments in the technique of the period are chiefly seen in pottery and metalwork, because these are the objects which most commonly survive. The pottery of La Tène is well made and symmetrical, commonly of a beautifully polished black surface, and balanced on a small and delicate foot. The metalwork is mostly of bronze, often of perforated design, and worked with great expertise into articles of jewelry, horse-trappings and harness and chariot-mounts, as well as arms and weapons. Scabbards are beautifully worked, especially the chapes. These bronze objects are rendered vivid by a liberal use of champlevé and red enamel.

Celtic art culminated at the height of the power of the Gauls. In the peripheral countries, especially in insular Britain, which drew their inspiration from this great development of La Tène culture, the main features continued to develop and expand in beauty and technique. But the power of growth and creation, of apprehending a new vision in the art of representation, died in Gaul herself after the Roman Conquest. The great developments in naturalistic sculpture of the Greek Classical world surpassed and by-passed Celtic art of the great creative period. We shall see that the Gauls were influenced and stimulated indirectly by naturalistic Greek sculpture, but only at a later period, and as a secondary development.

Early Celtic art is a linear art, essentially frontal, a two-dimensional rather than a three-dimensional expression. It aims at conveying a visual rather than a tangible impression. Whether as a cause or as a result of this linear character, the art of their stone sculpture is relatively elementary in the early period, and also relatively rare. The linear tradition still survives in the indication of the features, especially the mouth, of the stone figure from Holzgerlingen, Würtemberg [Jacobsthal, *Imagery*, Pl. 1*b*], and even in the stone heads from Entremont. Native free-standing sculpture in stone is crude, and suggests that Celtic craftsmen did not realize or develop the technique of artistic work in stone as a native art until the influence of Mediterranean sculpture had reached the north. This is especially true of the early representation of the human form, which is suggestive of a stele when upright, and is lifeless when seated. Even the human heads, which are capable of evoking a strong emotional appeal, are the creation of a type, strongly and often beautifully expressed; but they are neither individualized nor refined in surface treatment.

In general, Celtic representation of living figures in metalwork is superior to that of stone sculpture, but is confined to miniature figures in bronze, chiefly attached as handles or other adjuncts to some larger, commonly utilitarian, object. Heads and busts are highly stylized, with features similar to those of the stone sculptures and characteristically Celtic. A typical example is the bronze relief from Waldalgesheim (Jacobsthal, pl. 8, fig. 156) with the characteristic Celtic head 'broad above, narrow below', the prominent eyes, triangular nose, the emphasized eyebrows, the narrow slit mouth, absence of clearly marked ears, a framework of two leaves pointing downwards, and an upturned curl at the tip which may well have developed as a stylized form of hair, although commonly regarded as typifying a Celtic god.

Celtic stone animal sculpture is extremely rare and in bronze is also rare in naturalistic form. The most interesting examples are the bronze horse 12 cm. long from a Chariot-burial at Trier, which is a stiff and not competently anatomical model, and a boar from Budapest which would be a convincing animal if Celtic running spirals and half circles had not been substituted for bristles on the crest. A little bronze deer (10 cm. high) is pleasingly modelled but abstract in form (Jacobsthal, pl. 372). Its purpose is unknown, but certain details are reminiscent of Scythian technique. The use of birds as ornament, singly, in heraldic pairs, or in rows, is too widespread in the art of the Eurasian world from the Hallstatt period onwards to be regarded as purely Celtic, but was a prominent motif in Celtic art. The most effective example of the La Tène animal art is that of the conventionalized foxes (?) stalking the duck on the Lorraine flagon, a rare example of naturalistic grouping. The artist has caught to perfection the innocent unawareness of the duck and the eager predatory parent training her offspring to stalk. The details again show Oriental features and both coral and enamel are used, and conventional spirals indicate the leg joints, and line-hatchings, the natural hair; but this intimate little scene, on an object found, as is believed, on the Moselle, brings a rare homely touch into Gaulish art such as might well be used on an illuminated page for Ausonius's poem *Mosella*.

The convention of depicting an animal forming the handle is repeated in the Salzburg flagon (Jacobsthal pl. 382) and that from Borscher Aue near Geisa (Jacobsthal pls. 382, 383). In the latter the animal is standing on the shoulder of the jug and stretching up to the lip to drink. Despite the difference of motif it is impossible not to think of the dog, forming part of the handle of a spoon in the St Ninian's treasure from Shetland, and leaning forward to lick the contents greedily with protruding tongue.[5]

It was the expertise of the Greeks in the working of stone – the natural medium of their country – which first developed in Europe the art of surface modelling, and of stone architecture for domestic and religious buildings. In the Celto-Ligurian *oppida* the original simple Celtic tradition of fortification developed into more urban plans with regular streets and temples; but since the discovery of native wooden sculpture in Gaul, to which we shall refer later, we may expect to find traces of more elaborate indigenous Gaulish wooden architecture than has been recognized. In both Gaul and Britain the skill in detecting traces of early wooden remains is a relatively recent archaeological technique. We must be prepared for surprises.

The two regions where Celtic stone sculpture eventually developed are (1) Germany, where the art shows most originality, and where traces of foreign influence are relatively scarce; and (2) Provence, where foreign influence is traced through Marseilles, and where the earlier Ligurian culture has played a part. There can be no doubt that an important stimulus to the growth of stone statuary, especially in the south, was functional, and that it is closely bound up with the

362

development of the great sanctuaries, as we shall see. In the north the architectural function of the stone figure from Holzgerlingen, Würtemberg (cf. *sup.*) is suggested by the tenon-joint at the bottom, which Jacobsthal believed to have been inserted into a wall.

Several examples of stone sculpture are known from the Rhineland and Würtemberg. The chief centre is Pfalzfeld in Hunsrück in the land of the Treveri, where Celtic Mounds are numerous. Here a famous limestone obelisk is decorated on all its four sides with Celtic relief-motifs, and a human head, also in relief, is enclosed by great paired lobes or a bi-foliate leaf-shaped crown surmounted by scrolls. The pillar possibly terminated originally in a human head. The work is very archaic and may date from the fourth or third century BC (Filip, p. 161). The motif is peculiarly persistent, and may be compared with the design on the bronze plaque from Tal y Llyn, Merionethshire (Wales), of the early La Tène period.[6] The original Gaulish prototype is perhaps derived from fifth-century Etruscan designs on jewelry.

The sculpture of the south again forms two groups. The first and least numerous and significant is all closely associated with Marseilles and is directly inspired by Greek statuary. The second group is the work of native artists in the tradition known as Celto-Ligurian, a combination of the oldest indigenous culture of the Mediterranean sea-board east of the lower Rhône, and a later, third-century, Celtic superimposition. This group is very local and distinctive, differing widely from Greek and Roman statuary. Its products are all of local stone and the work of native artists. The most numerous and impressive have been found in the religious sanctuaries of Entremont and Roquepertuse north of Marseilles, of which the architectural features are discussed below. Other sanctuaries in the same area, such as that of Glanum (Greek *Glanon*), share a common chthonic feature as sanctuaries of the dead and the Underworld, which persisted in Glanum until the Augustan era. These ancient Celto-Ligurian sanctuaries have a history going back to Hallstatt times, and are of great architectural interest. Their lintels are deeply incised with geometrical figures and schematized horsemen. All have monumental porticos, *propylea*, decorated with painting and sculpture, and a primitive timber-work superstructure, characteristic of the domestic architecture of the region. The city-gate of Glanum is the oldest in Gaul, dating from the fourth century BC, with relief sculpture on the side-walls representing Gaulish captives.

At Roquepertuse the pillars are furnished with sculptured heads and still preserve remains of polychrome painting of geometrical designs, and designs of fish, birds, horses, and human beings, both painted and incised. At Entremont, at the base of the wall of the sanctuary, fifteen skulls were exhumed which had been exposed there. A fragment of a lintel shows two skull-shaped cells with a sculptured model of a *tête coupée*, the features of typical Celtic style but here without mouth, while one of the pillars is decorated with twelve heads of the same fashion. A later phase, still at Entremont, is represented by rounded pillars decorated on their sides with *têtes coupées* in relief, and, on their principal face, with a relief representing cavaliers armed with long rapiers of La Tène II type. The building is known as the 'Hall of the Skulls'. Lintels and pillars similarly furnished with cells occupied by sculptured and natural skulls are characteristic also of Glanum and of the great sanctuary of Roquepertuse.

Entremont dates from the third century, and was the religious capital of the Celto-Ligurian peoples who formed part of the confederation of the Salyens (Salluvii).[7] Indeed the situation of its *oppidum* and the quality of its statuary mark it out as the most important centre of the political and religious life of the Celto-Ligurian peoples, and demonstrate the close association of their native sculptures with religion and architecture.[8] The sanctuary of Roquepertuse belongs to the phase of La Tène II. The direct relationship with Gaulish civilization is emphasized by the prominence in both these sanctuaries of the human head, divorced from the human figure, and generally, to use the current French term, the *tête coupée*. These sanctuaries are sometimes furnished with actual human skulls fixed in the lintels or the pillars, or with substitutes in the form of sculptured models of masks of the dead, with closed eyes.

The numerous *têtes coupées* in the Celto-Ligurian sanctuaries suggest a cult of the skull, and illustrate what Diodorus and Strabo report on the authority of Posidonius of the early Gaulish custom of cutting off and preserving the heads of enemies. It is of special interest to note that *têtes coupées* are not found in all the sanctuaries, e.g. at Mouries, and that the pillars of Roquepertuse and the moulding of the lintel of Glanum had had their skull cells added after the building of the porticos, while at Entremont the 'Hall of the Skulls' belonged to the last phase of the *oppidum*, not long before its destruction in 123 BC. From this we might be tempted to conclude that the custom was not very ancient; but a considerable number of skulls bearing traces of suspension were found scattered on the surface of a road which had been metalled with the débris of great splendour from earlier buildings, perhaps indeed from an earlier occupation. Some of the heads, probably mummified, appear to have been cut off and pierced shortly after death. The cult of the head was widespread throughout the territory, and in the Celtic *oppidum* of Puig Castelar human skulls were found in which the nails from which they had hung were still present. The cult is associated with the period of La Tène II, and has possible wider affinities with the sculptured heads on the Cyclopean rampart at Tarragona, and in certain Spanish *oppida*, and also with the *têtes coupées* on the Etruscan gates of Perugia and Volterra. They are possibly not unconnected with the popularity of the mask as a motif in the Gaulish art of the same period.

The *têtes coupées* have been described as 'the first expression of naturalistic art which developed in the La Tène culture under the influence of Greco-Roman sculpture.'[9] It was in this Celto-Ligurian area that the Celts of the later La Tène period learned the art of stone sculpture in the round. These monuments are by no means all naturalistic, and, in fact, the most impressive, the Monster of Noves, is a highly imaginative group, generally regarded as a symbol of death. The composition is an expert production, representing a monster with lion-like body and hideous head and gaping jaws from which protrudes a human limb, while its forelegs rest on two realistic stone models of *têtes coupées*. We are familiar with monsters from whose jaws human forms project in the art of Este and Watsch and other sites of the Hallstatt period, where it was a favourite motif, and we may look for a common centre of origin, – but where? The sculptor of the Monster of Noves was no amateur, and had nothing to learn about the technique of group sculpture. It can be viewed from all sides, and is as competent in its three-fold composition as the Greek statue group of the Laocoön.

It was believed in the past that it was from the wealth of statuary in these great southern sanctuaries of the mouth of the Rhône that the Gauls first learnt the art in the later La Tène period of naturalistic human stone sculpture in the round. Entremont, in particular, was

365

rich not only in natural human heads (Benoit, pl. 35), but also in entire human figures. The heads show the typical Celtic traits with which we are familiar from the Irish sagas – the face 'broad above, narrow below' – and the typical prominent eyes, straight triangular nose, and wide slit-like mouth characteristic of Gaulish heads in all sculptures, and reproduced in the Celtic stone head from Gloucester. The busts are reminiscent of Herms. At Entremont, however, we have also in native stone natural life-size statues of the tribal heroes, chiefs, and queens, clad in contemporary costumes and leather armour and weapons denoting their rank, possibly actual portraits.

The temple site of Roquepertuse is rich in statues of the human form even more directly associated with its religious cult. Four or five human figures, squatting in the cross-legged 'Buddha attitude', with which we are also familiar from the attitude of the God Cernunnus on the Gundestrup bowl, have been recovered from the actual interior of the sanctuary. Their arms and legs are bare, but the torso is clad in a short tunic, decorated with rectilinear geometrical patterns in light relief or incised and painted. The posture is erect and the figures are slim and well-proportioned, but stiff and lifeless, although the arm in at least two of the statues is separated freely from the torso. The stiff and hieratic posture may be partly accounted for functionally by their position in the sanctuary itself. Presumably they were not intended to be scrutinized at close range, but to impress the communal imagination of the worshippers.

In recent years discoveries have been coming to light which have revolutionized our ideas of Celtic figure sculpture and are forcing us to reconsider the problems of its origin and relationship. While it still remains true that the most important influences on stone free-standing figure sculpture of Gaul are from the great Celto-Ligurian sanctuaries at the mouth of the Rhône, it is now clear to us that central Gaul posessed indigenous wooden sculpture which by the first century BC reached a comparatively high standard of development, and which was localized in religious sanctuaries. This localization and religious association may be in part due to the accident of our record. The survival of wooden sculpture is so precarious that our specimens are naturally restricted to important sites which have demanded excavation in their own rights. The oldest wooden sculptures are often reminiscent of the statuary of Entremont and Roquepertuse.[10] A wooden head, the features crudely moulded and

366

incised, has been found in a Gaulish sacred enclosure at Montbouy (Loiret); and in a sacred well on the same site a full-size wooden figure of equally elementary art. A hooded statue of oak more than three metres high, believed to be pre-Roman, has been excavated on the shore of Lake Geneva.[11] All the wooden full-length figures so far found, however, are reminiscent of tree-trunks, and recall perhaps the *simulacra* in the sacred wood referred to by Lucan.

The most important collection of Gaulish wooden sculpture so far unearthed is from the well-known Gallo-Roman sanctuary of Sequana at the source of the Seine, in which extensive excavations have been taking place since 1953, and are still in progress.[12] During the excavations of 1956–7, 190 pieces of wooden sculpture came to light in the marshy precincts, constituting, as Professor Martin assures us (p. 16), by their diversity, their originality, and the quality of their preservation, one of the most astonishing discoveries of Gallo-Roman archaeology. This initial find produced 27 statues or statuettes of half a metre to 1.25 metres in height; 40 heads from life- to half life-size; 16 pieces with 2 or 3 heads carved in relief on a single stave; 14 torsos, naked, draped, or schematized; about 30 limbs and some representations of the human internal organs; 12 representations of animals, including a fine bull; etc. Men and women were both represented – men being in the majority – and travellers (perhaps pilgrims) recognizable by their cloaks and hoods. The heads are the cream of the collection, ranging from blocks with only sparse and elementary modelling, with incised features and hair, to the realistic modelling governed by the bone structure of the face and massed hair in relief which, in spite of the characteristically Celtic slit-like mouth, present a realistic human head.

The head of a woman, in its modelling of structure, features, and the arrangement of the hair, has achieved complete mastery. The locality and the nature of the sculptures, and especially the single human limbs and organs, leave no doubt that this School of sculpture belongs to a medical sanctuary, but as yet the precise function of the artist and his atelier have to be determined. Was his status an official one, associated with the sanctuary, or a commercial adjunct? Certain features, e.g. the rows of heads carved on a single stave, suggest comparison with Entremont, and the close association of realistic sculpture with religion is established by all these Gaulish Schools of sculpture.

367

The importance of the indigenous wooden sculpture from Gaul demonstrates the independence of the artists, and the close relationship between art and the local material. The stone which had given permanence to the sculpture of the Mediterranean countries was naturally represented by wood in the more afforested countries of Central Europe. Our knowledge of Celtic sculpture and its history has accordingly been impoverished and even distorted by the perishable wood in which this sculpture is modelled.

In our endeavour to estimate the true significance of this Gaulish wooden sculpture it is important to bear in mind

(1) that as yet we are only on the verge of the subject. The excavations of Sequana are still in progress, and we are only in possession of the earliest results.

(2) That the specimens before us date from the Gallo-Roman Period, apparently from the first half of the first century AD. We do not know the date of the earliest development of this wooden sculpture.

(3) That the specimens before us give little indication of advanced treatment of the human form as a whole. The arms are not detached from the torso. The figure of the traveller is still not wholly free from the tree-trunk effect, although the cloak and position of the right arm is a common convention of Roman and Greek statues.

(4) This important school of Celtic wooden statuary which we know to have been flourishing in Gaul in the first century AD, whatever its origin, is not traceable in insular Celtic art, which is in general identical with that of the corresponding phase in Gaul. It would seem to strengthen the traditional view that Gaulish sculpture was profoundly modified in the late La Tène and Gallo-Roman Period by indirect Greek influences through Marseilles and the Celto-Ligurian sphere of the mouth of the Rhône. It was the early Celtic art of Gaul preceding that of the Gallo-Roman period which moulded the art of the insular Celtic countries and to which we must now turn.

During the period when early Celtic art was at its height in Gaul it penetrated to the Celtic people of Britain, where it flourished and developed an independent life of its own, always recognizable as fundamentally La Tène in origin and basic characteristics, but capable of taking original styles and local specialization in form. These local styles were the work of local schools which flourished in different parts of Britain in response to local demands, to the needs of different classes of the population, and to the nature of tribal relations with the Continent. We can distinguish the northern School working doubtless under the patronage of the Parisi and Brigantes, an eastern School in the territory of the Iceni, and a southern School under some more direct influence from the art centres of the Continent, especially the Belgae. This Celtic art, generally referred to as La Tène in its continental connexions, is commonly referred to as 'Late Celtic' in Britain, owing to the fact that it lingered here throughout the Roman period, and revived again to a new blossoming in the countries of northern and western Britain after the close of the Roman domination. Celtic art had already been introduced into Britain, chiefly by imports, throughout the Early Iron Age of the Hallstatt Period, but it was not till the later Iron Age in Gaul that the full wealth of Celtic art developed in the British Isles.

Continental La Tène art at its best is believed to have been introduced into Britain by imports during the third century BC but from the second century BC British Schools of Celtic art were producing independent works which, at least till the period of the Roman Conquest, were fully equal to the continental works. In Ireland, which the Romans never reached, the La Tène art had an unbroken and splendid development from its earliest beginnings till the Norman Conquest, even surviving and absorbing influences from the Vikings, to whose own art Celtic art had made heavy contributions. After the Norman Conquest of Ireland old traditional art forms continued to influence the new art forms introduced from the Continent by the Cistercian Order.

The La Tène art of Britain is identical with, and fully equal to that of Gaul at its best period. Emphasis has already been laid (p. 360 above) on the high quality of its metal work and its generous development of polychrome, particularly on the development in horse trappings and chariot mounts in arms and armour of which the shields from the Thames at Battersea and from the Witham near Lincoln are magnificent examples.[13] The Battersea shield is believed to date from *c*. 75 BC. That from the Witham is perhaps earlier, and is even finer in its workmanship, and has been held to be superior in technique to any contemporary work of continental Celtic art. The shield boss from the Thames at Wandsworth, while less spectacular than the Battersea and Witham shields, is of even greater beauty and grace. The Celtic chieftains of the north shared this splendid panoply of the Celtic warrior chiefs of the south. One of the finest pieces of La Tène bronze armour in Britain is the bronze pony cap from Torrs, Kircudbrightshire, dating, as is believed, from the second half of the third century BC.[14] In or close by the Stanwick fortifications in the North Riding of Yorkshire, over ninety pieces of metalwork have been found, consisting largely of bronze horse trappings and chariot mounts, some retaining traces of enamel, and the presence of iron tyres suggests that they formed elements of chariot burial like the famous group in the East Riding.[15]

Somewhat later come the more elaborate moulded objects, such as the anthropoid hilted swords and daggers; and here we must remember the highly original naturalistic mannikin on the lost dagger – again from the Witham (Fox, *P. and P*. pl. 10, e); the most beautiful of all tankards – that from Trawsfynydd, Merioneth, with its elaborately moulded handle (Fox, pl. 64); the gold twisted torc with heavy moulded terminals from Medwood Forest, Staffordshire (Fox, pl. 25); the moulded gold bracelet and electrum torc from the Snettisham treasure, in north-west Norfolk (Fox, pl. 32, fig. 33). The territory of the Iceni, though yielding ample remains which testify to the survival of the traditional chariot warfare, is relatively poor in military weapons, but is extraordinarily rich in objects of personal adornment, and Snettisham has yielded the largest accumulation of precious metal hitherto recorded from Britain in the Iron Age. Some of the material in this find is believed to have come from between south Suffolk and the Thames; but other torcs of gold alloyed with silver and copper, also found in north-west Norfolk, point to the use of such personal ornaments in the first century BC, and to the wealth of the ruling dynasty. Indeed this group of hoards contained over fifty torcs – more than from all the rest of Britain.[16]

More delicate in workmanship, and perhaps more closely linked with the earlier Classical tradition of the continent, are the beautifully incised bronze mirrors which were made in the last quarter of the first century BC and were widely distributed in southern Britain. Their decoration has adapted to perfection the La Tène curvilinear technique with linked spirals and expanding ends, and is admirably suited to the shape of the circular groundwork of the mirror. The

370

lobes and expanded leaf-like patterns are made to dominate the entire design by incised hatchings within the intervening spaces. The designs are sometimes regular, as in the mirrors from Birdlip, Gloucs., and from Desborough, Northants (Fox, pl. 57, c); but more often an illusion of regularity is effected by a subtle assemblage of asymmetrical curves, as in the superb unprovenanced mirror in the Meyer museum at Liverpool (Fox, pl. 55). The harmony is maintained by an almost incredible sureness of taste and draughtsmanship. As Françoise Henry observes, we are familiar with this harmony achieved from irregularity of line in La Tène art, e.g. in the scabbard from Cernon-sur-Coole, Marne,[17] 'mais dans les Iles cette fantaisie semble s'ériger en loi'.[18] These bronze mirrors, and many other fine specimens decorated with La Tène type of ornament, are without parallel on the continent, and have not been found among the Parisi and the Brigantes in the north. One naturally thinks of the Etruscan bronze mirrors of earlier times, but there appears to be no link.

From about the middle of the first century BC come the two most famous examples of bronze repoussé work in Britain, the so-called stave-buckets from Aylesford in Kent, and Marlborough in Wiltshire. The former is thought to be perhaps slightly the earlier of the two, and is certainly the more refined in workmanship. It is only 10 inches in height, and is formed of wooden staves, held in position by three bronze hoops, the topmost of which is decorated with delicate 'leaf-comma' whorls, and delicious little fantastic horses, horned and beaked, with bi-furcated tails. A handle is attached by two human masks. The vessel was found in a grave in a Belgic cemetery and contained cinerary remains, and in the same grave were found a flagon of Classical provenance – Italo-Greek – and other grave-goods of both Classical and Belgic type, including cinerary urns – in fact a funerary group. The incomplete Marlborough 'bucket' belongs to the same type as that from Aylesford, and is believed to have been used, like the latter, to contain cremated bones. It is twice as tall as the Aylesford 'bucket', and was decorated with repoussé designs on all three metal bands, but less refined in detail than the Aylesford ornament. Here also we have stylized elongated animals, including sea-horses, and a naturalistic moustached head, together with several masks which have been compared with the head on the Gundestrup bowl. Details on both buckets recall designs on Armorican coinage,

371

and the Marlborough bucket in particular is thought to have been probably an importation into this country from Armorica.

At this period Armorica shared in the art of the early Celtic styles of Gaul, and must have served in some degree as a link between the La Tène art of the Continent and that of Britain. In Brittany the curvilinear designs typical of this La Tène art, and of the pedestal vases characteristic of the Marne burials, are found also on the painted pottery,[19] and though the poverty of Armorica has left relatively few examples of the La Tène art on objects of outstanding value, the pottery shares both the design and the shapes characteristic of Gaulish La Tène, types II and III. The Celtic crannogs of Glastonbury and Meare in Somerset have left a wealth of pottery and wooden vessels incised with typical La Tène curvilinear designs (Fox, fig. 76) characteristic of that found in the cemeteries and *oppida* of Finistère, which are again characteristic of the pottery of Hunsbury in Northamptonshire,[20] and that found at Hengistbury Head with Armorican coins of the Coriosolitae and the Andecavi.[21]

It is interesting to reflect that Armorica also shares with Ireland a rare type of monument decorated with ornament of a La Tène tradition similar to that on the bronze mirrors and to the designs on the pottery just discussed, but presumably of earlier date. This is the independent and free-standing incised stone sculpture, of which the two best known Irish examples are the Turoe stone, an almost hemispherical block, referred to by Francoise Henry (*S.I.*, p. 35 f.) as the *doyenne* of stone sculptures, and the Castle Strange stone. With them we may compare the Kermaria stone from Pont l'Abbé, Finistère in Armorica, now in the museum of Saint-Germain.[22] The Turoe stone, like many later Celtic sculptures, is carved in only two planes – the depth of the ground-work and the external plane of the design, cut in very slight relief, the treatment closely reminiscent of that of Pfalzfeld[23] (cf. p. 363 above). The design is unmistakably that of the La Tène tradition, and the delicacy and perfection of technique is typical of Celtic work at its best, and betokens a high standard of achievement which – in regard to relief sculpture – does not necessarily imply a lengthy preceding local school of workmanship. The Castle Strange stone is in a different technique from that of the Turoe stone, being of the nature of a surface engraving with a design composed of related spirals, and it may also be later in date. Another much larger monument of the same class has been recently

372

discovered at Killycluggin (Cavan). Its design, of great elegance, consists of finely engraved curves and spirals.

The earliest surviving monuments of Irish art are stone sculpture. Human figures are traced back to the Neolithic period, both as free-standing sculpture and as incised on wall-slabs. The earliest Irish Christian stone crosses, the thin incised slabs of Carndonagh and Fahan Mura in the neighbourhood of Inishowen in the north, dating probably from the second half of the seventh century, may perhaps represent an unbroken tradition from this Neolithic art. In general, however, there would seem to have been at least a partial break between the megalithic art and that of later times, which would naturally come about by the introduction of importations from both the Continent and Britain; but a break in art does not necessarily imply a total discontinuance of old motifs, and the technique of stone carving must certainly have had a continuous history, as is implied by the Turoe and other carved stones, bearing La Tène designs.

In the Rath of the Synods on Tara Hill remains have been found of habitations with traces of the work of smiths and enamellers, and of Roman importations from the first to the third century AD showing contacts with both Britain and Gaul. Only a few yards away the Mound of the Hostages was found on excavation to have been originally built over a megalithic tomb, which had been covered later with numerous Bronze Age burials, indicating for Tara an origin as a necropolis and a prehistoric sanctuary, adapted by the Celts later as a royal residence. Ireland is a museum of the life of the past, and continuity can never be ruled out.

The La Tène art of the Continental Celts of the second Iron Age is believed to have been introduced into Ireland in the second century BC. Close contacts at this period were taking place with Britain, which exported a number of objects to Ireland; but the most important Irish contacts were with the Continent. Contacts with Britain came about naturally enough by trade and raiding; but the earliest Irish sculptured stones all have affinities with well-known Continental Celtic stone sculptures. The Turoe stone is very close in its technique to the stone from Pfalzfeld, while the two crude yet impressive self-standing human figure sculptures from Boa Island, Fermanagh [*A.I.*, p. 50] and the screaming figure from Tanderagee, Armagh [*A.I.*, p. 51] with moustache and horned helmet, have more in common with the Continental Celtic statue from Holzgerlingen, or the fragment from Echterdingen than with the more advanced type of Celto-Ligurian statuary of the Mouth of Rhône. It has been suggested that these Irish sculptured stones and statues imply a cult introduced from Gaul by Gaulish refugees fleeing in the face of the Roman invasions (Henry, *A.I.*, p. 18). These early sculptured heads from Ireland are in striking contrast to the limestone head of a young Celtic man of the Roman period from Gloucester[24], where the features and the treatment of the hair and the shape of the face are typically Celtic, but the plastic form has mastered the Classical Greco-Roman statuary presentation of the southern Gaulish sanctuaries at the mouth of the Rhône.

The chronology of the proto-historic phases of early Celtic art in Ireland is at present imprecise, and can only be determined by comparison with more or less parallel British and continental styles. The absence of Roman criteria and of Roman and continental coin evidence in Ireland is here a serious hiatus, and the long tradition of Celtic art in Ireland from the second century BC to the Norman Invasion, uninterrupted by any Roman conquest, makes questions of internal relative chronology within Ireland itself arbitrary and almost irrelevant. The masterly curvilinear art of the decorated bronze scabbards from the ruins of the Lisnacroghera *crannóg* (Co. Antrim) (Fox, *P. and P.*, pl. 73, b), and others closely related from the R. Bann at Toome and Coleraine, are all variations of the continental styles of La Tène II and III, and their close relationship with the style, incised on the Aylesford bucket and the Glastonbury wooden bowl, both of the pre-Roman period in Britain, suggest an approximate date of *c.* 175 BC for the opening phase of La Tène art in Ireland on metal objects (Fox, *P. and P.*, figs. 26 and pl. 73, b). Though these objects are possibly later than their continental equivalents, owing to time-lag, they are not later than the beginning of our era. These Irish scabbards are perhaps the product of a single school, a later atelier, since they are not found anywhere else in Ireland, and they suggest that the early La Tène art of Ulster was particularly close to that of the Continent. The decoration on these Irish scabbards resembles closely that on the slightly later Bugthorpe scabbard from the East Riding of Yorkshire, which is the earliest example in Britain of the 'shaded' technique produced by hatching reserved areas of the pattern (cf. p. 371 above). It should be noted, however, that this

374

technique is also a prominent feature on a shield-boss from Llyn Cerrig Bach in Anglesey (Fox, *P. and P.*, fig. 28).

We can only conjecture the manner in which the best La Tène art of this early period reached Ireland. Fox attributes the close relationship between the somewhat later Bugthorpe and Hunsbury scabbards and that of the Lisnacroghera style in part to cross-channel traffic, and 'a flourishing British settlement in Galloway, retaining early traditions for which the only known evidence is the Torrs pony-cap and horns' (*P and P.*, p. 43). Kuno Meyer had long ago suggested[25] on literary evidence, that Gaulish mercenaries had entered Ireland in the service of Irish kings during the early centuries of our era, but his conclusions point rather to the south. Possibly both routes were used.

Among the earliest evidence of imports derived from Britain are the bronze pins and penannular brooches, the former perhaps slightly the earlier, the latter derived from Roman models. Both have a long life, and from at least as early as the beginning of our era were often elaborately decorated with enamel. The bronze pins are as frequent in Scotland as in England, and the penannular brooches are of wide distribution throughout the British Isles. From South Wales we have a bronze penannular brooch, and from a hut site at Pant y Saer, Anglesey, a silver example, complete with its long pin on a loose swivel[26]. Its closest parallels are in the coastal districts of Scotland and date from the fourth to the sixth centuries.

Many of these pins and brooches are richly enamelled. A particularly interesting enamelled pin comes from a hoard on Norrie's Law in Fife. It is decorated with enamel and Celtic and Pictish designs surmounted by a tiny cross, and it can be dated to the late seventh century by Byzantine coins within the hoard. A large silver penannular brooch comes from the same hoard.[27]

From the second century AD the Celtic revival, following upon Roman decline, had brought about a closer union between Ireland and Scotland, and a consequent common artistic development, and from the foundation of the Irish kingdom of Argyll in the fifth century this closer union may be said to have developed into a common culture. During this period, and especially during the following centuries under the stimulus and patronage of the Christian Church, ornamentation on metal work and jewelry was enriched with a great wealth of new resources. Not only was the use of red enamel greatly

375

extended, but the surface was encrusted with semi-precious stones, garnets and even amber, and with coloured glass, and the technique of millefiori was introduced from Gallo-Roman jewelry. It was probably at this period that the Irish artists learnt to solder and to mount fine gold filigree, a technique admirably appropriate to the persistent traditional Celtic curvilinear decorative art.

Of this splendid development of native Celtic jewelry the two chief treasures are the Hunterston brooch in Scotland and the Tara brooch in Ireland. The former[28] is $4\frac{1}{2} \times 4\frac{3}{4}$ inches in diameter, and what remains of its pin is $5\frac{1}{2}$ inches long. Its form is a flattened closed ring of silver, divided by ridges into panels, the larger ones filled with zoomorphic interlaced decoration and Celtic spirals and trumpet patterns, formed of filigree set on gold plates, and the corner spaces and the smaller panels are set with amber studs. The delicacy and tact and the sense of proportion with which the crowded ground is treated show the same unerring sense of composition which is characteristic of Celtic art everywhere, and which we shall find repeated in the manuscript illuminations. An interesting detail is the claim to private ownership made by two names scratched on the plain surface of the back of the brooch in runic letters of Scandinavian type peculiar to the Hebrides, and probably dating from about the tenth century. The inscriptions are in Scandinavian, and may be translated 'Olfriti owns this brooch'; and 'Maelbritha owns this brooch'. The names, the former Scandinavian and the latter Irish, carry us to the mixed Norse-Irish kingdom of the Hebrides.

The most outstanding of all the brooches, indeed the most precious gem of all the Irish jewelry, is the so-called Tara brooch. Like the Hunterston brooch, it is a closed-ring penannular brooch with a long pin working on a loose ring, and it is assigned to the early eighth century.[29] It is relatively small, indeed one of the smallest of the ornamental brooches, only $3\frac{1}{2}$ inches in diameter, and it originally formed one of a pair connected by a thick chain of wire, probably intended to be worn on the shoulders as fasteners of some garment. It is made of a ring of moulded bronze, and is decorated on front and back, its surface divided into compartments by relief mouldings, filled with decorative work of great refinement and elegance. The designs within the smaller panels are curvilinear conventional motifs formed by the application of fine gold filigree wire interspersed with minute gold knobs, while the larger panels are filled by an intertwisted elongated bird form in a similar technique. Bird and beast heads project outward from the raised margin, the bird forms being unique on jewelry of this kind, and closely resembling many in the borders of the Lindisfarne Gospels. Red enamel and amber, small discs of blue and red glass, and tiny human heads carved in amethyst add polychrome splendour to the refinement and delicacy of this gem of art and craftsmanship.

It is impossible in our brief space to do more than hint at the splendour and wealth of the metal work of the Early Christian art of the eighth and ninth centuries in Ireland. In particular, the Church enriched its furnishings with objects which must have done worlds to arouse the imaginations of an illiterate congregation and to associate the Church with beauty and splendour lacking in their homely domestic dwellings. Everything shone and gleamed. On the altars chalices were adorned with gold and silver, and studded with jewels. The Gospels were bound in richly decorated covers, and encased in *cumdachs*, or shrines, studded with ornaments valuable enough to be ripped off and stolen. Reliquaries were valued as heirlooms, sometimes in the form of house-shrines, such as the one found in a Viking grave at Copenhagen, undoubtedly Irish loot (Henry, *I.A.C.P.*, pl. 27b), and the reliquary from Monymusk (Aberdeenshire), adorned with red and yellow enamel and elaborately decorated. This treasured heirloom is doubtless the *Brechbrennoch*, traditionally associated with St Columba, and had a function analogous to that of the *Cathach* in Ireland. Croziers were adorned with skilled bronze work. The Kells crozier, now in the British Museum, is a particularly instructive example.[30] The close association of this industry in bronze and enamels with the Church is illustrated by the founders' hoards of crucibles, tongs, and other tools found in monastic precincts, e.g. in the monastery of Nendrum on Mahee Island in Strangford Lough. The small size of the objects, and the fragments of red enamel still remaining in the crucibles prove their purpose to have been for only such small objects as we have been discussing.

The Ardagh Chalice is deservedly the most famous piece of early Irish Christian metal-work, and must obviously have been a valued treasure of some church altar. It is a large two-handled cup of beaten silver on a silver stem, decorated with gold, gilt bronze and enamel (Henry, *A.I.*, pl. 120 f., pls. 107, 108). The design would be massive, were not one's eye directed to the symmetry and balance of the bowl

377

and foot beautifully united by its golden collar, the polished simplicity of the silver surface, and the dazzling insistence of the red and blue enamel and gold filigree of its single band of decoration near the top of the bowl, and of the surface and attachment of the handles. In subtle contrast with these bold effects are light and delicate engravings in double ribbon lines with intervening lightly punched dots, on the plain surface of the bowl outlining the attachment of the handles. Similar delicate engraving on the surface of the bowl records the names of the apostles and has added suggestive touches of animal ornament. The function of contrast and of the value of the reserved space in composition are blended with perfect artistic taste.

It is difficult for us to imagine the society in which such a masterpiece of ecclesiastical art as the Ardagh Chalice and the great illuminated manuscripts could be adequately appreciated and recompensed by an aristocracy governed by institutions as archaic as the Brehon Laws, and still upholding the heroic standards of society. The Ardagh Chalice belongs to the world of the hermit poetry. The introduction of Christianity had brought about a complete dichotomy in the ideals of early Christian Ireland. Yet both ideals are completely Irish, and the infusion of a new and higher culture in the art and poetry of the Church alongside the retention of the heroic standards and oral literary forms of the ancient Celtic world are fused in the first millennium of our era in an individual form of idealism and culture which is the greatest gift of this remote Western Island to European society.

The art of the jewels and the bronze Church pieces constantly reminds us of its close association with the great illuminated manuscripts of the seventh to the ninth centuries. The correspondence between certain details of the art of the Tara brooch and the art represented by the Lindisfarne Gospels, the latter probably attributable to a date about AD 710–20, has already been emphasized. The similarity of the lettering of the inscription of the Ardagh Chalice to that of the big initial letters of the Lindisfarne Gospels not only constitutes a close link in date, but establishes the two objects as products of a single artistic phase. On the other hand, some objects, notably the belt-buckles in the Sutton Hoo ship-burial, now dated to approximately 625,[31] employ similar motifs, and it is becoming clearer that a common development is taking place in the artistic life of the whole of the British Isles from the middle of the seventh century.

378

To this same period and artistic phase we owe the rise of the great school of manuscript illumination in Ireland, the finest flower of Celtic art.[32] The vernacular Celtic style reached its highest development from the seventh to the end of the eighth or beginning of the ninth century, that is to say until its first encounter with the Vikings. It is to this great period of the native Celtic art style that we owe the masterpieces of the *Book of Durrow* and the *Book of Kells*. From the end of the eighth century there is a gradual decline until about 850.

The Celtic manuscripts of the period are of two types, (1) the large Gospel books carefully written in uncial or half-uncial script, intended to lie on the altar; and (2) small portable books, in cursive hand for ready reference or private reading, 'pocket editions'. Almost all the decorated manuscripts are Gospels, and having striking decoration on the first page of each Gospel, composed chiefly of immense initial monograms covered with decoration. The left-hand page facing the beginning of the text is almost always covered entirely with decoration, which shows considerable variation and is known as a 'carpet page'. In addition, to, or instead of, the carpet page, there is also at the beginning of each Gospel the symbol of the Evangelist or his portrait. The carpet pages and the symbol pages are often framed in running patterns of interlaced ribbon designs of the traditional Coptic style (Henry, *A.I.*, pl. 31, 60), while the monograms make use exclusively of spirals and fine twists (ibid., pl. 61).

The earliest of the fine illuminated manuscripts is the small Gospel book known as the *Book of Durrow*, attributed to about 650, or only a little later.[36] In its reserve and complete mastery of composition and design it attains perhaps the high-water-mark of Irish illumination. These qualities of maturity in the *Book of Durrow* indicate the culmination of a tradition, whatever its origin. The art of the *Book of Durrow* employs the traditional linear spiral ornament in the great initials to the opening of the Gospels, but the decoration of the carpet pages, and the pages of the symbols of the Evangelists, are bordered with the interlacing early ribbon form comparable with the Carndonagh and Fahan Mura crosses, and betray the influence of enamel in some of the discs. The range of colours is limited to four – brown, red, yellow and green – and the total effect is of the mellow beauty of autumn leaves, in contrast with the brilliant polychrome of the later manuscripts, especially the jewelled effect of the *Book of Kells* with its liberal use of blue. Neither book employs gold leaf – that is for the future; but it is interesting to note that the Durrow colours are identical with those of Syrian manuscripts of a later date and probably of archaic tradition, and are similar in their use of these colours for broad ribbon meanders. The manuscript contains several pages devoted wholly to ornamentation, reminding one of the beautiful Oriental carpets which may indeed have been one means of transmitting their designs, owing to the ready portability of fabrics.

Perhaps the most individual feature in the Book is the pages devoted to symbols of the Evangelists, both those devoted to the single figures and those divided into compartments containing the symbols. Here the Durrow manuscript shares with the Ardagh Chalice the relatively advanced sense of the value of the blank background to throw the principal design into higher relief. The human figures are particularly striking, deliberately eschewing naturalism and achieving an effect completely iconographical. The figure of St Matthew without arms and with both feet parallel, and at right angles to the axis of his body, stiffly clad in a single chequered garment, is reminiscent of a mosaic rather than of a painting, but on its blank white vellum ground-work, surrounded by the frame of ribbon meanders, it is a work of mature art, not so much the beginning of a tradition as its culmination. These figure panels, as we might call them, and the Canons of Concordances of the Gospels framed in arcading, have their nearest analogies in the Syrian Gospels written by the monk Rabula in the sixth century,[34] and, like many features in the early Celtic Church, undoubtedly owe their inspiration to Eastern Mediterranean influences.

Of all Irish works of art the *Book of Kells* is by common consent the chief treasure, and among the great Gospel Books ranks with the *Book of Durrow*. Its precise origin is unknown, whether in the Irish Columban monastery of Iona, or in Ireland, and its date is uncertain, but the early ninth century is probable. Kells was heavily raided and pillaged from late in the ninth century and throughout the tenth, but when we have our first historical reference to the manuscript itself it is preserved in the church at Kells, for we read in the Annals of Ulster, s.a. 1006 'the great Gospel of Columcille was wickedly stolen in the night out of the western sacristy of the great stone church of Kells – the chief relic of the western world on account of its ornamental cover', and that it was found later, stripped of its gold, and buried under a sod. In 1661 the manuscript passed to Trinity College, Dublin, where it has remained ever since.

The codex[35] is of relatively large size, and consists of thick polished vellum on which the text is written in a beautiful round half-uncial hand characteristic of the best large Irish manuscripts. The contents are very varied. The first leaf contains some Hebrew words and their Latin equivalents, and the symbols of the Evangelists – the man or angel for St Matthew, the lion for St Mark, the calf for St Luke, the eagle for St John. The next eight illuminated pages are filled with the Eusebian Canons, written in narrow columns in an arcading of decorated pillars. Folio 7v contains a full-page illustration of the Virgin and Child with attendant angels and elaborately decorated border. The drawing of the figures, both here and in the portraits of the evangelists St Matthew and St Mark, while anatomically far in advance of those of Durrow, are deliberately stylized, and carefully avoid any suggestion of naturalism. We are again reminded of enamelled and metal ikons, or of mosaic work, and the art is as remote from the Classical ideal as are the serpents, fish and birds in the interlacing design of the border from zoological reality. It is an art of suggestion rather than of delineation, and the suggestion is the creation of the Celtic imagination passing beyond the prescribed borders of science.

This iconographical treatment of the larger human figures is, of course, a deliberate piece of advanced sophistication. Paradoxically enough many of the smaller angels and human figures introduced into the ornament are convincingly natural. The little human figure at the top of the splendid illumination of the opening words of St Matthew's Gospel, and the charming head which terminates the curl of the letter P. in the great monogram page, take their place without the slightest incongruity amid the rich and varied tapestry of these great pages of pure ornament. It is perhaps in this great monogram page more than any other that the artist shows his skill in harmonizing the most disparate elements into his design. In a small space at the foot of the great initial *Chi* is a quiet little miniature of two rats gnawing a Church wafer, watched by two cats, carefully distinguished by the artist as a tortoise-shell and a brindled, with two more rats perched on their backs. Is it a symbol of the peace by which the lion and the lamb shall lie down together? Is it merely an artistic whimsey like the marginalia of many of the scribes?

It is in these great ornamental pages that the Irish artists'combined resourcefulness and tact is seen in its highest perfection. Whether it be confined in a rigid frame-work, as in the great eight-circled cross (fo. 33v), or whether it twists and turns in tiny circles, filling with studied splendour and dazzling brilliance the great monogram page of St Matthew's Gospel (fo. 34r); or whether it be restrained within a more geometrical enclosure recalling the leaded lights of a stained glass window, as in the opening words of St Mark's Gospel, the rich scrolls, the trumpet patterns, and the ribbon meander interlock, and resolve themselves, flow, intertwine and concentrate, only to uncurl again in endless and effortless variety exquisitely controlled and subordinated to the main design and purpose of the page. The lines of the ornament constantly put us in mind of the fine wire-work, and of the rich polychrome, of jewelry. We are far removed from the grave dignity, the mature restraint of the Durrow art, or its sombre autumnal colouring. The genius of Kells has the prodigal brilliance of easy mastery and unlimited resource. This profuse decoration, this prodigality of ornament, is scattered throughout the work, and is a perpetual delight as it appears, often with no apparent motive, in margins and interlinear figures, bright, fantastic, graceful, throughout the text.

From the seventh and eighth centuries the great Irish convents, the source of our early Irish art treasures, were the objects of heavy Viking depredations, and the monks were often forced to move to safer centres, sometimes taking their books with them, and it becomes increasingly difficult to pin-point the home of a given manuscript. The monks from Lindisfarne, the prey of the Vikings in the ninth century, eventually settled at Durham, where the fragmentary *Durham Gospels* combines survivals of the *Book of Durrow* and the closely related Lindisfarne style of decoration. The famous *Book of St Chad* now at Lichfield (Moreau, pl. 103; Henry, *A.I.*, pl. 98), but known to have been in Wales probably before the end of the eighth century, has close affinities with these earliest Irish manuscripts.[36] The *Rushworth* or *Mac Regol Gospels* (Henry, *A.I.*, pls. 110, 287), which were in the north of England in the tenth century, probably came originally from the Abbey of Birr in County Offaly. The art of the splendid *Echternach Gospels* is so closely allied to that of the *Book of Lindisfarne* and the *Durham Gospels* that it is commonly thought that the *Echternach Codex* was written and decorated in Northumbria in the early eighth century, and carried to the Continent; but the

382

details are equally close to the Irish art of the *Book of Durrow*. As F. Henry observes, the big lion, the symbol of St Mark 'which bounds, flame-like, shaking a cluster of golden curls, across a pavement of straight lines' behaves as 'one would expect the Durrow animal symbols to behave as soon as they had got bold enough to move' (*I.A.E.C.P.*, p. 129).

The influence of the art of this period was carried by Irish monks to continental monasteries, some of which kept in close touch with Ireland in the eighth and ninth centuries. Others, such as Luxeuil, St Gall, and Bobbio, were actually Irish foundations of the seventh century. It is commonly believed that the monks fleeing to the Continent to escape the Vikings carried their books with them, and no doubt this happened in some cases; but Irish influence in the continental books is more probably to be accounted for on the whole by the fact that under the monastic stimulus in Ireland in the preceding period art, learning, writing and the production of books had become a national accomplishment and trade. What the monks took to the Continent was their intellectual and artistic monopoly and means of livelihood, and all that appertained to the scholars' life, and to ecclesiastical art.

From the end of the eighth century the essential Celtic style, with its abundance of spiral and trumpet patterns and purely geometrical interlacings, began to decline, and was increasingly mingled with interlacing animals and birds which native Celtic art shared with the Teutonic art of the period. About 850 the art of the Vikings began to modify the Irish style of the period by the introduction of the so-called 'Jellinge style' from Norway, which had itself originated largely from imitation of Irish ornament. The resulting Hiberno-Viking style had a vigorous life in Ireland and the Isle of Man, and after the Irish victory of Clontarf in 1014 the revival of the Church stimulated zeal in restoration and in the creation of splendid new objects of Church use. Most of the *cumdachs*, or book-shrines, and the croziers were repaired and re-embellished during the period from about 1000 to 1125, and it is to the later part of the time that we owe the richest and the most elaborately ornamental ones, the shrine of St Patrick's bell, the cross of Cong, the shrine of St Lachtin's arm, and the Lismore Crozier.

In fact, after the middle of the tenth century, the art of Ireland seems to have passed almost entirely into ecclesiastical channels, and when the Anglo-Norman conquest actually took place the introduction of foreign Orders and the part played by Canterbury in the 'Hiberno-Danish' bishoprics had already prepared the way for a new style of art and architecture derived from continental sources. Only rare traces of the ancient Celtic traditions may have modified the new Norman styles, possibly, for example, the stone heads on Cormac's Chapel at Cashel, where Celtic *têtes coupées* may have imposed themselves against the current of Norman and medieval types.

The vigour of Irish tradition, indeed the vigour of Celtic tradition throughout the British Isles, is most fully represented by the sculptured stone crosses. We have already seen that the art and technique of stone sculpture which developed in the La Tène period continues in close union with the art of the succeeding periods in an unbroken tradition until the Middle Ages. The great number of the crosses and the wealth of their decoration are a valuable supplement to our knowledge of the art of the rarer and more perishable objects in metal and on vellum. A few examples, like the crosses of Fahan Mura and the Muiredach Cross of Monasterboice, afford us some chronological guidance by their inscriptions. More often by their numbers and precise localities they can be classified into Schools and periods, and so help us by comparison to discern the affinities of smaller portable objects whose provenance is unknown.

The earliest type of Irish sculptured crosses are carved on the flat stone surfaces of upright slabs, suggesting comparison with a picture on a manuscript page. The background of the sculptures consists of upright independent slabs or steles on which are either incised or carved in shallow relief a simple cross or a crucifixion group and other figures, mostly human (Henry, *A.I.*, pls. 49–56). In view of the manifest influence of the Eastern Mediterranean Christian Church on early Irish Christianity it is natural to suspect an ultimate influence from Coptic steles on these early Irish monuments. In Ireland crosses of this type are not rare or confined to one period, and are sometimes found side by side with later types. The most interesting and elaborate are the crosses from Fahan Mura and Carndonagh, both from the neighbourhood of Inishowen in Donegal.

These form a coherent group, the relationship being clear from both the treatment of the figures and the wide interlacing ribbons which, bordered by a double line, occupy the whole of the interior of the cross of Fahan Mura on both the east and west faces. The eastern face is austere in treatment, and recalls Coptic steles in certain details; the western face is much freer, the ribbon interlace encroaching on the ribbed border, and the stem of the cross is flanked with two rigid little figures recalling by their stiff garments, and the absence of delineation of the arms, the figure of St Matthew in the *Book of Durrow*. The Fahan Cross is of unusual interest in that it bears an inscription in clear Greek letters, being the Greek version of a formula of the *Gloria Patri*: 'Glory and honour to the Father and to the Son and to the Holy Spirit'. The formula on the Fahan cross is the one mentioned in canons 13 and 15 of the fourth Council of Toledo, held in 633, which was perhaps replaced about that time by the more modern form 'Glory to the Father', but which continued in use in the Mozarabic liturgy, and was widely used in Greek liturgies until at least the ninth century. The formula was probably copied at Fahan from a page of a Greek manuscript, perhaps during the course of the seventh century, a date favoured by other evidence (Henry, *A.I.*, p. 162 f.).

Fahan was a very important monastery in the Columban tradition of the seventh century, and was under the direct patronage of the branch of the northern Uí Néill whose seat nearby was the fortress of Ailech. The Carndonagh Cross, on the other hand, only a few miles to the north, is a much cruder piece of work, both in execution and design, a provincial poor relation of the refined and carefully executed work of Fahan, yet it clearly belongs to the same School and period. It is a tall thin slab of sandstone, one side entirely covered with double contour ribbons, the other with sharply incised figures forming a continuous design, the whole centred upon an oval containing a head of Christ in Glory. Other stylized figures, without indication of arms, are grouped on this same (eastern) face of the Cross, and the cross is associated with two little pillars (*A.I.*, pl. 59) bearing incised and lightly modelled figures of varying types – a warrior, an ecclesiastic, a harpist, and Jonah emerging from the whale. We are on the threshold of the narrative scenes of the later high crosses, and in the neighbouring cemetery is another cross of the same school. Meanwhile this Donegal school is not confined to Fahan and Carndonagh, but had left survivals on Inishkeel and on Caher and Tory islands.

With the high crosses we leave the slab crosses and find ourselves in a different world, a local Celtic milieu, for the high crosses are a

385

specialized development of the British Isles. They have no parallels in contemporary continental sculpture, but they are found widespread from the eighth to the twelfth centuries throughout the British Isles, not only in Ireland, especially in the centre and south, but throughout England, in Cornwall, Wales, the Isle of Man, and Western Scotland. These local developments do not imply a uniform character. The art of the Cornish[37] and Welsh crosses[38] and of those of south-western Scotland is largely geometrical interlacing ribbon and knot-work, and is artistically poor in comparison with the Irish and the highly original Pictish crosses; but the technique is generally faultless, which is all the more remarkable since these geometrical designs, especially of the angular variety (cf. the Carew Cross), are more exacting for the carver's skill than freer designs. A slip of the chisel can ruin an entire panel. This localization of art styles – we may refer to the unique slab from the Calf of Man – and still more this perfection of technique in the high crosses of Britain, is again the more remarkable since there are no indications of preliminary stages, or of gradual development and decline. Even if we postulate preliminary designs in metalwork, their faultless transference to stone is none the less puzzling. It is probable that the origins of the high cross, as of the stele, are to be sought in Mediterranean Christian lands, Armenia or elsewhere in the Byzantine empire, where political upheavals like the Arabic conquest and the Iconoclastic Controversy must certainly have driven many expert artists into exile.

The Irish high crosses are heavy stone erections, generally mounted on a solid, sometimes lofty stepped plinth. They fall into wide groups. The first group is best represented by the two Ahenny Crosses in Tipperary, which date at latest from about 750 (Henry, *A.I.*, p. 170). The crosses of Lorrha and the two south crosses of Clonmacnoise are from later in the century. The Moone Cross has also been assigned to the eighth century from its similarity to the crosses of Group I. All the crosses of this group are closely related in style to the metal work of the early eighth century, and can occasionally be dated by their close relationship to metal work found in Viking graves of the early ninth century.[39] The entire surface of the stone tends to be covered with running ornament resembling embroidery, each ornament being contained in a bordered panel. The ornament frequently combines spirals with interlace and animal heads, and Greek key patterns. On the Ahenny and Kilkieran and the Lorrha crosses

386

the entire surface is covered with spirals and interlaces, and it is only on the pedestals that scenes with human beings occur. On the North Ahenny cross horsemen and processions are found. Others, such as Kilrea and Killamery, have scenes on the cross itself and even on the arms. The 'south cross' of Clonmacnoise has a crucifixion scene below the head of the cross. All these scenes, as well as the figures on the cross of Moone, are in very low relief, and with little moulding. The cross of Moone is of a remarkable style, a small head and slender shaft rising from a high though narrow pyramidal base. There is hardly any ornament, the surface being largely divided into panels containing geometrical figures and animals. In its economy of detail and bold and rigorously simple figures, it is one of the most original and impressive of the crosses.

To the second group belong the Clonmacnoise school. This school is assigned approximately to the end of the eighth century or the beginning of the ninth by an inscription on the Bealin Cross, which has been transferred from this original milieu to Bealin near Athlone.[40] This date receives support from the similarity of details in their decoration and animal designs to those of the Books of Kells and of Armagh. The mouldings and carvings are still in very low relief, and their abundant ornaments are of fine interlacing and complicated spirals, and interlacing animals. To these motifs are added 'narrative' hunting scenes, mostly in panels, of which the Cross of Banagher has fine examples. These striking cavalcades of horsemen and hunters are sometimes almost identical with the superimposed processions of warriors and huntsmen on the Pictish crosses which are almost unique in the Western art of the period. In the Pictish sculptures they are infinitely varied. Their immediate inspiration is obscure, but horsemen continue until the eleventh and twelfth centuries on the Irish crosses.

On the other hand, the crosses of Iona and the Irish kingdom of Argyll have developed the bolder form and design which is found already in the cross of Bealin, and which develops more fully later. In this style the crosses are enclosed in a circle, which may form a part of the solid head or may be perforated. The carving is in deeper relief and a striking development is the great bosses standing out in high relief from the central disc and from the extremities of the arms. These are clearly reminiscent of metal work, in which bosses formed of coral, or enamel were used to mask a metal stud, as can be seen in the

387

Snettisham treasure from Norfolk, the great belt buckle from Sutton Hoo, and elsewhere.

Apart from the remarkable series of mounted horsemen and hunting scenes the great majority of figure and narrative scenes on the crosses are scriptural. The central theme is the Crucifixion, but apart from that, and doubtless leading up to it, the majority both in Ireland and Scotland illustrate scenes from the Old Testament. Especial favourites are the Fall, Daniel in the lions' den, Jonah and the whale, the three young men in the Fiery Furnace (from the Apocrypha), the sacrifice of Abel, David as harpist and warrior, and some episodes from the life of St Antony.

This general narrative repertoire, which Mlle. Henry aptly calls a 'theology in stone' (*S.I.*, p. 160), continues on the Irish crosses throughout the ninth and tenth centuries, after which it disappears without a trace. It is entirely absent from the crosses of the eleventh and twelfth centuries, and crosses like that of Dysert O'Dea revert to a covering of ornament – no longer spirals, but animal interlace – taking their place in the national revival which is reflected in the literature and scribal activity of the period, and looks back nostalgically to pre-Viking Ireland.

It is indeed a remarkable fact that in the first half of the ninth century the Viking invasions were at their height, and the destruction of the Irish monasteries was taking place on a great scale; yet, inexplicable as it seems to us, some seem to have been left immune, and an interlude of comparative peace in the late ninth and early tenth centuries has left us some of our finest crosses, notably those of Kells and Monasterboice. The crosses of this group seem to have formed a homogeneous Leinster tradition with a central School of sculpture at Monasterboice, and a continuous tradition until the twelfth century.

The treatment of the Crucifixion varies greatly in both time and place, but a constant feature in the Irish crosses is the presence on either side of the foot of the cross of two little figures, one lifting up the sponge, the other bearing a lance, as on the unfinished cross at Kells. We have seen them already on the steles from Fahan and Carndonagh (p. 384), and they occur on the eighth century Athlone gilded bronze plaque. They serve once more to illustrate the close correspondence between the motifs on metal and stone. On the Irish crosses St John and the Virgin never appear in this position. In the early crosses the Crucifixion is generally represented in low relief on quite a small scale, and sometimes placed relatively low, and surmounted by a Christ in Glory, as on the Moone and Carndonagh crosses. In this and some other details, e.g. the meeting of St Paul and St Antony, and the flight into Egypt, the iconography of the Irish crosses have points in common with the Ruthwell Cross of Dumfriesshire.

They rarely make use of foliage, however, and we have nothing corresponding to the foliage panels of the great English and Scottish Border crosses – Ruthwell, Bewcastle, Jedburgh and Acca. Amid the scenes on the Irish crosses in direct transition from Carolingian and Byzantine iconography we find both on the Irish and Scottish sculptures realistic hunting scenes which may possibly have a symbolic significance, but are certainly elements of the traditional repertoire of the sculptor. What is the direct inspiration of the motifs in which monsters wage perpetual warfare against one another, against serpents, devour human heads, even human beings, recalling to our memories the old Celtic art of Watsch and Este, and the Celto-Iberian statue of the Monster of Moves? How are we to interpret the juxtaposition of a panel on the Ahenny Cross depicting warriors on horseback and men in a chariot setting out with their dogs, apparently on a hunting expedition, with a neighbouring panel depicting a funeral procession, in which a headless corpse is carried on horseback, followed by a man bearing the head, and preceded by others carrying crosses?

The form of the cross and the presentation of the Crucifixion have undergone a complete transformation in the course of centuries. In our earliest examples, we have seen that the cross itself formed only a lightly incised symbol on a flat stone surface resembling a page of manuscript. Gradually the relief develops, the carving grows steadily bolder, and the page effect disappears, for example on the Pictish slab crosses of Glamis and Aberlemno. The architectural structure of the cross becomes fundamental. In Ireland the head of the high crosses is generally surrounded and strengthened by a circle or 'wheel'. This type of cross is confined in Scotland to the Irish districts – Argyll and the Hebrides, and assigned to the ninth and tenth centuries.[41] Heavy bosses protrude from the arms and head of the wheel crosses, e.g. on the Iona crosses of St Martin and St John, and from the centre of the Kildalton cross on Islay. In most of these great wheel crosses the

389

figure of Christ occupies the chief position, the central space of the intersection of the arms, even encroaching on the limbs and the arms, e.g. at Castledermot (Henry, *I.H.C.*, pl. 23), and on the Kells market cross (*ib.*, pl. 31), the cross of Muiredach at Monasterboice and the 'Cross of the Scriptures' at Clonmacnoise. In Ireland the cross becomes a crucifix on which the figure of Christ is sometimes sculptured in high relief, virtually an independent statue, as on the cross of Dysert O'Dea (*I.H.C.*, pl. 62), and the defaced cross on the Rock of Cashel (*ib.*, p. 64).

In our discussion of insular Celtic art we have dwelt most fully on the art of Ireland, for Celtic traditional art, like Celtic traditional literature, is preserved in its richest and most conservative form in this Western Isle. In Great Britain Celtic art and technique have a more strictly regional history. Wales has a wealth of stone crosses, both in relief and free-standing, dating from the seventh to the ninth centuries. Most of them are flat, but the most famous is the pillar-stone at Valle Crucis Abbey near Llangollen, which bears an inscription commemorating a certain Eliseg who probably lived in the eighth century. The high cross on a stepped base is found in both Wales and Cornwall, but figure scenes are not common, the sculptor's art being generally confined to geometrical designs covering the entire surface, and his artistic skill is revealed by the exact adaptation of his design to its framework, and the flawless execution of his work. The Whithorn and Kirkmadrine stones illustrate the unity of the Strathclyde School with this Western Border tradition. It is not until the great Northumbrian School of the early ninth century that we find a new stimulus from contemporary continental motifs, both the foliate tracery of Merovingian art, and the majestic dignity and serenity of the fully clothed Christ of the Crucifixion in the Ruthwell and Bewcastle crosses.

These carved tomb-stones of western Britain have a special value for us in that, unlike the Irish, they are rich in inscriptions, which tell us something of contemporary personnel. In Wales some of these records have specified the professions and the official status of the defunct, a doctor (*medicus*), a magistrate (*magistratus*), or, as on a memorial tablet with a tiny incised cross at Llangadwaladr in Anglesey, the early seventh century king Cadfan (*Catamanus*), *sapientis(s)imus opinatis(s)imus omnium regum* 'most learned and renowned of all kings'. Cornwall has nine stone inscriptions, mostly in Roman capitals, and a few in ogams. One near Fowey is of especial interest for it possibly commemorates the Trystan of early Cornish romantic legend. The Cornish wheel-headed crosses, sculptured in the round, date from the tenth century and are attributed to direct Irish influence; but the art in general is geometrical, like that of Wales.

The Isle of Man has more than ninety carved stones,[42] mostly undecorated commemorative slabs with incised crosses. A particularly interesting one bearing five prominent bosses, commemorates a certain Guriat, in all probability a member of the family from which descended Rhodri Mawr ('the Great'), king of North Wales (d. AD 878). A rare form of inscribed slab of probably the eighth century from Maughold, the earliest and most important Manx Church, is inscribed with two little archaic crosses, and above them a circle enclosing the marigold design of Mediterranean origin. The Island has at all times been a centre of the cultures of the surrounding lands, and it has a wealth of stone sculptures illustrating heathen Scandinavian mythology and dating from Viking times. In contra-distinction to this heathen repertoire is the unique little incised slab of the Crucifixion, assigned to the eighth or ninth century, found on the Calf of Man on the site of an early Celtic Chapel, doubtless a little Celtic monastery. The man holding the spear stands at the foot of the Cross, and the side which is broken away doubtless bore the man with the sponge. The detail of the iconography has no known parallel. It is a living Christ, with open eyes, carefully trimmed hair and forked beard, fully clad, not in a single vestment like a shroud, but in elaborate garments of many embroidered and otherwise varied patterns. The nails are emphasized in feet and hands, but the figure impresses one, not as a dead saviour but rather as a living king, only recently crucified.

With southern and western Britain we leave the Celtic traditional art behind. Indeed with this Manx crucifixion we have already left it. Northern and eastern Scotland possess a richly furnished album in stone which knows no predecessors, no close affinities. This is the art of the Picts. Its earliest form is that of a series of symbols, chiefly geometrical, but partly of conventionalized animals and birds, incised with supreme art on the undressed surface of boulders. These symbols are widespread, but have never yet been interpreted. Over a hundred survive, believed to date from the sixth to the eighth centuries, and their range extends from the Shetlands and the

Hebrides to the Firth of Forth. They also form incised tapestries on the walls of certain of the Fifeshire caves, and are found on small objects such as the bronze plate from the Laws, Angus;[43] and a silver leaf-shaped plate from Largo, Fife,[44] both now in the National Museum of Scotland.

The Pictish stone sculptures are never found free-standing, but a later class of Pictish carving, dating from the seventh to the ninth centuries, consists of upright dressed slabs bearing relief sculpture of a wider range and foreign influence – Celtic ornament, and the figure of the cross, though the Crucifixion never appears. Here the principal subjects are naturalistic animals and narrative scenes from the life of human beings, and though symbols still occur they are of a different range from those of our previous class. Indeed the stereotyped form of the symbols of class I, which is characteristic of the Northern Picts, has given place during the eighth century among the Southern Picts of the Tay Valley to a predominantly naturalistic art. The intrusion of interlace and scroll and knot-work is suggestive of the growing influence of Celtic political relations. Later in date are the similar sculptured slabs of greater size which have rejected the symbols but now combine with the naturalistic designs of class II stones features more especially characteristic of the art of Northumbria and Ireland. In fact the art of the Pictish people is a close parallel to their history, which we first meet at the height of their power in the sixth century under their great king, Brude mac Maelchon, the *rex potentissimus* of Bede's *Ecclesiastical History*. Only a powerful and highly organized realm could have been responsible for the runity, the wide range, and the high quality of early Pictish art. Only a high standard of refinement could have set the standard of its austere, possibly hieratic art. The origin of this art, like that of the pre-Celtic language of the earliest Picts, remains wholly unknown and almost beyond conjecture. The early Pictish sculptures carry us beyond the confines of the Celtic Realms.

NOTES

1 Jacobsthal, *E.C.A.* (Oxford, 1944), I, p. 160.
2 A. Varagnac, *A.G.*, *passim*.
3 T. Powell, *The Celts*, p. 168.
4 Filip, *C.C.*, p. 170.
5 Chadwick, *C.B.*, notes and references to Plate 54.
6 See H. N. Savory, 'A New hoard of La Tène metalwork from Wales', *Celticum* XII (1965), 163.
7 F. Benoit, *A.M.V.R.*, p. 9.
8 Benoit, *A.M.V.R.*, p. 17.
9 *Ibid.*, p. 24.
10 Moreau, *W.K.*, pl. 77.
11 F. Stahelin, *Die Schweiz in Römischer Zeit* (Basle, 1948), p. 544, fig. 157.
12 The following account of the wooden figures from Sequana, and the Plates, are from R. Martin, *Sculptures en bois découvertes aux Sources de la Seine* (Dijon, 1964). We are indebted to Dr Glyn Daniel for procuring this work for us.
13 C. Fox, *P. and P.*, p. 26 ff. The Battersea shield, in colour, forms the frontispiece of the *British Museum Guide to the Antiquities of the Early Iron Age* (1925).
14 See Fox, *op. cit.*, p. 22 ff.; pl. 19; cf. fig. 16.
15 *British Museum Guide to Early Iron Age Antiquities*, p. 138 ff., R. E. M. Wheeler, *Stanwick*, p. 2 ff.
16 R. Rainbird Clarke, *East Anglia* (London, 1960), p. 104 f.
17 See Déchelette, *Manuel* II, part iii, fig. 463, 2.
18 *S.I.*, p. 35.
19 Déchelette, II, figs. 660–1, 663, 667, 668.
20 Fox, fig. 77, c.
21 H. Hubert, *The Rise of the Celts* (London, 1934), fig. 218 f.
22 Figured in Déchelette, *Manuel* II, fig. 709.
23 F. Henry, *A.I.*, p. 20; *I.A.*, 6.
24 J. M. C. Toynbee, *Art in Roman Britain* (London, 1962), pl. 8, Fig. 7.
25 *L.I.F.C.*, 8, n. 16.
26 See N. K. Chadwick, *C.B.*, Plate 33; and references there cited.
27 Joseph Anderson, *S.E.C.T.*, II, p. 314 ff.
28 See J. Anderson, *S.E.C.T.*, II, p. 1 ff.; figs. 1–3.
29 Françoise Henry, *I.A.E.C.P.*, pp. 119; 150 f.
30 For details see M. and L. de Paor, *E.C.I.*, pp. 154, 166, and pl. 58–60.
31 C. Hawkes, *Antiquity*, XXXCIII (1964), p. 252 ff.
32 The great facsimile reproduction in colour of the *Book of Durrow* (published in two volumes, 1960) and the *Book of Kells* (published in three volumes in 1940) are done by the Urgraf Verlag of Bern.
33 F. Henry, *S.I.*, p. 47; ibid. *I.A.E.C.P.*, p. 63.

34 See O. M. Dalton, *Byzantine Art and Archaeology* (Oxford, 1911), figs. 266 and 267.
35 An inventory of the contents and 24 plates of coloured reproductions in Sir Edward Sullivan, *The Book of Kells* (published by the Studio, 1914).
36 On this MS and the related style of decoration in the MSS of Durrow and Lindisfarne see the important study by F. Henry, 'The Lindisfarne Gospels', *Antiquity* XXXVII (1963), especially p. 104 ff.
37 Notably the Cardinham and the Sancreed Crosses (H. O'N. Hencken, *ACS*, figs. 50 and 51).
38 Notably the Carew and Pemmon Crosses, and one in Brecon Museum and the smaller Margam Cross. For the whole Series see V. E. Nash-Williams, *E.C.M.W.*, passim.
39 F. Henry, *I.H.C.*, p. 59.
40 Henry, *A.I.*, p. 172; pl. 88. For the 'north cross' of Clonmacnoise, *ibid.*, pl. 91; for one of the little pillars, pl. 95.
41 S. Cruden, *E.C.P.M.S.*, p. 14 f.
42 For details and plates see P. M. C. Kermode, *Manx Crosses* (London, 1907).
43 Chadwick, *C.B.*, fig. 28.
44 *Ibid.* fig. 29.

EPILOGUE

We found the Celts in south central Europe in the Bronze Age, perhaps as early as 2000 BC, and saw them later spreading west to the Atlantic and into the British Isles, and east as far as Asia Minor. By the fourth century BC they were, in numbers and in the extent of Celtic territory, the greatest people in Europe. Then came a period of decline when the Gauls of north Italy were conquered by the Romans, and the tribes north of the Alps were subjugated or expelled by the Germans. Caesar's Gallic War ended with the heroic effort of Vercingetorix at Alesia. His defeat and capture in 52 BC marks the end of Gaulish independence. But the Gauls quickly took advantage of Roman citizenship and Roman education, so that by the close of the fourth century Gaul was the principal intellectual area of the western Empire. The Gauls became known for their eloquence in public speaking and their gift for poetry: the poet Ausonius, and Sidonius Apollinaris, bishop and writer, are well-known names, and St Jerome himself speaks of 'the richness and splendour of Gaulish oratory'.[1] This is in accord with the comment of Cato the Elder that the ancient Gauls specially wished to be able to speak well (p. 32).

The great contribution of the Celts in the prehistoric period was in the field of decorative art in stone and metal-work. The art-form called La Tène which is peculiar to them is abstract art, pure decoration, in contrast to the grander art of Greece and Rome where Man is at the centre. There is even a refusal of representation, for when animal forms are brought into the pattern, they are in fantastic shapes, mere elements in the scheme of curves and spirals and interlacements in which the artists took delight. La Tène art is usually considered to end soon after Roman influence became dominant in Celtic territory, c. AD 100, but the imaginative quality and decorative sense that mark it did not disappear without leaving a trace behind; and the tools and monuments of Roman Gaul owe much of their worth to the tradition.

In Ireland Roman influence was never established, and here the old style was preserved, and it put on more magnificence in the Middle Ages. The splendid metal-work of the Ardagh Chalice and the Tara Brooch, the manuscript illumination of the Book of Durrow and the Book of Kells, the decorative panels of the Cross of Muredach at Monasterboice, are in the tradition of La Tène.

The Celtic realms of the historic period are Ireland and Wales, with their respective outlying countries in Scotland and the Isle of Man, Cornwall and Brittany. And in the British Isles the Celtic genius found its fullest expression and realized its greatest achievement under the stimulus of Christianity. Ireland received Christianity from Britain, and 'by the sixth century Irish Christianity surpassed that of every other land in western Europe, not only in intensity and sanctity, but also in passionate devotion to learning and missionary enthusiasm ... The passionate enthusiasm with which the Irish devoted themselves to the study of sacred learning and the liberal arts from the seventh century is without parallel in the rest of Europe ... Before the eighth century there were at least fifty important centres where Irish influence was dominant, ranging from Brittany in the north-west to Würzburg and Salzburg in the east, and from the English Channel ... to Bobbio.'[2]

The sudden growth of learning and holiness in Ireland in the sixth century is an extraordinary fact which suggests some efficient cause, and it is possible that Ireland was a place of refuge for scholars fleeing from the barbarians in Gaul, even perhaps for refugees from Egypt fleeing from the Moors, who brought with them these monastic virtues.[3] In the sixth century St Columba converted the Picts of Scotland, and Columbanus was on his way towards establishing the tradition of the *Scotti peregrini*. From the founding of Clonmacnoise in 548 to the founding of the Irish monastery at Ratisbon in 1090, the Irish were a powerful influence in the western Church. Toynbee claims for them a degree of cultural superiority in western Europe during all this long time,[4] and, while that may be too bold a claim, the known facts prove a very high level of piety and of scholarship at home and abroad. Virgilius of Salzburg († 784), called The Geometer, was abbot of St Peter's, and governed the diocese of Salzburg for more than thirty years. He was apparently learned in cosmography, and was denounced by St Boniface for teaching the existence of the Antipodes. Clemens Scottus was head of the Palace School under Louis the Pious. His contemporary, Dícuil, was the author of the *Liber de Mensura Orbis Terrae*, said to be the best book on geography in the early Middle Ages.[5] Dúngal of St Denis wrote a treatise on an eclipse of the sun. Donatus, bishop of Fiesole from 826 to 877, was an accomplished poet. The two greatest names, Sedulius and Eriugena, have been introduced earlier (pp. 237–41). And these are only some of the poets, scholars and saints whom Traube and his disciples have made known.[6] To the list of names must be added the witness of Bobbio and of St Gall. 'It is impossible for the classical scholar to exaggerate the significance of the part played by the Irish in the work of preserving classical literature.'[7]

During the ninth and tenth centuries Ireland was being ravaged by the Norsemen, and the monastic schools were plundered again and again, so that there must have been hundreds of refugees who now in turn sought the quiet of Irish monasteries in France and Germany, from Péronne, Laon and Rheims to Fulda and Würzburg. Their zeal for learning did not fail, and the scholarship of the Irish on the continent was never at a higher level than in the ninth century, when most of those mentioned above were active.

Even at home, however, learning, literature and art survived, and even prospered, in spite of the Viking raids. It was during the Viking period that some of the grandest High Crosses were made, and fine metal-work was still being done. Indeed it is in some measure to this danger from the Norsemen that we owe the building of the handsome bell-towers which give dignity and grace to so many monastic sites. The early 'round towers', such as those of Clonmacnoise, Kells and Monasterboice, are thought to have been built in the tenth century, mainly as strongholds in which relics, treasures, and books could be housed, and in which the monks took refuge on occasion. The raised doorway, which can be approached only by a ladder, and the form and disposition of the windows, prove their defensive character. The annals record the burning of the tower of Slane in 948, when all the relics were destroyed and some of the monks were killed, and similar disasters are told repeatedly during the latter part of the tenth century. Some towers, those of Kildare, Timahoe and Devenish, show roman-esque features, and are thus not earlier than the twelfth century. The round tower was now perhaps regarded as a necessary part of the monastic buildings, even when the monasteries were not in constant danger. The beautiful tower at Ardmore is an example from this period.[8]

In literature as in life, the Celtic peoples have given more to others than they managed to harvest for themselves. Two themes are prominent in early Irish literature, nature and tragic love. Kuno Meyer said well that the Irish were quick to take an artistic hint, and had a liking for the half-said thing: the early nature poetry that we have presented is evidence of it. The motif of the Doomed Lovers was carried from Wales to Brittany and became one of the great matters of medieval and renaissance literature. Arthurian romance, *la matière de Bretagne* in its wider extension, is known to be another gift of Wales to Europe, although the Welsh sources are lost. After a splendid beginning, with heroic themes not unworthy of Homer, Irish literature perished in the manuscripts. The habit of oral recitation in the houses of the great may have died out as literacy began to spread, and the written form of the stories degenerated quickly into tedious wordiness. Only in the peasants' cottages were the old stories still recited, and there, as folk-tales, they became overlaid with international *märchen*-motifs, and the matter itself changed. Finn replaced Cú Chulainn, and the ballad appeared beside the folk-tale. The Fenian warriors are good-humoured giants.

Maybe society itself was somehow fossilized in Ireland and Wales even before the Normans came. The future lay with the Normans, and the native genius stood still. In the eleventh century there had been a revival of learning in Ireland, and a period of reform under Brian Boru. A Welshman, Sulien, came to Ireland to study *c.* 1045, and stayed there for several years before returning to Wales to teach at Llanbadarn Fawr.[9] The second great mission to Germany began at this time. In 1067 an Irish monk from Donegal, Muiredach mac Robartaig, went on pilgrimage to Rome with two companions. They stopped at Ratisbon on their journey and were asked to stay; and they established themselves at Weih-Sankt-Peter outside the city, living in separate huts in the Irish manner. Muiredach, or Marianus by his Latin name, stayed there till his death in 1080. Soon afterwards some of his monks made a new foundation, St James of Ratisbon, and adopted the Rule of St Benedict. This was the first of the Irish Benedictine abbeys on the Continent, the *Schottenklöster* as they were called. From Ratisbon foundations were made at Würzburg and Vienna, at Nüremberg, Bamberg and Eichstätt. There was even a

398

monastery at Kiev for some time until the Mongol invasion in 1241. These abbeys kept in touch with Ireland, and drew their monks from the home country for three hundred years, a strange and almost accidental renewal of the great tradition of Columbanus. Then the supply of monks from Ireland failed, and the foundations passed, one by one, into other hands. St James is now the diocesan seminary of Ratisbon, Eichstätt is in the hands of German Capuchins; only the *Schottenklöster* of Vienna preserves its name, and there the Benedictines are still in possession, but they are no longer Irish.[10]

In Ireland the school of historical poets known as 'synthetic historians' appears at this time. Cinaed Ua Hartacáin († 975), Cúán Ua Lothcháin († 1024), Fland Mainistrech († 1056) and Gilla Coemáin († 1072) deserve mention, and if Fland were really the author of the great recension of *Táin Bó Cualnge* in the Book of Leinster, as Zimmer thought, he would have special honour.

The spirit of reform and the literary activity were most notable in the twelfth century, under the leadership of St Malachy, when diocesan rule was established in the Church, and the Cistercians came from Clairvaux and founded Mellifont. The literary men were now engaged in compiling old traditions and inventing new tales.[11] Down to the end of the twelfth century Irish literature is the greatest vernacular literature in Europe, and Welsh literature is next to it.

In Wales likewise there was a movement of recovery and reform. Here the Normans were already established in the south as conquerors, and everywhere along the Border there was the threat of foreign domination. The death of Henry I in 1135 was the occasion for a general effort to shake off the enemy. 'A new spirit of daring and independence seems to have seized the whole Welsh race.'[12] It was the age of Gruffydd ap Cynan, who had been building up the strength of Gwynedd and extending its territory. His son, Owain, became the most powerful of the Welsh princes, and added Ceredigion to the country under his control. The Normans suffered a disastrous defeat at Cardigan in 1136, and fled with heavy losses; and in the two following years Owain and his brother Cadwaladr again went south and completed their victory. Under Owain the Welsh nation attained the full measure of national consciousness,[13] and he lived to see the collapse of Henry II's expedition in 1165, after which the king abandoned hope of conquering Wales. The first Eisteddfod was held in

1176 in the new castle of Rhys ap Gruffydd at Aberteifi, and competitors were invited from Ireland and Scotland.

There may have been an impulse of response in both countries to the challenge of the Normans. A notable result of it was the increased activity of the bardic schools, an attempt to give new life to a very ancient custom; but no great writer appeared at that time anywhere in the Celtic countries in the native tradition. In Wales Meilyr and Gruffydd ap yr Ynad Coch were the chief poets of the time. One might add, for literature, the author of the Four Branches of the Mabinogion, if we could identify him.

Whatever the cause, the ancient practice of court poetry was the one literary *genre* that flourished in the later Middle Ages and down to modern times, in Scotland and Wales and Ireland, in forms more polished and more powerful than ever, *dán dírech* in Irish, *cynghanedd* in Welsh. This praise-poetry seems to have been all that the Welsh and Irish chieftains wanted to hear, and they were willing to pay for it. The poets were professional parasites, but they were more than that. They were custodians of a very old tradition, and the chief upholders of the honour and self-esteem of Irish noblemen; and they were highly trained in the craft of poetry.

It has not been part of our plan to follow the fortunes of the Celtic peoples beyond the twelfth century. In Ireland old Celtic institutions lived on at least in the west and north until the end of the sixteenth century, Celt and Norman side by side, some of the Norman lords now Irish in speech and habit. In Wales the end of independence came in 1282 (p. 341), but there have been several periods of revival, and Wales is still strongly Celtic in speech and strongly separatist – or at least particularist – in feeling. In Scotland, where there never was a conquest, old Gaelic custom survived in the Highlands and Islands even longer than in Ireland. A bardic elegy in strict form was composed for James MacDonald who died in 1738.[14] Brittany was formally annexed to France only in 1532, and there, as in Wales, the people have clung to old tradition in language and culture with great loyalty. This recent history is beyond our competence, and outside the scope of our endeavour. Our endeavour has been to tell what is known of the Celts in prehistoric times, and of the Celtic peoples later in their separate realms, the founding of the Celtic kingdoms, their institutions, their languages and literatures, their art, and the part that they have played in the history of Europe.

400

NOTES

1 See *PLECG* 26, 47 f., 296 f.
2 S. J. Crawford, *Anglo-Saxon Influence on Western Christendom* 11, 17, 88.
3 See Lynn White, *Latin Monasticism in Northern Sicily* (Cambridge, Mass., 1938), p. 21, n. 7, and pp. 16 f.
4 *Study of History* (ed. Somervell) 155.
5 L. Bieler, *Ireland, Harbinger of the Middle Ages* 125.
6 See also L. Weisgerber, 'Eine Irenwelle an Maas, Mosel und Rhein in Ottonischer Zeit', *Geschichte und Landeskunde* (Forschungen u. Darstellungen Franz Steinbach . . . gewidmet), Bonn, 1960.
7 E. Norden, *Die antike Kunstprosa* ii 667. There is no history of classical scholarship in Irish monasteries on the Continent.
8 For an account of the Round Towers see F. Henry, *L'Art irlandais* 71–76.
9 See *HW* ii 460.
10 See D. A. Binchy, 'Irish Benedictines in Medieval Germany', *Studies* xviii (1929), 194 ff.
11 G. Murphy, *Ossianic Lore* 16–17; F. Henry, *op. cit.* iii 17.
12 J. E. Lloyd, *History of Wales* ii 462, 523.
13 *Ibid.* 487.
14 A. Cameron, *Reliquiae Celticae* ii 274.

Abbreviations

Periodicals

N.B. Abbreviations for periodicals are in roman type to distinguish them from abbreviations of book titles, which are in italics.

AA	Archaeologia Aeliana
AB	Analecta Bollandiana
AC	Archaeologia Cambrensis
AJ	The Antiquaries Journal
APAW	Abhandlungen der preussischen Akademie der Wissenschaften
Arch J	The Archaeological Journal
BBCS	The Bulletin of the Board of Celtic Studies
Beitr.	Beiträge zur Geschichte der deutschen Literatur
BSHAB	Bulletin de la Société d'Histoire et d'Archéologie de Bretagne
BSL	Bulletin de la Société de Linguistique de Paris
CHAJ	Cork Historical and Archaeological Journal
DR	The Dublin Review
ÉC	Études Celtiques
JA	Journal Asiatique
JBAA	Journal of the British Archaeological Association
JRIC	Journal of the Royal Institute of Cornwall, Second Series
JRS	Journal of Roman Studies
JRSAI	Journal of the Royal Society of Antiquaries of Ireland
MA	Medieval Archaeology
MSHAB	Mémoires de la Société d'Histoire et d'Archéologie de Bretagne
MSL	Mémoires de la Société de Linguistique
NA	Neues Archiv für Sächsische Geschichte
NTS	Norsk Tidsskrift for Sprogvidenskap
PBA	Proceedings of the British Academy
PRIA	Proceedings of the Royal Irish Academy
PSAS	Proceedings of the Society of Antiquaries of Scotland
RC	Revue Celtique

SÉC	Société d'Émulation des Cotes-du-Nord, Bulletins et Mémoires
SGS	Scottish Gaelic Studies
SH	Studia Hibernica
SHR	The Scottish Historical Review
SR	The Scottish Review
TCWS	Transactions of the Cumberland and Westmorland Antiquarian Society
TDGS	Transactions of the Dumfriesshire and Galloway Natural History and Antiquarian Society
THSC	Transactions of the Honourable Society of Cymmrodorion
TLCAS	Transactions of the Lancashire and Cheshire Antiquarian Society
TPS	Transactions of the Philological Society
ZCP	Zeitschrift für Celtische Philologie
ZDMG	Zeitschrift der deutschen morgenlandischen Gesellschaft
ZfdA	Zeitschrift für deutsches Altertum

Books

N.B. Books referred to only once in the text are generally specified fully in the notes, and not entered in this list of abbreviations.

AB	*Angles and Britons* (O'Donnell Lectures, Cardiff, 1963).
ABR	J. M. C. Toynbee, *Art in Britain under the Romans* (Oxford, 1964).
ACS	H. O'Neill Hencken, *The Archaeology of Cornwall and Scilly* (London, 1932).
AG	A. Varagnac, *L'Art Gaulois* (Yonne, 2nd ed., 1964).
AI	F. Henry, *L'Art Irlandais*, 3 vols. (Yonne, 1963, 1964).
ÄID	K. Meyer, *Über die älteste irische Dichtung*, I–II (APAW Jahrgang 1913, Berlin 1913–14).
A. Inisfallen	*The Annals of Inisfallen*, edited and translated by Seán Mac Airt (Dublin, 1951).
AIP	K. Meyer, *Selections from Ancient Irish Poetry* (2nd ed., London, 1913).
AL	*Ancient Laws of Ireland*, vol. 1–6, edited by W. M. Hennessy, W. N. Hancock, T. O'Mahony, A. G. Richey, R. Atkinson (Dublin, 1856–1901).
ALI	*Ancient Laws and Institutes of Wales*, edited by Aneurin Owen (London, 1841).
ALMA	*Arthurian Literature in the Middle Ages*, edited by R. S. Loomis (Oxford, 1959).
AMVR	F. Benoit, *L'Art Méditerranéen de la Vallée du Rhone* (Aix-en-Provence, 1955).

ARB   J. M. C. Toynbee, *Art in Roman Britain* (London, 1962).

AS   N. K. Chadwick, *The Age of the Saints in the Early Celtic Church* (O.U.P., 1961, reprinted 1963).

ASC   D. Whitelock, *The Anglo-Saxon Chronicle. A Revised Translation* (London, 1961).

ASE   F. M. Stenton, *Anglo-Saxon England* (2nd ed., Oxford, 1947).

ASG   J. M. Clark, *The Abbey of St Gall* (Cambridge, 1926).

AT   *The Annals of Tigernach*, edited and translated by Whitley Stokes, R.C., vols. XVI, 1895, 170 ff.; XVII, 1896, 6 ff.

AU   *The Annals of Ulster*, in 4 vols. Vol. I edited and translated by W. M. Hennessy (Dublin, 1887); Vols. II–IV, B. MacCarthy (Dublin, 1893, 1895, 1901).

Bagendon   E. M. Clifford, *Bagendon* (Cambridge, 1961).

BB   *Book of Ballymote*, facsimile edition by R. Atkinson (Dublin, 1887).

Bede   C. Plummer, *Venerabilis Baedae Opera Historica*, 2 vols. (Oxford, 1896).

Bordeaux   C. Jullian, *Histoire de Bordeaux depuis les Origines jusqu'en 1895* (Bordeaux, 1895).

BRA   G. Simpson, *Britons and the Roman Army* (London, 1964).

Bruchst.   K. Meyer, *Bruchstücke der älteren Lyrik Irlands* (APAW, Berlin, 1919).

CA   Ifor Williams, *Canu Aneirin*, Cardiff, 1938.

Caspari   Caspari, *Briefe Abhandlungen und Predigten* (Christiania, 1890). English translation by R. S. Haselhurst, under the title: *The Letters of Fastidius* (London, 1927). Our page references are to the English translation.

CB   N. K. Chadwick, *Celtic Britain* (London, 1964).

CB   John Rhŷs, *Celtic Britain* (London, 1904).

CC   Olivier Loyer, *Les Chrétientés Celtiques* (Paris, 1965).

CCH   Jan Filip, *Celtic Civilization and its Heritage* (Prague, 1960, English translation by R. F. Samsour, 1962).

CCL   Louis Gougaud, *Christianity in Celtic Lands*. Translated from the author's MS. by Maud Joynt (London, 1932).

CE   I. Ll. Foster and L. Alcock, *Culture and Environment* (London, 1963).

CG   D. A. Binchy, *Críth Gablach* (Dublin, 1941).

CGG   *Cogadh Gaedhel re Gallaibh*, edited and translated by J. H. Todd (London, 1867).

CI   E. MacNeill, *Celtic Ireland* (Dublin, 1921).

CIIC   R. A. S. Macalister, *Corpus Inscriptionum Insularum Celticarum*, 2 vols. (Dublin, 1945, 1949).

CIL   *Corpus Inscriptionum Latinarum*.

CK   Myles Dillon, *The Cycles of the Kings* (Oxford, 1946).

CM   K. H. Jackson, *A Celtic Miscellany* (London, 1951).

CPS   W. J. Watson, *History of the Celtic Place-Names of Scotland* (Edinburgh, 1926).

CRB   Hugh Williams, *Christianity in Roman Britain* (Oxford, 1912).

CS   W. F. Skene, *Celtic Scotland*, 3 vols. (Edinburgh, 1886–1890).

DF   *Duanaire Finn*, Irish text and translation by E. MacNeill and Gerard Murphy, 3 vols. (London, 1908, 1933, 1953).

DHC   M.–L. Sjoestedt, *Dieux et Héros des Celtes* (Paris, 1940). English translation with additional notes by Myles Dillon (London, 1949).

EA   Episcopal Acts and cognate documents relating to Welsh Dioceses 1066–1272, 2 vols., edited by James Conway Davies (Hist. Soc. Church in Wales, 1, 3, 4, 1946–48).

ÉB   J. Loth, *L'Émigration Bretonne en Armorique du Ve au VIIe Siècle de Notre Ère* (Paris, 1883).

EC   *The Early Cultures of North-West Europe*, edited by Sir C. Fox and B. Dickins (Cambridge, 1950).

ECA   P. Jacobsthal, *Early Celtic Art* (Oxford, 1944).

ECI   M. and L. de Paor, *Early Christian Ireland* (London, 1958).

ECMW   V. E. Nash-Williams, *The Early Christian Monuments of Wales* (Cardiff, 1950).

ECPM   S. Cruden, *The Early Christian and Pictish Monuments of Scotland* (Edinburgh, 1957).

EGC   T. H. Bindley, *The Epistle of the Gallican Churches* (London, 1900).

EHC   L. Duchesne, *The Early History of the Church*. English translation of the first edition, reprinted (London, 1950).

EIHM   T. F. O'Rahilly, *Early Irish History and Mythology* (Dublin, 1946).

EIL   Myles Dillon, *Early Irish Literature* (Chicago, 1948).

EIS   *Early Irish Society*, edited by Myles Dillon (Dublin, 1954).

ES   H. M. Chadwick, *Early Scotland* (Cambridge, 1949).

ESEM   *Essays and Studies presented to Professor E. MacNeill*, edited by Rev. J. Ryan (Dublin, 1940).

ESSH   A. O. Anderson, *Early Sources of Scottish History*, 2 vols. (Edinburgh, 1922).

EWP   Ifor Williams, *Lectures on Early Welsh Poetry* (Dublin, 1944).

FABW   W. F. Skene, *The Four Ancient Books of Wales*, 2 vols. (Edinburgh, 1868). Vol. I Translation, Vol. II Welsh texts.

FCL   *The Fate of the Children of Lir*, edited and translated by R. J. O'Duffy (5th ed., Dublin, 1908).

FCT   *The Fate of the Children of Tuireann*, edited and translated by R. J. O'Duffy (Dublin, 1901).

FCU   *The Fate of the Children of Uisneach*, edited and translated by R. J. O'Duffy (Dublin, 1914).

FEIA   C. Fox, *A Find of the Early Iron Age from Llyn Cerrig Bach, Anglesey* (Cardiff, 1946).

Fontes   I. Zwicker, *Fontes Historiae Religionis Celticae*, 3 parts (Berlin, 1934–36).

FPRB   P. Salway, *The Frontier People of Roman Britain* (Cambridge, 1965).

FWS   *Festschrift für Whitley Stokes* (Leipzig, 1900).

GC   Élie Griffe, *La Gaule Chrétienne à l'Époque Romaine*, I (Paris and Toulouse, 1947).

GL   H. M. and N. K. Chadwick, *The Growth of Literature*, 3 vols. (Cambridge, 1932–1940).

GLL   M. Manitius, *Geschichte der lateinische Literatur des Mittelalters*, 3 vols. (Munich, 1911, 1923, 1931).

Groupement   H. Pedersen, *Le Groupements des Dialectes Indo-Européens* (København, 1925).

HB   H. Waquet, *Histoire de la Bretagne* (Paris, 1950).

HB   L. A. Le Moyne de la Borderie, *Histoire de Bretagne*, 6 vols. (Rennes and Paris, 1896–1914).

HB   E. Durtelle de Saint-Sauveur, *Histoire de Bretagne*, 2 vols. (4th ed., Rennes, 1947).

HB   A. Rebillon, *Histoire de Bretagne* (Paris, 1957).

Heldensage   R. Thurneysen, *Die irische Helden- und Königsage* (Halle (Saale), 1921).

HG   C. Jullian, *Histoire de la Gaule*, 8 vols. (Paris, 1908–1926).

Hill-Forts   R. E. M. Wheeler and K. Richardson, *Hill-Forts of Northern France* (Oxford, 1957).

HIM   R. H. Kinvig, *A History of the Isle of Man* (2nd edition, Liverpool, 1950).

Hist. Brit.   *The Historia Brittonum* by Nennius. Ed. by T. Mommsen, Monumenta Germaniae Historica, auctores antiquissimi, t. XIII (Berlin, 1898, reprinted 1961); also by F. Lot (Paris, 1934). Translated by A. W. Wade-Evans, *Nennius's History of the Britons* (London, 1938).

HW   J. E. Lloyd, *History of Wales*, 2 vols. (3rd ed., London, 1939).

HWL   T. Parry, *A History of Welsh Literature*. Translated by H. I. Bell (Oxford, 1955).

IA   F. Henry, *Irish Art in the Early Christian Period to A.D. 800* (London, 1965).

IAECP   F. Henry, *Irish Art in the Early Christian Period* (2nd ed., London, 1947).

ICCS　　　　*Proceedings of the International Congress of Celtic Studies* (Dublin, 1962).

IDPP　　　　T. F. O'Rahilly, *Irish Dialects Past and Present* (London, 1932).

IHC　　　　F. Henry, *Irish High Crosses* (Dublin, 1964).

IM　　　　　J. Ryan, *Irish Monasticism* (Dublin and Cork, 1931).

Invasions　　L. Musset, *Les Invasions: Les Vagues Germaniques* (Paris, 1965).

IPD　　　　C. S. Boswell, *An Irish Precursor of Dante* (London, 1908).

IPG　　　　E. MacNeill, *Early Irish Population Groups* (PRIA xxix C 1911).

Irland　　　L. Bieler, *Irland* (Lausanne and Freiburg, 1961). English edition, *Ireland* (London, 1963).

Ir. T　　　*Irische Texte*, ed. W. Stokes and E. Windisch (Leipzig, 1880–1905).

IT　　　　　R. Flower, *The Irish Tradition* (Oxford, 1947).

LB　　　　　*Leabhar Breac, the Speckled Book*, facsimile edition by S. Ferguson (Dublin, 1876).

LBS　　　　S. Baring-Gould and J. Fisher, *The Lives of the British Saints*, 4 vols. (London, 1907–1913).

LC　　　　　*Lebor na Cert (The Book of Rights)*, edited and translated by Myles Dillon (Dublin, 1962).

Lec.　　　　*The Book of Lecan*, facsimile edition by Kathleen Mulchrone (Dublin, 1937).

Légende　　J. Marx, *La Légende Arthurienne et le Graal* (Paris, 1952).

LHEB　　　K. H. Jackson, *Language and History in Early Britain* (Edinburgh, 1953).

LIFC　　　　K. Meyer, *Learning in Ireland in the Fifth Century and the Transmission of Letters* (Dublin, 1913).

LIS　　　　　C. Plummer, *Bethada Náem nÉrenn (Lives of Irish Saints)*. 2 vols. (Oxford, 1922).

LL　　　　　*The Book of Leinster*, facsimile edition by R. Atkinson (Dublin, 1880).

LP　　　　　M. P. Charlesworth, *The Lost Province* (Cardiff, 1949).

LRB　　　　A. Birley, *Life in Roman Britain* (London, 1964).

LRE　　　　A. H. M. Jones, *The Later Roman Empire*, 3 vols., + one vol. maps (Oxford, 1964).

LRV　　　　G. W. Meates, *Lullingstone Roman Villa* (London, 1955).

LS　　　　　D. A. White, *Litus Saxonicum* (Madison, Wisconsin, 1961).

LU　　　　　*Lebor na hUidre*, ed. R. Best and O. Bergin (Dublin, 1929).

Lughnasa　Máire MacNeill, *The Festival of Lughnasa* (Oxford, 1962).

Manuel　　J. Déchelette, *Manuel d'Archéologie Préhistorique Celtique et Gallo-Romaine*, II (Paris, 1914).

407

Manuel   G. Dottin, *Manuel pour servir à l'Étude de l'Antiquité Celtique* (2nd ed., Paris, 1915).

Math   W. J. Gruffydd, *Math vab Mathonwy* (Cardiff, 1928).

MD   *The Metrical Dindshenchas.* Edited and translated by E. Gwynn in 5 parts (Dublin, R.I.A., 1903–1935).

ND   O. Seeck (editor), *Notitia Dignitatum* (Berlin, 1876).

OCR   P. W. Joyce, *Old Celtic Romances* (London, 1914).

OEN   H. M. Chadwick, *The Origin of the English Nation* (Cambridge, 1907).

OIT   K. H. Jackson, *The Oldest Irish Tradition: A Window on the Iron Age* (Cambridge, 1964).

ON   P. Hunter Blair, *The Origins of Northumbria* (Gateshead-on-Tyne, 1948).

Onomasticon E. Hogan, *Onomasticon Goidelicum* (Dublin, 1910).

P and P   C. Fox, *Pattern and Purpose* (Cardiff, 1958).

P and S   W. F. Skene, *Chronicles of the Picts and Scots* (Edinburgh, 1867).

Pélage   G. de Plinval, *Pélage, Ses Écrits, Sa Vie, et Sa Réforme* (Lausanne, 1943).

Pelagius   J. Ferguson, *Pelagius* (Cambridge, 1956).

Phases   E. MacNeill, *Phases of Irish History* (Dublin, 1920).

PLECG   N. K. Chadwick, *Poetry and Letters in Early Christian Gaul* (London, 1955).

PP   *The Problem of the Picts*, edited by F. T. Wainwright (Edinburgh, 1965).

Rawl.   Rawlinson B 502, facsimile edition, ed. K. Meyer (Oxford, 1909).

RB   I. A. Richmond, *Roman Britain* (Harmondsworth, 1955; 2nd ed., 1963).

RBEE   P. Hunter Blair, *Roman Britain and Early England* (Edinburgh, 1963).

RBES   F. G. Collingwood and J. N. L. Myres, *Roman Britain and the English Settlements* (Oxford, 1936).

RC   I. A. Richmond and O. G. S. Crawford, *The British Section of the Ravenna Cosmography* (Oxford, 1949).

RCB   G. Webster and D. R. Dudley, *The Roman Conquest of Britain* (London, 1965).

RG   O. Brogan, *Roman Gaul* (London, 1953).

RIB   R. G. Collingwood and R. P. Wright, *The Roman Inscriptions of Britain* (Oxford, 1965).

RIN   C. G. Starr, *The Roman Imperial Navy* (Ithaca, N.Y., 1941).

RNNB   I. A. Richmond, *Roman and Native in North Britain* (Edinburgh, 1958).

ROB   F. Haverfield and G. Macdonald, *The Roman Occupation of Britain* (Oxford, 1924).

RRB   F. Haverfield, *The Romanization of Roman Britain.*

(Revised by G. Macdonald, Oxford, 1923).

SC   *Sanas Cormaic, An Old-Irish Glossary*, edited by Kuno Meyer (Anecdota from Irish Manuscripts iv, Halle, 1912).

Schools of Gaul   T. Haarhoff, *Schools of Gaul: A Study of Pagan and Christian Education in the Last Century of the Western Empire* (Oxford, 1920).

SCO   G. S. M. Walker, *Sancti Columbani Opera* (Dublin, 1957).

SEBC   *Studies in the Early British Church*, by N. K. Chadwick, K. Hughes, Christopher Brooke, K. Jackson (Cambridge, 1958).

SEBH   *Studies in Early British History* by H. M. Chadwick and others (Cambridge, 1954, reprinted 1959).

SECT   J. Anderson, *Scotland in Early Christian Times* (Edinburgh, 1881).

SG   S. H. O'Grady, *Silva Gadelica* (London, 1892). Vol. I Irish Texts. Vol. II Translations.

SI   F. Henry, *La Sculpture Irlandaise* (Paris, 1933).

SILH   J. Carney, *Studies in Irish Literature and History* (Dublin, 1955).

SM   G. Murphy, *Saga and Myth in Ancient Ireland* (Dublin, 1961).

Sources   J. F. Kenney, *The Sources for the Early History of Ireland* (New York, 1929).

SS   S. Hellmann, *Sedulius Scottus* (Munich, 1906).

ST   Stith Thompson, *Motif-Index of Folk Literature*, 6 vols. (Copenhagen, 1955–58).

Stanwick   R. E. M. Wheeler, *The Stanwick Fortifications* (Oxford, 1954).

Táin   *Die altirische Heldensage Táin Bó Cúalnge*, edited and translated by E. Windisch (Leipzig, 1905). [New edition and translation by C. O'Rahilly, Dublin, 1967.]

TIG   *Three Irish Glossaries*, edited by Whitley Stokes (London, 1862).

TL   M. L. W. Laistner, *Thought and Letters in Western Europe A.D. 500–900* (2nd ed., London, 1957).

TP   T. F. O'Rahilly, *The Two Patricks* (Dublin, 1942).

Triads   *Trioedd Ynys Prydein. The Welsh Triads*, edited and translated by R. Bromwich (Cardiff, 1961).

Tripartite Life   *The Tripartite Life of Patrick with other Documents relating to that Saint*, 2 vols., edited by Whitley Stokes (London, 1887). I. Tripartite Life, Irish text and translation. II. Documents concerning S. Patrick, Irish text and translation.

TRS   O. G. S. Crawford, *Topography of Roman Scotland* (Cambridge, 1949).

TSC　　　J. Earle and C. Plummer, *Two Saxon Chronicles*, 2 vols. (Oxford, 1899).

TT　　　A. O. Curle, *The Treasure of Traprain*: *A Scottish Hoard of Roman Silver* (Glasgow, 1923).

VA　　　*Viking Antiquities in Great Britain and Ireland*, 6 parts (Oslo, 1940–54).

VB　　　K. Meyer, *The Voyage of Bran*, 2 vols. (Dublin: I, 1895, II, 1897).

VSBG　　A. W. Wade-Evans, *Vitae Sanctorum Britanniae et Genealogiae* (Cardiff, 1944).

VSH　　　C. Plummer, *Vitae Sanctorum Hiberniae*, 2 vols. (Oxford, 1910).

WK　　　J. Moreau, *Die Welt der Kelten* (3rd ed., Stutthart, 1961).

YBL　　　*The Yellow Book of Lecan*.

Map 1

Legend:
- //// Belgic districts
- //// Probable Belgic districts
- REGNI Pro-Roman
- CORITANI Neutral
- SILURES Active opponents of Rome
- ═══ Roman roads
- ──► Routes of advance
- 0 10 20 30 40 50 Miles

Map 2

Legend:
- Coloniae
- Cantonal Capitals
- Legionary fortresses
- Roman Province AD 47
- 0 10 20 30 40 50 Miles

Hadrian's Wall

MANAU

BRIGANTES
Isurium
Eburacum
PARISI
Petuaria

Deva

ORDOVICES   CORNOVII
Viroconium
Lindum

CORITANI
Ratae
CENI
Venta

TRINOVANTES

DEMETAE
Moridunum   SILURES   Glevum
DOBUNNI
CATUVELLAUNI
Camulodunum

Venta
Isca
Corinium
Verulamium
Londinium

ATREBATES
Calleva
BELGAE
Venta
Durovernum
CANTIACI

REGNENSES
Noviomagus

Lindinis
DUROTRIGES
Durnovaria

Isca
DUMNONII

Map 3

C.R.—24

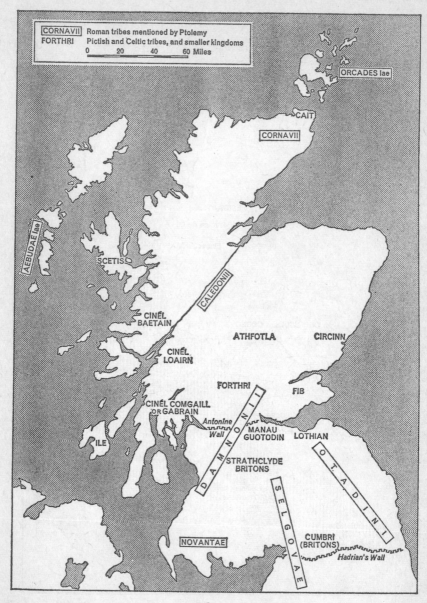

CORNAVII — Roman tribes mentioned by Ptolemy
FORTHRI — Pictish and Celtic tribes, and smaller kingdoms

0   20   40   60 Miles

ORCADES Iae

CAIT

CORNAVII

AEBUDAE Iae

SCETIS

CALEDONII

CINÉL BAETAIN

ATHFOTLA

CIRCINN

CINÉL LOAIRN

FORTHRI

FIB

CINÉL COMGAILL or GABRAIN

Antonine Wall

MANAU GUOTODIN

LOTHIAN

ILE

DAMNONII

STRATHCLYDE BRITONS

OTADINI

SELGOVAE

NOVANTAE

CUMBRI (BRITONS)

Hadrian's Wall

Map 4

Map 5

Map 6

Map 7

Map 8. Plan of Cruachain

INDEX

Dufnewestan.21

428

THE WORLD OF THE PHOENICIANS
Sabatino Moscati

A comprehensive survey of the culture, history and social life of the Phoenicians, one of the most enigmatic peoples of antiquity.

£1 *Illustrated*

THE GREEK EXPERIENCE
C. M. Bowra

'To succeed in giving the Greeks a fresh life is a hard task, but Sir Maurice Bowra has achieved it'

75p *Illustrated*   *Books of the Year, Sunday Times*

THE AGE OF RECONNAISSANCE
J. H. Parry

'Dr Parry's book is an admirable survey of this dynamic period in European history as well as a solid contribution to our knowledge of the circumstances which made it possible'

£1 *Illustrated*   *Times Literary Supplement*

THE AGE OF REVOLUTION
E. J. Hobsbawm

'A brilliant account of Europe in its revolutionary age. . . . No one could ask for more'

£1 *Illustrated*   *A. J. P. Taylor, New Statesman*

All Sphere Books are available at your bookshop or
newsagent, or can be ordered from the following address:

Sphere Books, Cash Sales Department,
P.O. Box 11, Falmouth, Cornwall.

Please send cheque or postal order (no currency), and allow
7p per copy to cover the cost of postage and packing
in U.K. or overseas.